D1356470

The Calculus of Retirement Income

Financial Models for Pension Annuities and Life Insurance

This book introduces and develops—from a unique financial perspective—the basic actuarial models that underlie the pricing of life-contingent pension annuities and life insurance. The ideas and techniques are then applied to the real-world problem of generating sustainable retirement income toward the end of the human life cycle. The roles of lifetime income, longevity insurance, and systematic withdrawal plans are investigated within a parsimonious framework. The underlying technology and terminology of the book are based on continuous-time financial economics, merging analytic laws of mortality with the dynamics of equity markets and interest rates. Nonetheless, the text requires only a minimal background in mathematics, and it emphasizes examples and applications rather than theorems and proofs. *The Calculus of Retirement Income* is an ideal textbook for an applied course on wealth management and retirement planning, and it can serve also as a reference for quantitatively inclined financial planners. This book is accompanied by material on the Web site ⟨www.ifid.ca/CRI⟩.

Moshe A. Milevsky is Associate Professor of Finance at the Schulich School of Business, York University, and the Executive Director of the IFID Centre in Toronto, Canada. He was elected Fellow of the Fields Institute in 2002. Professor Milevsky is co-founding editor of the *Journal of Pension Economics and Finance* (published by Cambridge University Press) and has authored more than thirty scholarly articles in addition to three books. His writing for popular media received a Canadian National Magazine Award in 2004. He has lectured widely on the topics of retirement income planning, insurance, and investments in North America, South America, and Europe, and he is a frequent guest on North American television and radio.

The Calculus of Retirement Income

*Financial Models for Pension Annuities
and Life Insurance*

MOSHE A. MILEVSKY

Schulich School of Business

CAMBRIDGE
UNIVERSITY PRESS

CAMBRIDGE UNIVERSITY PRESS
Cambridge, New York, Melbourne, Madrid, Cape Town, Singapore, São Paulo

Cambridge University Press
40 West 20th Street, New York, NY 10011-4211, USA

www.cambridge.org
Information on this title: www.cambridge.org/9780521842587

© Moshe A. Milevsky 2006

This publication is in copyright. Subject to statutory exception
and to the provisions of relevant collective licensing agreements,
no reproduction of any part may take place without
the written permission of Cambridge University Press.

First published 2006

Printed in the United States of America

A catalog record for this publication is available from the British Library.

Library of Congress Cataloging in Publication data
Milevsky, Moshe Arye, 1967–
The calculus of retirement income : financial models for pension
annuities and life insurance / Moshe A. Milevsky.
p.   cm.
ISBN 0-521-84258-1 (hardback)
1. Old age pensions – Mathematical models.   2. Annuities – Mathematical
models.   3. Retirement income – Mathematical models.   I. Title.

HD7105.3.M54   2006
368.3′701 – dc22   2005029455

ISBN-13   978-0-521-84258-7 hardback
ISBN-10   0-521-84258-1 hardback

Cambridge University Press has no responsibility for
the persistence or accuracy of URLs for external or
third-party Internet Web sites referred to in this publication
and does not guarantee that any content on such
Web sites is, or will remain, accurate or appropriate.

Contents

List of Figures and Tables   *page* x

I   MODELS OF ACTUARIAL FINANCE

1	Introduction and Motivation	3
	1.1 The Drunk Gambler Problem	3
	1.2 The Demographic Picture	5
	1.3 The Ideal Audience	9
	1.4 Learning Objectives	10
	1.5 Acknowledgments	12
	1.6 Appendix: Drunk Gambler Solution	14
2	Modeling the Human Life Cycle	17
	2.1 The Next Sixty Years of Your Life	17
	2.2 Future Value of Savings	18
	2.3 Present Value of Consumption	20
	2.4 Exchange Rate between Savings and Consumption	22
	2.5 A Neutral Replacement Rate	26
	2.6 Discounted Value of a Life-Cycle Plan	27
	2.7 Real vs. Nominal Planning with Inflation	28
	2.8 Changing Investment Rates over Time	30
	2.9 Further Reading	32
	2.10 Problems	33
3	Models of Human Mortality	34
	3.1 Mortality Tables and Rates	34
	3.2 Conditional Probability of Survival	35
	3.3 Remaining Lifetime Random Variable	37
	3.4 Instantaneous Force of Mortality	38
	3.5 The ODE Relationship	39
	3.6 Moments in Your Life	41

3.7   Median vs. Expected Remaining Lifetime   44
3.8   Exponential Law of Mortality   45
3.9   Gompertz–Makeham Law of Mortality   46
3.10   Fitting Discrete Tables to Continuous Laws   49
3.11   General Hazard Rates   51
3.12   Modeling Joint Lifetimes   53
3.13   Period vs. Cohort Tables   55
3.14   Further Reading   59
3.15   Notation   60
3.16   Problems   60
3.17   Technical Note: Incomplete Gamma Function in Excel   61
3.18   Appendix: Normal Distribution and Calculus Refresher   62

4   Valuation Models of Deterministic Interest   64

4.1   Continuously Compounded Interest Rates?   64
4.2   Discount Factors   66
4.3   How Accurate Is the Rule of 72?   67
4.4   Zero Bonds and Coupon Bonds   68
4.5   Arbitrage: Linking Value and Market Price   70
4.6   Term Structure of Interest Rates   72
4.7   Bonds: Nonflat Term Structure   73
4.8   Bonds: Nonconstant Coupons   74
4.9   Taylor's Approximation   75
4.10   Explicit Values for Duration and Convexity   76
4.11   Numerical Examples of Duration and Convexity   78
4.12   Another Look at Duration and Convexity   80
4.13   Further Reading   81
4.14   Notation   82
4.15   Problems   82

5   Models of Risky Financial Investments   83

5.1   Recent Stock Market History   83
5.2   Arithmetic Average Return versus Geometric Average
       Return   86
5.3   A Long-Term Model for Risk   88
5.4   Introducing Brownian Motion   91
5.5   Index Averages and Index Medians   97
5.6   The Probability of Regret   98
5.7   Focusing on the Rate of Change   100
5.8   How to Simulate a Diffusion Process   101
5.9   Asset Allocation and Portfolio Construction   102
5.10   Space–Time Diversification   104
5.11   Further Reading   107
5.12   Notation   108
5.13   Problems   108

6   Models of Pension Life Annuities   110

  6.1   Motivation and Agenda   110
  6.2   Market Prices of Pension Annuities   110
  6.3   Valuation of Pension Annuities: General   114
  6.4   Valuation of Pension Annuities: Exponential   115
  6.5   The Wrong Way to Value Pension Annuities   115
  6.6   Valuation of Pension Annuities: Gompertz–Makeham   116
  6.7   How Is the Annuity's Income Taxed?   119
  6.8   Deferred Annuities: Variation on a Theme   121
  6.9   Period Certain versus Term Certain   123
  6.10 Valuation of Joint and Survivor Pension Annuities   125
  6.11 Duration of a Pension Annuity   128
  6.12 Variable vs. Fixed Pension Annuities   130
  6.13 Further Reading   134
  6.14 Notation   136
  6.15 Problems   136

7   Models of Life Insurance   138

  7.1   A Free (Last) Supper?   138
  7.2   Market Prices of Life Insurance   138
  7.3   The Impact of Health Status   139
  7.4   How Much Life Insurance Do You Need?   140
  7.5   Other Kinds of Life Insurance   142
  7.6   Value of Life Insurance: Net Single Premium   143
  7.7   Valuing Life Insurance Using Pension Annuities   145
  7.8   Arbitrage Relationship   147
  7.9   Tax Arbitrage Relationship   148
  7.10 Value of Life Insurance: Exponential Mortality   149
  7.11 Value of Life Insurance: GoMa Mortality   149
  7.12 Life Insurance Paid by Installments   150
  7.13 NSP: Delayed and Term Insurance   150
  7.14 Variations on Life Insurance   151
  7.15 What If You Stop Paying Premiums?   154
  7.16 Duration of Life Insurance   157
  7.17 Following a Group of Policies   159
  7.18 The Next Generation: Universal Life Insurance   160
  7.19 Further Reading   162
  7.20 Notation   162
  7.21 Problems   162

8   Models of DB vs. DC Pensions   164

  8.1   A Choice of Pension Plans   164
  8.2   The Core of Defined Contribution Pensions   165
  8.3   The Core of Defined Benefit Pensions   169

8.4 What Is the Value of a DB Pension Promise?   172
8.5 Pension Funding and Accounting   176
8.6 Further Reading   180
8.7 Notation   181
8.8 Problems   182

II   WEALTH MANAGEMENT:
APPLICATIONS AND IMPLICATIONS

9 Sustainable Spending at Retirement   185
9.1   Living in Retirement   185
9.2   Stochastic Present Value   187
9.3   Analytic Formula: Sustainable Retirement Income   190
9.4   The Main Result: Exponential Reciprocal Gamma   192
9.5   Case Study and Numerical Examples   193
9.6   Increased Sustainable Spending *without* More Risk?   202
9.7   Conclusion   206
9.8   Further Reading   208
9.9   Problems   208
9.10 Appendix: Derivation of the Formula   209

10 Longevity Insurance Revisited   215
10.1   To Annuitize or Not To Annuitize?   215
10.2   Five 95-Year-Olds Playing Bridge   216
10.3   The Algebra of Fixed and Variable Tontines   218
10.4   Asset Allocation with Tontines   220
10.5   A First Look at Self-Annuitization   225
10.6   The Implied Longevity Yield   226
10.7   Advanced-Life Delayed Annuities   234
10.8   Who Incurs Mortality Risk and Investment Rate Risk?   241
10.9   Further Reading   244
10.10 Notation   245
10.11 Problems   245

III   ADVANCED TOPICS

11 Options within Variable Annuities   249
11.1   To Live and Die in VA   249
11.2   The Value of Paying by Installments   252
11.3   A Simple Guaranteed Minimum Accumulation Benefit   257
11.4   The Guaranteed Minimum Death Benefit   258
11.5   Special Case: Exponential Mortality   259
11.6   The Guaranteed Minimum Withdrawal Benefit   262
11.7   Further Reading   268
11.8   Notation   269

12 The Utility of Annuitization 270

   12.1 What Is the Protection Worth? 270

   12.2 Models of Utility, Value, and Price 271

   12.3 The Utility Function and Insurance 272

   12.4 Utility of Consumption and Lifetime Uncertainty 274

   12.5 Utility and Annuity Asset Allocation 278

   12.6 The Optimal Timing of Annuitization 281

   12.7 The Real Option to Defer Annuitization 282

   12.8 Advanced RODA Model 287

   12.9 Subjective vs. Objective Mortality 289

   12.10 Variable vs. Fixed Payout Annuities 290

   12.11 Further Reading 291

   12.12 Notation 292

13 Final Words 293

14 Appendix 295

Bibliography 301

Index 309

Figures and Tables

FIGURES

2.1 The human financial life cycle: Savings, wealth &
consumption (constant investment rate) *page* 25
2.2 The human financial life cycle: Savings, wealth &
consumption (varying investment rate) 32
3.1 RP2000 mortality table used for pensions 36
3.2 Relationships between mortality descriptions 40
3.3 The CDF versus the PDF of a "normal" remaining lifetime R.V. 42
3.4 The hazard rate for the normal distribution 42
3.5 The CDF versus the PDF of an "exponential" remaining
lifetime R.V. 47
3.6 RP2000 (unisex pension) mortality table vs. best Gompertz fit
vs. exponential approximation 50
4.1 Evolution of the bond price over time 69
4.2 Model bond value vs. valuation rate 71
4.3 The term structure of interest rates 73
4.4 "Taylor's D" as maturity gets closer 77
4.5 How good is the approximation? 81
5.1 Visualizing the stochastic growth rate 89
5.2 Sample path of Brownian motion over 40 years 92
5.3 Another sample path of Brownian motion over 40 years 93
5.4 Sample paths: BM vs. nsBM vs. GBM 94
5.5 What is the Probability of Regret (PoR)? 99
5.6 Space–time diversification 107
6.1 Pension annuity quotes: Relationship between credit rating and
average payout (income) 113
6.2 One sample path – Three outcomes depending on h 135
8.1 Pension systems 165
8.2 Salary/wage profile vs. weighting scheme: Modeling pension
vesting & career averages 169

8.3	ABO vs. PBO vs. RBO	174
9.1	The retirement triangle	186
9.2	Stochastic present value (SPV) of retirement consumption	189
9.3	Minimum wealth required at various ages to maintain a fixed retirement ruin probability	200
9.4	Probability given spending rate is not sustainable	201
9.5	Expected wealth: 65-year-old consumes $5 per year but protects portfolio with 5% out-of-the-money puts	204
9.6	Ruin probability conditional on returns	205
10.1	I want a lifetime income	228
10.2	Advanced life delayed annuity	235
11.1	Three types of puts	250
11.2	Titanic vs. vanilla put	260
12.1	Expected loss	271

TABLES

1.1	Old-age dependency ratio around the world	6
1.2	Expected number of years spent in retirement around the world	7
2.1	Financial exchange rate between $1 saved annually over 30 working years and dollar consumption during retirement	23
2.2	Government-sponsored pension plans: How generous are they?	26
2.3	Discounted value of life-cycle plan = $0.241 under first sequence of varying returns	31
2.4	Discounted value of life-cycle plan = −$0.615 under second sequence of varying returns	31
3.1	Mortality table for healthy members of a pension plan	35
3.2	Mortality odds when life is normally distributed	41
3.3	Life expectancy at birth in 2005	43
3.4	Increase since 1950 in life expectancy at birth $E[T_0]$	44
3.5	Mortality odds when life is exponentially distributed	46
3.6	Example of fitting Gompertz–Makeham law to a group mortality table—Female	49
3.7	Example of fitting Gompertz–Makeham law to a group mortality table—Male	49
3.8	How good is a continuous law of mortality?—Gompertz vs. exponential vs. RP2000	50
3.9	Working with the instantaneous hazard rate	52
3.10	Survival probabilities at age 65	54
3.11	Change in mortality patterns over time—Female	56
3.12	Change in mortality patterns over time—Male	57
4.1	Year-end value of $1 under infrequent compounding	65
4.2	Year-end value of $1 under frequent compounding	65

4.3   Years required to double or triple $1 invested at various
      interest rates   67
4.4   Valuation of 5-year bonds as a fraction of face value   70
4.5   Valuation of 10-year bonds as a fraction of face value   70
4.6   Estimated vs. actual value of $10,000 bond after change in
      valuation rates   80
5.1   Nominal investment returns over 10 years   84
5.2   Growth rates during different investment periods   85
5.3   After-inflation (real) returns over 10 years   86
5.4   Geometric mean returns   87
5.5   Probability of losing money in a diversified portfolio   90
5.6   SDE simulation of GBM using the Euler method   102
6.1   Monthly income from $100,000 premium single-life pension
      annuity   111
6.2   A quick comparison with the bond market   112
6.3   Monthly income from $100,000 premium joint life pension
      annuity   112
6.4   IPAF $\bar{a}_x$: Price of lifetime $1 annual income   118
6.5   Taxable portion of income flow from $1-for-life annuity
      purchased with non–tax-sheltered funds   121
6.6   DPAF $_u\bar{a}_{45}$: Price of lifetime $1 annual income for 45-year-old   123
6.7   Value $V(r, T)$ of term certain annuity factor vs. immediate
      pension annuity factor   124
6.8   Duration value D (in years) of immediate pension annuity
      factor   129
6.9   Pension annuity factor at age $x = 50$ when $r = 5\%$ 131
6.10 Annuity payout at age $x = 65$ ($100,000 premium)   134
7.1   U.S. monthly premiums for a $100,000 death benefit   139
7.2   U.S. monthly premiums for a $100,000 death benefit—
      50-year-old nonsmoker   140
7.3   Net single premium for $100,000 of life insurance protection   150
7.4   Net periodic premium for $100,000 of life insurance protection   151
7.5   Model results: $100,000 life insurance—Monthly premiums
      for 50-year-old by health status   153
7.6 $100,000 life insurance—Monthly premiums for 50-year-old
      by lapse rate   156
7.7   Duration value D (in years) of NSP for life insurance   158
7.8   Modeling a book of insurance policies over time   159
8.1   DC pension retirement income   171
8.2   DC pension: Income replacement rate   171
8.3   DB pension retirement income   172
8.4   DB pension: Income replacement rate   173
8.5   Current value of sample retirement pension by valuation rate
      and by type of benefit obligation   175

8.6	Change in value (from age 45 to 46) of sample retirement pension by valuation rate and by type of benefit obligation	177
8.7	Change in pension value at various ages assuming $r = 5\%$ valuation rate	177
8.8	Change in PBO from prior year	178
8.9	Change in ABO from prior year	178
9.1	Probability of retirement ruin given (arithmetic mean) return μ of 7% with volatility σ of 20%	195
9.2	Probability of retirement ruin given μ of 5% with σ of 20%	197
9.3	Probability of retirement ruin given μ of 5% with σ of 10%	197
9.4(a)	Maximum annual spending given tolerance for 5% probability of ruin	198
9.4(b)	Maximum annual spending given tolerance for 10% probability of ruin	198
9.4(c)	Maximum annual spending given tolerance for 25% probability of ruin	199
9.5	Probability of ruin for 65-year-old male given collared portfolio under a fixed spending rate	202
9.6	Probability of ruin for 65-year-old female given collared portfolio under a fixed spending rate	203
10.1	Algebra of fixed tontine vs. nontontine investment	218
10.2	Investment returns from fixed tontines given survival to year's end	219
10.3	Algebra of variable tontine vs. nontontine investment	220
10.4	Optimal portfolio mix of stocks and safe cash	224
10.5	Monthly income from immediate annuity ($100,000 premium)	231
10.6	Cost for male of $569 monthly from immediate annuity	231
10.7	Cost for female of $539 monthly from immediate annuity	232
10.8	Should an 80-year-old annuitize?	232
10.9	ALDA: Net single premium ($_u a_x$) required at age x to produce $1 of income starting at age $x + u$	236
10.10	ALDA income multiple: Dollars received during retirement per dollar paid today	239
10.11	Lapse-adjusted ALDA income multiple	240
10.12	Profit spread (in basis points) from sale of ALDA given mortality misestimate of 20%	244
11.1	BSM put option value as a function of spot price and maturity—Strike price = $100	252
11.2	Discounted value of fees	256
11.3	Annual fee (in basis points) needed to hedge the death benefit—Female	258
11.4	Annual fee (in basis points) needed to hedge the death benefit—Male	259

11.5	Value of exponential Titanic option	262
11.6	GMWB payoff and the probability of ruin within 14.28 years	265
11.7	Impact of GMWB rate and subaccount volatility on required fee k	268
12.1	Relationship between risk aversion γ and subjective insurance premium I_γ	275
12.2	When should you annuitize in order to maximize your utility of wealth?	288
12.3	Real option to delay annuitization for a 60-year-old male who disagrees with insurance company's estimate of his mortality	289
12.4	When should you annuitize?—Given the choice of fixed and variable annuities	291
14.1(a)	RP2000 healthy (static) annuitant mortality table—Ages 50–89	296
14.1(b)	RP2000 healthy (static) annuitant mortality table—Ages 90–120	296
14.2	International comparison (year 2000) of mortality rates q_x at age 65	297
14.3(a)	2001 CSO (ultimate) insurance mortality table—Ages 50–89	298
14.3(b)	2001 CSO (ultimate) insurance mortality table—Ages 90–120	298
14.4	Cumulative distribution function for a normal random variable	299
14.5	Cumulative distribution function for a reciprocal Gamma random variable	299

PART ONE

MODELS OF ACTUARIAL FINANCE

ONE

Introduction and Motivation

1.1 The Drunk Gambler Problem

A few years ago I was asked to give a keynote lecture on the subject of retirement income planning to a group of financial advisors at an investment conference that was taking place in Las Vegas. I arrived at the conference venue early—as most neurotic speakers do—and while I was waiting to go on stage, I decided to wander around the nearby casino, taking in the sights, sounds, and smells of flashy cocktail waitresses, clanging coins, and musty cigars. Although I'm not a fan of gambling myself, I always enjoy watching others get excited about the mirage of a hot streak before eventually losing.

On this particular random walk around the roulette tables, I came across a rather eccentric-looking player smoking a particularly noxious cigar, though seemingly aloof and detached from the action around him. As I approached that particular table, I noticed two odd things about *Jorge*; a nickname I gave him. First, Jorge appeared to be using a very primitive gambling strategy. He was sitting in front of a large stack of red $5 chips, and on each spin of the wheel he would place one—and only one—of those $5 chips as a bet on the black portion of the table. For those of you who aren't familiar with roulette, this particular bet would double his money if the spinning ball landed on any one of the 18 black numbers, but it would cost him his bet if the ball came to a halt on any of the 18 red numbers or the occasional 2 green numbers. This is the simplest of all possible bets in the often complicated world of casino gambling: black, you win; red or green, you lose.

Yet, watching him closely over a number of spins, I noticed that—regardless of whether the ball landed on a black number (yielding a $10 payoff for his $5 gamble) or landed on red or green numbers (causing a loss of his original $5 chip)—he would continue mechanically to bet a $5 chip on black for each consecutive round. This seemed rather boring and pointless

3

to me. Most gamblers double up, get cautious, react to past outcomes, and take advantage of what they suppose is a hot streak. Rarely do they do the exact same thing over and over again.

Even more peculiar to me was what Jorge was doing in between roulette rounds, while the croupier was settling the score with other players and getting ready for the next spin. In one swift motion, Jorge would lift a rather large drinking glass filled with some unknown (presumably alcoholic) beverage, take a deep gulp, and then put the glass back down next to him. But, immediately upon his glass touching the green velvet surface, a waitress would top up the drinking glass and Jorge would mechanically hand her one of the $5 chips from his stack of capital. *This process continued after each and every spin of the wheel.* Try to imagine this for a moment. The waitress waits around for the wheel to stop spinning so that she can pour Jorge another round of gin—or perhaps it was scotch—so that she can get yet another $5 tip from this rather odd-looking character.

As I was standing there mesmerized by Jorge's hypnotic actions and repeated drinking, I couldn't help but wonder whether Jorge would pass out drunk and fall off his stool before he could cash in what was left of his chips.

There was no doubt in my mind that, if he continued with the same strategy, his stash of casino chips would continue to dwindle and eventually disappear. Note that after each round of spinning and drinking, his investment capital would either remain unchanged or would decline by $10. If the ball landed on black and he then paid $5 for the drink, he would be back where he started. If the ball landed on red and he then paid $5, the total loss for that round was $10. Thus, his pile of chips would never grow. The pattern went something like this: 26 chips, 26 chips, 26 chips, 24 chips, 22 chips, 22 chips, 20 chips, and so forth.

In fact, I was able to develop a simple model for calculating the odds that Jorge would run out of chips before he ran out of sobriety. From where I was standing, it appeared that he had about 20 more chips or $100 worth of cash. There was a 47.4% chance (18/38) he would get lucky with black on any given spin, and I loosely assumed a 10% chance he would pass out with any swig from the glass. Working out the math—and I promise to do this in detail in Section 1.6—there is a 15% chance he'd go bankrupt while he was still sober. Stated from the other side, I estimated an 85% chance he would pass out and fall off his chair before his stack of chips disappeared. That would be interesting to observe. Obviously, the model is crude and the numbers are rounded—and perhaps Jorge could hold his liquor better than I assumed—but I can assure you the waitress wanted Jorge's blacks to last forever.

I was planning to stick around to see whether my statistical predictions would come true, but time was running short and I had to return to my speaking engagement. As I was rushing back, weaving through the many tables, it occurred to me that I had just experienced a quaint metaphor on financial planning and risk management as retirees approach the end of the human life cycle.

With just a bit of imagination, think of what happens to most people as they reach retirement after many years of work—and hopefully with a bit of savings—but with little prospect for future employment income. They start retirement with a stack of chips that are invested (wagered or allocated) among various asset classes such as stocks, bonds, and cash. Each week, month, or year the retirees must withdraw or redeem some of those chips in order to finance their retirement income. And, whether the roulette wheel has landed on black (a bull market) or on green or red (flat or bear market), a retiree must consume. If the retiree lives for a very long time, there is a much greater chance that the chips will run out. If, on the other hand, the retiree spends only five or ten years at the retirement table, the odds are that the money will last. The retiree can obviously control the number of chips to be removed from the table (i.e., the magnitude of retirement income) as well as the riskiness of the bets (i.e., the amount allocated to the various investments). Either way, it should be relatively easy to compute the probability that a given investment strategy and a given consumption strategy will lead to retirement ruin.

So, in some odd way, we are all destined to be Jorge.

1.2 The Demographic Picture

In mid-2005 there are approximately 36 million Americans above the age of 65, which is approximately 13% of the population. By the year 2030 this number is expected to double to 70 million. Indeed, the fastest-growing segment of the elderly population is the group of those 85+ years old. The aging of the population is a global phenomenon, and many from the over-65 age group will continue working on a part-time basis well into their late sixties and seventies. A fortunate few will have earned a defined benefit (DB) pension that provides income for the rest of their natural life. Most others will have likely participated in a defined contribution (DC) plan, which places the burden of creating a pension (annuity) on the retiree. All of these retirees will have to generate a retirement income from their savings and their pension wealth. How they should do this at a sustainable rate—and what they should do with the remaining corpus of funds—is the impetus for this book.

Table 1.1 provides some hard evidence, as well as some projections, on the potential size and magnitude of the retirement income "problem." Using

Table 1.1. *Old-age dependency ratio[a]*
around the world

Country	Year[b]		
	2000	2010	2030
Australia	29.1%	34.7%	51.4%
Austria	36.6%	42.9%	77.3%
Belgium	40.5%	44.7%	68.5%
Canada	29.1%	35.2%	58.8%
Denmark	35.3%	45.5%	65.0%
Finland	35.9%	47.0%	70.6%
France	37.9%	43.0%	63.0%
Germany	41.8%	46.0%	76.5%
Greece	42.5%	46.8%	69.2%
Ireland	28.0%	30.7%	42.5%
Italy	42.7%	49.7%	78.5%
Japan	41.4%	58.4%	79.0%
Mexico	13.9%	16.2%	28.7%
New Zealand	28.6%	33.9%	54.9%
Poland	29.8%	31.4%	50.8%
South Korea	18.3%	23.9%	53.0%
Spain	38.2%	42.2%	69.7%
Sweden	41.7%	51.0%	72.5%
Switzerland	37.6%	48.9%	84.4%
Turkey	16.4%	17.8%	28.6%
United Kingdom	38.1%	43.3%	66.1%
United States	29.3%	33.2%	52.0%

[a] Size of population aged at least 60 divided by size of
population aged 20–59.
[b] Figures for 2010 and 2030 are estimated.
Source: United Nations.

data compiled by the United Nations across different countries, the table shows the number of people above age 60 as a fraction of the (working) population between the ages of 20 and 59. The larger the ratio, the greater the proportion of retirees in a given country. This ratio is often called the old-age dependency ratio, since traditionally the older people within a society are dependent on the younger (working) ones for financial and economic support. Stated differently, a larger dependency ratio creates a larger burden for the younger generation.

In the year 2000, the old-age dependency ratio hovered around 30% for the United States and Canada, but by 2030 this number will jump to 52% in the United States and to 59% in Canada, according to UN estimates. At

Table 1.2. *Expected number of years spent in retirement around the world*

Country	Males			Females		
	2000	2010	2030	2000	2010	2030
Australia	19.0	19.7	21.0	27.1	27.8	29.1
Austria	21.1	22.1	23.8	27.3	28.6	30.2
Belgium	22.0	23.1	24.8	29.8	30.9	32.5
Canada	18.5	19.2	20.5	25.5	26.2	27.5
Denmark	17.3	18.0	19.3	22.9	24.1	25.7
Finland	20.3	20.9	22.3	25.2	26.0	27.2
France	20.5	21.4	23.2	26.7	27.5	29.0
Germany	19.4	20.2	22.1	25.3	26.6	28.2
Greece	18.4	18.9	20.2	23.7	24.4	25.7
Ireland	16.9	17.4	18.7	22.7	23.6	25.2
Italy	19.5	20.1	21.4	27.0	27.8	29.1
Japan	16.3	17.3	18.9	23.5	24.7	26.8
New Zealand	18.3	18.8	20.2	24.8	25.5	26.9
Spain	18.8	19.3	20.7	25.7	26.4	27.7
Sweden	18.7	19.4	20.6	23.2	23.9	25.4
Switzerland	16.6	17.2	18.4	24.3	24.9	26.2
Turkey	14.8	15.4	16.7	15.3	15.9	17.0
United Kingdom	18.0	18.9	20.5	23.8	25.0	26.8
United States	16.8	17.6	19.4	22.0	23.2	24.9

Notes: The actual retirement age varies by country. Figures for 2010 and 2030 are estimated.
Sources: Watson Wyatt and World Economic Forum.

the other extreme are countries like Mexico and Turkey, whose dependency ratios are currently in the low to mid-teens and should grow only to 28% by 2030. Despite the variations, these numbers are increasing in all countries.

According to a recent report prepared by the consulting firm of Watson Wyatt for the World Economic Forum, the main causes for the projected increases in the dependency ratio are a lower fertility ratio and the unprecedented increases in the length of human life. People live longer—beyond ages 60, 70, and 80, as demonstrated in Table 1.2—but they aren't born any earlier. So, the ratio of older people to younger people within any country continues to increase.

Human longevity is a fascinating topic in its own right. According to Dr. James Vaupel, Director of the Max Planck Institute for Demographic Research, the average amount of time that females live in the healthiest countries has been on the rise during the last 160 years at a steady pace of three months per year. For example, in 2005 Japanese women are estimated to have a life expectancy of approximately 85 years. Currently, Japanese women are the record holders when it comes to human longevity, and the projection is that—four years from now, in 2009—Japanese women will have a life expectancy of 86 years. Now let your imagination do the mathematics. What will the numbers look like in twenty or thirty years?

The oncoming wave of very long-lived retirees—who will possibly be spending more time in retirement than they did working—will require extensive and unique financial assistance in managing their financial affairs. Moreover, financial planners and investment advisors, who are on the front line against this oncoming wave, are hardly ignorant of this trend. Some have begun to retool themselves to better understand and meet the needs of this unique group of retirees. They are pressuring insurance companies, investment banks, and money managers to design, sell, and promote retirement income (a.k.a. pension) products that go beyond traditional assets.

For thirty years the financial services industry has focused on the *accumulation* phase for millions of active workers. Mutual fund and investment companies were falling all over themselves to provide guidance on the right mix of mutual funds, the right savings rate, and the most prudent level of risk to build the largest nest egg with the least amount of risk. The terms "asset allocation" and "savings rate" have become ubiquitous. Most investors understand the need for diversified investment portfolios.

What consumers and their advisors have less of an appreciation for are the interactions between longevity, spending, income, and the right investment portfolio. In part, the fault for this intellectual gap lies at the doorsteps of those instructors who teach portfolio theory within a static, one-period framework in which everybody lives to the end of the period. In fact, I have been teaching undergraduate, graduate, and doctoral students in business finance for over fifteen years and am continuously dismayed by their lack of knowledge about (and interest in) actuarial and insurance matters. Of course, learning about pensions or term life and disability insurance is not the most enjoyable activity when the competing course in the other lecture hall is teaching currency swap contracts, exotic derivatives, and hedge funds. Death and disability can't compete. For the most part, the students lack a framework that links the various ideas in a coherent manner. I hope this book helps make some of these actuarial issues more palatable and interesting to financial "quants."

Against this backdrop of financial demographics, product innovation, and human longevity, this book will attempt to merge the analytic language of modern financial theory with actuarial and insurance ideas motivated by what we may call the retirement income dilemma.

1.3 The Ideal Audience

The ideal audience for this book is ... me. Yes, me. I know it might sound a bit odd, but writing this book has most basically given me a wonderful opportunity to collect and organize my thoughts on the topic of retirement income planning. I suspect that most authors will confirm a similar feeling and objective. Researching, organizing, and writing this book have helped me establish the financial and mathematical background needed to understand the topic with some rigor and depth. I am using this book also as a textbook for a graduate course I teach at the Schulich School of Business at York University (Toronto) on the topic of financial models for pension and insurance.

On a broader and more serious level, this book has two intended audiences. The first group consists of the growing legion of financial planners and investment advisors who possess a quantitative background or at least a numerical inclination. This group is in the daily business of giving practical advice to individual investors. They need a relevant and useful framework for explaining to their clients the risks they incur by either spending too much money in retirement, not having a diversified investment portfolio, or not hedging against the risks of underestimating their own longevity. And so I hope that the numerous stories, examples, tables, and case studies scattered throughout this book can provide an intuitive foundation for the underlying mathematical ideas. Yes, I know that some parts of the book, especially those involving calculus, may not be readily accessible to all. But as Dr. Roger Penrose—a world-renowned professor of mathematical physics at Oxford University—said in the introduction to his recent book *The Road to Reality: A Complete Guide to the Laws of the Universe*: "Do not be afraid to skip equations or parts of chapters when they begin to get a mite too turgid! I do this often myself ...."

The second audience for this book consists of my traditional colleagues, peers, and fellow researchers in the area of financial economics, pensions, and insurance. There is a growing number of scholars around the world who are interested in furthering knowledge and practice by focusing on the *normative* aspects of finance for individuals. Collectively, they are creating scientific foundations for personal wealth management, quite similarly to the fine tradition of personal health management and the role of personal physicians. Indeed, work by such luminaries as Harry Markowitz (1991) and Robert Merton (2003) has emphasized the need for different tools when addressing personal financial problems as opposed to corporate financial problems.

1.4 Learning Objectives

This book is an attempt to provide a theory of applied financial planning over the human life cycle, with particular emphasis on retirement planning in a stochastic environment. My objective is not necessarily to analyze what people are doing or the positive aspects of whether they are rational, utility maximizing, and efficient in their decisions, but rather to provide the underlying analytic tools to help them and their advisors make better financial decisions. If I could sum up—in a half-joking manner—the educational objectives and underlying theme that run through this book, it would be to guide Jorge on his investment/gambling strategy so that he could continue tipping the waitress after every spin of the wheel and, it is hoped, pass out before his money is depleted. On a more serious note, this book is about developing the analytic framework and background models to help retiring individuals—and those who are planning for retirement—manage their financial affairs so that they can maintain a comfortable and dignified lifestyle during their golden years.

The main text consists of twelve chapters (an appendix of tables and a bibliography are also included). An ideal background for this book would be a basic understanding of the rules of differential and integral calculus, some basic probability theory, and familiarity with everyday financial instruments and markets.

Here is a brief chapter-by-chapter outline of what will be covered.

Part I Models of Actuarial Finance

1. *Introduction and Motivation.* This chapter.
2. *Modeling the Human Life Cycle.* I review the basic time value of money (TVM) mathematics in discrete time as it applies to the human life cycle. I present some deterministic models for computing the amount of savings needed during one's working years to fund a given standard of living during the retirement years. I briefly discuss how this relates to pension plans and the concept of retirement income replacement rates. The modeling is done without any need for calculus and requires only a basic understanding of algebra.

3. *Models of Human Mortality.* I introduce actuarial mortality tables and hazard rates using the tools of continuous-time calculus and probability. I present the analytic mortality workhorse of the book, which is the Gompertz–Makeham (GoMa) and exponential model for lifetime uncertainty. This chapter should help develop a thorough understanding of the *remaining lifetime* random variable, which is critical to all pension and insurance calculations.

4. *Valuation Models of Deterministic Interest.* I review the basics of continuous-time versus discrete interest rates as well as the term structure of interest rates. I provide valuation formulas for coupon bonds under a deterministic interest rate curve in continuous time. I introduce the concept of duration and convexity in continuous time and show how this can be used to approximate changes in bond prices.

5. *Models of Risky Financial Investments.* I develop models for understanding the long-term trade-off between risk and reward in the stock market. The analytics of portfolio diversification and the probability of losing money are examined. I start with some historical data and evidence on asset class investment returns. I then motivate portfolio growth rates and introduce the Brownian motion model underlying the lognormal distribution of investment returns. The chapter ends with a discussion of the difference between space and time diversification.

6. *Models of Pension Life Annuities.* I start by illustrating current market quotes of pension annuities and then move on to the valuation of life and pension annuities that provide income for the remainder of one's life. This is done by merging the concepts of interest rates, mortality rates, and pensions. This chapter can also be understood within the context of the valuation of bonds with a random maturity. The models are implemented for Gompertz–Makeham mortality; also, variable immediate annuities and joint life annuities are valued.

7. *Models of Life Insurance.* Features of real-world insurance prices and contracts are introduced. I then provide valuation formulas for basic term life insurance. I discuss how these formulas relate to pension annuities as well as the arbitrage relationship between them. Also discussed are the taxation treatment of insurance and its various permutations such as whole life, variable life, universal life, and so on.

8. *Models of DB vs. DC Pensions.* This chapter reviews the basic forms of public and private pensions. I develop some models for computing the value of a defined benefit (DB) pension promise and then compare this to a defined contribution (DC) pension. I discuss basic pension

funding and accounting issues, such as the accumulated benefit obligation (ABO) and projected benefit obligation (PBO) in continuous time. This chapter links ideas of mortality, annuities, and life-cycle savings.

Part II Wealth Management: Applications and Implications

9. *Sustainable Spending at Retirement.* What is the most a retiree can safely spend during retirement without running the risk of ruin? How much do you need at retirement in a random and uncertain world? Introducing the stochastic present value (SPV), a simple little formula.
10. *Longevity Insurance Revisited.* An in-depth examination of the age-related benefits from annuitization. I quantify mortality credits and the Implied Longevity Yield (ILY). Recent and future innovations in longevity insurance are discussed.

Part III Advanced Topics

11. *Options within Variable Annuities.* An analysis of exotic put options that are embedded within variable annuity policies (insurance savings accounts). I show how to value and price options that have a random maturity date and are paid by installments.
12. *The Utility of Annuitization.* The utility function of wealth, and the differences between value, price, and cost. I discuss the microeconomic foundations of the demand for insurance and annuities. This chapter gives another perspective on the best age at which to annuitize, using the tools and framework of "real option" pricing. Valuation of the option to wait is also discussed.

1.5 Acknowledgments

This is not the first book I have written and hopefully it will not be the last, which is why I have learned to start the acknowledgments by thanking my dear wife Edna who—well into our second decade of marriage—continues to tolerate my odd and moody work habits. She carefully read large portions of the book, or at least the parts written in English, and provided valuable feedback and inspiration at important junctures. My four daughters Dahlia, Natalie, Maya, and Zoe deserve a special thank-you for putting up with dad, who locked himself in his office for hours on end instead of doing the usual fatherly things on evenings, weekends, and vacations. I'm especially grateful to baby Zoe, who was born in late 2004—just when I was getting into the swing of things with this book—and would wake me up at about 3:00 every morning. Unknowingly, and with grudging admission on my part, she arranged for me to have large chunks of time each day to work on the book, well before the sun came up.

After my immediate family, I must start by thanking Anna Abaimova—from The IFID Centre at the Fields Institute in Toronto—who carefully edited, corrected, and then reviewed various portions of the manuscript as it was being written by the (often sloppy) author. Along the same lines, Matt Darnell and the excellent staff at Cambridge University Press, especially Scott Parris and Brianne Millett, deserve a special thank-you for their patience and hard work.

From an academic point of view, I can trace the intellectual lineage of large portions of this book to my research collaborations—in the field of actuarial finance and quantitative wealth management—with Sid Browne, Narat Charupat, Peng Chen, Kwok Ho, Huaxiong Huang, Amin Mawani, Kristen Moore, Steven Posner, David Promislow, Chris Robinson, Tom Salisbury, Hans Tuenter, and Jenny Young. Most of the ideas, models, and analysis within the core of the book had their genesis in joint research papers with these co-authors. In some sense I should be described as an editor who is compiling joint research ideas, not as the author of an original work. And, although I have learned a tremendous amount from working with each of these thirteen co-authors, I must single out Tom Salisbury and Chris Robinson for their mentorship and guidance ever since my days as a Ph.D. student.

Also, I owe a special thank-you to my co-editors at the *Journal of Pension Economics and Finance,* which, like this book, is published by Cambridge University Press. Jeff Brown, Steve Haberman, and Mike Orszag have taught me a lot about pension economics and retirement planning during many years of joint editorial work. Their own research on the topic of retirement income has influenced my thinking and writing as well.

In addition, I would like to thank reviewers of the manuscript: Narat Charupat, Dale Domian, Jim Dunlea, Gady Jacoby, Marie-Eve Lachance, Joanne Lui, Mike Orszag, Scott Robinson, Mark Schell, Kevin Zhu, and Jun Zhuo for their careful reading, quick turnaround, and helpful comments.

Finally, I owe a debt of gratitude to the thousands of practicing financial planners, wealth managers, and investment advisors who have attended my public lectures and keynote presentations on the analytics of retirement income planning. They are the ones who have encouraged me to continue thinking, talking, and writing about these practical issues from a distinctly mathematical perspective. There is nothing more gratifying than hearing their practical questions, translating them into the language of financial probabilities, and then returning to the ivory tower I inhabit in order to share these fresh and relevant problems with my research colleagues.

1.6 Appendix: Drunk Gambler Solution

For those of you who are wondering how to "solve" the drunk gambler problem, here is the answer. The gambler starts the evening in a casino with initial capital denoted by w_0, in dollars. On each spin of the roulette wheel the gambler bets exactly \$1 on Black, which has a probability denoted by p of paying \$2 at the end of the spin; there is a probability of $1 - p$ of paying zero if the ball lands on either Red or Green. Then, after every spin, the gambler pays \$1 for a drink, regardless of whether he won or lost. The same idea can be scaled up to \$5, \$10, or even \$100 individual bets, as long as the amount wagered on each spin is precisely the amount paid for the drink.

Either way, at the end of each round of spinning and drinking, the gambler is left with capital (i.e. chips) in the amount of $w_i = w_{i-1} + X_i - 1$, where X_i is a random variable with $\Pr[X_i = +1] = p$ and $\Pr[X_i = -1] = 1 - p$. Or, put another way: $w_i = w_{i-1}$ with probability p when the ball lands on Black, and $w_i = w_{i-1} - 2$ with probability $1 - p$ when the ball lands on Red or Green.

Also, each time the gambler buys (and immediately consumes) a drink for \$1, there is a constant probability q that he "passes out" and thus effectively ends the game (as well as the evening). Likewise, the probability that he remains "sober" and survives to the next round is $1 - q$. My critical assumption in all of this—which simplifies the mathematics greatly—is that sobriety is independent across drinks and so the odds of being sober after i rounds is $(1 - q)^i$; this is what happens under independent coin tosses or with the roulette wheel itself.

Note that this person will eventually be "ruined" and run out of gambling chips—even if he is still sober—provided that $p < 0.5$, which is the case for most roulette wheels that are tilted in the house's favor. Indeed, even on a relatively honest table with 18 Blacks, 18 Reds, and 2 Greens, the odds of getting Black is $p = 18/38 = 47.3\%$.

The underlying random variable X_i, which here "moves the chips" from one round to the next, is called a *Bernoulli* random variable. And the sum of identical and independent Bernoulli random variables is (defined as) binomially distributed. The probability of being solvent after n rounds, where $n > w_0/2$, is the probability of getting at least $n - w_0/2$ Blacks in a collection on n Bernoulli trials. For example, if the gambler starts with $w_0 = 20$ dollars, then the probability of being solvent after $n = 30$ rounds (ignoring whether the gambler is still sober or not) is equivalent to the probability of getting $n - w_0/2 = 20$ Blacks in a collection of $n = 30$ Bernoulli trials. Note that if $n < w_0/2$ then it is mathematically impossible to become ruined, since at worst the gambler has had a streak of $n < w_0/2$ Reds and paid only $w_0/2$ for drinks. This still adds up to less than w_0.

I now denote the probability of being ruined at precisely time i by R_i. It is the probability of having $w_{i-1} = 1$ or $w_{i-1} = 2$ at the end of round $i - 1$, multiplied by $1 - p$. Note that if w_0 is odd then w will equal 1 just before ruin. But if w_0 is even, then w will be equal to 2 just before ruin. The probability I am trying to compute is the probability of being sober exactly when the money runs out. This Ruined while Sober probability can therefore be written as:

$$\text{RwS} := \sum_{i=1}^{\infty} R_i (1 - q)^i. \tag{1.1}$$

To start with, let k be the largest integer strictly less than $w_0/2$—that's the largest number of Reds the gambler can have without being ruined. For example, if $w_0 = 20$ then $k = 9$, since if he gets more than 9 Reds the chips are gone. The probability of becoming ruined precisely at time i can be computed explicitly via

$$R_i = (1 - p) \binom{i - 1}{k} p^{i-1-k} (1 - p)^k. \tag{1.2}$$

This formula is based on elementary combinatorial arguments. The number of ways to get k Reds from a total of $i - 1$ spins is equal to $i - 1$ "choose" k. This is then multiplied by the probability of getting k Reds and $i - 1 - k$ Blacks, which is $p^{i-1-k}(1 - p)^k$. The product of both these terms is then multiplied by $1 - p$, which is the probability of getting ruined on the ith round. Putting all the bits and pieces together by adding up the infinite number of terms in equation (1.2), the formula for the Ruined while Sober probability can be expressed as

$$\text{RwS} := \left(1 - \frac{q}{1 - p + pq}\right)^{k+1}, \tag{1.3}$$

which is equal to 1 when $q = 0$ and is less than 1 as long as $q > 0$.

For example, when $p = 18/38$ and $q = 10\%$ and $k = 9$, then the relevant probability is 14.7%, which is the number I mentioned in the body of the chapter. On the other hand, if the probability of passing out is a lower $q = 5\%$ in any given round, then the Ruined while Sober probability is a higher 38.5%. Also, if the gambler starts with $w_0 = 25$ dollars, then the largest number of Reds he can get and not be ruined is $k = 12$, so that RwS = 8.2% under a $q = 10\%$. This is because the gambler is starting with a larger capital base and so it is more likely he will get drunk prior to the inevitable point at which all his chips vanish. Indeed, under the same $w_0 = 25$ and $k = 12$, if the chances of passing out in any given round are reduced to $q = 5\%$ then the Ruined while Sober probability is increased to RwS $=$ 28.9%. Finally, if $q = 0$ and the gambler never gets drunk, then (1.3) collapses to RwS $= 100\%$ regardless of either the value of p (getting Black) or the value of w_0, since the gambler is destined for ruin.

TWO

Modeling the Human Life Cycle

2.1 The Next Sixty Years of Your Life

Suspend your disbelief for a moment and bear with me as I imagine the next sixty years of your financial life. Assume that you enter the labor force or start working at the age of 35. Your job is expected to pay a fixed and predictable $50,000 per year for the next thirty years, after which you retire at age 65. This job provides no pension or retirement benefits. Rather, it is your personal responsibility to make sure you *save* enough during your thirty working years so that you can maintain a dignified standard of living or *consumption* during your retirement years. For the moment, let us ignore inflation and income taxes—two important issues I shall address in detail later—and finally, imagine you die at the ripe old age of 95.

What fraction of your salary must you save during your thirty years of work so that, when you retire with your accumulated nest egg, you can generate an equivalent income stream that will last for the remaining thirty years of life?

Note that if your saving rate is too high—say $20,000 per year, leaving you with only $50,000 − $20,000 = $30,000 annually to live off during your working years—then you might end up with a much better lifestyle when you are retired as compared to when you are working. That wouldn't make sense, would it? On the other hand, if you don't save enough while you are working then you might end up with a much lower standard of living when you retire. Would that be desirable? Obviously some people prefer a higher standard of living when they are young (especially if you ask them while they are still young). Others say that retirement is when they plan to "enjoy their money," which is why they might want to save (much) more during their working years. Yet another group will claim they just want a smooth and predictable standard of living during their entire life, and some

17

might argue that the point of saving money is to create a legacy and bequest for remaining generations. In any case, the point here is definitely not to tell you what you *should* do or should want. Rather, the point of this chapter and the models developed in the next few pages is to examine the savings needed to create a smooth profile of consumption over your entire life, assuming that your objective was to spend your last dollar on your last living day. This is often called the "die broke" strategy.

This rather artificial problem is actually at the heart of financial planning, and most textbooks on personal finance begin the discussion at precisely this point. For starters, I will develop a series of formulas to answer this question, *assuming* that interest rates or periodic investment returns are fixed and known in advance. This simple case will set the stage for the more advanced scenario involving random investment returns, unknown mortality (i.e., how long you will live in retirement), uncertain inflation, changing wages, and unavoidable income taxes. For now, let me start by introducing the following notation and symbols.

2.2 Future Value of Savings

Let $i = 1, \ldots, N$ denote the number of years you will be working, where N is your final year of work (a.k.a. the "retirement year"). Let W denote your constant wage or salary while you are working, let S denote your constant annual savings—which is assumed to take place in one lump sum at the end of each working year—and let C denote your desired consumption or spending once you are retired (this will likewise be withdrawn or consumed at the end of each retirement year). Note that, while you are saving S dollars during your working years, these funds will accumulate and grow at an effective annual investment rate of R. Therefore, at retirement you will have accumulated the *future value of savings*:

$$\text{FV}(S, R, N) = \sum_{i=1}^{N} S(1 + R)^{(N-i)}. \tag{2.1}$$

The intuition for this equation should be quite simple. The future value of the S dollars you save at the end of the first ($i = 1$) year of work will grow for a total of $N - 1$ years until retirement. This portion—or piece of savings—grows to $S(1+R)^{N-1}$. Then, the future value of the S dollars you save at the end of the second ($i = 2$) year of work will grow for $N - 2$ years to a total value of $S(1 + R)^{N-2}$, and so forth. Remember that savings are assumed to take place at the end of the year, and your last-portion

S is saved one instant prior to retirement and thus will not accumulate any interest. In other words, $S(1 + R)^{(N-i)}$ is exactly S when $i = N$.

Now, using no more than the basic algebraic formula for the sum of a finite geometric series,

$$1 + x + x^2 + x^3 + x^4 + \cdots + x^n = \frac{x^{n+1} - 1}{x - 1},$$

the right-hand side of (2.1) can be expressed in closed form (provided $R > 0$) and without a summation sign by

$$\mathrm{FV}(S, R, N) = S\frac{(1 + R)^N - 1}{R}. \tag{2.2}$$

For example, if you save \$1 at the end of each year for 30 years at a 5% rate of interest, then the future value of your savings at retirement will be $\mathrm{FV}(1, 0.05, 30) = \$66.44$. This expression scales linearly, so that the future value of \$1,000 saved for 30 years at the same 5% interest is \$66,439; if you save \$10,000 per year, you will have \$664,390 at retirement, and so forth.

Of course, if I double the investment rate to 10% per year, then the future value of savings increases by more than a factor of 2. The relationship is not linear in the investment rate R. The precise value is $\mathrm{FV}(1, 0.10, 30) = \$164.50$, which is roughly 150% more wealth at retirement when you earn $R = 10\%$ versus $R = 5\%$.

Observe that carelessly substituting $R = 0\%$ into (2.2) yields an error because of the zero in the denominator. This does not mean that there is no answer when $R = 0$. Rather, the correct way to approach a zero investment rate is by going back to equation (2.1) itself, or by taking the "calculus limit" of equation (2.2) as $R \to 0$. Either of these approaches leads to the obvious $\mathrm{FV}(S, 0, N) = SN$.

Note also that there is nothing special or unique about annual savings. The conscientious worker could save the same S dollars per year but on a monthly or weekly basis—in smaller pieces of $S/12$ or $S/52$. In this case, the relevant future value of savings at retirement would be denoted by $\mathrm{FV}(S/12, R/12, 12N)$ or $\mathrm{FV}(S/52, R/52, 52N)$, where the interest R is now defined as a nominal rate that is compounded 12 or 52 times per year. For example, if you save \$1 per year at a rate of $R = 5\%$ for 30 years, then $\mathrm{FV}(1, 0.05, 30) = \$66.44$. On the other hand, if you save \$0.25 per quarter at a rate of 1.25% per quarter for a period of 30 years (120 quarters), then the relevant value is $\mathrm{FV}(0.25, 0.0125, 120) = \$68.80$, which is more than what you get from saving the money annually. If the savings are deposited monthly then FV(1/12, 0.05/12, 360) = $69.36; if weekly, FV(1/52, 0.05/52, 1560) = $69.57. In each case the worker is saving a total of $1 per year, but the higher frequency of saving and compounding results in a higher future value of savings at retirement.

In sum, I have presented a versatile and general formula for computing the future value of your retirement nest egg, assuming you save S for the next N years. In any financial calculator, it is simply the future value of a constant annuity.

2.3 Present Value of Consumption

Now let's examine the retirement period in terms of income, spending, and consumption. Imagine you have reached retirement with the nest egg FV(S, R, N) and now intend to spend or consume C dollars per year from your accumulated savings. At the end of each year, you withdraw C dollars from your nest egg or investment account to finance your retirement needs.

I will now compute the present value (where the word "present" refers to the exact date of your retirement) of your consumption and spending needs. In terms of notation, let $j = 1, \ldots, D$ denote the years in retirement until the year of death, which is denoted by D. For example, $D = 30$ is 30 years of retirement. The formula we need now is the *present value of consumption*:

$$PV(C, R, D) = \sum_{j=1}^{D} \frac{C}{(1+R)^j}. \tag{2.3}$$

The present value of your planned consumption and spending during retirement is the value of each year's spending discounted by the relevant time period. The end-of-first-year's spending is discounted by $(1+R)^1$, the end-of-second-year's spending is discounted by $(1+R)^2, \ldots$. Add these pieces together and you are left with equation (2.3).

Once again, using basic algebra to add up the series on the right-hand side of (2.3), we arrive at

$$PV(C, R, D) = C\frac{1 - (1+R)^{-D}}{R}, \tag{2.4}$$

with a similar understanding that PV($C, 0, D$) = CD.

For instance, if you want a nest egg at retirement that is large enough to provide you with $D = 30$ years of $50,000 per year, then you need PV(1, 0.05, 30) = $15.37 per dollar of income, which is 50000 × 15.372 = $768,600 of savings at retirement. Remember that all of this is assuming your money earns a constant $R = 5\%$ per year in retirement. But if your money can earn a higher $R = 10\%$ per year during retirement, then you need only $PV(1, 0.1, 30) = \$9.43$ per dollar of retirement consumption spending, or $50000 \times 9.427 = \$471{,}350$ in retirement savings. Notice the dramatic impact of the investment rate on the required sum of money.

At the risk of repeating myself, the main point can be stated as follows. *If all of your money is invested in a savings account or investment fund earning R% per annum and you intend on spending \$1 per year for a period of D years during retirement, then you must have at least* $PV(1, R, D)$ *on the date of retirement. If you start with less than* $PV(1, R, D)$ *in your nest egg, then your consumption spending of \$1 per year will lead to financial ruin at some point prior to the end of the D years.*

Here is a more formal way to think about this statement. Assume that you enter the retirement years with a lump sum of X dollars (i.e., your nest egg). This money is then completely invested in a bank or savings account that earns an effective $R\%$ each and every year. At the end of the first year of retirement you spend or consume \$1 from the portfolio, which leaves you with the following wealth after your first year in retirement:

$$[\text{nest egg at year 1}] = X(1 + R) - 1.$$

You then continue investing the (large) remaining funds in the same account earning the same return of $R\%$ and spend another dollar at the end of the second year of retirement (the dollar value is irrelevant because the model scales linearly in wealth). Your wealth after your second year in retirement is

$$[\text{nest egg at year 2}] = (X(1 + R) - 1)(1 + R) - 1.$$

In the same manner, the wealth after your third year of retirement is

$$[\text{nest egg at year 3}] = ((X(1 + R) - 1)(1 + R) - 1)(1 + R) - 1.$$

Notice the pattern. Each year you subtract \$1 and then allow the remainder to grow at the exact same rate R. Do this for exactly D years and, after collecting some terms, you should be left with the following simplified expression for the wealth after your Dth year in retirement:

$$[\text{nest egg at year } D] = X(1 + R)^D - \sum_{j=1}^{D}(1 + R)^{D-j}. \qquad (2.5)$$

Now here is the crucial part. If this number is greater than zero, then your initial nest egg of X has lasted for D years. If this number is less than zero, you have been ruined prior to D years of retirement. More importantly, if your wealth—or portfolio—hits zero precisely at the end of the Dth year of retirement, then X must satisfy the following equation:

$$X := \sum_{j=1}^{D} \frac{1}{(1+R)^j}.$$

That is: If your initial retirement nest egg (exactly equal to X) is invested at a rate of $R\%$ per year and if you consume \$1 each year, then you will run out of money at time D. This value of X is precisely the present value of \$1 consumed during retirement as presented in (2.3) and (2.4). Notice the two distinct ways of arriving at the same statement. You need at least $\text{PV}(1, R, D)$ to finance D years of retirement consumption.

2.4 Exchange Rate between Savings and Consumption

We are well on our way to answering the main question posed earlier. We have an expression for the future (retirement) value of your savings, and we have an expression for the present (retirement) value of your spending or consumption plan. Retirement is the focal point. If we set these values equal to each other, then we can solve for the relationship between desired consumption and required savings. Of course, there are many ways to analyze the relationship between savings and consumption, and here I take a relatively simple approach. I will incorporate utility theory into retirement decision models in Chapter 12.

Equating (2.2) and (2.4) leaves us with

$$\text{FV}(S, R, N) = \text{PV}(C, R, D),$$

$$C = S \frac{\text{FV}(1, R, N)}{\text{PV}(1, R, D)}. \tag{2.6}$$

One unit of savings S multiplied by the ratio in the right-hand side of equation (2.6) provides us with the equivalent units of consumption.

At the risk of overwhelming the reader with too many symbols, I will define the *exchange rate* or ratio between the future value and the present value by the Greek letter alpha.

$$\alpha := \frac{\text{FV}(1, R, N)}{\text{PV}(1, R, D)} = \frac{(1+R)^N - 1}{1 - (1+R)^{-D}}. \tag{2.7}$$

The α-value can range from a small number near 0 to a large number much greater than 1. By carefully inspecting equation (2.7), you should come to

Table 2.1. *Financial exchange rate between $1 saved annually over 30 working years and dollar consumption during retirement*

Investment rate ($R\%$)	Number of years D over which retirement income is required					
	15	20	25	30	35	40
0.0	2.000	1.500	1.200	1.000	0.857	0.750
1.0	2.509	1.928	1.579	1.348	1.183	1.059
2.0	3.157	2.481	2.078	1.811	1.623	1.483
3.0	3.985	3.198	2.732	2.427	2.214	2.058
4.0	5.044	4.127	3.590	3.243	3.005	2.834
5.0	6.401	5.331	4.714	4.322	4.058	3.872
6.0	8.140	6.893	6.184	5.743	5.453	5.254
7.0	10.371	8.916	8.106	7.612	7.296	7.085
8.0	13.235	11.538	10.612	10.063	9.720	9.500
10.0	21.627	19.321	18.122	17.449	17.056	16.821
12.0	35.433	32.309	30.770	29.960	29.519	29.275
14.0	58.088	53.870	51.912	50.950	50.465	50.216

the realization that α will increase as R increases or as N increases and that α will decrease as D increases. Also, when $N = D$ and $R = 0$, the corresponding value is $\alpha = 1$. Think about it: If investment rates are zero and you are working for the same number of years you are retired, then you must save the exact amount that you wish to consume.

Table 2.1 displays the savings/consumption exchange rate α assuming $N = 30$ working years of saving under various values of the investment rate R and retirement period D.

For example, if you can earn $R = 5\%$ on your savings during each year of work and during 30 years of retirement, then each dollar of savings will translate into a retirement income of $4.32 per year. If under the same $R = 5\%$ investment rate you desire income for only 25 years, then you can afford to withdraw $4.71 per year during retirement. Thus, although 30 years of saving $1 per year under a 5% investment rate accumulates to the same $FV(1, 0.05, 30) = \$66.44$ nest egg, you can afford to spend $4.71 for 25 years because this is equivalent to $4.32 for 30 years. Note that (respectively) $PV(4.714, 0.05, 25) \approx \$66.44$ and $PV(4.322, 0.05, 30) \approx \$66.44$ for the present value of income, per equation (2.4).

Table 2.1 also confirms the intuition that when $R = 0\%$, the nest egg grows to the sum of savings NS. Moreover, the amount of income that one can extract during retirement is precisely $C = S$ when the number of years in retirement $D = N$. Note also the unbelievably high α multiples (i.e., the exchange rate) when the investment rate is $R = 14\%$. A single

dollar of savings for each of 30 working years will translate into $50 of an-
nual retirement income for 30 years. The $\alpha = 50$ exchange rate should be
encouraging to savers who can invest aggressively and earn high rates of
return over long periods of time. Remember, though, that for this 50-to-1
deal to work you must earn $R = 14\%$ each and every year during the next
60 years of your life. It is not enough to earn 14% on average† or most of
the time. You must earn 14% each year for 30 years of saving and 30 years
of retirement. Only then will $1 provide you with $50 of income. Later I
will address what happens when investment returns or interest rates are unknown and how to think about this problem, which is obviously the case
for actual 60-year horizons.

Note that I have avoided making any judgment on whether 4%, 8%, or
even 10% is a realistic investment rate over the long horizons we are discussing. I will return to this topic in Chapter 5. For now I will say only
that it would be ridiculous to assume you can earn *any* rate year after year,
since markets, interest rates, and bond yields are random and tend to fluc-
tuate over time.

Here is another way to use Table 2.1. Imagine that you contribute $1 to
a (personal pension plan) savings account during 30 working years in exchange for a lifetime pension income when you retire. If this pension plan
gives you $3 of retirement income for each $1 of contributions, or a 3-to-1
exchange rate, then the *implied* investment return from this pension arrangement is approximately 3% if you plan to be retired for 20 years (unhealthy
male) and 4% if you plan to be retired for 35 years (healthy female). The
greater the implied investment return, the more lucrative is the pension deal.

To conclude this discussion, an interesting number in Table 2.1 is the
exchange rate α for a 30-year retirement when the interest rate $R = 6\%$,
which some consider to be a reasonable long-term estimate for investment
returns after inflation is taken into account. In this case, $1 of saving per
year generates roughly $6 of retirement income per year, or $10,000 of saving per year provides almost $60,000 of income in retirement. Figure 2.1
provides a graphical illustration of the underlying financial life cycle in this
case. You can see the gradual change in wealth that is experienced during
30 years of saving $1 and 30 years of consuming $6, all under a constant
investment rate of 6%.

This idea of a savings/consumption exchange rate is at the core of most
government pension plans that require working citizens to save for retirement by imposing a payroll tax on their wages and then provide them with
a pension or lifetime income when they retire. Of course, most government

---

† This holds whether the average is arithmetic or geometric (see Chapter 5 for this distinction).

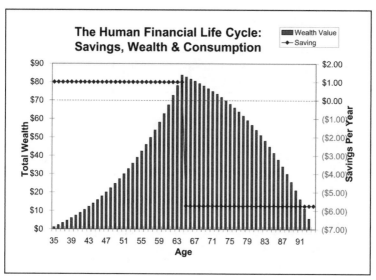

Figure 2.1. Constant investment rate

pension plans have elements of insurance and redistribution in addition to pure savings. Namely, the income it provides during retirement is not necessarily linked to your own savings and wages but rather to an average industrial wage earned by the working population. I will talk more about the insurance and redistributive aspects of social pension systems in Chapter 8.

Nevertheless, despite the caution one must exercise in generalizing our simple models, Table 2.2 provides a rough summary of the so-called exchange rate between savings and consumption from social (government-funded) pension plans around the world. It displays the total payroll tax paid by workers in various countries and compares it to the pension benefit as a percentage of an average worker's wages. For example, U.S. workers "save" roughly 12% of their wages via a payroll tax (half paid by the employer and half paid by the employee), and this entitles the worker to a consumption stream (pension benefit) of approximately 39% of their wage when they retire. Using our language, the exchange rate is a little more than 3-to-1. Mexico appears to have the highest exchange rate at 6-to-1 (which is the only exchange rate in Figure 2.2 close to the 6-to-1 value mentioned previously as a viable goal in retirement savings); Canada is not far behind with a 4-to-1 rate. In fact, the implied "return" numbers might be close to zero when you consider the long time over which the payroll taxes are collected (i.e. saved) and the relatively short period of time over which the pension income is paid out. Of course, any comparison between countries should be done very carefully, since each has its own caps, exclusions, and

Table 2.2. *Government-sponsored pension plans:*
How generous are they?

Country	Consumption rate $\approx C/W$	Saving (tax) rate $\approx S/W$	Exchange rate (α)
Belgium	34%	16%	2.08
Canada	33%	8%	4.23
France	26%	15%	1.76
Germany	39%	20%	2.00
Greece	46%	20%	2.30
Italy	73%	33%	2.23
Japan	42%	17%	2.40
Mexico	105%	18%	6.03
Netherlands	23%	24%	0.94
Poland	104%	33%	3.18
Portugal	77%	35%	2.22
Spain	61%	28%	2.16
Turkey	87%	20%	4.36
United Kingdom	14%	5%	2.75
United States	39%	12%	3.15

Source: Watson Wyatt calculations for World Economic Forum (data:
early 2000).

limits. But the general picture shows that savings (via payroll taxes) and
consumption (pension benefits) can be linked using a framework like the
one described here.

2.5 A Neutral Replacement Rate

I am now (finally) ready to answer the main question that initially sent us
down this path. I earn $W = \$50,000$ per year for $N = 30$ years and am
wondering how much I must save, denoted by S, so that my nest egg at retirement will be enough to provide the same exact standard of living I had
prior to retirement, which is $W - S$.

Equation (2.6) provides us with a relationship between saving S and the
desired consumption C, which in this case is $C = W - S$. This leads to

$$W - S = S\alpha \iff S = \frac{W}{1 + \alpha}, \tag{2.8}$$

where once again α denotes the savings/consumption exchange rate. We
are searching for a value of S such that $W - S$ is precisely equal to C, which
is αS. And so it all comes down to the investment rate R. When $R = 8\%$

and $N = D = 30$, we obtain $\alpha = 10.063$ and therefore $S = \$4{,}520$, according to (2.8).

Observe that by saving $S = \$4{,}520$ each year you are left with a net wage of \$45,480. The future value of $S = \$4{,}520$ is $FV(4520, 0.08, 30) \approx \$512{,}000$, and the present value of the net wage (retirement income) is also $PV(45480, 0.08, 30) \approx \$512{,}000$ in retirement. Stated differently, saving $4520/50000 = 9\%$ of your wages will lead to an identical standard of living at retirement, assuming you can earn $R = 8\%$ for 60 years.

If you can earn only $R = 5\%$ then the equivalent exchange rate is $\alpha = 4.32194$ and the required amount of saving is $50000/(1 + 4.32194) = \$9{,}395$ each year. This leaves you with a net wage of $\$50{,}000 - \$9{,}395 = \$40{,}605$ per year. The future value of your savings is $FV(9395, 0.05, 30) = \$624{,}200$, which is equivalent to $PV(40605, 0.05, 30) \approx \$624{,}200$. In this case, saving $9395/50000 \approx 18.8\%$ of your gross wage will create a retirement income stream that is equivalent to your net wage.

In sum: If over a period of 30 working years you save 9% of your (constant) gross salary, then you will have a large enough nest egg to create an identical retirement income stream that will last for your 30 golden years—assuming you can earn a consistent 8% on your investments. And if you are satisfied with a retirement income stream that is lower than the 91% net wage during your working years, you can obviously afford to save less.

2.6 Discounted Value of a Life-Cycle Plan

If we put both of the foregoing ingredients—savings and consumption phase—together into one large equation, then the total discounted value of both stages in the human life cycle can be expressed as the *discounted value of life-cycle plan*:

$$\mathrm{DVLP}(R, S, C, N, D) := \sum_{i=1}^{N+D} \frac{S_i - C_i}{(1 + R)^i}; \qquad (2.9)$$

here the variable $S_i = 0$ (and $C_i > 0$) during the retirement spending years whereas $C_i = 0$ (and $S_i > 0$) during the working (saving) years, and $i = 1, \ldots, N + D$. I am using the word "discounted" to remind you that we are discounting all cash flows (both inflows and outflows) to the current time 0. Earlier, my use of the words "present value" was meant to discount spending during retirement back to the point of retirement, which may still be far in the future from time 0. I will try to stick to this distinction for most of the book.

In any event, by appealing to both (2.2) and (2.4) and by holding S and C constant across all periods, the discounted value of the entire life-cycle plan can be written and solved as

$$\text{DVLP}(R, S, C, N, D) = \frac{S(1 - (1 + R)^{-N})}{R} - \frac{C(1 - (1 + R)^{-D})}{R(1 + R)^N}. \quad (2.10)$$

The first part of equation (2.10) discounts N years of savings back to time 0, and the second part discounts D years of spending to the retirement date and then discounts that entire quantity back N years to time 0. If the discounted value of savings equals the discounted value of consumption, the financial plan is feasible. On the other hand, if the DVLP quantity is negative then the plan is not sustainable. Either saving must be increased or spending must be reduced or the investment rate R must (somehow) be increased.

For example, $\text{DVLP}(0.05, 1, 10, 30, 30) = -20.19593$. This should be interpreted to mean that a life-cycle plan that saves \$1 for 30 years (work) and then spends or consumes \$10 for 30 years (retirement) is not sustainable at an $R = 5\%$ investment rate. The discounted value has a deficit of \$20.19. This person would have to either save more while working or consume less while retired. However, if we increase the investment rate to $R = 8\%$ then the discounted value of the same plan ($S = 1$, $C = 10$) is now $\text{DVLP}(0.08, 1, 10, 30, 30) \approx 0$, signifying that the financial plan is feasible.

2.7 Real vs. Nominal Planning with Inflation

In the previous few sections and in the models I have presented, wages W are assumed to be constant during the entire life cycle and so the level of savings S required to finance a consumption of C dollars was a constant percentage of the wage. Obviously, wages do not actually remain constant over the entire life cycle, in part because of productivity improvements but also because inflation tends to increase the price of everything (including wages) over time. So, I now move from a simple model in which wages and savings remain constant (in nominal terms) over the working years to a slightly more realistic framework in which wages increase each year owing to general price inflation. Either way, my objective is to convince you that—as long as you equally adjust all inputs for inflation—the structure of the equation remains the same.

Once I introduce price and wage inflation into this system, the symbol S_i will be used to denote the nominal dollar value of savings in period (or year) i and the symbol S_i^{π} to denote the real (after-inflation) value of savings in period i. One way to think about this distinction is by picking a baseline calendar year, say 2005, and then converting all inflation-adjusted dollars into year-2005 values. Thus, if you save $S_5 = 100$ nominal dollars in the year 2010 but inflation was 5% in each of the five years between 2005 and 2010, then the real value of savings in the year 2010 is $S_5^{\pi} = 100/(1.05)^5 = 78.35$ dollars. Conversely, if you save $S_5^{\pi} = 78.35$ real dollars in period $i = 5$ (the year 2010) and if the inflation rate was 5% during each year, then the nominal value of savings in the year 2010 is $S_5 = 100$.

Therefore, if you enter the labor force with a wage of W_0 at the start of period $i = 0$ (i.e., the year 2005) and if this wage increases each year owing to a constant inflation rate denoted by π, then your *nominal* wage at the start of period i will be

$$W_i = W_0(1+\pi)^i. \tag{2.11}$$

As a result, if you save S^{π} real (after-inflation) dollars during each of your N working years, then the amount of (nominal) dollars that you will have accumulated is given by the following expression:

$$S^{\pi}(1+\pi)(1+R)^{N-1} + S^{\pi}(1+\pi)^2(1+R)^{N-2}$$
$$+ S^{\pi}(1+\pi)^3(1+R)^{N-3} + \cdots + S^{\pi}(1+\pi)^N, \tag{2.12}$$

where R denotes the nominal investment rate earned in any given year. However, I can decompose this number into a "real" component and an "inflation" component to write the investment rate as

$$R = (1+R^{\pi})(1+\pi) - 1, \tag{2.13}$$

where R is the nominal rate and $R^{\pi} \leq R$ is the real inflation-adjusted rate. Then, a bit of algebra allows us to express the future value of savings as

$$FV^{\pi}(S, R, N) = S^{\pi}(1+R^{\pi})^N \sum_{i=1}^{N} \frac{(1+\pi)^i}{((1+R^{\pi})(1+\pi))^i}, \tag{2.14}$$

which collapses to the familiar

$$FV^{\pi}(S, R, N) = S^{\pi} \frac{(1+R^{\pi})^N - 1}{R^{\pi}}. \tag{2.15}$$

The same results will follow when the present value of consumption is computed at retirement. The relevant sum is replaced by

$$PV^{\pi}(C, R, D) = \frac{C^{\pi}(1 - (1+R^{\pi})^{-D})}{R^{\pi}}$$
$$= \sum_{j=1}^{D} \frac{C^{\pi}(1+\pi)^j}{((1+R^{\pi})(1+\pi))^j}. \tag{2.16}$$

Here is an example. You plan to save $10,000 in after-inflation dollars each year for the next 30 years until retirement. Thus, at the end of year 1 you will save $10000(1 + \pi)$ nominal dollars, and at the end of year 2 you will save $10000(1 + \pi)^2$ nominal dollars, and so on. These savings will be invested at a real inflation-adjusted rate of $R^\pi = 8\%$ per annum. The nominal investment rate will be $(1 + \pi)(1 + 0.08) - 1$. *Question:* What is the value—either real or nominal—of your retirement savings after 30 years? *Answer:* If you don't know what π is, then you won't be able to obtain a nominal (pre-inflation) value of your nest egg. However, the real (after-inflation) value can easily be calculated as follows:

$$10000\frac{(1.08)^{30} - 1}{0.08} = \$1,132,832; \tag{2.17}$$

the nominal value will be $1132832 \times (1 + \pi)^{30}$ dollars.

In sum, you are entitled to use the exact same equation and methodology to compute the future value of savings at retirement as for the present value of consumption at retirement, provided that you replace both savings (in dollars) and investment rates (in percent) to after-inflation values.

2.8 Changing Investment Rates over Time

When the interest (saving, valuation) rate R is *not* constant from one period to the next, equation (2.9) should be expressed as the discounted value of life-cycle plan:

$$\text{DVLP} = \sum_{i=1}^{N+D}(S_i - C_i)\prod_{j=1}^{i}(1 + R_j)^{-1}. \tag{2.18}$$

Here, as before, S_i and C_i denote (respectively) savings and consumption during time period i ($i = 1, \ldots, N + D$), but the new product term involving R_j replaces the old $(1 + R)^{-i}$. Thus, depending on the actual sequence of values for R_j, the value of equation (2.18) might be positive or negative. In fact, if the future R_j values are random or unknown then the DVLP will also be random.

To make this point clear, Tables 2.3 and 2.4 illustrate the DVLP values under two possible sequences of returns for R_j ($j = 1, \ldots, N + D$), where $N = 5$ and $D = 5$. One key point that should stand out is that—even though the 10-year average rate of return is identical in both scenarios (i.e., 8%)—the DVLP was positive in one case ($0.241) but negative in the other (−$0.615). In other words, you could not fully meet your consumption needs under the second scenario: your wealth would run out in the tenth year.

Table 2.3. *Discounted value of life-cycle plan = $0.241 under first sequence of varying returns*

Year (i)	$S_i - C_i$ ($)	R_j (%)	PV($S_i - C_i$) ($)	Wealth at year end ($)
1	1.0	8.68	0.92	1.00
2	1.0	−17.55	1.12	1.82
3	1.0	9.57	1.02	3.00
4	1.0	24.83	0.82	4.74
5	1.0	26.67	0.64	7.01
6	−1.5	42.66	−0.68	8.50
7	−1.5	−35.67	−1.05	3.97
8	−1.5	17.32	−0.90	3.15
9	−1.5	19.04	−0.75	2.25
10	−1.5	−15.53	−0.89	0.40

Note: Average $R = 8\%$.

Table 2.4. *Discounted value of life-cycle plan = −$0.615 under second sequence of varying returns*

Year (i)	$S_i - C_i$ ($)	R_j (%)	PV($S_i - C_i$) ($)	Wealth at year end ($)
1	1.0	10.34	0.48	1.00
2	1.0	26.65	0.72	2.27
3	1.0	−22.99	0.93	2.75
4	1.0	37.06	0.68	4.76
5	1.0	−3.63	0.70	5.59
6	−1.5	8.45	−0.97	4.56
7	−1.5	6.83	−0.91	3.37
8	−1.5	18.02	−0.77	2.48
9	−1.5	16.87	−0.66	1.40
10	−1.5	−17.61	−0.80	−0.35

Note: Average $R = 8\%$.

Figure 2.2 provides a graphical illustration of the financial life cycle when the underlying investment return R_j can vary from year to year. This particular graph is the outcome of a computer simulation that generated 60 years of investment returns with an average return in any given year of $E[R_j] = 6\%$ but with standard deviation (a.k.a. dispersion) of 20%. As in Figure 2.1, the assumption is that $1 is saved for 30 years (from age 35 to age 64) and then $5.74 is consumed for 30 years (from age 65 to age 94). The individual dies on his or her 95th birthday. Notice that in this simulation the individual ran out of money at age 77, since wealth becomes negative at that point

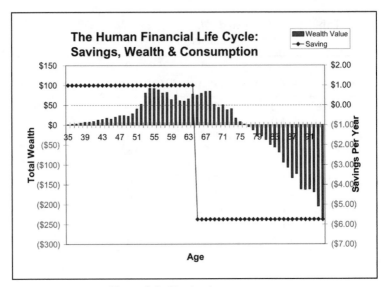

Figure 2.2. Varying investment rate

(and never recovers). The discounted value of this life-cycle plan was negative and thus the plan was not sustainable.

In order for the $S_i - C_i$ plan to be sustainable, the plotted wealth value must stay above zero all the way to the end of the life cycle. That is, the magnitude of the ruin (i.e., the amount by which the wealth value is below zero at age 95) is somewhat secondary to the fact that the plan resulted in ruin. Obviously, Figure 2.2 is but one of many possible outcomes from the computer simulation. In other scenarios—under the same expected investment return of $E[R_j] = 6\%$—the wealth value never hits zero, which is good news for the retiree. In later chapters I will explain how to quantify this risk that the wealth value hits zero prior to the random date of death.

2.9 Further Reading

This chapter covers material that is rather basic when compared to the remainder of this book. Yet the underlying ideas are most critical in setting the stage for the long-term nature of our models. The notion of a discounted value of a life-cycle plan will resurface again in later chapters.

The concept of a stochastic discounted value can be traced back in the actuarial literature to Buhlmann (1992) within the context of life-contingent cash flows. For additional reading on the personal finance aspects of the material presented here, I recommend the basic financial planning textbook by Ho and Robinson (2005). For a deeper understanding of the human life cycle from an economic perspective, see the classic paper by Modigliani (1986), which is a summary of his Nobel Prize lecture. Another classic piece on the human life cycle is Yaari (1965), which sets the tone for our later discussion on annuities. Finally, the papers by Bodie, Merton, and Samuelson (1992) and Viceira (2001) take the arguments in this chapter one step further by incorporating the discounted value of savings and human capital into asset allocation models (more on this later).

2.10 Problems

PROBLEM 2.1. Create a spreadsheet that models the next 60 years of your life. Assume that you save $1 (real) each year during 30 years of work and that you spend $8 (real) per year during 30 years of retirement. Generate ten sequences of 60 random returns that are normally distributed with an average of $E[R^\pi] = 8\%$ and a standard deviation of $SD[R^\pi] = 15\%$. Compute the average and standard deviation of the DVLP under these ten distinct sequences. For those sequences that resulted in a negative DVLP, identify precisely the year (or period) in which you ran out of money.

PROBLEM 2.2. Assume (a) that during your $D = 30$ years of retirement you plan to consume $C^\pi = \$100,000$ per year and (b) that during this entire period you will earn $R^\pi = 8\%$ on your money. However, instead of retiring with the appropriate value of PV(C, R, D) to fund your retirement, you have only 75% of PV(C, R, D). In other words, you are 25% underfunded at retirement. This obviously means that if you continue spending C^π then you will run out of money well before the age of death at period D. Compute the period during which you will run out of money. Derive a general expression for the "ruin period" if you retire with $z < 100\%$ of your required nest egg. Also derive a general expression for the ruin period if you retire with 100% of the required PV(C, R, D) nest egg but assuming you earn only $(R - z)\%$ (instead of $R\%$) during each year of retirement.

THREE

Models of Human Mortality

3.1 Mortality Tables and Rates

It is time to get a bit more technical. In this chapter I will cover most of what you need to know about mortality rates and tables in order to appreciate the valuation and pricing of mortality-contingent claims. At various points I will be using basic calculus to express the underlying mathematics. But please don't be discouraged if the material appears somewhat esoteric or theoretical. My main objective is to arrive at a collection of formulas that can be used independently of whether you understand every step of how they were derived.

To begin with, the basis of all pension and insurance valuation is the mortality table. A mortality table—perhaps better referred to as a vector or collection of numbers—maps or translates an age group x into a probability of death, q_x, during the next year. For example, q_{35} is the probability of dying before your 36th birthday, assuming you are alive on your 35th birthday. By definition, $0 \leq q_x \leq 1$ and $q_N = 1$ for some large enough $N \approx 110$. Table 3.1 displays a portion of one of the hundreds of different mortality tables. This one is called the RP2000 (where "RP" denotes retirement pension) healthy annuitant mortality table, which is available from the Society of Actuaries, $\langle$www.soa.org$\rangle$. This portion of the table displays conditional death rates from age $x = 50$ to age $x = 105$ only in increments of 5 years; the complete table is provided in Chapter 14 of this book. For an example of variation among the different available mortality tables, please review Table 14.3, which is a table that is used to price insurance policies. For an international comparison see Table 14.2, which lists q_{65} for different countries as of the year 2000.

Figure 3.1 provides a visual plot of what a mortality table looks like. The numbers start very low when you are young; they increase with age and

Table 3.1. *Mortality table for healthy members of a pension plan*

Age	Conditional probability of death at any age	
	Female q_x	Male q_x
50	0.002344	0.005347
55	0.003531	0.005905
60	0.006200	0.008196
65	0.010364	0.013419
70	0.016742	0.022206
75	0.028106	0.037834
80	0.045879	0.064368
85	0.077446	0.110757
90	0.131682	0.183408
95	0.194509	0.267491
100	0.237467	0.344556
105	0.293116	0.397886
110	0.364617	0.400000
115	0.400000	0.400000
120	1.000000	1.000000

Source: Society of Actuaries, RP2000 (static).

tend to flatten out near age 100. Then, they jump to $q_N = 1$ at the very last entry of the mortality table. The actuaries and demographers who compile these tables must make some assumptions and extrapolate at higher ages, since they have very little data (which is used to estimate the numbers) on which to base the death rates.

Note the difference between males and females. The annual death rate q_x for females is uniformly lower than the death rate for males at the same age. Sometimes the numbers for males and females are averaged together to create a "unisex" mortality table. Either way, the conditional probability of survival in year x is equal to the *complement* of q_x, or $1 - q_x$. Along the same lines, sometimes you will see $({}_1p_x)$ written as p_x in order to save space.

3.2 Conditional Probability of Survival

The mortality table provides the probability of death or the probability of survival within any one given year, but the conditional probability of survival goes a step further. That is: if an individual is currently aged x, then the probability of surviving n more years is denoted and defined by

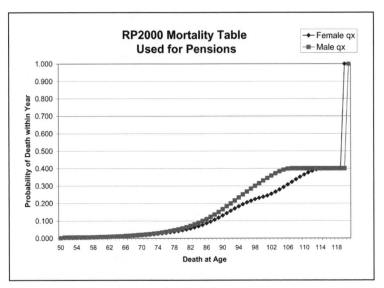

Figure 3.1

$$({}_n p_x) = \prod_{i=0}^{n-1} (1 - q_{x+i}).   \qquad (3.1)$$

Why is this the correct formula? Think of independent coin tosses. The odds of getting n heads in a row is the product of the probabilities of getting one head in one toss. If you think of getting heads as the conditional probability of survival $(1 - q_{x+i})$, then multiplying them together leads to the required quantity. If you stare at equation (3.1) long enough, you should be able to see the internal logic of the multiplications. You should also convince yourself that if you fix the age x then the probability $({}_n p_x)$ will decline as n increases, since the odds of surviving to more advanced ages declines as time progresses. Likewise, if you fix n and increase x, then $({}_n p_x)$ also declines with increasing age. For example, the probability of living for $n = 30$ more years is much higher when you are $x = 20$ years of age than when you are $x = 70$ years of age. In fact, $({}_{30} p_{20})$ is pretty close to 100% whereas $({}_{30} p_{70})$ is pretty close to zero. In terms of notation, I will use $n \leq N$ for discrete ages and $t \leq T$ for continuous ages. Needless to say, the quantity $({}_t p_x)$ or $({}_n p_x)$ is fundamental in actuarial finance and in the remainder of this book.

A research study by the Society of Actuaries identified a number of risk factors that have an immediate and direct impact on survival probabilities during retirement. Some are obvious and some are not. For example, the precise age and gender of a retiree bear directly on the respective mortality rates. Older males have higher mortality rates than younger females. In addition, (excessive) alcohol consumption, smoking, and obesity increase hazard rates when other factors are held constant. Perhaps more surprisingly, one's occupation has an impact on mortality rates and not solely because of "hazardous" jobs. Race and ethnicity affect mortality as well. For example, Asians and Pacific Islanders have lower mortality rates overall than either Whites or Blacks. In addition, religion (i.e., being part of a religious collective) and marriage (for males) lowers mortality. Of course, many of these factors are correlated with each other, making it hard to isolate the "essential" factor driving mortality. Nevertheless, it is important to stress that mortality is not homogenous across the population, and certainly a "mortality table" is not the final word on your particular odds of survival.

3.3 Remaining Lifetime Random Variable

Now I will introduce a random variable (R.V.) denoted by T_x and indexed by age x, which represents the *remaining lifetime* for an individual currently aged x. The R.V. T_x has a probability density function (PDF) denoted and defined by $f_x(t)$ when T_x is continuous and by $\Pr[T_x = x_i]$ when the random variable is discrete. Here, $x + x_i$ denotes the ages at which people are "allowed" to die. For example, a 60-year-old could die after x_i years, where $x_1 = 10$, $x_2 = 25$, and $x_3 = 35$. In this case $T_{60} = \{10, 25, 35\}$, and the probability mass function (PMF) replaces the PDF. I assume that $\Pr[T_{60} = 10] = 8/12$, $\Pr[T_{60} = 25] = 3/12$, and $\Pr[T_{60} = 35] = 1/12$ (and will return to this momentarily).

What does the cumulative distribution function of T_x look like? First, I will use the function $F_x(t)$ to denote the conditional probability of dying before the age of $x + t$. This probability must equal 1 when added to $({}_t p_x)$, the conditional probability of surviving t more years (as introduced in the previous section). Since

$$({}_t p_x) := 1 - F_x(t) = \Pr[T_x \geq t],$$

it follows that the cumulative distribution function (CDF), which is the probability that the remaining lifetime is *less than* a value of T_x, will simply be

$$F_x(t) := 1 - ({}_t p_x) = \Pr[T_x < t]. \tag{3.2}$$

To state this in another way: when the random variable T_x is continuous, the CDF is

$$F_x(t) = \int_0^t f_x(s)\, ds; \tag{3.3}$$

when the random variable T_x is discrete,

$$F_x(n) = \sum_{i=1}^{n} \Pr[T_x = x_i]. \tag{3.4}$$

Returning to my example where $T_x = \{10, 25, 35\}$, $F_x(10)$ would denote the probability of dying at or before the age of 70. The precise value of $F_x(10)$ would be

$$\Pr[T_{60} \le 10] = \frac{8}{12}.$$

Similarly, for $F_x(25)$ and $F_x(35)$ we have

$$\Pr[T_{60} \le 25] = \frac{8}{12} + \frac{3}{12} = \frac{11}{12} \quad \text{and}$$

$$\Pr[T_{60} \le 35] = \frac{8}{12} + \frac{3}{12} + \frac{1}{12} = 1,$$

respectively.

Observe also that the expected value of the remaining lifetime R.V. is equal to the average of the remaining lifetimes weighted by their probabilities. Once again using the same values, the expected remaining lifetime works out to

$$E[T_{60}] = \frac{8}{12} \times 10 + \frac{3}{12} \times 25 + \frac{1}{12} \times 35 = 15.833 \text{ years.}$$

3.4 Instantaneous Force of Mortality

Now that I have demonstrated the intuition behind the conditional probability of survival $(_t p_x)$, I will show how this probability can be represented in another way, which will be useful in defining the *instantaneous force of mortality* (IFM). As long as $(_t p_x)$ is constant or decreasing with respect to t, then this function can be represented as

$$(_t p_x) = \exp\left\{ -\int_x^{x+t} \lambda(s)\, ds \right\}, \tag{3.5}$$

where the curve $\lambda(s) \ge 0$ for all $s \ge 0$. Think of $\lambda(s)$ as the instantaneous rate of death at age s. If $t = 0$ then $(_t p_x) \to 1$, and when $t \to \infty$ we must have that $(_t p_x) \to 0$ so that $\int_x^{x+\infty} \lambda(s)\, ds \to \infty$. In English this means that adding up the "instantaneous killing force" will eventually kill the individual. The probability of surviving to infinity must go to zero because we cannot allow anyone to live forever. It might seem somewhat artificial to worry about these things, but the point is that—if I am working in continuous time—then I must make sure the functions are making sense even under the most extreme situations.

Note that by a simple change of variables $u = s - x$ we can rewrite equation (3.5) as

$$({}_t p_x) = \exp\left\{-\int_0^t \lambda(x + u)\, du\right\}. \tag{3.6}$$

Integrating the curve $\lambda(s)$ from a lower bound x to an upper bound $x + t$ is mathematically equivalent to integrating the curve starting at $\lambda(x + s)$ from a lower bound 0 to an upper bound t. However, this change of bounds will allow me to arrive at some important relationships.

Now that we have defined $({}_t p_x)$ in this (more restrictive) way, I may take the derivatives of both sides of equation (3.6) to arrive at

$$\frac{\partial}{\partial t}({}_t p_x) = -({}_t p_x)\lambda(x + t).$$

Therefore, the derivative of the cumulative distribution function $F_x(t)$ or $1 - ({}_t p_x)$ is the probability density function $f_x(t)$, which is equivalent to

$$f_x(t) = (1 - F_x(t))\lambda(x + t). \tag{3.7}$$

3.5 The ODE Relationship

Based on (3.7), the ordinary differential equation (ODE) for the function $F_x(t)$, we can represent the IFM as

$$\lambda(x + t) = \frac{f_x(t)}{1 - F_x(t)}, \quad t \geq 0. \tag{3.8}$$

Note that $F_x(t) \rightarrow 1$ as $t \rightarrow \infty$ (everyone dies eventually) and therefore $\lambda(t) \rightarrow \infty$ as $t \rightarrow \infty$, unless $f_x(t)$ approaches zero faster (in the numerator). Thus, the function $F_x(t)$ and its derivative $f_x(t)$ will determine the shape and behavior of $\lambda(x + t)$. Note also that the relationship implied by equation (3.8) leads to

$$F_x(t) = 1 - \frac{f_x(t)}{\lambda(x + t)}, \tag{3.9}$$

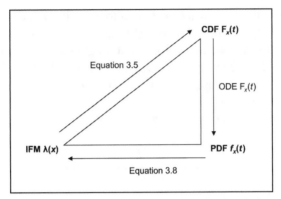

Figure 3.2. Relationships between mortality descriptions

which then implies

$$f_x(t) = ({}_tp_x)\lambda(x+t). \tag{3.10}$$

Collectively, these equations allow us to move from $F_x(t)$ to $f_x(t)$ to $\lambda(x+t)$ and back again without using too much calculus.

In sum, the preceding relationships allow us to "create" mortality laws in two different ways:

1. we can start with a CDF $F_x(t) = 1 - ({}_tp_x)$, take the derivative to create the PDF $f_x(t)$, and then use equation (3.8) to obtain the IFM $\lambda(x)$; or
2. we can start with the IFM, build the CDF $F_x(t) = 1 - ({}_tp_x)$ using equation (3.5), and then take derivatives to arrive at the PDF $f_x(t)$.

Figure 3.2 shows how to visualize the relationships between three possible descriptions of mortality.

Here is a question to ponder: Using some of the qualitative features we would expect from the IFM curve, can we use *any* functional form for $f_x(t)$ and $F_x(t)$, or are there some natural restrictions on the remaining lifetime random variable? For example, in the case of the familiar normal distribution, the CDF of the remaining lifetime random variable T_x is defined as

$$N(m,b,t) = \int_{-\infty}^{t} \frac{1}{b\sqrt{2\pi}} \exp\left\{-\frac{1}{2}\left(\frac{z-m}{b}\right)^2\right\} dz. \tag{3.11}$$

For a refresher on the CDF of the normal distribution see Section 3.18, which may also be of help for the material still to come.

Table 3.2. *Mortality odds when life is
normally distributed*

Year	$F(t)$	$f(t)$	$f(t)/(1 - F(t))$
1	5.48%	0.74%	0.78%
5	9.12%	1.09%	1.20%
10	15.87%	1.61%	1.92%
15	25.25%	2.13%	2.85%
20	36.94%	2.52%	3.99%
25	50.00%	2.66%	5.32%
30	63.06%	2.52%	6.81%
35	74.75%	2.13%	8.43%
40	84.13%	1.61%	10.17%
45	90.88%	1.09%	11.99%
50	95.22%	0.66%	13.88%

Note: $E[T_x] = 25$ years; $\sigma = 15$ years.

In order to assess how useful the normal distribution is for modeling T_x, we can rely on the Excel functions NORMDIST(t,mean,standard deviation,true) for $F_x(t)$ and NORMDIST(t,mean,standard deviation,false) for $f_x(t)$ and thereby generate Table 3.2. Figures 3.3 and 3.4 plot the complete data for the remaining lifetimes from 1 to 50 years. As an example of how to interpret the data, note that—for an individual alive today—the probability of dying *within* 15 years is 25.25% whereas the probability of dying *during* year 15 is 2.13%.

The shape of the hazard rate function $\lambda(x)$, shown in Figure 3.4, appears reasonable: the rate of death at any moment increases with age, which is what one might expect. However, given a sufficiently high standard deviation (15 years in our example), we have an anomaly. Note the shape of the PDF function in Figure 3.3; given the properties of a normal distribution, the shape of this curve implies that there is a chance of dying within a negative number of years, which of course is impossible. As a result, this distribution is not useful for modeling T_x and we will need to explore other alternatives.

3.6 Moments in Your Life

We can now define the concept of *moments* and then move on to life expectancy and standard deviation of the remaining lifetime. The word "moment" may seem like an odd word to use for describing this calculation, but it basically captures the dispersion around a central point of value. If

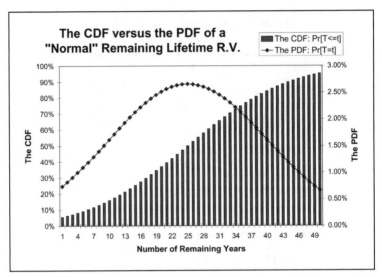

Figure 3.3

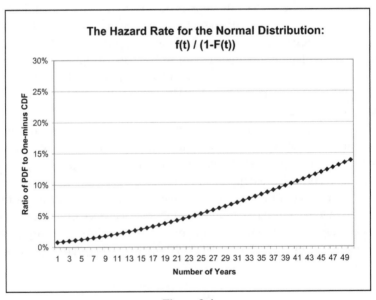

Figure 3.4

T_x is a continuous variable then the first moment of its distribution—or its expected value—is defined as

$$E[T_x] = \int_0^\infty t f_x(t)\, dt. \tag{3.12}$$

Table 3.3. *Life expectancy at birth in 2005*

Bottom 10 countries		Top 10 countries	
Swaziland	35.30	Japan	82.40
Lesotho	36.30	Sweden	80.70
Djibouti	37.60	Hong Kong	80.60
Botswana	38.20	Macao	80.07
Mozambique	38.40	Israel	79.97
Malawi	40.52	Iceland	79.91
Sierra Leone	42.37	Norway	79.73
South Africa	42.44	France	79.69
Burundi	42.66	Australia	79.64
Rwanda	43.33	Belgium	79.59

Source: Watson Wyatt.

Observe that this is equivalent to

$$E[T_x] = \int_0^\infty (_tp_x) \, dt. \tag{3.13}$$

If you need to convince yourself of this relationship, write down the expression for the expectation (or average) using equation (3.12) and then use integration by parts to convert the integrand, which can be stated as $F_x'(t)$ times t, to $F_x(t)$ itself. We will use this trick in several later chapters.

When T_x is a discrete random variable, the definition of the first moment is

$$E[T_x] = \sum_{i=1}^N x_i \Pr[T_x = x_i]. \tag{3.14}$$

Table 3.3 provides a sense of how the expected remaining lifetime at birth $E[T_0]$ varies throughout the world. Japan sits at the top of the list with a life expectancy of 82.4 years, and Swaziland is at the other end with a life expectancy of only 35.3 years. Despite this variation, life expectancy has been steadily improving throughout the world. The data in Table 3.4 illustrates the trend that has been observed since 1950.

Note that there is a difference between $E[T_0]$ and $E[T_1]$, for example. The former is life expectancy at birth, while the latter is life expectancy at the age of $x = 1$. In many countries there is a fairly large gap between these two numbers due to infant mortality. In fact, much of the increase in life expectancy over the last hundred years or so becomes more noticeable when computing $E[T_0]$ owing to the reduction in death during the first few days of life.

Table 3.4. *Increase since 1950 in life expectancy at birth $E[T_0]$*

Region	Years
Asia	27.70
North Africa	26.20
South America	19.20
Western Africa	17.60
Southern Europe	14.90
Africa	14.80
Western Europe	11.63
North America	9.62

Source: Watson Wyatt.

Now that we have developed a basic understanding of the first moment, or expected value, of T_x, we can move on to higher moments. The second moment, or the *square mean*, for the continuous R.V. is

$$E[T_x^2] = \int_0^\infty t^2 f_x(t)\, dt. \tag{3.15}$$

Taking the root of the difference between the second moment and the first moment squared yields the standard deviation of the random variable:

$$\mathrm{SD}[T_x] = \sqrt{E[T_x^2] - E^2[T_x]}. \tag{3.16}$$

Squaring this quantity results in the variance of the random variable. These important quantities will resurface at numerous points throughout the book.

3.7 Median vs. Expected Remaining Lifetime

A value distinct from the mean or expected remaining lifetime is the median remaining lifetime, which is related to T_x as follows:

$$\Pr[T_x < M[T_x]] = 0.5. \tag{3.17}$$

Another way to think of the median remaining lifetime is via

$$_{M[T]}p_x = 0.5. \tag{3.18}$$

The probability of living to the median is 50%. The median remaining lifetime (MRL) will be less than the expected remaining lifetime (ERL) in all cases. Here is the reason: since remaining lifetimes can only be positive—you can't live for additional negative years—it follows that the arithmetic average of a collection of positive numbers is always greater than the median of the same numbers. The bottom line is that one must be careful when using such phrases as "people are living on average to 80 years." This could be either a median value $M[T_0]$ or a mean value $E[T_0]$, and the former is less than the latter.

3.8 Exponential Law of Mortality

I've shown that modeling T_x using the normal distribution does not create a realistic approximation of the remaining lifetime. Now I will examine another possible model. Assume that the IFM curve satisfies $\lambda(x + t) = \lambda$, which is constant across all ages and times. In this case, let us "build" the $F_x(t)$ and $f_x(t)$ functions using equation (3.5).

Note that we have

$$(_tp_x) = \exp\left\{-\int_x^{x+t} \lambda(s)\,ds\right\} = e^{-\lambda t}. \tag{3.19}$$

The integral in the exponent collapses to (i.e., can be solved to produce) a linear function λt. This is because, since the function $\lambda(x)$ is a horizontal line, the area under the curve is simply the base $((x + t) - x)$ times the height λ. In this case the current age x does not really affect the probability of survival because all that matters is the magnitude λ of the IFM. In other words, $(_tp_x)$ is identical to $(_tp_y)$ for any x and y as long as the underlying λ is the same.

Think about what this means. At every age, the instantaneous probability of death is the same. Did you know that lobsters have a constant IFM? Their instantaneous probability of death is constant. In any event, thanks to the relationship summarized in Figure 3.2, a number of mathematical objects "fall" into our lap:

$$F_x(t) = 1 - e^{-\lambda t}; \tag{3.20}$$

$$f_x(t) = \lambda e^{-\lambda t}. \tag{3.21}$$

Remember that the expected remaining lifetime in the case of an exponential model is

$$E[T_x] = \int_0^\infty t\lambda e^{-\lambda t}\,dt = \frac{1}{\lambda}. \tag{3.22}$$

For example: when $\lambda = 0.10$ the ERL is $E[T_x] = 10$, and when $\lambda = 0.05$ the ERL is $E[T_x] = 20$. In contrast, the median remaining lifetime is obtained

Table 3.5. *Mortality odds when life is
exponentially distributed*

Year	$F(t)$	$f(t)$	$f(t)/(1 - F(t))$
1	3.92%	3.843%	4.00%
5	18.13%	3.275%	4.00%
10	32.97%	2.681%	4.00%
15	45.12%	2.195%	4.00%
20	55.07%	1.797%	4.00%
25	63.21%	1.472%	4.00%
30	69.88%	1.205%	4.00%
35	75.34%	0.986%	4.00%
40	79.81%	0.808%	4.00%
45	83.47%	0.661%	4.00%
50	86.47%	0.541%	4.00%

Note: $E[T] = 1/\lambda = 1/0.04 = 25$ years.

by integrating the PDF curve from time 0 to the median remaining lifetime
and then solving for $M[T_x]$:

$$\frac{1}{2} = e^{-\lambda M[T_x]} \iff M[T_x] = \frac{\ln[2]}{\lambda} < \frac{1}{\lambda}. \qquad (3.23)$$

Thus, when $\lambda = 0.05$ the MRL is $M[T_x] = \ln[2]/0.05 = 13.862$ years, in
contrast to the ERL of $1/0.05 = 20$ years. Notice the six-year gap between
the two measures. This gap is a result of the difference between means and
medians, which we will revisit later in the context of stock market returns.
The greater the volatility or dispersion of the numbers, the greater the variation between the mean and median. Here the mean is skewed (to the right)
by one or two outliers, but the median is not affected by that.

Now, Table 3.5 and Figure 3.5 can be used to assess the exponential law
of mortality relative to the normal distribution data presented earlier.

The exponential model of mortality appears to overcome some of the
problems of the normal model, and we will use the former in a number
of places throughout the book. There is, however, another model that also
provides a solution to the unrealistic assumption of a constant hazard rate.

3.9 Gompertz–Makeham Law of Mortality

As in the case of the exponential law of mortality, the Gompertz–Makeham
(GoMa) law of mortality is "built" using the IFM curve $\lambda(x)$. In the GoMa
case, the definition is:

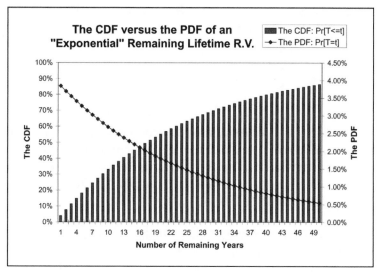

Figure 3.5

$$\lambda(x) = \lambda + \frac{1}{b}e^{(x-m)/b}, \quad t \geq 0, \tag{3.24}$$

where m is the modal value of life and b is the dispersion coefficient. I shall often return to the source and value of (m, b) within this book. According to (3.24), the instantaneous force of mortality is a constant λ plus a time-dependent exponential curve. The constant λ aims to capture the component of the death rate that is attributable to accidents, while the exponentially increasing portion reflects natural death causes. This curve increases with age and goes to infinity as $t \to \infty$.

When the individual is exactly $x = m$ years old, the GoMa–IFM curve is $\lambda(m) = \lambda + 1/b$, but when the individual is younger $(x < m)$ the GoMa–IFM curve is $\lambda(x) < \lambda + 1/b$, and when the individual is older $(x > m)$ the GoMa–IFM curve is $\lambda(x) > \lambda + 1/b$. Thus, $x = m$ is a special age point on the IFM curve—it is the modal value.

The convention is to label equation (3.24) the *Gompertz–Makeham* law when $\lambda > 0$ and simply *Gompertz* when $\lambda = 0$. In the Gompertz case, typical numbers for the parameters are $m = 82.3$ and $b = 11.4$, under which $\lambda(65) = 0.01923$ and $\lambda(95) = 0.26724$. You should note that, for the most part, I will assume that $\lambda = 0$ whenever I work with the GoMa law. Although certainly convenient from a mathematical perspective, this assumption is also realistic because λ tends to have a very small value in practice.

By the construction specified in equation (3.5), the conditional probability of survival under the GoMa–IFM curve is equal to

$$(_tp_x) = \exp\left\{-\int_x^{x+t}\left(\lambda + \frac{1}{b}e^{(s-m)/b}\right)ds\right\}$$

$$= \exp\{-\lambda t + b(\lambda(x) - \lambda)(1 - e^{t/b})\}, \qquad (3.25)$$

and $F_x(t) = 1 - (_tp_x)$. Notice how the probability of survival declines, in time, at a rate faster than λ. The additional terms in the exponent are less than zero and thus accelerate the decline. For example: when $\lambda = 0$, $m = 82.3$, and $b = 11.4$, equation (3.25) results in $F_{65}(20) = 0.6493$ and $F_{65}(10) = 0.2649$ as well as $F_{75}(30) = 0.9988$.

By taking derivatives of $F_x(t)$ with respect to t, we recover the probability density function of the remaining lifetime random variable $f_x(t) = F'_x(t)$, which is left as an exercise problem.

We can also take the "easy" route by appealing to (3.10), which leads us to

$$f_x(t) = \exp\{-\lambda t + b(\lambda(x) - \lambda)(1 - e^{t/b})\}\left(\lambda + \frac{1}{b}e^{(x+t-m)/b}\right); \qquad (3.26)$$

this is the $(_tp_x)$ of the Gompertz–Makeham law multiplied by the IFM curve $\lambda(x + t)$.

The expected remaining lifetime under the Gompertz–Makeham law of mortality is

$$E[T_x] = \int_0^\infty \exp\{-\lambda t + b(\lambda(x) - \lambda)(1 - e^{t/b})\}\,dt$$

$$= \frac{b\Gamma(-\lambda b, b(\lambda_x - \lambda))}{e^{(m-x)\lambda + b(\lambda - \lambda_x)}}, \qquad (3.27)$$

where

$$\Gamma(a,c) = \int_c^\infty e^{-t}t^{(a-1)}\,dt$$

is the *incomplete Gamma function,* which can be easily evaluated for the parameters a and c using the GAMMADIST function in Excel. A brief technical note on this expression can be found in Section 3.17.

Tables 3.6 and 3.7 provide numerical examples of the expected life span of males and females of age x under a variety of values for m and b. Note that I have used different m, b values at different ages. Think of m and b as parameters in a flexible functional form, with values selected that best fit the survival probabilities at any given age.

Table 3.6. *Example of fitting Gompertz–Makeham law to a group mortality table—Female*

Age (x)	m	b	$x + E[T_x]$
30	88.8379	9.213	83.61
40	88.8599	9.160	83.82
50	88.8725	9.136	84.21
60	88.8261	9.211	84.97
65	88.8403	9.183	85.69

Table 3.7. *Example of fitting Gompertz–Makeham law to a group mortality table—Male*

Age (x)	m	b	$x + E[T_x]$
30	84.4409	9.888	78.94
40	84.4729	9.831	79.31
50	84.4535	9.922	79.92
60	84.2693	10.179	81.17
65	84.1811	10.282	82.25

3.10 Fitting Discrete Tables to Continuous Laws

What is the best way to locate the Gompertz–Makeham or exponential parameters for the IFM that best fit a given mortality table such as Table 3.1? Here are some possible techniques:

- equalize the ERL or the MRL so that they are the same under both distributions;
- pick one or two given survival points ($_t p_x$) on the mortality table and then locate parameters that "fit" this probability;
- minimize the distance between the theoretical $f_x(t)$ and the empirical (population) $f_x(t)$ over a given range; or
- any combination of these.

Table 3.8 and Figure 3.6 compare the survival probability ($_t p_{65}$) under a Gompertz (i.e. $\lambda = 0$) and exponential specification that have been fit to the unisex RP2000 table by matching the MRL (to equal 19 years across the three data sets). Note the large difference between the exponential curve and the other (Gompertz, RP2000) curve. The exponential model overestimates

Table 3.8. *How good is a continuous law of mortality?—*
Gompertz vs. exponential vs. RP2000

| | Survival probability | | |
Age	Gompertz[a]	Exponential[b]	Unisex RP2000
65	1.000	1.000	1.000
70	0.929	0.837	0.929
75	0.821	0.701	0.822
80	0.666	0.587	0.667
84	0.509	0.509	0.509
85	0.467	0.491	0.466
90	0.256	0.411	0.249
95	0.092	0.344	0.088
100	0.016	0.288	0.020
105	0.001	0.241	0.003

[a] $m = 86.34, b = 9.5; \lambda = 0.$ [b] $\lambda = 3.555\%.$

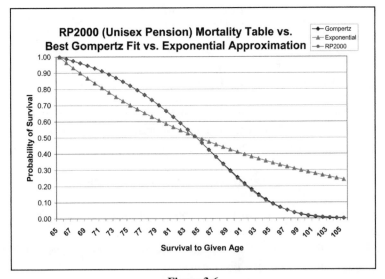

Figure 3.6

the probability of living to very advanced ages and underestimates the probability of living to younger ages. In contrast, the Gompertz curve is virtually indistinguishable from the RP2000.

I have just presented three general models for mortality. Two of them—the normal and the exponential—are convenient to work with but are somewhat unrealistic. The third model, the Gompertz–Makeham distribution, is the more realistic of the three because (as demonstrated in Figure 3.6) it can be "force fitted" to any number of true mortality tables at middle age. Note though that at advanced ages the q_x tend to flatten out (see Figure 3.1) and so the Gompertz–Makeham law, which implies exponential growth, might then not be a suitable model.

3.11 General Hazard Rates

The idea that the conditional survival probabilities can be generated via the instantaneous force of mortality can be extended to more general event probabilities. For example, the probability that someone is still working in a given job, or the probability they are still contributing to a pension, can be modeled via the *instantaneous hazard rate* (IHR). We will use the term IFM when dealing specifically with death and use IHR when dealing with other "decrements."

For instance, it is common to model the rate at which people "lapse" or "surrender" an insurance, annuity, or pension contract by using the curve

$$\eta(t) = \eta - \frac{\eta_1}{t + \eta_2}, \quad t > 0, \tag{3.28}$$

where $\eta \geq 0$, $\eta_1 \geq 0$, and $\eta_2 > 0$. The hazard rate starts off at time 0 with a value of $\eta - \eta_1/\eta_2$ and then increases at a rate of $\eta_1/(t + \eta_2)^2$ until it approaches the value η asymptotically. Hence, for this hazard rate function to be positive and well-defined, we must impose the additional restriction that $\eta - \eta_1/\eta_2 > 0$. From the construction provided by equation (3.8) we have

$$\eta(t) = \frac{h(t)}{1 - H(t)}, \tag{3.29}$$

where $H(t) = \Pr[L \leq t]$ is the cumulative distribution function and $h(t) = H'(t)$ is the probability density function of the random variable L. This leads to the following solution:

$$H(t) = 1 - \exp\left\{ -\int_0^t \eta(s) \, ds \right\}. \tag{3.30}$$

Some algebra and calculus then yield

$$H(t) = 1 - \exp\left\{ -\int_0^t \eta \, ds \right\} \exp\left\{ \int_0^t \frac{\eta_1}{s + \eta_2} \, ds \right\}$$

$$= 1 - e^{-\eta t} \left(\frac{t}{\eta_2} + 1 \right)^{\eta_1}. \tag{3.31}$$

Table 3.9. *Working with the instantaneous hazard rate*

Year	Annual lapse rate	Hazard rate: $\eta(s)$	Integral of $\eta(s)$: $\int_0^t \eta(s)\, ds$	Probability of nonlapse: $\exp\{-\int_0^t \eta(s)\, ds\}$
1	2.0%	2.020%	2.020%	98.00%
2	2.0%	2.020%	4.041%	96.04%
3	3.0%	3.046%	7.086%	93.16%
4	4.0%	4.082%	11.169%	89.43%
5	5.0%	5.129%	16.298%	84.96%
6	6.0%	6.188%	22.486%	79.86%
7	7.0%	7.257%	29.743%	74.27%
8	10.0%	10.536%	40.279%	66.85%
9	12.0%	12.783%	53.062%	58.82%
10	14.0%	15.082%	68.144%	50.59%
11	18.0%	19.845%	87.989%	41.48%
12	20.0%	22.314%	110.304%	33.19%
13	20.0%	22.314%	132.618%	26.55%
14	20.0%	22.314%	154.932%	21.24%
15	20.0%	22.314%	177.247%	16.99%
16	20.0%	22.314%	199.561%	13.59%
17	20.0%	22.314%	221.876%	10.87%
18	20.0%	22.314%	244.190%	8.70%
19	20.0%	22.314%	266.504%	6.96%
20	100.0%	1000.000%	1266.504%	0.00%

This expression obviously collapses to $1 - e^{-\eta t}$ when $\eta_1 = 0$. Finally, the PDF for the future lapse-time random variable can be written explicitly as

$$h(t) = \left(\eta - \frac{\eta_1}{t + \eta_2}\right)\left(e^{-\eta t}\left(\frac{t}{\eta_2} + 1\right)^{\eta_1}\right). \tag{3.32}$$

Once again we have used the convenient relationship between the CDF, PDF, and IHR.

The same ideas can be applied to discrete "lapsation" tables as well, and this is shown in Table 3.9. Here, the second column contains the annual lapse rates in percentage format. For example, during the first year, 2% of the population discontinue their coverage and surrender their policies. In the second year, 2% of the remaining (unlapsed) population surrender their policies. In the third year 3% surrender, and so forth. The final row contains a lapse rate of 100%, which implies that anyone still holding a policy after 19 years will—at the end of the twentieth year—lapse or surrender the policy with 100% certainty. View these rates as q_x-values applied to lapsation and surrender as opposed to life and death. Remember that

$q_x = 1 - \exp\{-\int_0^1 \eta(s)\,ds\}$ by (3.5), and if we assume that $\eta(s)$ is constant over the interval from 0 to 1 then $\eta = -\ln[1 - q_x]$ over the period in question. In other words, the IHR curve is a step function that jumps each year to a new level η and stays there until the end of the year. The third column in the table converts these numbers into instantaneous lapse rates $\eta(s)$ by taking logarithms as mentioned previously. The fourth column computes the integral portion $\int_0^t \eta(s)\,ds$, which is simply the sum of the individual lapse rates from year 1 to year t; and the last column computes the conditional probability of survival, which (using our previous notation) is $\Pr[L > t]$.

Of course, you can go directly from the second column to the last column by multiplying 1 minus the annual lapse rates until the relevant year; the result would be exactly the same. My point and objective are to illustrate how one can merge the continuous and discrete frameworks together.

Finally, the expected holding period $E[L]$, which can be viewed as the analogue of the expected remaining lifetime, is the integral (sum) of the nonlapse probability from year 0 to year 20. In this example, the expected remaining holding period is equal to 9.72 years. Note that larger values for the annual lapse rates would reduce the expected remaining holding period.

Here's a problem to consider. People purchase life insurance and must pay premiums on a regular basis. Assume they lapse (cease paying) their premiums at a rate of

$$\eta(t) = 0.10 + \frac{0.09}{t+1}.$$

The instantaneous force of mortality is Gompertz with parameters $m = 82.3$ and $b = 11.4$, so that

$$\lambda(x) = \frac{1}{11.4} \exp\left\{\frac{x - 82.3}{11.4}\right\}.$$

What is the probability of dying while the insurance policy is still in force (unlapsed)?

3.12 Modeling Joint Lifetimes

Table 3.10 provides (reasonable) survival probabilities at age 65. It uses the Gompertz law of mortality under parameters $m = 88.18$ and $b = 10.5$ for males and $m = 92.63$ and $b = 8.78$ for females. These numbers are optimistic projections and come directly from equation (3.25) under $x = 65$. Imagine a married couple, both aged 65, who are interested in computing joint survival probabilities. What is the probability that they *both* survive from the current age 65 to age 90?

Table 3.10. *Survival probabilities[a]*
at age 65

Survive to age	Male	Female
70	0.935	0.967
75	0.839	0.912
80	0.705	0.823
85	0.533	0.686
90	0.339	0.497
95	0.164	0.281
100	0.023	0.103

[a] Using "optimistic" mortality projections and continuous law of mortality.

The answer can be obtained by using the simple calculation

$$(_{25}p_{65}^{male}) \times (_{25}p_{65}^{female}) = 0.339 \times 0.497 = 16.84\%.$$

This assumes we are dealing with independent events. But are they? Some researchers have found a "broken heart" syndrome whereby the death of one's spouse increases the mortality rate of the survivor.

Next, what is the probability that at least one of the couple survives from the current age 65 to age 90? The answer is:

$$1 - (1 - (_{25}p_{65}^{male})) \times (1 - (_{25}p_{65}^{female})) = 1 - (1 - 0.339) \times (1 - 0.497)$$
$$= 66.75\%.$$

Here, the probability is almost four times larger. The intuition is that the only excluded event is the one in which both people die, which has only a $(1 - 0.339)(1 - 0.497) = 33.25\%$ chance of occurring. Subtract this from 1 and you have the probability that either the male, female, or both survive.

Note that the probability of an x-year-old male and a y-year-old female both surviving t more years can be written as

$$(_{t}p_x^{male}) \times (_{t}p_y^{female}) = \exp\left\{ -\left(\int_x^{x+t} \lambda^{male}(s)\, ds + \int_y^{y+t} \lambda^{female}(s)\, ds \right) \right\}.$$

Now using the same change of variables used to derive (3.6), the integral portion can be represented as

$$-\int_0^t (\lambda^{male}(x + s) + \lambda^{female}(y + s))\, ds, \qquad (3.33)$$

and the two IFM curves can be combined into one IFM curve:

$$\lambda^{\text{combined}}(s) = \lambda^{\text{male}}(x+s) + \lambda^{\text{female}}(y+s). \qquad (3.34)$$

Finally, if both are the same age $x = y$ and if the parameters for m and b are the same, then the combined IFM is simply double the individual IFM.

3.13 Period vs. Cohort Tables

Up to this point in the discussion, I have treated the death rate q_x and the survival rates $(_tp_x)$ as universal variables that depend only on a current age x but not on a particular calendar year or birth year. Thus, for example, q_{65} is a general probability that a 65-year-old will die in the next year, which can also be interpreted as that fraction of a group of 65-year-olds who will not survive to see their 66th birthday. However, I have been silent on the issue of when, exactly, this 65-year-old person (or group) was born. This person could have born in 1940, in which case q_{65} is the probability he or she will die in 2005. Or this person could have been born in 1955, in which case q_{65} is the probability of dying in 2020. In fact, it is quite feasible that q_{65} for the 1940 cohort will be higher than q_{65} for the 1955 cohort, since the health of a typical 65-year-old is projected to improve over time given advances in medicine, nutrition, and the like. According to a study by Tillinghast (2004), life expectancy at birth for females in the United States has increased by nearly 30 years for those born in the new millennium as compared to those born in 1900.

The principal thrust of this section is that sometimes it is important to keep track of an actual cohort (birth year) as opposed to a generic person of age, say, 65. Thus, in this section I will add a superscript to remind the reader of the exact group and cohort to which I refer. For instance, q_{65}^{1940} denotes the death probability for a 65-year-old born in the year 1940, while q_{65}^{1955} denotes the death probability for the group born in 1955. Generally speaking, q_x^z will denote the age-x death probability for the z-year cohort. The same notation will be applied to $(_tp_x^z)$, which denotes the probability that an x-year-old who was born in the year z will survive t more year(s) to age $x+t$.

What this means is that—in order to compute accurately the probability of survival for someone who was born in 1940 and is currently 65 years of age—we must evaluate

$$(_5p_{65}^{1940}) = (1 - q_{65}^{1940})(1 - q_{66}^{1940})(1 - q_{67}^{1940})(1 - q_{68}^{1940})(1 - q_{69}^{1940})$$

when dealing with a discrete table of values.

Along the same lines, the (generic) instantaneous force of mortality will also exhibit a cohort superscript z indicating the year of birth and will thus be denoted by $\lambda^z(x)$. The survival probability would then be represented as

Table 3.11. *Change in mortality patterns*
over time—Female

x + t	Individual survival probabilities ($_{t}p_{55}$)		
	1971	1983	1996
55	100.0%	100.0%	100.0%
60	97.6%	98.2%	98.5%
65	93.8%	95.6%	96.2%
70	88.9%	91.4%	92.6%
75	81.2%	84.9%	89.9%
80	68.9%	74.5%	77.5%
85	50.4%	58.6%	62.8%
90	28.1%	37.9%	42.7%
95	10.3%	18.1%	22.1%
100	2.6%	5.9%	8.2%
$E[T_{55}]$	31.76	34.03	35.22

$$(_{t}p_{x}^{z}) = \exp\left\{-\int_{0}^{t} \lambda^{z}(x+s)\,ds\right\}.$$

Here is yet another way to think about the cohort effect. If you track a large and diverse population of individuals at different ages during the next year and keep track of the number of deaths, you should be able to obtain a reasonably good estimate for q_{x}^{2005-x}. You would count the number of x-year-olds alive at the beginning of the year and divide this number into the number of x-year-olds who survived to the end of the year; 1 minus this ratio would provide a contemporaneous estimate of q_{x}^{2005-x}.

After all, the 55-year-olds who died during the year 2005 would have been born in the year 1950, so you would have an estimate for q_{55}^{1950}. The 75-year-olds who died during the year would have been born in the year 1930, so you would have an estimate for q_{75}^{1930}, et cetera. This process would be generating a *period* mortality table as opposed to a *cohort* mortality table. In fact, Tables 3.11 and 3.12 were created from the same kind of period mortality tables of q_{x}^{1971-x}, q_{x}^{1983-x}, and q_{x}^{2000-x} values for three baseline years. Thus, to be precise, the $(_{t}p_{x})$ values are not representative of any particular cohort. To compute true $(_{t}p_{x}^{z})$ would require converting, for $0 \leq x \leq 120$, the q_{x}^{1971-x} values to q_{x}^{z} values by making some sort of assumption about how q_{x} changes over time.

This brings us to a discussion of *how to model* mortality improvements, which is distinct from *the reasons why* q_{x}^{z1} might differ from q_{x}^{z2}, where

Table 3.12. *Change in mortality patterns over time—Male*

x + t	Individual survival probabilities ($_t p_{55}$)		
	1971	1983	1996
55	100.0%	100.0%	100.0%
60	95.2%	96.6%	97.4%
65	88.6%	91.9%	93.7%
70	79.9%	84.8%	88.0%
75	68.2%	74.2%	79.1%
80	53.0%	59.6%	66.3%
85	35.3%	41.5%	49.6%
90	18.1%	23.4%	31.3%
95	5.6%	10.0%	15.4%
100	0.7%	2.89%	5.55%
$E[T_{55}]$	27.49	29.70	31.93

$z1 > z2$ are two different cohorts. One easy way to link the two death rates is by assuming that, for any given age, mortality improves (i.e., death rates decline) at a constant rate denoted by the Greek letter xi, $\xi \geq 0$, so that

$$q_x^{z1} = q_x^{z2} e^{-\xi(z1-z2)}. \tag{3.35}$$

Hence, the greater the distance in time between the two cohorts, the greater the mortality improvement. For example, if we arbitrarily assume that $\xi = 0.02$ and $q_{65}^{1940} = 0.015$ then, under the simple model specified in equation (3.35), $q_{65}^{1955} = 0.015 e^{-0.02(15)} \approx 0.011$; this is a reduction of approximately four deaths per thousand exposed. Note that for simplicity I have used the $e^{-\xi(z1-z2)}$ structure for projecting mortality, though I could have done the same via $(1 + \xi)^{(z1-z2)}$ instead. In that case the improvement would be stated with effective as opposed to continuous compounding. Most commonly used projection scales or factors are often expressed in annual terms. This is obviously a question of taste as opposed to substance.

In any case, when you think about it, this model is rather simplistic in that ξ is not assumed to be age dependent (yielding, e.g., the same rate of improvement for 99-year-olds and 19-year-olds)—and that, in the limit, all q_x^{z1} values go to zero as $z1$ increases. A more sophisticated model would not assume a constant ξ for all ages but instead would assume ξ_x^z, which varies with x and z and is based on other demographic and environmental factors. We won't be doing much of that in this book, but it is an important area of focus for actuaries who study mortality.

In fact, one might go so far as to argue that, if we are currently in the year 2005, then it is nearly impossible to predict q_x^z values for any z cohort born anywhere near 2005. This is why some researchers (see the references listed in Section 3.14 for more information) have developed models to randomly project q_x^{z1} values using biostatistical methods. In the most general terms, there is a substantial amount of research being conducted to understand the behavior of the function ξ^z, which is how the z birth-year cohort's health differs from previous and future generations. The study of this topic is also of great importance to insurance companies, since major underestimates of mortality improvements can adversely affect profitability. I will revisit this topic in Chapter 10 and provide an example of the implications of such a misestimation.

Just to make sure this concept is clear, here is an example of how to convert a *period* mortality table to a *cohort* mortality table. In order to do this, we must have a rule for projecting mortality.

So, for the sake of argument, assume the baseline period table is for the year 2000 and that it contains the following mortality rates:

$$q_{65}^{1935} = 0.0103, \quad q_{66}^{1934} = 0.0114, \quad q_{67}^{1933} = 0.0125,$$
$$q_{68}^{1932} = 0.0137, \quad q_{69}^{1931} = 0.0151.$$

(By the way, these numbers are from the female RP2000 mortality table; see Table 14.1.) Note that in each case the subscript x and superscript z add up to a value of 2000, which is consistent with the structure of a period table. These people—of different ages—are all alive in the year 2000 and will experience different (hazard) mortality rates in the next year depending on their current age. The main question I would like to address is: What is the probability that a person born in the year 1935 (who is 65 years old in 2000) will survive to age 70?

Prior to our discussion about cohort versus period tables, the answer to this question would have been simply to multiply 1 minus the q_x-values for $x = 65, \ldots, 69$. However, now I must convert the q_x-values to those that are relevant for the 1935 cohort. Obviously, if I make the trivial assumption that the projection factor $\xi = 0$ in equation (3.35) then the q_x^z-values are identical for all birth cohorts, so (for example) $q_{66}^{1935} = q_{66}^{1936}$ and $q_{68}^{1935} = q_{68}^{1937}$. In this case, the period table is treated as a cohort table and the relevant survival probability is

$$(_5p_{65}) = (1 - 0.0103)(1 - 0.0114)(1 - 0.0125)(1 - 0.0137)(1 - 0.0151)$$
$$= 0.9385,$$

where I have deliberately not used a superscript on the survival probability $(_5p_{65})$ to remind the reader that we are not distinguishing between period tables and cohort tables. However, if we make the projection assumption that mortality will improve by a constant $\xi = 0.01$ each year for each successive generation, then the cohort survival probability is

$$
\begin{aligned}
(_5p_{65}^{1935}) &= (1 - 0.0103)(1 - 0.0114e^{-0.01})(1 - 0.0125e^{-0.02}) \\
&\quad \times (1 - 0.0137e^{-0.03})(1 - 0.0151e^{-0.04}) \\
&= 0.9398
\end{aligned}
$$

as opposed to the lower 0.9385, reflecting the "improvement" in mortality.

Of course, I could have performed the same calculation for other ages and other birth years. Not to belabor the point, but a true cohort mortality table is actually a matrix, not a vector, since we must keep track not only of ages but also birth years. Once again, the numbers displayed in Tables 3.11 and 3.12 are based on period mortality tables—for the baseline years 1971, 1983, and 2000—that have been converted into survival probabilities from age 65 assuming $\xi = 0$ improvement factors.

In sum, the take-away from this section is as follows. Although I will not make mortality improvement adjustments throughout the chapters, when using a mortality table in practice it is important to be crystal clear on whether these numbers capture a particular z-birth cohort q_x^z or are meant to represent a period, in which case q_x^{C-x}; here C is the baseline calendar year, and everyone dies at age 120 ($0 \le x \le 120$).

3.14 Further Reading

Obviously it is impossible for me to cover all the relevant and important aspects of actuarial modeling of mortality in one chapter. For those who want to learn (much) more, or those who want to become actuaries, the master reference is *Actuarial Mathematics* by Bowers et al. (1997), published by the Society of Actuaries. That book is truly an encyclopedia of actuarial valuation, a topic we shall see more of in Chapter 6 and Chapter 7. However, I warn you that the notation and symbols in Bowers can be daunting and that certain sections are impenetrable to the layman (like myself).

For more information about the Gompertz–Makeham law of mortality, see Carriere (1992, 1994). For a discussion of whether people are able to estimate their own "subjective" mortality rates, see Hurd and McGarry (1995). For an examination of general mortality tables and how they are revised over time, see Johansen (1995); see also Johansson (1996) for an analysis, using the Gompertz–Makeham distribution, of the economic value of decreasing hazard rates.

The GoMa model is widely used by economists, actuaries, and insurance researchers to model mortality. A popular model for projecting and forecasting mortality was developed by Lee and Carter (1992), and a related paper by Olivieri (2001) examines the same issue from a continuous-time perspective. For a discussion of current estimates of longevity and of how long people are expected to live in the future, see Olshansky, Carnes, and Cassel (1990) as well as Olshansky and Carnes (1997). Finally, for more information about the Factors Affecting Retirement Mortality (FARM) project, please visit the Society of Actuaries Web site, ⟨www.soa.org⟩.

3.15 Notation

q_x—probability of death within the given year at age x

$(_t p_x)$—conditional probability of an x-year-old surviving t more years

T_x—remaining lifetime random variable for an individual currently aged x

$f_x(t)$—probability density function (PDF) of the R.V. T_x

$F_x(t)$—cumulative distribution function (CDF) of the R.V. T_x (note: $F_x'(t) = f_x(t)$)

$\lambda(x + t)$—instantaneous force of mortality

$e^{-\lambda t}$—the $(_t p_x)$ under exponential law of mortality

m, b—Gompertz–Makeham parameters

$\exp\{-\lambda t + b(\lambda(x) - \lambda)(1 - e^{t/b})\}$—the $(_t p_x)$ under Gompertz–Makeham law of mortality

$\Gamma(a, c)$—incomplete Gamma function with parameters a and c

η—general hazard or lapse rate when the PDF is $h(t)$ and the CDF is $H(t)$

3.16 Problems

PROBLEM 3.1. Provide a simplified expression for the Gompertz–Makeham $f_x(t)$ and plot its shape in Excel from $x = 0$ to $x = 110$. Assume $m = 82.3$ and $b = 11.4$, as well as $m = 75$ and $b = 11.4$. Note the qualitative differences.

PROBLEM 3.2. Using the same $m = 82.3$ and $b = 11.4$ parameters, compute the median value $M[T_{65}]$ and compare with the mean value $E[T_{65}]$.

PROBLEM 3.3. Using the Gompertz law of mortality under parameters $m = 88.18$ and $b = 10.5$ for males and $m = 92.63$ and $b = 8.78$ for females, compute the probability that at least one member of a married couple currently aged 62 (female) and 67 (male) will survive to age 95.

3.17 Technical Note: Incomplete Gamma Function in Excel

Recall that to obtain the expected remaining lifetime of the Gompertz–Makeham law of mortality, we required

$$\Gamma(a,c) := \int_c^\infty e^{-t} t^{(a-1)} \, dt,$$

which is the incomplete Gamma function. This function is available in Excel, with a slight modification, using the CDF of the Gamma random variable G together with the standard Gamma function $\Gamma(a)$ via the relationship

$$1 - G_a(c) = \int_c^\infty \frac{e^{-t} t^{(a-1)}}{\Gamma(a)} \, dt,$$

where $G_a(c)$ is the CDF of a Gamma density with parameters c and a (i.e., $G_a(c) = \Pr[G < c]$).

This leads to:

$$\Gamma(a)(1 - G_a(c)) = \int_c^\infty e^{-t} t^{(a-1)} \, dt = \Gamma(a,c). \qquad (3.36)$$

In order to calculate $\Gamma(a,c)$, the actual syntax in Excel would be

EXP(GAMMALN(a))*(1-GAMMADIST(c,a,1,TRUE)).

For example, the value of $\Gamma(2,3) \approx 0.199$ and $\Gamma(3,2) \approx 1.353$. These numbers can also be obtained by computing $\Gamma(2) = 1.0$ and multiplying by (1-GAMMADIST(3,2,1,TRUE)) = 0.199 to recover the first expression $\Gamma(2,3)$.

In the event that $-1 < a \leq 0$, which results in an undefined $\Gamma(a)$ value, we can perform an integration by parts to obtain

$$\int e^{-t} t^{(a-1)} \, dt = \frac{1}{a} t^a e^{-t} + \frac{1}{a} \int e^{-t} t^a \, dt. \qquad (3.37)$$

This is equivalent to

$$\Gamma(a,c) = -\frac{c^a e^{-c}}{a} + \frac{1}{a}\Gamma(a+1,c). \qquad (3.38)$$

In our context, one iteration should be enough to make the implicit Gamma parameter positive. The syntax in Excel would then be

(EXP(GAMMALN(a+1))*(1-GAMMADIST(c,a+1,1,TRUE)))/a
-((c^a)*EXP(-c))/a

Finally, in the event we need another "round", we use the identity

$$\Gamma(a, c) = -\frac{c^a e^{-c}}{a} + \frac{1}{a}\left(\frac{-c^{(a+1)} e^{-c}}{a+1} + \frac{1}{a+1}\Gamma(a+2, c)\right). \quad (3.39)$$

In later chapters I will rely on these functions when the a parameter is negative.

3.18 Appendix: Normal Distribution and Calculus Refresher

Assume that you are interested in evaluating the following integral:

$$\Phi(a, b \mid c) = \int_{-\infty}^{c} \frac{1}{\sqrt{2\pi b^2}} \exp\left\{-\frac{1}{2}\left(\frac{x-a}{b}\right)^2\right\} dx, \quad (3.40)$$

where a, b, c can represent any constant or even a complicated function as long as it does not depend on the integrating variable x. From a graphical perspective, this expression should be recognized as the "area under a curve" between $-\infty$ and c for a normal distribution with a mean or expected value of a and a standard deviation of b. This also means that, as $c \to \infty$, the integral value $\Phi(a, b \mid c) \to 1$ regardless of the precise values of a or b.

The rules of calculus allow me to make any number of substitutions within the integrand—as long as I make equivalent substitutions over the upper and lower bounds of integration and the integrator—without affecting the value of the integral $\Phi(a, b \mid c)$. The reason I would want to make these changes is to simplify or perhaps collapse the integrand into an expression that is easier to work with or that might be available analytically.

For example, I can define a new "integrator" variable $z = (x - a)/b$, which of course means that $x = zb + a$. This means that every x in the integral should be replaced with $zb + a$ and that every dx in the integral should be replaced with $b \times dz$. This also affects the upper and lower bounds of integration. Instead of c we now must write $(c - a)/b$ and instead of $-\infty$ we must write $(-\infty - m)/b$, which is the same order of infinity.

The process of changing variables in calculus always proceeds along the same lines. You start with a new symbol in the original integral in equation (3.40) as the integrating variable, for example z, which is expressed in terms of the old integrating variable, x. The upper and lower bounds of integration are changed according to the new function defined by z. The function is inverted so that the original x is expressed in terms of the new z, and then dx is expressed as a function of dz. Finally the substitution is made for both x and dx, which leads to the new integral that involves only the integrating variable z. This allows us to write

$$\Phi(a, b \mid c) = \int_{-\infty}^{(c-a)/b} \frac{1}{\sqrt{2\pi}} \exp\left\{-\frac{z^2}{2}\right\} dz, \qquad (3.41)$$

an expression that is much cleaner and easier to use. This is the area under the standard normal curve from $-\infty$ to $(c-a)/b$. Statisticians often refer to the process of subtracting the mean and dividing by the standard deviation as *standardizing the random variable,* but it is a simple change of variable from calculus.

Notice how the $b \times dz$ was canceled by the b in the denominator of the fraction. This cancellation would have happened regardless of how complicated the expression b is, as long as it is not a function of x. Thus, for example, the combination $a = vt$ and $b = \sigma\sqrt{t}$ would not preclude one from making the exact same substitution, since the functions a and b do not depend on the critical integrating variable x. In this case the upper bound of integration would be $(c - vt)/\sigma\sqrt{t}, \ldots$.

FOUR

Valuation Models of Deterministic Interest

4.1 Continuously Compounded Interest Rates?

Our models will mostly be developed in continuous time. This means that money grows as a result of the force of interest in a continuous manner. To maintain consistency, I will use the letter r to denote the current continuously compounded (CC) rate of interest. The relationship between the nominal CC rate r and the effective annual rate $R = e^r - 1$ is, via the exponential operator (or its inverse), the natural logarithm. For example, if the effective annual rate is 10% then the continuously compounded rate will be (a lower) $\ln[1 + 0.10] = 9.531\%$ per annum. This 0.5% gap between the rates (47 basis points, to be exact) is substantial when compounded over long periods of time. Note that each basis point is *one hundredth* of a percentage point. Caution is therefore warranted when using a generic interest rate in any calculation or formula. Make sure you confirm the compounding period.

Tables 4.1 and 4.2 show the growth of one dollar under different compounding frequencies and effective annual rates. Of course, the more frequently we compound interest, the greater the sum of money available at the end of the year. Notice that a 12% rate compounded continuously yields a gain of 75 basis points (1.12750 vs. 1.12) over a 12% rate compounded annually.

When working with the continuously compounded rate, mathematically we are building on the relationship

$$\lim_{n \to \infty} \left(1 + \frac{r}{n}\right)^n = e^r. \tag{4.1}$$

This can be formally proved by defining a new variable,

$$y := \left(1 + \frac{r}{n}\right)^n, \tag{4.2}$$

Table 4.1. *Year-end value of $1 under infrequent compounding*

Rate	Annual ($n = 1$)	Quarterly ($n = 4$)
4%	$\left(1 + \frac{0.04}{1}\right)^1 = 1.04$	$\left(1 + \frac{0.04}{4}\right)^4 = 1.04060$
5%	$\left(1 + \frac{0.05}{1}\right)^1 = 1.05$	$\left(1 + \frac{0.05}{4}\right)^4 = 1.05095$
6%	$\left(1 + \frac{0.06}{1}\right)^1 = 1.06$	$\left(1 + \frac{0.06}{4}\right)^4 = 1.06136$
7%	$\left(1 + \frac{0.07}{1}\right)^1 = 1.07$	$\left(1 + \frac{0.07}{4}\right)^4 = 1.07186$
8%	$\left(1 + \frac{0.08}{1}\right)^1 = 1.08$	$\left(1 + \frac{0.08}{4}\right)^4 = 1.08243$
10%	$\left(1 + \frac{0.10}{1}\right)^1 = 1.10$	$\left(1 + \frac{0.10}{4}\right)^4 = 1.10381$
12%	$\left(1 + \frac{0.12}{1}\right)^1 = 1.12$	$\left(1 + \frac{0.12}{4}\right)^4 = 1.12551$

Table 4.2. *Year-end value of $1 under frequent compounding*

Rate	Daily ($n = 365$)	Continuous ($n = \infty$)
4%	$\left(1 + \frac{0.04}{365}\right)^{365} = 1.04081$	$e^{0.04 \times 1} = 1.04081$
5%	$\left(1 + \frac{0.05}{365}\right)^{365} = 1.05127$	$e^{0.05 \times 1} = 1.05127$
6%	$\left(1 + \frac{0.06}{365}\right)^{365} = 1.06183$	$e^{0.06 \times 1} = 1.06184$
7%	$\left(1 + \frac{0.07}{365}\right)^{365} = 1.07250$	$e^{0.07 \times 1} = 1.07251$
8%	$\left(1 + \frac{0.08}{365}\right)^{365} = 1.08328$	$e^{0.08 \times 1} = 1.08329$
10%	$\left(1 + \frac{0.10}{365}\right)^{365} = 1.10516$	$e^{0.10 \times 1} = 1.10517$
12%	$\left(1 + \frac{0.12}{365}\right)^{365} = 1.12747$	$e^{0.12 \times 1} = 1.12750$

and then taking natural logarithms of both sides so that

$$\ln[y] = n \ln\left[1 + \frac{r}{n}\right].$$

The result is

$$\lim_{n \to \infty} \ln[y] = \lim_{n \to \infty} \frac{\ln[1 + r/n]}{1/n}.$$

We now invoke L'Hôpital's rule from calculus, which allows us to compute limits of fractions by taking derivatives of both the numerator and denominator and then calculating the limit of the "derived" fraction. If we take derivatives of the numerator and denominator, we are left with

$$\lim_{n\to\infty} \frac{\ln[1+r/n]}{1/n} = \lim_{n\to\infty} \frac{r}{1+r/n} = r,$$

which then leads to

$$\lim_{n\to\infty} \ln[y] = r$$

and therefore

$$\lim_{n\to\infty} \left(1+\frac{r}{n}\right)^n = e^r.$$

The point of this little bit of calculus is to thoroughly convince you of the following.

- Compounding interest more frequently—once you get down to the daily level—does not lead to "more money" in the limit. In fact, there is only a *1-basis-point* difference between compounding interest daily and compounding interest continuously.
- The mathematical technique was predicated on being able to take the derivative of $\ln[1+r/n]$ and then limits to arrive at e^r. This could be a problem when the main argument in the function is random, in which case it becomes impossible to take formal derivatives.

4.2 Discount Factors

Using our terminology, the discounted value of a dollar to be received at time t is

$$d(t) = e^{-rt}. \tag{4.3}$$

This $d(t)$ will often be referred to as a *discount factor,* which can be envisioned as an exchange rate between a dollar at time t and its value today. With a discount factor (function) in our hands we don't have to worry about the precise interest rate r, and we can compute the present value of any cash flow C simply by multiplying it by $d(t)$.

For example, when $r = 5\%$ and $t = 10$ years we obtain a discount factor of $d(10) = e^{-0.05\times 10} = 0.6065$; but when $r = 3\%$ and $t = 10$ years, the discount factor is a higher $d(10) = e^{-0.03\times 10} = 0.7408$. Stated differently, a dollar in ten years is worth 60.65 cents today when the interest rate is 5% but is worth 74.08 cents today when the interest rate is 3%.

Remember that there is an inverse relationship between the interest rate and the discount factor. If r increases then $d(t)$ decreases, and $d(t)$ decreases also when t increases.

Table 4.3. *Years required to double or triple $1 invested at various interest rates*

Rate	Double ($C = \$2$)	Triple ($C = \$3$)
4%	$\frac{1}{0.04} \ln[2] = 17.3286$	$\frac{1}{0.04} \ln[3] = 27.4653$
5%	$\frac{1}{0.05} \ln[2] = 13.8629$	$\frac{1}{0.05} \ln[3] = 21.9722$
6%	$\frac{1}{0.06} \ln[2] = 11.5524$	$\frac{1}{0.06} \ln[3] = 18.3102$
7%	$\frac{1}{0.07} \ln[2] = 9.9021$	$\frac{1}{0.07} \ln[3] = 15.6944$
8%	$\frac{1}{0.08} \ln[2] = 8.6643$	$\frac{1}{0.08} \ln[3] = 13.7326$
10%	$\frac{1}{0.10} \ln[2] = 6.9314$	$\frac{1}{0.10} \ln[3] = 10.9861$
12%	$\frac{1}{0.12} \ln[2] = 5.7762$	$\frac{1}{0.12} \ln[3] = 9.1551$

How long does a dollar have to be invested before it doubles, triples, and quadruples in value, assuming it is invested at a rate of r (CC) per annum? Well, if we are interested in a dollar growing into C then we must solve

$$e^{rT} = C \iff T = \frac{1}{r} \ln[C]. \tag{4.4}$$

With continuous compounding the variable t is expressed in decimal form (or as a fraction of one year), which means that if we want to obtain its value in months then we must calculate $12t$, for weeks we must calculate $52t$, and so on. Notice, again, the inverse relationship between the interest rate r and the time needed to grow to a fixed dollar sum of C.

Thus (and as shown in Table 4.3), at a 12% interest rate you must wait about 5.78 years for your money to double; at 4%, the wait is about 17.33 years.

4.3 How Accurate Is the Rule of 72?

Practitioners often invoke something called the "rule of 72," which claims that you can divide 72 by the *effective* annual interest rate to yield an estimate for the number of years it takes for your money to double. In order to compare this popular rule with the results in Table 4.3, I must first convert the 4% and 12%, which are continuously compounded rates, into $e^{0.04} - 1 = 0.0408$ and $e^{0.12} - 1 = 0.1274$, which are effective rates.

Using the rule of 72, we get $72/4.08 = 17.647$, which is a bit higher than the correct 17.33 years, and $72/12.74 = 5.65$, which is slightly lower than the correct 5.78 years.

Note that if we use the rule of 72 with a denominator that is continuously compounded instead of effective, the error in this approximation can be written as

$$[\text{error in rule of } 72] := \frac{1}{r}\left(\frac{72}{100} - \ln[2]\right) = \frac{0.02685}{r}.$$

If the valuation rate is greater than 2.68% then the "approximation bias" is less than one year, and if the valuation rate is less than 2.68% then this bias is greater than one year. Under this implementation, the error declines with r and is always positive, which means that the rule overestimates the waiting time.

Interestingly enough, since $100\ln[2] \approx 69.3$, a more accurate rule would have been the "rule of 69" for an interest rate that is continuously compounded. In this case, the error between the correct result and approximation would be smaller.

4.4 Zero Bonds and Coupon Bonds

Imagine a bond that matures in T years and pays annual coupons of c times the face value. Assume these coupons are paid every day in the amount of $c/365$. What is this bond "worth" today when interest rates in the market are at r? The present value of the cash flows paid to the holder of the bond (per $1 of face value) can be stated as

$$[\text{PV of bond}] = \sum_{i=1}^{365T} \frac{c/365}{(1 + R/365)^i} + \frac{1}{(1 + R/365)^{365T}}.$$

However, if we assume these coupons are paid in *continuous time* instead of daily—and this won't make a big difference, as we saw earlier—then a model value of this bond can be written as

$$V(c, r, T) = \int_0^T ce^{-rs}\, ds + e^{-rT}. \tag{4.5}$$

Thus, a $10,000 face-value bond, which pays annual coupons of $10000c$, would have a model value of $10000V(c, r, T)$. Similarly, a $100,000 face-value bond, which pays annual coupons of $100000c$, would have a model value of $100000V(c, r, T)$.

Stare at this equation for a while. Do you see why it makes sense to integrate the discount factor $d(s) = e^{-rs}$ against the coupon yield c? If we are modeling a portfolio of zero-coupon bonds—each of which is paying

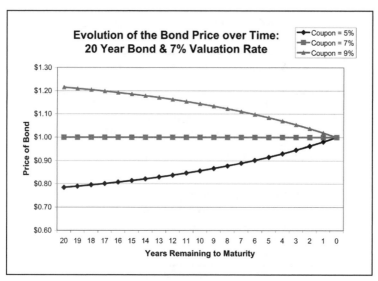

Figure 4.1

only the face value, $1dt$, as it matures between time 0 and T—then $c = 1$ in the main equation. And if we are modeling only one zero-coupon bond that pays \$1 at time T, then $c = 0$.

In either event, after some simple calculus is applied to the valuation equation (4.5), we obtain that the model value of a "generic" bond can be written as

$$V(c, r, T) = \frac{c}{r}(1 - e^{-rT}) + e^{-rT}. \tag{4.6}$$

This may look familiar. As we saw in Chapter 2, the PV of consumption at retirement is calculated in much the same way as the first term in equation (4.6), while the second term is simply the discount factor for the face value of the bond to be paid at time T. Note that if $c = r$ then $V(r, r, T) = 1$. In words, when the valuation rate is precisely equal to the coupon yield on the bond, it will have a "par" (equal to face) model value. When $c > r$, the bond will have a model value of $V(c, r, T) > 1$, and when $c < r$ the value of the bond will be $V(c, r, T) < 1$; see Figure 4.1 for an illustration.

To make sure you understand the basics of bond valuation, think about the following questions.

- How do changes in c, r, and T affect the bond pricing equation?
- What happens as $T \to \infty$ and the bond is perpetual?
- Where, in the calculus, is the constant valuation rate used?

Table 4.4. *Valuation of 5-year bonds as a fraction of face value*

Valuation rate (r)	Value
4%	$V(0.05, 0.04, 5) = 1.0453$
5%	$V(0.05, 0.05, 5) = 1.0000$
6%	$V(0.05, 0.06, 5) = 0.9568$

Note: Coupon yield $c = 5\%$, maturity $T = 5$ years.

Table 4.5. *Valuation of 10-year bonds as a fraction of face value*

Valuation rate (r)	Value
4%	$V(0.05, 0.04, 10) = 1.0824$
5%	$V(0.05, 0.05, 10) = 1.0000$
6%	$V(0.05, 0.0, 10) = 0.9248$

Note: Coupon yield $c = 5\%$, maturity $T = 10$ years.

Tables 4.4 and 4.5 provide values for generic bonds as functions of the valuation rate r, the coupon yield c, and the maturity T. When we increase the maturity from $T = 5$ years to $T = 10$ years, notice the impact on the bond value. Remember also that these numbers are fractions of "face value." So, for example, a 5-year 5% bond is worth $9,568 when the face value is $10,000 and the valuation rate is $r = 6\%$.

The impact of a varying r, c, and T can also be demonstrated graphically. Figure 4.2 shows that, if a set of bonds has coupon rates that are higher than the valuation rate (i.e., they are premium bonds), then bonds with larger coupons will, of course, have higher values than those with lower coupons; but given two bonds with the same coupon, the bond with the longer maturity will have a higher value. The opposite is true in a "discount" situation: given two bonds with the same coupon rate, the bond with the shorter maturity will be more valuable.

4.5 Arbitrage: Linking Value and Market Price

Note that I am careful to distinguish between the *model value* of the generic bond, which is based on formulas and assumptions, and the *market price* of the bond, which is an actual number at which investors can buy and sell

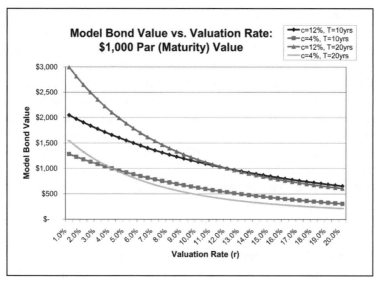

Figure 4.2

the bond. In many cases the model value of a financial instrument can differ from the market price of the same instrument, and later in the analysis we will discuss the reasons for such differences.

However, when the valuation rate is *r and* an investor can borrow as well as lend money at this valuation rate, then the aforementioned model value $V(c, r, T)$ must also be the market price of the bond. If not, there is an *arbitrage* or opportunity for riskless profit. This imbalance cannot persist for long—would you leave a $100 bill on the floor?—and eventually the market price will converge to the model value.

If the market price of a bond were actually higher than its model value as dictated by equation (4.6), then an arbitrageur would short sell the (over-priced) bond and invest the proceeds at the valuation rate r in order to pay off the coupons due along the way. The selling pressure (on the bond) would drive the market price down toward its model value. Conversely, if the market price of the bond were lower than dictated by the model value in (4.6), then arbitrageurs would purchase the underpriced bond by borrowing the required funds at the rate of r and slowly paying back the loan as the bond paid coupons and finally matured. In this case, the cash flows received from the bond contract would exceed the debt owed to the bank. The buying pressure would eventually force the market price of the bond up to its model value. Or it is also possible that the borrowing pressure would force the market interest rate r up, and the model value would be forced down to the market price.

For example, if a $T = 10$-year maturity coupon bond pays an annual coupon yield of $c = 5\%$ when interest rates in the market are at $r = 6\%$, then the model value of this bond is $V(0.05, 0.06, 10) = 92.48\%$ of its face value. Thus, if the face value of the bond is \$10,000 and the annual coupon of \$500 is paid daily in amounts of $500/365$ dollars per day, then the model value of the bond is \$9,248. The reason this bond has a value lower than its face amount of \$10,000 is because the 5% coupon rate is too low relative to the current interest rate in the market. Hence, to compensate for this deficiency, the model value is only 92.48% of the face value.

Now imagine this bond actually existed and was trading in the market for a price of \$9,500, which is higher than the model value. If you could short sell this relatively expensive bond for \$9,500 and use the entire proceeds of the short sale, you could immediately pocket \$252 and use the remaining \$9,248 to invest at 6%. This would generate the required $500/365$ each day, and the bulk of the funds would provide exactly \$10,000 to pay off the bond at maturity. It's easy to see why an opportunity like this can't stick around forever, so the bond price must eventually fall to the model value of \$9,248.

4.6 Term Structure of Interest Rates

In our earlier discussion we assumed that the CC interest rate r at which money is growing over time is constant during the entire period of analysis. In practice, the valuation rate can depend on the maturity time t. Therefore, when using a time-dependent interest rate, I will use the notation $r(t)$ to remind the reader that the interest rate curve depends on the maturity. In this case the discount factor would retain the same functional form:

$$d(t) = e^{-r(t)t}, \tag{4.7}$$

with the understanding that stating the valuation rate as simply r will imply a constant or flat valuation curve.

For example, assume that the time-dependent continuously compounded interest rate $r(t)$ is

$$r(t) = a - \frac{b}{t+1}, \quad t \geq 0. \tag{4.8}$$

This is just one of many ways of modeling the time-dependent rate. In this case, when $a = 5\%$ and $b = 2\%$ we have $r(10) = 0.04818$, and when $a = 6\%$ and $b = 2\%$ we have $r(10) = 0.05818$. Note that, in this model, as

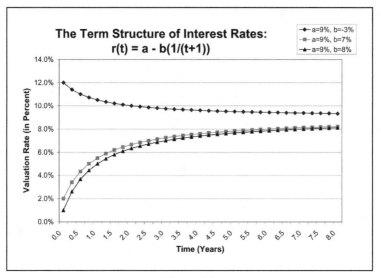

Figure 4.3

$T \to \infty$ the interest rate converges to a from below because the second portion converges to zero. In this case the discount factor would be

$$d(t) = e^{-at+bt/(t+1)}.$$

Think about what this "term structure" of interest rates—or the relationship between interest rates and various maturities—looks like graphically. Figure 4.3 displays the valuation rate $r(t)$ over 30 years for three values of $\{a, b\}$ in the equation just displayed. Observe the effect on the "big picture" of changing b.

Note that $r(t)$ being a function of time is separate from the fact that the $r(t)$ itself can change over time. That is, the curve might look one way today, but tomorrow it could take on a different shape. I will not delve too much into this issue right now, but keep this in mind as we move forward.

4.7 Bonds: Nonflat Term Structure

When the continuously compounded valuation rate $r(t)$ is a function of time, the fundamental bond valuation equation (4.6) must be written as

$$V(c, r(t), T) = c \int_0^T e^{-r(s)s} \, ds + e^{-r(T)T}. \tag{4.9}$$

For example, if we assume that

$$r(t) = a - b\left(\frac{1}{t+1}\right),$$

then

$$V(c, r(t), T) = c \int_0^T e^{-(a - b/(s+1))s} \, ds + e^{-(a - b/(T+1))T}.$$

Of course, there is never any guarantee that we can "solve" the integral and arrive at a closed-form expression for the bond value, regardless of how simple an interest rate curve $r(t)$ we use.

4.8 Bonds: Nonconstant Coupons

If the coupon yield $c(t)$ is also a function of time, then the fundamental bond valuation equation (4.6) must be written as

$$V(c(t), r(t), T) = \int_0^T c(s) e^{-r(s)s} \, ds + e^{-r(T)T}. \tag{4.10}$$

For instance: if a 20-year bond with a face (or principal) value of $10,000 pays an annual coupon of $1,000 that declines by 7% each year, then it follows that, under a constant valuation rate of $r = 10\%$, the model bond value would be expressed as

$$V = \int_0^{20} 1000 e^{-(0.07)s} e^{-(0.10)s} \, ds + 10000 e^{-(0.10)(20)}$$

$$= \$7,039.39. \tag{4.11}$$

The first term in the integrand captures the declining coupon, and the second term is the present value factor that brings all the coupons back to time 0.

More generally, a bond with a face value of F that pays a coupon of cF that declines by λ each year would have a value of

$$V = cF \int_0^T e^{-(r+\lambda)s} \, ds + F e^{-rT}$$

$$= \frac{cF}{r + \lambda} (1 - e^{-(r+\lambda)T}) + F e^{-rT}. \tag{4.12}$$

Note that, when the bond becomes a perpetuity (which means that $T \to \infty$), the bond value will converge to a simple $V = cF/(r + \lambda)$.

It might seem artificial and unrealistic to have a bond that pays coupons in this way, but later we shall see a number of applications of this concept.

4.9 Taylor's Approximation

In this section I investigate the sensitivity or impact of the valuation rate r on the generic bond equation $V(c, t, T)$. Specifically, I am interested in how *much* the bond value will change when we increase or decrease the rate r by a small amount Δr.

Economic intuition dictates that if $\Delta r > 0$ then the change in the value of the bond will be negative and if $\Delta r < 0$ then the change in the value of the bond will be positive. And, if you remember your calculus, we can approximate the change in the value of any continuous function by taking derivatives of the given function and applying Taylor's theorem. According to the Taylor approximation,

$$V(c, r + \Delta r, T) - V(c, r, T)$$
$$\approx (\Delta r)V'(c, r, T) + \frac{(\Delta r)^2}{2}V''(c, r, T), \quad (4.13)$$

where $V'(c, r, T)$ and $V''(c, r, T)$ denote (respectively) the first and second derivative of the bond equation (4.6) relative to the valuation rate r. The intuition for this relationship is that a small change in the rate r will trigger a small change in the bond, where the relationship between these two changes is determined by how quickly the bond function $V(c, r, T)$ moves when plotted against r.

It is convenient to rewrite (4.13) by dividing both sides by the bond value $V(c, r, T)$, which leads to

$$\frac{V(c, r + \Delta r, T) - V(c, r, T)}{V(c, r, T)}$$
$$\approx (\Delta r)\frac{V'(c, r, T)}{V(c, r, T)} + \frac{(\Delta r)^2}{2}\frac{V''(c, r, T)}{V(c, r, T)}. \quad (4.14)$$

In English, the relative change in the bond value (as a result of a movement in the rate r) can be approximated by the sum of two quantities on the right-hand side of (4.14). Finally, given the centrality of this approximation in a number of places throughout the material, I will use the notation $D(c, r, T)$ as follows:

$$D(c, r, T) = -\frac{\partial V(c, r, T)/\partial r}{V(c, r, T)}; \quad (4.15)$$

also,

$$K(c, r, T) = \frac{\partial^2 V(c, r, T)/\partial r^2}{V(c, r, T)}. \quad (4.16)$$

In both definitions, the derivative with respect to the rate r is now stated explicitly. Later I will explain why I have decided to define $D(c, r, T)$ as "negative" the derivative, which might seem odd at first glance. Some readers will recognize the expression $D(c, r, T)$ as the modified duration of the bond and $K(c, r, T)$ as the (modified) convexity of the bond, assuming the valuation rate is equal to the bond's internal yield. By *internal yield* I mean the value of r that leads to an expression for $V(c, r, T)$ that is equivalent to the market price of the bond. Note that there are several different ways in which duration is defined in the financial literature. Sometimes the derivative of $-V(c, r, T)$ with respect to r itself is called the duration; in other places, $-D(c, r, T)$ times e^r is defined as duration. To avoid confusion, in this book *duration* is as defined by equation (4.15).

These definitions and terms lead us from (4.14) to the abbreviated approximation

$$[\% \text{ change in bond value}] \approx -(\Delta r)D + \frac{(\Delta r)^2}{2}K. \qquad (4.17)$$

Observe also that nowhere in this approximation do we explicitly use the functional form of the bond value itself. Indeed, even if the pricing equation is some complicated function of valuation rates, coupon yields, and time horizons, the relationship (4.17) should still hold.

4.10 Explicit Values for Duration and Convexity

Recall equation (4.6), where the explicit definition of the bond value in the generic case was

$$V(c, r, T) = \frac{c}{r}(1 - e^{-rT}) + e^{-rT};$$

this is the result of integrating the coupon rate c against the discount function e^{-rs} and then adding the discounted face value. Using this expression, we can obtain explicit values for D and K by taking the appropriate partial derivatives in (4.15) and (4.16). This leads to

$$D(c, r, T) = -\frac{c(e^{-rT} - 1 + rTe^{-rT}) - r^2Te^{-Tr}}{cr(1 - e^{-Tr}) + r^2e^{-Tr}} \qquad (4.18)$$

and

$$K(c, r, T) = \frac{c(2 - e^{-rT}(2 + 2rT + r^2T^2)) + r^3T^2e^{-rT}}{cr^2(1 - e^{-Tr}) + r^3e^{-rT}}. \qquad (4.19)$$

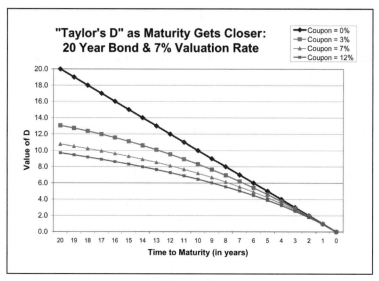

Figure 4.4

Despite the messy-looking expressions for both D and K, a number of important insights can be obtained from "staring" at the equations long enough. Figure 4.4 provides some graphical intuition for the relationship between V, K, and D as a function of c, r, and T.

First, with regards to $D(c, r, T)$—which can be interpreted as the bond value's derivative scaled by the bond value's price—notice that if the valuation rate r is equal to the coupon yield c then (4.18) simplifies to

$$D(c, c, T) = \frac{1 - e^{-cT}}{c},$$

which converges to T as $c \to 0$.

Along the same lines, note that if $c = 0$ (which, recall, is a zero-coupon bond) then the value of D simplifies to

$$D(0, r, T) = T$$

independently of r, which happens to be the exact maturity of the zero-coupon bond. This is why it is common to measure D in units of years. Later I will derive a deeper connection between D and actual units of time.

Moving on to $K(c, r, T)$—the bond value's second derivative scaled by the bond value's price—observe that when the coupon yield c is equal to the valuation rate r, we obtain the much simpler

$$K(c, c, T) = \frac{2(1 - Tce^{-cT} - e^{-cT})}{c^2}.$$

Furthermore, when $c = 0$ and the bond is of the zero-coupon variety, the value collapses to

$$K(0, r, T) = T^2;$$

hence it is common to measure K in units of years squared.

4.11 Numerical Examples of Duration and Convexity

Let's start with two bonds. Bond 1 has a face value of $10,000 paying a continuous coupon yield of $c = 11\%$ and maturing in $T = 17.20$ years. The current (valuation) rate in the market is assumed to be $r = 7\%$, and the bond value is therefore

$$10000V(0.11, 0.07, 17.2) \approx \$14,000.$$

At the same time, another $10,000 face-value bond (bond 2), paying a coupon of $c = 10\%$ and with maturity in $T = 38.69$ years, is also "worth" $14,000 under the current $r = 7\%$ valuation rate because

$$10000V(0.10, 0.07, 38.69) \approx \$14,000.$$

Our second bond is worth the same as the first bond—even though it has a lower (10% versus 11%) coupon yield—because it has a (much) longer maturity. Both bonds are obviously worth much more than their $10,000 par value as a result of the generous coupon yields (10% and 11%), which are much higher than current market rates of $r = 7\%$.

The D and K values of the two bonds are as follows. For bond 1, equation (4.18) leads to $D(0.11, 0.07, 17.2) = 9.1185$ years and equation (4.19) leads to $K(0.11, 0.07, 17.2) = 119.002$ years squared. Note that the D value is much lower than the maturity of $T = 17.2$ years and that the K value is much lower than $T^2 = 295.84$ years squared.

The D and K values of bond 2 are $D(0.10, 0.07, 38.69) = 12.8162$ years and $K(0.10, 0.07, 38.69) = 283.010$ units, respectively. Of course, the larger values come from the longer maturity of bond 2. Interestingly, the 20 additional years of maturity of bond 2 adds less than four years to the D value. In other words, the sensitivity of the bond value to changes in the rate r is not that much greater for bond 2 than for bond 1.

Now let us return to our approximation. Both bonds are "worth" \$14,000. Assume the valuation (or market) interest rate $r = 7\%$ changes from $r = 7\%$ to $7\% + \Delta r$ over a (very) short period of time, so that the maturities of the two bonds are still 17.2 years and 28.69 years, respectively.

Using the Taylor D-and-K method—as presented in (4.17)—the change in the value (or price) of the bond will be approximated by

$$V(c, r, T)\left(-(\Delta r)D + \frac{(\Delta r)^2}{2}K\right). \tag{4.20}$$

For example, if $\Delta r = 0.01$, which is a 1% (or 100-basis-point) increase in the valuation rate, then the value of bond 1 becomes

$$\approx 14000 + 14000\left(-(0.01)(9.1185) + \frac{(0.01)^2}{2}119.002\right)$$

$$= \$12{,}806.71; \tag{4.21}$$

for bond 2, we get

$$\approx 14000 + 14000\left(-(0.01)(12.8162) + \frac{(0.01)^2}{2}283.010\right)$$

$$= \$12{,}403.84. \tag{4.22}$$

The value of both bonds will fall when interest rates increase, but the impact of this change on bond 2 will be greater than its impact on bond 1. In fact, bond 2 will drop in value by \$400 more as a result of the greater sensitivity of D to changes in rates.

Note that by using the precise generic bond formula for the value of both bonds under the new interest rate $r = 8\%$, we obtain

$$10000V(0.11, 0.08, 17.2) = \$12{,}802.80 \tag{4.23}$$

and

$$10000V(0.10, 0.08, 38.69) = \$12{,}386.84, \tag{4.24}$$

respectively. The message is clear. Taylor's D-and-K approximation gives us numbers that are within a few dollars of the true bond value. Table 4.6 provides a more extensive example of how well (or poorly) the approximation works when we compare to the correct bond value. In the second column I have computed the new bond value using only the first derivative D in Taylor's approximation, and in the third column I have used both the first and second derivatives.

Table 4.6. *Estimated vs. actual value of $10,000 bond after change in valuation rates*

	Approximation using[a]		
Δr	D only	D & K	Exact value[b]
+2.5%	$6,865.92	$7,657.22	$7,520.64
+1.0%	$8,746.37	$8,872.98	$8,863.40
+0.5%	$9,373.18	$9,404.83	$9,403.60
+0.1%	$9,874.64	$9,875.90	$9,875.89
0.0%	$10,000.00	$10,000.00	$10,000.00
−0.1%	$10,125.36	$10,126.63	$10,126.64
−0.5%	$10,626.82	$10,658.47	$10,659.79
−1.0%	$11,253.63	$11,380.24	$11,391.17
−2.5%	$13,134.08	$13,925.39	$14,115.33

[a] "D only" is first derivative; "D & K" is first and second derivative.
[b] $10000V(c, r + \Delta r, T)$.
Note: $c = 7\%$, $r = 7\%$, $T = 30$ years.

Notice that for relatively small (i.e., 10-basis-point) changes in the valuation rate, the D-only and the D-and-K approximations produce numbers that are remarkably close to the correct bond value under the new valuation rate. However, as Δr grows—either positively or negatively—the D-only approximation can be off by hundreds of dollars and the D-and-K approximation is biased by over $100.

Figure 4.5 graphically summarizes the characteristics of the two approximations. Note also that the D-only approximation *always* leads to a smaller bond value than the correct answer, regardless of whether Δr is large or small, positive or negative. Adding the second derivative, which is the K term, partially closes the gap or bias and brings the total D-and-K approximation closer to the correct number. Even so, if $\Delta r > 0$ then the Taylor D-and-K method overestimates the new bond price, and if $\Delta r < 0$ then Taylor's D-and-K method (still) underestimates the price.

4.12 Another Look at Duration and Convexity

Let us go back to first principles and carefully examine the definition of Taylor's D, using the integral representation of the generic bond value:

$$D(c, r, T) = \frac{-\frac{\partial}{\partial r}\left(\int_0^T ce^{-rs}\, ds + e^{-rT}\right)}{\int_0^T ce^{-rs}\, ds + e^{-rT}}. \tag{4.25}$$

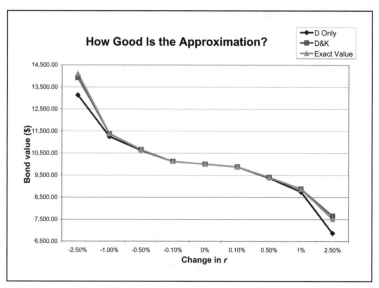

Figure 4.5

The numerator is (minus) the first derivative of the bond price with respect to the valuation rate, and the denominator is the bond value itself. Remember that the derivative "operator" can be moved inside the integral and then used on the integrand, so that the entire $D(c, r, T)$ can be rewritten as

$$D(c, r, T) = \int_0^T s\left(\frac{ce^{-rs}}{V(c, r, T)}\right) ds + T\left(\frac{e^{-rT}}{V(c, r, T)}\right). \tag{4.26}$$

Stare at this expression for a while. We see that the $D(c, r, T)$ function can also be identified as a type of weighted average. *The duration of the bond value is the weighted average of the time to payment,* where the weights are the share of the bond's cash flow in present value terms.

This is why we call $D(c, r, T)$ the bond's duration. Likewise, $K(c, r, T)$ is called the bond's convexity. The word "convexity" comes from measuring the curvature of a plot of the bond price as a function of the interest rate.

4.13 Further Reading

There are tens if not hundreds of books and articles that have been written in the last century that develop a formal model of bond pricing and fixed-income products. Clearly it is impossible to do justice to the numerous and respected authors who have written on this topic. However, if you are interested in reading and learning more about duration, convexity, and sophisticated models of the yield curve—and if you are willing to tolerate some more advanced mathematics—then I would recommend you get a copy of de La Grandville's *Bond Pricing and Portfolio Analysis* (2001). Alternatively, you can read Fabozzi's *Fixed Income Mathematics* (1996). Between these two books, you should have your theoretical bases covered.

4.14 Notation

$V(c, r, T)$—value of a generic coupon bond, which pays a coupon of c, matures after time T, and is valued using the discount rate r

$D(c, r, T)$—duration of the generic coupon bond

$K(c, r, T)$—convexity of the generic coupon bond

4.15 Problems

PROBLEM 4.1. A perpetual bond with a face value of $F = \$100{,}000$ pays coupons of $cF = \$10{,}000$ per year, but these coupons decline at a rate of $\lambda = 5\%$ each year. The current valuation rate in the market is $r = 7\%$, yet the bond is trading for $96{,}000$. Please describe in detail how you would arbitrage this price, assuming you could borrow and lend at $r = 7\%$.

PROBLEM 4.2. Take derivatives of the basic bond value with respect to the interest rate r, and confirm you recover the expressions for D and K.

PROBLEM 4.3. Let c_A and c_B denote the coupons on a $100{,}000$ face-value bond that mature at time T_A and T_B, respectively. You are long two bonds $\{A, B\}$ and short a third bond $\{G\}$ with coupon c_G that matures at time T_G. The model value of bond $\{G\}$ is equal to the sum of the bonds $\{A, B\}$. Interest rates move from r to $r + \Delta r$. Derive an expression for the change in the model value of your position.

FIVE

Models of Risky Financial Investments

5.1 Recent Stock Market History

In this chapter I will introduce models for investments that are more risky than the relatively safe fixed-income bonds introduced in the previous chapter. My objective is to develop a limited set of formulas for computing the probabilities of various investment outcomes over long-term horizons.

Table 5.1 starts us down this path by providing a 10-year history of the stock market as proxied by the widely cited Standard & Poor's index of the 500 largest companies traded in the United States. I will label this the SP500 index, or sometimes just "the index." Although this index captures only 500 of more than 5,000 investable stocks and common shares in the United States, these 500 are quite influential because they account for roughly 60%–70% of the market capitalization (i.e., the market value of all companies) in the country.

Of course, many other developed countries have their own stock market and indices—and the financial models we develop can be applied to any one of them—but I have selected the U.S. market because of its overwhelming influence in the global economy.

For example, if at the open of trading in January 1995 you invested $100 spread amongst these 500 companies—or if you purchased $100 of an open-ended mutual fund or exchange-traded mutual fund that invested in the SP500 index—then at the close of trading in December 1995 your money would have grown to $100(1 + 0.3743) = 137.43$ dollars. This growth would have come from dividends (roughly two or three percentage points) but mostly from capital gains. If you then continued investing in the SP500 during the year 1996, your $137.43 would have grown by 23.07% to $137.43(1 + 0.2307) = 169.14$ dollars by the end of 1996. In fact, at the end of the 10-year period from early January 1995 to late December

Table 5.1. *Nominal investment returns*
over 10 years

Year	Stocks (SP500)	Cash (T-bills)	Inflation (CPI)
1995	37.43%	5.60%	2.54%
1996	23.07%	5.21%	3.32%
1997	33.36%	5.26%	1.92%
1998	28.58%	4.86%	1.61%
1999	21.04%	4.68%	2.68%
2000	−9.11%	5.89%	3.39%
2001	−11.88%	3.83%	1.55%
2002	−22.10%	1.65%	2.38%
2003	28.70%	1.02%	1.88%
2004	10.87%	1.20%	3.26%

Source: Ibbotson Associates.

2004, your original $100 would have grown to more than $312. The effective compound annual growth rate (CAGR) was thus $(3.125)^{1/10} - 1 = 12.07\%$. Converting this number to continuous compounding yields a growth rate of $\ln[1.1207] = 11.40\%$. As in earlier chapters of the book, I will do my best to use continuous compounding whenever possible.

A number of additional insights from Table 5.1 are worth pointing out. First, if we take a simple arithmetic mean (average) of the ten numbers—that is, we add them up and divide by ten—the result is a value of 14.00%, which is about two percentage points higher than the CAGR. Later I will return to this number and discuss its relevance and importance in forecasting returns.

Note also that the last few years of the 1990s was an extraordinary and historically unprecedented period in the stock market, both U.S. and global. For five years in a row the market went up by more than 20% per year. It is hard to believe this feat will ever be repeated, and the first few years of the twenty-first century reminded investors about the other side of this coin.

Table 5.1 has two additional columns that display the investment returns from holding cash as proxied by U.S. Treasury bills and the inflation rate as measured by the Consumer Price Index. The "cash" series should be interpreted in the same way as the "stocks" series. A sum of $100 invested in early 1995 would have grown to $105.60 by the end of 1995, and so forth. Note that cash is much less volatile than stocks because its returns never exceeded 6% but never fell below zero. Cash performed better than stocks in three of the ten years, and stocks outperformed cash in the seven other

Table 5.2. *Growth rates during different investment periods*

Invested in January of	Value of $1 invested in SP500 index				
1995	$1.000				
1996	$1.374				
1997	$1.691	$1.000			
1998	$2.256	$1.334			
1999	$2.900	$1.715	$1.000		
2000	$3.510	$2.076	$1.210		
2001	$3.191	$1.886	$1.100	$1.000	
2002	$2.812	$1.662	$0.969	$0.881	
2003	$2.190	$1.295	$0.755	$0.686	$1.000
2004	$2.819	$1.667	$0.972	$0.883	$1.287
2005	$3.125	$1.848	$1.078	$0.980	$1.427
Growth (CC)	11.40%	7.67%	1.25%	−0.52%	17.78%

years. This pattern is not just an artifact of the last ten years. Indeed, over the last 75 years for which reliable stock market data is available, stocks have done better than cash, on average. Every once in a while, however, stocks experience a "shock" in which bad returns can wipe out years of gains. This is a brief snapshot of the relationship between risk and return in the capital markets.

Table 5.2 provides a slightly different perspective on the risk aspects of investing. It displays the evolution of $1 invested at the start of 1995, 1997, 1999, 2001, and 2003—assuming it was invested in the SP500 index.

For example, the 1995 dollar grew to $3.125 by the open of trading in 2005, which was more than triple the original investment. And as previously shown, the annual growth rate (continuously compounded) for the 10-year period was 11.40%.

Notice that the 1997 dollar experienced a growth rate of 7.67% during the eight years in which it was exposed to the market, whereas the 2001 dollar never quite recovered from the bear market and started 2005 at $0.98 for a negative four-year growth rate of −0.52%. Finally, the 2003 dollar earned a growth rate of 17.78% over the two-year period of 2003 and 2004. Observe how the growth rate depends on when you "get in" as well as the ending period, of course.

Now, back to the previous table, the last column in Table 5.1 displays the U.S. inflation rate during the same 10-year period, as proxied by the Consumer Price Index. Over this 10-year period, inflation eroded purchasing power by no more than 3.5% in any given year. These numbers are tame

Table 5.3. *After-inflation (real) returns over 10 years*

Year	Stocks (SP500)	Cash (T-bills)
1995	34.03%	2.98%
1996	19.12%	1.83%
1997	30.85%	3.28%
1998	26.54%	3.20%
1999	17.88%	1.95%
2000	−12.09%	2.42%
2001	−13.23%	2.25%
2002	−23.91%	−0.71%
2003	26.33%	−0.84%
2004	8.37%	0.49%

compared to the inflation rates of the 1970s and early 1980s. Usually inflation is lower than the T-bill return, although 2002 and 2003 were exceptions to this rule.

In fact, Table 5.1 can be converted from "nominal" pre-inflation numbers to "real" after-inflation numbers by dividing 1 plus the investment return by 1 plus the inflation rate and then subtracting 1; mathematically, $(1 + R)/(1 + \pi) - 1$. The intuition for the division—versus subtracting inflation from the return—is the same logic as for compounding interest. Table 5.3 displays the converted numbers.

One of the most fundamental beliefs in financial economics—some even consider it the religion's dogma—is that we never know what next year's, next month's, or even next week's investment return will be. It is random, uncertain, and stochastic. All we can do is try to estimate the odds or the probability distribution.

5.2 Arithmetic Average Return versus Geometric Average Return

Given that we don't know what the future will bring, let's start simple and imagine that next year will yield one of three outcomes: $\{10\%, 35\%, -15\%\}$. Furthermore, assume that the outcome $R = 10\%$ has a $1/2$ chance, that $R = 35\%$ has a $1/4$ chance, and that $R = -15\%$ has a $1/4$ chance. You could generate (or simulate) these outcomes by tossing a fair coin. If it falls heads, register a $+10\%$ gain. If it falls tails, toss the coin again and then, depending on whether it falls heads or tails the second time, register a $+35\%$ or -15%, respectively. What is the average or expected outcome for next year?

Table 5.4. *Geometric mean returns*

Probability of listed outcome			Geometric mean
1/2	1/4	1/4	
10%	42%	−15%	10.00%
10%	35%	−15%	8.55%
10%	40%	−20%	7.89%
10%	45%	−25%	7.10%
10%	50%	−30%	6.17%
10%	70%	−51%	0.00%

The arithmetic mean or average of the three possible returns is:

$$\tfrac{1}{2}(+10\%) + \tfrac{1}{4}(+35\%) + \tfrac{1}{4}(-15\%) = 10.0\%. \tag{5.1}$$

What does this number actually mean? One way of looking at the arithmetic average is to say that if you kept tossing the coin a large number of times and kept a record of the frequency of each outcome you saw, then the arithmetic average, calculated as in (5.1), would equal a number that is close to 10.0%. In fact, the longer you perform this experiment, the closer your result would approach 10.0%. So states the law of large numbers. Hence, the arithmetic average of these possible returns would also equal the expected return.

Mathematically, if R_1 and R_2 are independent random variables then the expected value of the investment return can be expressed in the following two ways:

$$E[(1 + R_1)(1 + R_2)] = E[1 + R_2] \times E[1 + R_2].$$

Furthermore, if $E[R_1] = E[R_2]$ then we are allowed to make the following statement:

$$E[(1 + R_1)(1 + R_2)(1 + R_3) \cdots (1 + R_n)] = E^n[1 + R_1]. \tag{5.2}$$

In contrast, the geometric mean is:

$$(1 + 0.10)^{(1/2)}(1 + 0.35)^{(1/4)}(1 - 0.15)^{(1/4)} - 1 = 8.55\%. \tag{5.3}$$

Table 5.4 displays the geometric mean of a number of related "gamble" or investment opportunities.

Another way to think of the geometric mean is as a midpoint between losses and gains that are multiplicative rather than additive. Note that, if you lose 10% in the stock market in any given year, then you must earn

$1/(0.9)-1 = 11.1\%$ the next year just to break even. The product $(0.9)(1.111)$ is exactly 100%, and you are back where you started.

Keep in mind this distinction between the arithmetic and geometric average throughout the chapters.

5.3 A Long-Term Model for Risk

I am now ready to present the model we will use to describe the long-term evolution of indices or investment portfolios for (most of) the remainder of the analysis. We start with an initial investment of $S_0 = 100$, for example, and after T years this capital amount grows to a random value:

$$S_T = S_0 e^{\tilde{g}T}, \tag{5.4}$$

where $\tilde{g}$ denotes the annualized *growth rate* of the portfolio during the T-year period. That is, the time-scaled log-price ratio is $\ln[S_t/S_0]/T = \tilde{g}$. Thus, for example, after $T = 10$ years the random growth rate might be a realized 8.5% yet after $T = 20$ years be only 7.0%. In this case, the portfolio or index might grow from $S_0 = 100$ to $S_{10} = 100e^{(0.085)(10)} = 233.96$ after 10 years and to $S_{20} = 100e^{(0.07)(20)} = 405.52$ after 20 years. This, of course, is just one possible realization of the growth-rate path of $\tilde{g}$ during the next 20 years. Another possible realization is that $\tilde{g} = 10\%$ for the first 10 years and $\tilde{g} = -5\%$ for the entire 20 years. In this (unfortunate) case, the portfolio grows from $S_0 = 100$ to $S_{10} = 100e^{(0.10)(10)} = 271.83$ after 10 years but then plummets to $100e^{(-0.05)(20)} = 36.788$ by the end of the 20 years.

Once again, $\tilde{g}$ is a random variable whose evolution is unknown in advance. Compare it to the risk-free interest rate r in the previous chapter. Both are multiplied by t and then placed in the exponent of e to "grow" the initial investment over time; however, whereas r is known, $\tilde{g}$ is stochastic. In theory, it can range anywhere from $-\infty$ to $+\infty$, although either extreme is far from likely.

There is, of course, a multitude of statistical distributions that we could select to describe the annualized growth rate $\tilde{g}$, and you might be surprised to learn that there are many different distributions that have been proposed for $\tilde{g}$ over the last century of scholarly writing, during which thousands of research papers have been written on this topic. Forecasting the evolution of $\tilde{g}$ over time is something of a holy grail in the field of financial economics. Although I could probably write an entire book on models and calibration of $\tilde{g}$, I will take the easy path and assume that $\tilde{g}$ satisfies the most ubiquitous of all statistical quantities: the normal distribution. I will assume that $\tilde{g}$ is normally distributed with an expected value of ν (Greek letter nu) and a variance of σ^2/T, or standard deviation of $\sigma/\sqrt{T}$ for T the horizon over

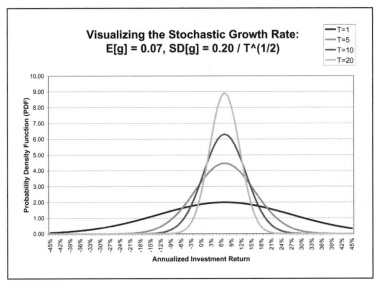

Figure 5.1

which we are forecasting investment returns. Later I will justify why I have placed a "time horizon" variable T in the denominator of the variance, but for now think of it as a reduction in the uncertainty of the growth rate over time. Note that, by the laws of probability, the expected value of the cumulative growth $\tilde{g}T$ is $E[\tilde{g}T] = \nu T$ and the variance of $\tilde{g}T$ is $\text{Var}[\tilde{g}T] = (\sigma^2/T)T^2 = \sigma^2 T$. To summarize more formally, I will assume that

$$\tilde{g} \sim N(\nu, \sigma^2/T) \tag{5.5}$$

and therefore $\tilde{g}T \sim N(\nu T, \sigma^2 T)$.

For example, I might say that over the next year the (annualized) growth rate of the SP500 index is expected to be $E[\tilde{g}] = 7\%$ with a variance of $\text{Var}[\tilde{g}] = (0.20)^2$ or a standard deviation of $\text{SD}[\tilde{g}] = 0.20 = 20\%$. Under these assumptions, during the next 10 years the annualized growth rate is still $E[\tilde{g}] = 7\%$ but with a variance of $\text{Var}[\tilde{g}] = (0.20)^2/10 = 0.004$ units and a standard deviation of $0.20/\sqrt{10} = 6.32\%$. By our "normality" assumption this implies that, two thirds of the time, the annualized return will fall between $0.07 - 0.063 = 0.7\%$ and $0.07 + 0.063 = 13.3\%$. Likewise, during the next 25 years, the annualized growth rate is still expected to be $E[\tilde{g}] = 7\%$ and the standard deviation is $\text{SD}[\tilde{g}] = 0.20/5 = 4\%$. Along the same lines, two thirds of the time the annualized return will fall between $0.07 - 0.04 = 3\%$ and $0.07 + 0.04 = 11\%$.

Figure 5.1 provides a graphical illustration of the probability density function (PDF) curves of $\tilde{g}$ for the various values of T. Now the role of T in the

Table 5.5. *Probability of losing money in a diversified portfolio*

v	σ	$T = 1$	$T = 5$	$T = 10$	$T = 20$	$T = 30$
12%	20%	0.274	0.090	0.029	0.004	0.001
12%	10%	0.115	0.004	0.000	0.000	0.000
7%	20%	0.363	0.217	0.134	0.059	0.028
7%	10%	0.242	0.059	0.013	0.001	0.000
5%	20%	0.401	0.288	0.215	0.132	0.085
5%	10%	0.309	0.132	0.057	0.013	0.003

denominator becomes apparent. As T increases, the dispersion around the 7% declines in proportion to $1/\sqrt{T}$, which is equivalent to saying that, as the term over which you hold an investment increases, so do your chances of earning a growth rate that is closer to the expected value.

Table 5.5 provides some additional insight into the time-dependent structure of $\tilde{g}$. It answers the question: What is the probability that you will lose money over a T-year horizon?—assuming various parameter combinations of v and σ that drive the growth rate. Recall that losing money means that the annualized growth rate was negative. Thus we are effectively computing the probability that a normally distributed random variable, with a mean value v and a standard deviation of $\sigma/\sqrt{T}$, is less than (or equal to) zero. In the language of Excel, we are using the function NORMDIST(0,nu,sigma/sqrt(T), TRUE) with different values of v, σ, and T.

For instance, if the expected annualized growth rate is 12% and the standard deviation of this growth rate over one year is 20%, then the probability of losing money over a one-year investment period is 0.274, which is roughly a 27% chance. However, over a 20-year period the probability drops to 0.004, which is less than a 1% chance. This is a dramatic reduction in the probability of loss as the time horizon increases. Yet, when the expected annualized growth rate is reduced to 5% with the same 20% standard deviation parameter, the probability of loss over one year is close to 40% and over 20 years is 13%. This should make intuitive sense. Also, we are careful not to make the overaggressive claim that financial risk is declining with the time horizon—even though all of the numbers in the table are decreasing as T gets larger—mainly because we have ignored the magnitude of the shortfall itself. In other words, people care about more than just the chances of losing money, they want to know how *much* they can lose, how bad it can get. This is where (and why) standard deviation is another important measure of risk. It helps us measure the magnitude in addition to just the probability.

5.4 Introducing Brownian Motion

The quantity $\tilde{g}t$, which can be treated as a total return expressed using continuous compounding, is extremely important in its own right. The product of the (random) growth rate and time—which reduces to $\ln[S_t/S_0]$, using our first definition—often has its own notation and description amongst financial specialists. I will adopt their convention and define a new expression,

$$B_t^{(\nu,\sigma)} := \tilde{g}t \sim N(\nu t, \sigma^2 t). \tag{5.6}$$

The object $B_t^{(\nu,\sigma)}$ is normally distributed with an expected value of νt and a standard deviation of $\sigma\sqrt{t}$. I will abbreviate this object by B_t when $\nu = 0$ and $\sigma = 1$, instead of using $B_t^{(0,1)}$.

It might appear unnecessarily cumbersome to introduce yet another set of symbols and objects to describe investment returns. But B_t—which has its own name, Brownian motion—is of interest not only to finance and investment specialists. The term B_t is part of a large family of mathematical objects called *continuous-time stochastic processes,* which are fundamental in the areas of physics and biology as well as classical probability theory.

Formally, B_t models *standard Brownian motion* (SBM) if the following statements are all true:

1. $\Pr[B_0 = 0] = 1$;
2. $\Pr[B_t \text{ varies continuously with } t] = 1$; and
3. the increments $\Delta_i B := B_{t_i} - B_{t_{i-1}}$ are independent—and have normal (Gaussian) distributions with mean $E[\Delta_i B] = 0$ and with variance $\text{Var}[\Delta_i B] = \Delta_i t := t_i - t_{i-1}$—when $0 \leq t_0 < t_1 < \cdots < t_n$.

The Gaussian assumption (discussed in Section 3.18) implies the following probability statements:

$$\Pr[a \leq B_t \leq b] = \int_a^b \frac{1}{\sqrt{2\pi t}} e^{-z^2/2t} \, dz;$$

$$E[f(B_t, \underbrace{B_{t+s}}_{B_t + \Delta B})]$$

$$= \int_{-\infty}^{\infty} \int_{-\infty}^{\infty} f(u, u + v) \frac{1}{\sqrt{2\pi t}} e^{-u^2/2t} \frac{1}{\sqrt{2\pi s}} e^{-v^2/2s} \, dv \, du.$$

Figure 5.2 provides one possible realization of the standard Brownian motion B_t over the next 40 years. To create a sample path, remember that $B_0 = 0$, $B_1 = N(0,1) \cdot \sqrt{\Delta t}$, and $B_{t_i} = B_{t_{i-1}} + N(0,1) \cdot \sqrt{\Delta_i t}$, where $\Delta_i t$ (the change in time) is expressed as a fraction of a year.

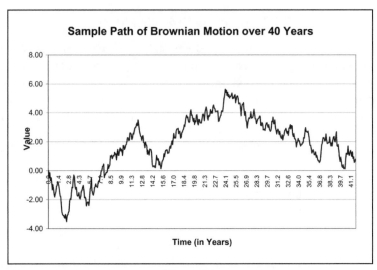

Figure 5.2

Though all the plotted paths start at a value of zero, some wander up while others wander down. The expected value $E[B_t \mid B_0 = 0] = 0$ and the standard deviation $SD[B_t \mid B_0 = 0] = \sqrt{\Delta t}$. Figure 5.2 might give the impression of describing a market that moved upward for 25 years and then declined for the next 15, but in fact these numbers are completely random. There was no trend, no momentum, and no direction. Figure 5.2 is just one of infinitely many paths possible. Each data point should be interpreted as the total return earned after t years. Figure 5.3 shows another one of many possible paths. In this case the standard Brownian motion spent most of its time in negative territory and recovered only at the very end.

The standard Brownian motion process B_t can be used to construct the more complex $B_t^{(v,\sigma)}$, which is a nonstandard Brownian motion with varying values of v and σ, via the linear relationship defined by

$$B_t^{(v,\sigma)} = \sigma B_t + vt. \tag{5.7}$$

At first it might seem odd, but think about this for a while. You start with a regular Brownian motion B_t, which will move up and down randomly, and you multiply by a constant σ. If this constant $\sigma < 1$ then it will shrink the path (value), and if this constant $\sigma > 1$ then it will increase the path (value). But the expected value of this "mapped" process σB_t is still zero; it is only stretching and compressing, not shifting the actual path. That is

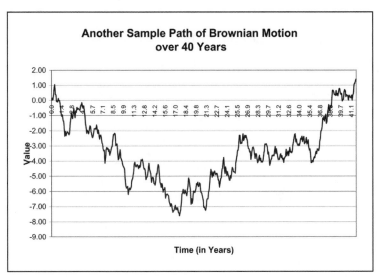

Figure 5.3

where v times t comes in. It takes the mapped process and adds a drift term to the σB_t.

Finally, whereas standard and nonstandard Brownian motion may govern the growth of the investment, the price of the asset is governed by *geometric Brownian motion* (GBM), the workhorse of financial economic theory. We'll see why it's worthy of this title when we can eventually write down its stochastic differential equation. For now, remember that GBM has the form

$$S_t = S_0 e^{vt + \sigma B_t},$$

where B_t is a standard Brownian motion, S_0 the initial value (i.e., the value of S_t when $t = 0$), $\sigma > 0$ the volatility, and v the expected growth rate. Note that S_t is *lognormally* distributed: that is, $\ln S_t = \ln S_0 + vt + \sigma B_t$ is *normally* distributed. Figure 5.4 demonstrates how the path can vary depending on whether you are working with the standard B_t, nonstandard B_t, or geometric B_t.

Here is yet another eclectic way to think about the behavior and path of Brownian motion over time. Assume that time is measured in units of years and that you are now standing in the middle of your living room or back yard with a measuring stick in your hand. Now, imagine that every $\Delta t = \frac{1}{525600}$ year units—which is exactly one minute—you toss a fair coin. If it comes up heads, you move $\sqrt{\Delta t} = 1/\sqrt{525600} \approx 1/725$ kilometer to the

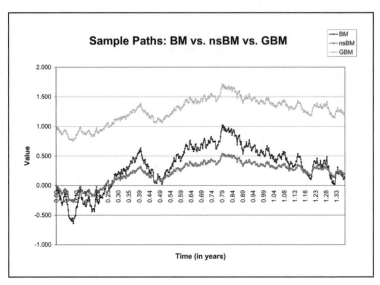

Figure 5.4

north of your current position; if it falls on tails, you move $1/725$ kilometer to the south. In this thought experiment, every minute you move slightly more than a meter, to either the north or the south. Consider your movement over time, which I will index and label using the (new) symbol Z_i, where $Z_0 = 0$. Here is one possible sequence (or realization) of the stochastic process Z:

$$Z_0 = 0, \quad Z_{\Delta t} = \sqrt{\Delta t}, \quad Z_{2\Delta t} = 0,$$

$$Z_{3\Delta t} = -\sqrt{\Delta t}, \quad Z_{4\Delta t} = -2\sqrt{\Delta t}, \quad Z_{5\Delta t} = -\sqrt{\Delta t}.$$

In this particular experiment, you got heads, tails, tails, tails, and then a final heads to end up in a position of $-\sqrt{\Delta t}$ after five coin tosses.

Where will you be after N coin tosses? Well, the expected value in any given toss can be formally computed as $\frac{1}{2}\left(+\frac{1}{725}\right) + \frac{1}{2}\left(-\frac{1}{725}\right) = 0$, and thus in N tosses you can expect to be in the exact same position as you started. What about the variance or standard deviation of this estimate? Here is where it gets interesting, since formally the variance per toss will be $\frac{1}{2}\left(+\frac{1}{725}\right)^2 + \frac{1}{2}\left(-\frac{1}{725}\right)^2 = \frac{1}{525600}$. By construction, the variance (of the estimate) of where you will be after one time step is exactly the time increment Δt. The variance after N tosses will be $N\Delta t$. And finally, the variance after one year—which is $N = 525600$ coin tosses—will be exactly 1 kilometer.

After two years, which is 2×525600 coin tosses, the variance will be two kilometers. You expect to stay exactly where you are on average, but the uncertainty (as measured by the variance) increases by one kilometer per year. Does this look familiar? We have just constructed a crude approximation of a Brownian motion. Sure, a mathematician would still have to prove that the distribution of the uncertainty is indeed normal (i.e. Gaussian) or close to normal, but the central limit theorem (CLT) assures us that this will be the case.

More generally, if our coin toss moves us by $1/\sqrt{N}$ units every $\Delta t = 1/N$ years and if we let $N \rightarrow \infty$ (which implies that $\Delta t \rightarrow 0$), then we have constructed a Brownian motion. This is why it is often common to see the statement that

$$\Delta B \approx \pm \sqrt{\Delta t}, \tag{5.8}$$

where ΔB denotes the change in the value of a Brownian motion during a time increment Δt. The (wild) oscillations of the Brownian motion almost cancel each other out—which is why you can expect to go nowhere with time—but the uncertainty adds up and you can expect to wander quite far.

Here is another way to think about the relationship in (5.8). If you divide both sides by $\sqrt{\Delta t}$ (which is not exactly kosher when $\Delta t \rightarrow 0$, but bear with me anyway) then you can think of the ratio $\Delta B / \Delta t$ as a rate of change or instantaneous derivative. But the right-hand side is random, since it can be either positive or negative depending on the outcome of the coin toss. Thus, one consequence that arises is the *nondifferentiability* of the Brownian motion. Stated more formally:

$$\frac{dB_t}{dt} \approx \frac{\Delta B}{\Delta t} \approx \frac{\pm 1}{\sqrt{\Delta t}} \rightarrow \pm \infty \text{ as } \Delta t \rightarrow 0. \tag{5.9}$$

In contrast to a deterministic function of time, the derivative of the Brownian motion simply does not exist. It's not large or infinite, it is just not defined. Intuitively, the Brownian motion is moving too much over a short period of time for there to be a smooth rate of change. It is positive and negative infinity at the same time.

Going back to our thought experiment and the Δt coin toss, another important characteristic of the Brownian motion is its *infinite variation*. Imagine that, instead of moving up (north) or down (south) depending on the outcome of the coin toss, you always moved north. In other words, you always took the absolute value of the outcome $\left| \pm \sqrt{\Delta t} \right| = \Delta t$. In this case, you would quickly (and obviously) find yourself moving north. The sum of the Brownian motion increments will continue to grow as the time intervals become smaller, which mathematically can be stated as:

$$\sum |\Delta B| \approx N\sqrt{\Delta t}, \quad \text{where} \quad N \cdot \Delta t = 1$$

$$= \frac{1}{\sqrt{\Delta t}} \rightarrow \infty \quad \text{as} \quad \Delta t \rightarrow 0. \tag{5.10}$$

This may at first seem like an esoteric mathematical property. But in fact, when you compare this situation to a smooth function, you will see the impact of uncertainty. Generally, when you add up the absolute value of the increments of a smooth function—no matter how small the increments—the summation adds up to a finite quantity. Think about breaking up the function $f(x) = x^2$ into small pieces based on Δx. If you add the $|f(x_i) - f(x_{i-1})|$ values together for $x = 1, \ldots, N$, the summation will converge. Not so when the function oscillates wildly the way Brownian motion does.

Finally, there is an important limiting property of Brownian motion B_t that has some investment implications and is therefore worth discussing. What happens when time gets very large and $t \rightarrow \infty$? How will the B_t behave? We have already discussed its mean and variance, but how fast will it move toward a (possible) large value? The answer is as follows:

$$\lim_{t \to \infty} \frac{B_t}{t} \rightarrow 0. \tag{5.11}$$

The limiting value of the ratio of the standard Brownian motion to time is zero. In other words, time itself "moves faster" than a Brownian motion. In investment terms, think of the left-hand side of (5.11) as the annualized growth rate of an investment $\tilde{g}$, but where the expected value of the growth rate is zero. *As time increases, the realized growth rate converges to the expected growth rate, which is zero.*

Along the same lines, recall the definition and discussion of the nonstandard Brownian motion $B_t^{(\nu,\sigma)}$, which was constructed from the standard Brownian motion B_t scaled by σ before adding νt. We have:

$$\lim_{t \to \infty} \tilde{g} = \frac{B_t^{(\nu,\sigma)}}{t} = \nu + \sigma \frac{B_t}{t} \rightarrow \nu. \tag{5.12}$$

The intuition is the same. In this case, the realized growth rate converges to ν, which is the expected growth rate. Stated differently, the probability approaches 100% that the annualized return from investing in an asset whose value follows a geometric Brownian motion will be very close to the geometric mean.

5.5 Index Averages and Index Medians

At this point you should have a decent idea of how the fundamental object B_t behaves over time. In this section we delve into the behavior of e^{B_t}, which represents the evolution of the index (or portfolio) value itself. Remember the various stages in our definition:

$$S_t = S_0 e^{\tilde{g}t} := S_0 e^{B_t^{(v,\sigma)}} = S_0 e^{vt+\sigma B_t}. \tag{5.13}$$

The last two equalities come from the construction of the Brownian motion. When $\sigma = 0$, the index or portfolio will grow at a fixed rate of v with zero uncertainty or randomness.

I am now interested in some of the probabilistic properties of S_t. The median value of the index at time t is the simple and intuitive

$$M[S_t] = S_0 M[e^{vt+\sigma B_t}] = S_0 e^{vt}.$$

Thus, 50% of the time S_t will be above $S_0 e^{vt}$ and 50% of the time S_t will be below $S_0 e^{vt}$. As time $t \to \infty$, the median value of the index or portfolio grows without bound provided that $v > 0$. If $v = 0$ then the median value of $S_t = S_0$ for all values of t, since there is no growth.

You can verify that the median value for S_t is indeed $S_0 e^{vt}$ by going through the following steps. First, given that S_t is lognormally distributed, note that the general probability

$$\Pr[S_t \leq u] = \Pr[\ln[S_0] + vt + \sigma B_t \leq \ln[u]]$$

$$= \Pr\left[\frac{B_t}{\sqrt{t}} \leq \frac{\ln[u/S_0] - vt}{\sigma\sqrt{t}}\right]. \tag{5.14}$$

By construction and definition of the standard Brownian motion, the term $B_t/\sqrt{t}$ is normally distributed with an expected value of 0 and a standard deviation of 1. This leads to

$$\Pr[S_t \leq u] = \int_{-\infty}^{(\ln[u/S_0]-vt)/\sigma\sqrt{t}} \frac{\exp\{-\frac{1}{2}z^2\}}{\sqrt{2\pi}} \, dz, \tag{5.15}$$

where the integrand should be recognized as the basic Gaussian (or normal) probability density function. Thus, if we make the substitution $u = S_0 e^{vt}$ then the upper bound of integration collapses to zero, which by symmetry of the normal distribution around zero leads to an integral value of $\Pr[S_t < S_0 e^{vt}] = 1/2$ and hence this value of u is the median value.

In contrast, to obtain the expected value $E[S_t]$ I will rely on the following general statement about how to compute expectations of functions. In equation (5.16), $\mathcal{F}_t$ represents the information or knowledge that you have available at time t. The idea is that if the present state is known then the rest of the past is irrelevant:

$$E[h(S_{t+s}) \mid \mathcal{F}_t] = E[h(S_{t+s}) \mid S_t]. \qquad (5.16)$$

For example,

$$\begin{aligned} E[h(B_{t+s}) \mid \mathcal{F}_t] &= E[h(B_t + \Delta B) \mid \mathcal{F}_t] \\ &= \int_{-\infty}^{\infty} h(B_t + z) \frac{1}{\sqrt{2\pi s}} e^{-z^2/2s} \, dz. \end{aligned}$$

In the case of $S_t = S_0 e^{\nu t + \sigma B_t}$ we have

$$\begin{aligned} E[h(S_{t+s}) \mid \mathcal{F}_t] &= E[h(S_0 e^{\nu(t+s)+\sigma B_{t+s}}) \mid \mathcal{F}_t] \\ &= E[h(S_0 e^{\nu t + \sigma B_t} e^{\nu s + \sigma \Delta B}) \mid \mathcal{F}_t] \\ &= \int_{-\infty}^{\infty} h(S_t e^{\nu s + \sigma z}) \frac{1}{\sqrt{2\pi s}} e^{-z^2/2s} \, dz. \end{aligned}$$

The expected value $E[S_t]$ must be computed by integrating:

$$\begin{aligned} E[S_t] &= \int_{-\infty}^{+\infty} S_0 (e^{\nu t + \sigma \sqrt{t} z}) \frac{\exp\{-\frac{1}{2} z^2\}}{\sqrt{2\pi}} \, dz \\ &= S_0 \exp\{(\nu + \tfrac{1}{2}\sigma^2) t\}. \qquad (5.17) \end{aligned}$$

The first portion of the integrand contains the exponentiation, which is then multiplied by the normal density. At this point you might wonder why and how the exponent has suddenly "grown" a factor of $\frac{1}{2}\sigma^2$ within the νt. This is a legitimate question that is tied to the difference between the geometric mean and the arithmetic mean: the $\nu + \frac{1}{2}\sigma^2$ denotes the arithmetic mean whereas the ν denotes the geometric mean. The difference between the two is equal to half of volatility squared.

5.6 The Probability of Regret

We can now derive an easy-to-use expression for the probability that an index or portfolio satisfying the exponential Brownian motion model will earn less than a risk-free interest rate r. I have labeled this the "probability

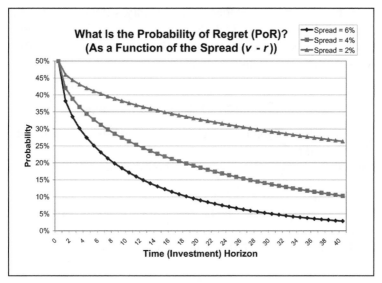

Figure 5.5

of regret" because an investor will regret not having invested in the safe
asset when the earned growth rate $\tilde{g}$ is less than the risk-free rate r.

Based on the same logic used earlier to compute median and mean values, we have

$$\Pr[S_t \le S_0 e^{rt}] = \Pr\left[\frac{B_t}{\sqrt{t}} \le -\left(\frac{v-r}{\sigma}\right)\sqrt{t}\right]$$

$$= \varphi\left(-\left(\frac{v-r}{\sigma}\right)\sqrt{t}\right), \qquad (5.18)$$

where $\varphi(z)$ denotes the CDF of the standard normal distribution. The probability of regret (PoR) can be obtained by integrating the area under the
standard normal curve from $-\infty$ to $\frac{r-v}{\sigma}\sqrt{t}$. Note that when $r < v$, which
would be expected in practice, the probability would be less than 50%.
When $r = v$ the probability is exactly 50%, and when $r > v$ the probability
is greater than 50%. Observe that, as $t \to \infty$, the probability goes either
to 0 (if the risk-free rate is less than the expected growth rate) or to 1 (if the
risk-free rate is greater than the expected growth rate). The standard deviation parameter σ, sometimes known as volatility, has the opposite effect as
it approaches infinity.

Figure 5.5 plots the probability of regret as a function of time t for different values of the risk premium $(v - r)$. For example, if $t = 10$ years,

$\nu - r = 6\%$, and $\sigma = 20\%$, then the probability that the (risky) index S_{10} is worth less than $S_0 e^{r10}$ is 17.1%. Note that this probability value does not depend on the exact value of either ν or r itself but rather on the difference between the two, or the *spread*.

5.7 Focusing on the Rate of Change

We are now in a position to investigate the rate of change of the index or portfolio over time.

Recall that a first-order ordinary differential equation (ODE) has the form

$$\begin{cases} \frac{dz}{dt} = f(t, z), \\ z(0) = z_0. \end{cases}$$

For instance, in the case of exponential growth or decay, the ODE allows us to arrive at Z_t from Z_0:

$$\frac{dz}{dt} = kz \text{ has the solution } z(t) = z_0 e^{kt}.$$

In contrast, in order to obtain stochastic differential equations we must take an ODE and then add random noise. But because $dB_t/dt = \pm\infty$, as we saw in (5.9), the expression

$$\frac{dS_t}{dt} = \mu(t, S_t) + \sigma(t, S_t)\frac{dB_t}{dt}$$

makes no sense as written. Note that we are using μ and σ as functions, not as constants.

Mathematicians developed the notion of a stochastic integral and later used it to show convergence of solutions to the difference equation

$$\Delta S_t = \mu(t, S_t)\Delta t + \sigma(t, S_t)\Delta B_t. \tag{5.19}$$

In the limit, equation (5.19) gives meaning to the *stochastic differential equation* (SDE):

$$dS_t = \mu(t, S_t)dt + \sigma(t, S_t)dB_t,$$

or

$$\frac{dS_t}{S_t} = \mu dt + \sigma dB_t. \tag{5.20}$$

The solution is a *diffusion* process. It should be thought of as a standard Brownian motion but with position-dependent drift and volatility:

$$\frac{\Delta S_i}{S_i} = \left(\nu + \frac{1}{2}\sigma^2\right)\Delta t + \sigma\Delta B_i. \qquad (5.21)$$

The expression $\left(\nu + \frac{1}{2}\sigma^2\right)$ is central to a number of formulas in finance, which is why it is common to see this expression defined as follows:

$$\mu = \nu + \frac{1}{2}\sigma^2 \iff \nu = \mu - \frac{1}{2}\sigma^2. \qquad (5.22)$$

The parameter μ is often called the (continuously compounded) arithmetic mean and ν the (CC) geometric mean. Recall once again that the arithmetic mean is larger than the geometric mean by a factor of $\frac{1}{2}\sigma^2$. I will move between the two notations, using μ and ν depending on need and context.

5.8 How to Simulate a Diffusion Process

In theory, there are two possible ways to simulate a collection of sample paths or a diffusion process. The first method is to solve the stochastic differential equation and then represent the process in closed form as an explicit function of pure B_t values. Thus, for example, if you can generate sample paths for B_t—by generating random numbers that are normally distributed—then you can also generate sample paths of B_t^2, e^{B_t}, $2B_t$, or any other explicit function of B_t. However, in most cases the diffusion process cannot be explicitly solved and written as a function of B_t. As a result, we must usually create sample paths by generating small changes for the value of the process. Here is how this is done.

Consider the general diffusion process satisfying the stochastic differential equation

$$dS_t = \mu(t, S_t)dt + \sigma(t, S_t)dB_t$$

on the interval $0 \le t \le T$. We can discretize time so that

$$0 = t(0) < t(1) < t(2) < t(3) < \cdots < t(N) = T.$$

An *Euler approximation* is a stochastic process, denoted by Y_t, that satisfies the iterative system

$$Y_{j+1} = Y_j + \mu(t(j), Y_j)(t(j+1) - t(j)) + \sigma(t(j), Y_j)(B_{t(j+1)} - B_{t(j)})$$

for $j = 0, \ldots, N - 1$ with initial value $Y_0 = X_0$. Furthermore, if we let $t(j) = j\tau$ where $\tau = T/N$, then

$$E[B_{t(j+1)} - B_{t(j)}] = 0$$

Table 5.6. *SDE simulation of GBM using the Euler method*

Period $j+1$	Time	$N(0,1)$	ΔB_t	$\sigma \times Y_j \times \Delta B_t$	$\mu \times Y_j \times \Delta t$	Y_{j+1}
1	0.004	−0.3002	−0.0190	−0.3798	0.0400	99.6602
2	0.008	−1.2777	−0.0808	−1.6107	0.0399	98.0894
3	0.012	0.2443	0.0154	0.3031	0.0392	98.4317
4	0.016	1.2765	0.0807	1.5893	0.0394	100.0604
5	0.020	1.1984	0.0758	1.5167	0.0400	101.6172
6	0.024	1.7331	0.1096	2.2277	0.0406	103.8855
7	0.028	−2.1836	−0.1381	−2.8694	0.0416	101.0577
8	0.032	−0.2342	−0.0148	−0.2994	0.0404	100.7988

Note: $Y_0 = \$100$, $\mu = 10\%$, $\sigma = 20\%$, $\Delta t = 0.004$ years.

and

$$E[(B_{t(j+1)} - B_{t(j)})^2] = \tau;$$

we can simulate the underlying diffusion using standard techniques.

Table 5.6 presents an example of the diffusion process simulation using the Euler approximation. The table shows simulated end-of-period asset values for eight periods.

5.9 Asset Allocation and Portfolio Construction

In this section I will provide some guidance on how to analyze a portfolio of securities or asset classes whose individual dynamics obey the models described so far. Our objectives are to examine the combined time dynamics of portfolio diversification and to investigate the impact of holding more investments versus holding them for longer periods of time.

I start with a collection of n securities and let S_t^i denote the price of the ith security at time t. The evolution of each individual S_t^i is modeled by the stochastic differential equation from Section 5.7, which can be rewritten as

$$dS_t^i = \mu_i S_t^i dt + \sigma_i S_t^i dB_t^i, \tag{5.23}$$

where B_t^i is now a vector of standard Brownian motions and where, without loss of generality, I scale $S_0^i = 1$ for all securities $i \leq n$. The parameters $\{\mu_i, \sigma_i\}$ denote the instantaneous drift rate (mean) and diffusion coefficient (volatility) of the ith security. The correlation coefficient is then denoted by $d\langle B^i, B^j \rangle = \rho_{ij} dt$, with the understanding that $\rho_{ij} = \rho_{ji}$ and $\rho_{ii} = \rho_{jj} = 1$ for all $i, j \leq n$.

We may use (5.22) to rewrite equation (5.23) as

$$S_t^i = \exp\left\{\left(\mu_i - \tfrac{1}{2}\sigma_i^2\right)t + \sigma_i B_t^i\right\} = \exp\{(v_i)t + \sigma_i B_t^i\}, \tag{5.24}$$

with expectation $E[S_t^i \mid S_0^i = 1] = e^{\mu_i t}$ and standard deviation SD$[S_t^i \mid S_0^i = 1] = \exp\{\mu_i t\}\sqrt{\exp\{\sigma_i^2 t\} - 1}$. Once again, the log-price is normally distributed with mean $E[\ln[S_t^i]] \mid S_0^i = 1] = \left(\mu_i - \tfrac{1}{2}\sigma_i^2\right)t$ and standard deviation SD$[\ln[S_t^i]] \mid S_0^i = 1] = \sigma_i\sqrt{t}$.

An investor can construct a diversified portfolio by partitioning an initial wealth of $W_0 = w$ amongst the n available securities in proportions α_i. Furthermore, I assume that the investor continuously rebalances the portfolio in order to maintain a dollar value of $\alpha_i W_t$ in the ith security at all times.

By simple construction, the portfolio process W_t will obey a stochastic differential equation denoted by

$$dW_t = \sum_{i=1}^{n} \alpha_i W_t \left(\frac{dS_t^i}{S_t^i}\right)$$
$$= \sum_{i=1}^{n} \alpha_i \mu_i W_t\, dt + \sum_{i=1}^{n} \alpha_i \sigma_i W_t\, dB_t^i. \tag{5.25}$$

Under this representation, the aggregate portfolio process W_t is driven by n correlated standard Brownian motion factors B_t^i, where $i = 1,\ldots,n$. However, equation (5.25) can be simplified by combining the n distinct factors into one independent source of risk.

Toward this end, we can define a new portfolio drift coefficient as

$$\mu_p(n) = \sum_{i=1}^{n} \alpha_i \mu_i. \tag{5.26}$$

Also, we can simplify the Brownian components in (5.25) by defining an aggregate portfolio standard deviation of volatility via

$$\sum_{i=1}^{n} \alpha_i \sigma_i\, dB_t^i = \left[\sqrt{\sum_{i=1}^{n}\sum_{j=1}^{n} \alpha_i \sigma_i \rho_{ij} \sigma_j \alpha_j}\,\right] dB_t$$

$$= \left[\sqrt{\sum_{k=1}^{n} \alpha_k^2 \sigma_k^2 + \sum_{i=1}^{n}\sum_{\substack{j=1 \\ i \neq j}}^{n} \alpha_i \sigma_i \rho_{ij} \sigma_j \alpha_j}\,\right] dB_t$$

$$= \sigma_p(n)\, dB_t. \tag{5.27}$$

The new combined (source-of-risk) term dB_t is a standard one-dimensional Brownian motion. The new $\sigma_p(n)$ is the portfolio volatility, which is an explicit function of the size (space dimension) n of the portfolio as well as an implicit function of the volatility and correlation structure and the individual security weights.

The resulting SDE obeyed by the (total wealth) portfolio can be represented by

$$dW_t = \mu_p(n)W_t dt + \sigma_p(n)W_t dB_t, \quad W_0 = 1. \tag{5.28}$$

Akin to the case for individual securities, the explicit solution to the stochastic differential equation (5.28) is

$$W_t = \exp\{(\mu_p(n) - \tfrac{1}{2}\sigma_p^2(n))t + \sigma_p(n)B_t\}, \tag{5.29}$$

where we now use the definition

$$v_p(n) := \mu_p(n) - \tfrac{1}{2}\sigma_p^2(n). \tag{5.30}$$

What does all this "buy" me?—I now have the expected growth rate needed to compute the relevant probabilities.

5.10 Space–Time Diversification

We can now put two ideas together. If a portfolio consisting of n securities is held for a period of t years, then the probability of regret is defined as

$$\text{PoR}(n,t) := \Pr[W_t \le e^{rt}] = \Pr[\ln[W_t] \le rt], \tag{5.31}$$

which is the probability of doing *worse* than the interest rate r. By the definition of W_t from (5.29), we arrive at

$$\text{PoR}(n,t) = \Pr\left[\frac{B_t}{\sqrt{t}} \le -\left(\frac{v_p(n)-r}{\sigma_p(n)}\right)\sqrt{t}\right]$$

$$= \varphi\left(-\left(\frac{v_p(n)-r}{\sigma_p(n)}\right)\sqrt{t}\right), \tag{5.32}$$

which is identical in form to (5.18) in Section 5.6.

To obtain more precise results we now assume that $\alpha_i = 1/n$, which means that the initial wealth $W_0 = w$ is portioned and invested equally amongst the n securities and is maintained in those proportions during the entire time $[0,t]$. Furthermore, assume that all securities in the portfolio have the same drift rate μ, the same volatility σ, and a uniform correlation structure denoted by ρ. In other words, the covariance matrix Σ for the n securities can be represented as

$$\Sigma := \begin{pmatrix} \sigma^2 & & & \cdots & \rho\sigma^2 \\ & \sigma^2 & & \cdots & \rho\sigma^2 \\ & & \sigma^2 & \cdots & \rho\sigma^2 \\ \cdots & \cdots & \cdots & \ddots & \vdots \\ \rho\sigma^2 & \rho\sigma^2 & \rho\sigma^2 & \cdots & \sigma^2 \end{pmatrix}. \tag{5.33}$$

This structure may seem odd at first. However, my objective is to examine the effect on $\text{PoR}(n, t)$ of adding more securities (space) and holding them for longer periods (time). In any event, by (5.27) the portfolio variance, which we denote explicitly by $\sigma_p^2(n \mid \sigma, \rho)$, collapses to

$$\sigma_p^2(n \mid \sigma, \rho) = \sum_{k=1}^{n} \left(\frac{1}{n}\right)^2 \sigma^2 + \sum_{i=1}^{n} \sum_{\substack{j=1 \\ i \neq j}}^{n} \left(\frac{1}{n}\right)^2 \rho\sigma^2$$

$$= n\frac{\sigma^2}{n^2} + (n^2 - n)\rho\frac{\sigma^2}{n^2}$$

$$= \frac{\sigma^2}{n} + \left(1 - \frac{1}{n}\right)\rho\sigma^2 = \sigma^2\left(\frac{1}{n}(1 - \rho) + \rho\right). \tag{5.34}$$

Hence the portfolio volatility, which is the diffusion coefficient of the wealth process W_t, is

$$\sigma_p(n \mid \sigma, \rho) = \sigma\sqrt{\rho + \frac{1 - \rho}{n}}. \tag{5.35}$$

As one expects intuitively, the derivative of the portfolio volatility $\sigma_p(n \mid \sigma, \rho)$, with respect to the space variable n, is:

$$\frac{\partial \sigma_p(n \mid \sigma, \rho)}{\partial n} = \frac{\sigma(\rho - 1)}{2n^2\sqrt{\rho + (1 - \rho)/n}}$$

$$= \frac{\sigma^2(\rho - 1)}{2n^2\sigma_p(n \mid \sigma, \rho)} < 0 \quad \forall \rho < 1, \tag{5.36}$$

which implies the obvious conclusion that a portfolio with a greater number of securities reduces volatility.

Along the same lines, we have that

$$\frac{\partial \sigma_p(n \mid \sigma, \rho)}{\partial \rho} = \frac{\sigma(n-1)}{2n\sqrt{\rho + (1-\rho)/n}}$$

$$= \frac{\sigma^2(n-1)}{2n\sigma_p(n \mid \sigma, \rho)} > 0 \quad \forall n > 1, \qquad (5.37)$$

which implies that, ceteris paribus, a larger correlation coefficient leads to a larger portfolio volatility and a corresponding increase in the shortfall PoR(n,t). Finally, it should be obvious from equation (5.35) that the derivative of $\sigma_p(n \mid \sigma, \rho)$ with respect to σ is positive.

As a result of the square root in equation (5.35), we are forced to accept that

$$\rho + \frac{1-\rho}{n} \geq 0 \implies \rho \geq \frac{1}{1-n}. \qquad (5.38)$$

A relatively large collection of securities can have a constant correlation structure between them as long as $\rho \geq 1/(1-n)$. Thus, for example, if $n = 2$ (a portfolio of two securities) then the correlation coefficient must be at least $\rho \geq -1$ and thus any structure is acceptable. If $n = 3$ then $\rho \geq -0.5$, and if $n = 10$ then $\rho \geq -0.111$. In the limit, when $n \to \infty$, we obtain that $\rho \geq 0$ as the lower bound for the correlation structure, which is our sufficient condition.

In the same vein, when $n \to \infty$ we have that $\sigma_p(n \mid \sigma, \rho) \to \sigma\sqrt{\rho}$; this implies that the portfolio volatility converges to a constant value, which will be zero only when $\rho = 0$. The limiting value of $\sigma_p(\infty \mid \sigma, \rho)$ is the so-called market volatility. Stated in terms of modern portfolio theory, when $\rho > 0$ we have a nondiversifiable market factor. And, after a certain point, additional *space* diversification provides no further value in reducing portfolio volatility or, by extension, equity shortfall risk. Thus, when $n \to \infty$, the portfolio volatility will approach the market volatility, which in our context will be $\sigma\sqrt{\rho}$. This fact is consistent with standard textbook illustrations of the portfolio variance approaching—and converging to—the market variance as the number of securities increases.

Finally, the probability of regret, per equation (5.31), will be

$$\text{PoR}(n,t \mid r, \mu, \sigma, \rho) = \varphi\left(\frac{r - \mu + \frac{1}{2}\sigma^2(\rho + (1-\rho)/n)}{\sigma\sqrt{\rho + (1-\rho)/n}}\sqrt{t}\right), \qquad (5.39)$$

where the explicit variables r, μ, σ, ρ are introduced to denote the homogenous case of constant parameters and equal portfolio weights.

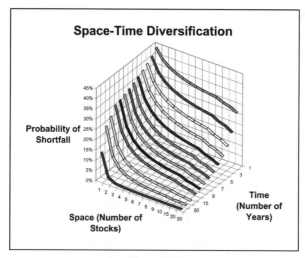

Figure 5.6

Observe that if $\rho = 0$ then the denominator on the right-hand side of (5.39) will go to zero as $n \to \infty$. Thus, in the presence of completely independent securities, the volatility and the equity shortfall risk can be driven to zero with a large enough portfolio provided that $r < \mu$. Of course, in practice the financial risk can never be entirely "squeezed" out of the system, and there is always a chance of falling short of the risk-free rate. This is analogous to (identifying a market factor and) stating that $\rho > 0$. Furthermore, the PoR will decrease as the term of the portfolio increases if the drift effect offsets the volatility (which increases with time)—that is, if $r - \mu > \frac{1}{2}\sigma^2(\rho + (1 - \rho)/n)$.

Figure 5.6 shows the impact of space and time by displaying the PoR curve assuming an expected growth rate of $v = 10\%$, volatility of $\sigma = 25\%$, a risk-free (personal benchmark) rate of $r = 6\%$, and a correlation coefficient of $\rho = 15\%$ between individual returns.

Clearly, the longer the individual holds the portfolio (assuming $r - \mu > \frac{1}{2}\sigma^2(\rho + (1 - \rho)/n)$) and the greater the number of securities in the portfolio, the lower is the probability of regret. In sum, I hope to have illustrated how the tools of continuous-time finance can be used to compute the relevant probabilities.

5.11 Further Reading

As in previous chapters, I have only scratched the surface of models for financial markets and risky investments. Of course, all these models began with Markowitz (1959), which is the first and most important reference for this chapter. For the mathematically inclined reader I would recommend Baxter and Rennie (1998) for a deeper analysis of these models with applications to derivative security pricing. On the empirical side—for those who want to learn much more about how to calibrate and estimate parameters for the various models—I recommend the book by Campbell, Lo, and MacKinlay (1997). For a more recent analysis of the difference between geometric and arithmetic means with regard to their proper estimation and use in financial economics, see Jacquier, Kane, and Marcus (2003).

Bodie (1995) has an interesting and controversial critique of the notion that "time" reduces investment risk. Boyle (1976) was one of the first to model investment returns as random variables within the context of pensions and insurance. Browne (1999) further develops the concept of shortfall risk and probability of loss. Campbell and colleagues (Campbell et al. 2001; Campbell and Viciera 2002) provide a number of models for asset allocation within the context of individual investors and the human life cycle. Levy and Duchin (2004) conduct an extensive investigation of historical equity and bond returns, comparing the suitability of various statistical models. Leibowitz and Kogelman (1991) pursue the idea of shortfall risk within a portfolio context, and Rubinstein (1991) derives the portfolio dynamics under lognormal security returns.

The final part of this chapter—which introduces the concept of space–time diversification—draws heavily from Milevsky (2002), where a large number of additional examples are provided in addition to a more in-depth analysis of the effect that the individual variables have on the shortfall probability. Finally, thanks to Ibbotson Associates (2005) for compiling and providing the historical return data.

5.12 Notation

$\tilde{g}$—annualized growth rate random variable with expected value ν

$B_t^{(\nu, \sigma)}$—a stochastic process with an expected value of νt and a standard deviation of $\sigma\sqrt{t}$, used in this book to model the fluctuation of risky investments

5.13 Problems

PROBLEM 5.1. Assume that the annualized growth rate $\tilde{g}$ of your investments satisfies a normal distribution (as discussed in this chapter) with an expected value of $\nu = 7\%$ and a standard deviation of $\sigma = 20\%$. What is the probability that you will triple your money after 5 years of investing? After 10 years?

PROBLEM 5.2. Build a simple computer simulation in Excel that will generate five different sample paths for a standard Brownian motion B_t over a 20-year period. Use a time increment of $\Delta t = \frac{1}{52}$ years (i.e., each simulated change is one week) and plot these sample paths against each other. Assume that $\nu = 10\%$ and $\sigma = 20\%$, and use these five paths to manufacture sample paths for $B_t^{(\nu,\sigma)}$. Then use these values to generate five sample paths for $\tilde{g}$ (which is defined, you will recall, by $B_t^{(\nu,\sigma)}/t$).

PROBLEM 5.3. Use $\nu_i = \{10\%, 15\%, 12\%\}$ and $\sigma_i = \{15\%, 35\%, 20\%\}$ to construct the portfolio $\nu_p(3)$ with volatility $\sigma_p(3)$ when the correlation between all securities is $\rho = +20\%$. What is the probability of regret from holding this portfolio after 20 years? (Assume that $r = 5\%$ is the threshold for regret.)

SIX

Models of Pension Life Annuities

6.1 Motivation and Agenda

An insurance company or pension fund promises to pay you $1 for the rest of your life, no matter how long you live. Or they promise to pay you and your spouse $1 for as long as *at least one* of you is still alive.

How can they promise something like that? How much is this promise worth today? How much was this worth yesterday, and how much will it be worth tomorrow? These are the topics of this chapter, which brings together all the ideas that were introduced and motivated in previous chapters. We are finally ready to discuss pensions.

6.2 Market Prices of Pension Annuities

Table 6.1 displays the actual prices (quotes) of pension or life annuities for individuals at various ages. These quotes are based on a $100,000 *premium* or deposit that is paid at the time of purchase with funds from a tax-sheltered savings plan. I have displayed the payouts based on the average of the "best" U.S. companies quoting in early January 2005.

The $100,000 premium entitles annuitants to receive monthly income for the rest of their lives. In some cases, they are entitled to the guarantee that if they die "early" then their spouse or family receives some payments. For example, a 65-year-old male will receive $655 per month for the rest of his life if he selects a pension annuity with *no* guarantee (or "certain") period; should the annuitant die one year (or even one month) after buying the annuity, his heirs receive nothing. On the other hand, if this 65-year-old male uses his $100,000 premium to purchase a life annuity with a 10-year certain period then the monthly payments will be only $630 (instead of $655) per month. This is because the contract stipulates that, if the annuitant dies

Table 6.1. *Monthly income from $100,000 premium single-life pension annuity*

Period certain	Age 50		Age 65		Age 70		Age 80	
	M	F	M	F	M	F	M	F
0-year	$514	$492	$655	$605	$747	$677	$1073	$961
10-year	$509	$490	$630	$592	$694	$649	$841	$812
20-year	$498	$484	$569	$555	$591	$583	$585	$585

Notes: M = male, F = female. Income starts one month after purchase.
Source: CANNEX, January 2005.

within 10 years, the beneficiary will receive $630 until a total of 10 years (or 120 months) of payments have been made. So, for example, if the annuitant dies after 4 years (48 months) of payments—that is, at the start of age 69—then the beneficiary will be paid an additional 6 years (72 months) of $630 dollars. Stated differently, in the worst-case scenario, the annuitant together with the beneficiary are assured they will get at least $630 × 120 = $75,600 back from the insurance company in exchange for the $100,000 annuity premium. This is why the monthly payment is lower than the zero-year certain payment of $655.

A number of additional qualitative insights are worth noting. Obviously there is an age effect. The older the annuitant at the time of purchase, the larger are the monthly payments. This, of course, is because the expected (or median) remaining lifetime is lower and hence the $100,000 must be returned over a shorter period of time.

Also, at any given starting age, females always receive less per month (for the same $100,000 premium) than males. This is because females live longer on average and hence the company will be making more payments. Note that the gender gap is $514 − $492 = $22 at age 50, when the guaranteed period is zero, but a much larger $1,073 − $961 = $112 at age 80. Furthermore, this gender premium increases as a percentage of the male's monthly income from $22/$514 = 4.2% at age 50 to $112/$1,073 = 10.4% at age 80. At age 60, the gender premium is 7.6% and at age 70 it is 9.4%. Finally, the gender effect is slightly reduced as the certain period is increased, since a portion of the payment is no longer life contingent and hence is independent of whether the annuitant is a male or a female. For example, note that an 80-year-old male and female each get only $585 per month if they both want a 20-year period certain. The odds of either of them living to 100 is quite slim, so one can think of this particular pension annuity as

Table 6.2. *A quick comparison with the bond market*

Coupon yield	Approximate maturity (years)	Price of bond ($)	Yield to maturity (%)
$3\frac{1}{8}$	2	99.78	3.24
$3\frac{5}{8}$	5	99.72	3.68
$4\frac{1}{4}$	10	100.88	4.14
$7\frac{1}{2}$	20	136.69	4.64
$5\frac{3}{8}$	30	111.56	4.61

Source: Wall Street Journal, January 2005.

Table 6.3. *Monthly income from $100,000 premium joint life pension annuity*

Period certain	Age of male and female			
	50	65	70	80
0-year	$465	$545	$597	$791
10-year	$465	$544	$594	$753
20-year	$465	$533	$565	$601

Note: Income starts immediately after purchase.
Source: CANNEX, January 2005.

a generic bond with a minuscule amount of longevity insurance. For the interested reader, Table 6.2 compares the actual yields of bonds with maturities comparable to the periods guaranteed by annuities.

There are many possible variations on the pension annuity theme. One popular one is for the annuitant to specify that, upon death, a surviving spouse will continue to receive income for as long as the spouse lives. This is known as a joint life or a *joint and survivor* (J&S) annuity. In this case the underlying random lifetime variable consists of the maximum of the two lives. This type of guarantee is different from a period certain because it is contingent on the life of the surviving spouse and not on some fixed horizon, such as 10 or 20 years.

Table 6.3 shows the payouts of various J&S annuities. For instance: if two 65-year-olds (here, one male and one female) purchase a $100,000 joint life pension annuity without a guaranteed period then the monthly income will be $545, which is lower than either the $655 or the $605 that a male

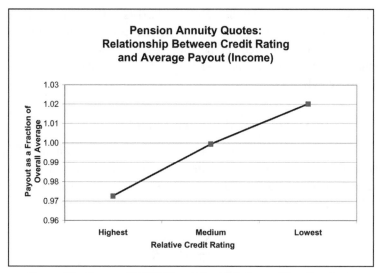

Figure 6.1. *Source:* CANNEX and The IFID Centre (Canadian data).

or a female could have obtained individually (cf. Table 6.1). The reason for this should be clear. In the single-life case, all payments cease once the annuitant dies. But with the joint life pension annuity, both annuitants must die before payments cease and so, to compensate, the monthly payments must be lower.

Some companies allow you to purchase the right to a stream of income that is adjusted for inflation using the Consumer Price Index (CPI) as a basis. In this case, each year your payments would be either linked to the index, which tracks inflation, or increased by a fixed cost-of-living adjustment (COLA) rate. To compensate the company for offering this inflation protection, the initial monthly payment would be lower than it would be had you not selected this feature. True inflation-linked annuities are quite rare, and few consumers purchase them.

Note also that not all insurance companies quote the same rates. Some companies are notoriously stingy and promise 5%–10% less in annual income as compared to the competition. Other firms are quite generous and pay 5%–10% more than the average company. Why the variation? One hypothesis concerns the company's credit rating, and Figure 6.1 provides evidence. The figure illustrates the relationship between credit (agency) rating and the average payouts offered on annuities in Canada. Notice that companies with lower credit ratings tend to have higher (average) annuity payouts and vice versa.

Although it is not clear if the same effect exists in U.S. or other markets, strong anecdotal evidence suggests that consumers are willing to trade off and thus receive less retirement income in exchange for a stronger guarantee that the income will actually be provided (i.e., that the company stands little risk of default).

6.3 Valuation of Pension Annuities: General

Let's say that the insurance company commits to pay the annuitant $1 per year for the rest of the annuitant's life. Assuming an effective valuation rate of R per annum, the *stochastic present value of a pension annuity* (SPV-PA), which I will denote as a_x, is

$$a_x = \sum_{i=1}^{D} \frac{1}{(1+R)^i}, \tag{6.1}$$

where D is the random (integer) number of years until death. The integral version of this expression for payments that are made in continuous time is

$$a_x = \int_0^{T_x} e^{-rt}\, dt = \int_0^{\infty} e^{-rt} 1_{\{T_x \geq t\}}\, dt, \tag{6.2}$$

where T_x is the remaining lifetime random variable defined in Chapter 3 and the "indicator function" $1_{\{T_x \geq t\}}$ takes on the value of 1 when $T_x \geq t$ and 0 when $T_x < t$. I stress that a_x is a random variable.

Now imagine that an insurance company sells hundreds and thousands of these pension annuity contracts to different people—all of whom are age x, for example. Some of these people will live a very long time, and so the insurance company will have to pay out quite a lot over the course of their lives. Other customers will not live as long and the payments will be much less. On average, though, the insurance company will be paying out an amount that can be computed by taking expectations of equation (6.1). In fact, the more policies they sell, the smaller the variance around this number.

The expected value of this random variable is often called the *immediate pension annuity factor* (IPAF):

$$\bar{a}_x = E\left[\int_0^{T_x} e^{-rt}\, dt \right] = \int_0^{\infty} e^{-rt} (_t p_x)\, dt$$

$$= \int_0^{\infty} \exp\left\{ -\left(rt + \int_0^t \lambda(x+s)\, ds \right) \right\} dt, \tag{6.3}$$

where the word "immediate" comes from the fact that payments start immediately upon paying the premium $\bar{a}_x$ (pronounced "ey bar ex"). Note that the annuity factor $\bar{a}_x$ can also be thought of as a variation of the exchange rate between savings and consumption, introduced in Chapter 2. However, now the "savings" are made in one lump sum and "consumption" occurs until a random time T_x. Later I will introduce a deferred PAF, whose payments don't begin until after some years have elapsed.

The expectation in (6.3) can be converted to a survival probability curve since $E[1_{\{T_x \geq t\}}] = (_t p_x)$. The second equality comes from the definition of the survival probability, which was also introduced in Chapter 3.

6.4 Valuation of Pension Annuities: Exponential

If T_x is exponentially distributed, which (as you may recall from Chapter 3) implies that $(_t p_x) = e^{-\lambda t}$, then the annuity factor from equation (6.3) collapses to

$$\bar{a}_x = \int_0^\infty e^{-(r+\lambda)t} \, dt = \frac{1}{r + \lambda}. \tag{6.4}$$

For example, when $r = 5\%$ and $\lambda = 5\%$, the annuity factor is $1/(0.05 + 0.05) = \$10.0$ per dollar of lifetime income. If $r = 4\%$ and $\lambda = 6\%$ then the annuity factor is (still) $10, and the same is true if $\lambda = 4\%$ and $r = 6\%$. Observe how only the sum of r and λ matters and not the individual components. The interest rate r and the instantaneous force of mortality (IFM) λ have the exact same effect on the annuity factor: they both discount the future to the present, but one adjusts for the value of money while the other adjusts for the value of mortality. Even though (6.4) holds only under exponential mortality, the tight connection between r and the general $\lambda(x)$ curve will appear again many times.

6.5 The Wrong Way to Value Pension Annuities

A common mistake is to value pension annuities by arguing that income will be received "on average" throughout the expected remaining lifetime (ERL), which in our notation is $E[T_x]$. This incorrect approach then "adds up" the discounted value of income for the ERL and uses this as the annuity factor. To understand why this is wrong (or, at best, a biased approximation), think of the remaining lifetime random variable under an exponential distribution. In this case, the discounted value of income until the end of the ERL is

$$\int_0^{1/\lambda} e^{-rt}\, dt = \frac{e^{-r/\lambda}}{-r} + \frac{1}{r} = \frac{1}{r}(1 - e^{-r/\lambda}). \tag{6.5}$$

Approximating the exponential term by $e^{-r/\lambda} \approx 1 - r/\lambda$ leaves us with an approximate integral value of $1/\lambda$, which is larger than the correct annuity factor of $1/(r + \lambda)$.

For example: if $r = 5\%$ and $\lambda = 4\%$, which leads to an expected remaining lifetime of 25 years, then by (6.4) the correct annuity factor is $1/0.09 = \$11.111$ per dollar of lifetime income. However, under the incorrect formula (6.5), the annuity factor would be $\$14.27$, which is higher by more than $3 per dollar of lifetime income. Stated differently, a fixed premium of \$100,000 converted into a pension annuity should provide, under exponential mortality, an annual income of $\$100,000/11.11 = \$9,000$, not $\$100,000/14.27 \approx \$7,000$. Using the erroneous method will lead to less annual income. In fact, this error will persist regardless of the particular law of mortality that is used for valuation purposes.

Another common misconception is to multiply the correct \$9,000 annual income by the life expectancy of 25 years and thus claim that the annuitant "gets back" $\$9,000 \times 25 = \$225,000$ on average, which is more than double the original premium. This is misleading because the time value of money has been ignored, and it also clearly illustrates the importance of using the entire survival curve $(_tp_x)$ as opposed to just the expected remaining lifetime $E[T_x]$.

On a slightly more technical level, we conclude our discussion here by stating that

$$\int_0^{E[T_x]} e^{-rt}\, dt > E\left[\int_0^{T_x} e^{-rt}\, dt\right], \tag{6.6}$$

which is a general way of arguing that the incorrect annuity factor on the left-hand side is always greater than the correct annuity factor on the right-hand side. This fact is also a corollary of Jensen's inequality in the mathematical literature.

6.6 Valuation of Pension Annuities: Gompertz–Makeham

Recall from Section 3.9 that, under the Gompertz–Makeham (GoMa) law of mortality, the IFM obeys the relationship

$$\lambda(x) = \lambda + \frac{1}{b} \exp\left\{\frac{x - m}{b}\right\}. \tag{6.7}$$

The survival probability was shown to be

$$({}_t p_x) = \exp\{-\lambda t + b(\lambda(x) - \lambda)(1 - e^{t/b})\}. \tag{6.8}$$

Consequently, by (6.3) the annuity factor under GoMa can be expressed as

$$\bar{a}_x = e^{b(\lambda(x) - \lambda)} \int_0^\infty e^{-(\lambda + r)t - b(\lambda(x) - \lambda)e^{t/b}} \, dt. \tag{6.9}$$

We now substitute using the change of variable $s = e^{t/b}$ and $ds = dt e^{t/b}/b$, so that $ds/s = dt/b$ and $s^b = e^t$, which leaves us with

$$\bar{a}_x = b e^{b(\lambda(x) - \lambda)} \int_1^\infty s^{-(\lambda + r)b - 1} e^{-b(\lambda(x) - \lambda)s} \, ds. \tag{6.10}$$

Finally, we use a second change of variable and let $w = b(\lambda(x) - \lambda)s$, so that $dw = b(\lambda(x) - \lambda)ds$; therefore,

$$\bar{a}_x = \frac{b(b\lambda(x) - \lambda)^{(\lambda + r)b + 1}}{b(\lambda(x) - \lambda)} e^{b(\lambda(x) - \lambda)} \int_{b(\lambda_x - \lambda)}^\infty w^{-(\lambda + r)b - 1} e^{-w} \, dw$$

$$= b(b\lambda(x) - b\lambda)^{(\lambda + r)b} e^{b(\lambda(x) - \lambda)} \Gamma(-(\lambda + r)b, b(\lambda(x) - \lambda)). \tag{6.11}$$

Recall from Chapter 3 that $\Gamma(\cdot, \cdot)$ denotes the incomplete Gamma (IG) function, defined as

$$\Gamma(a, c) = \int_c^\infty e^{-t} t^{(a-1)} \, dt.$$

This finally leads to the main expression:

$$\bar{a}_x = \frac{b\Gamma\left(-(\lambda + r)b, \exp\left\{\frac{x - m}{b}\right\}\right)}{\exp\left\{(m - x)(\lambda + r) - \exp\left\{\frac{x - m}{b}\right\}\right\}}. \tag{6.12}$$

The last part of our story is recognizing that $(b\lambda(x) - b\lambda)^{(\lambda + r)b}$ can be simplified to $e^{(x - m)(\lambda + r)}$ by using the original definition of the IFM $\lambda(x)$ in equation (6.7).

These derivations may seem overwhelming at first, so here are some numerical examples to help develop an intuition for the formulas. Assume in these examples that $\lambda = 0, m = 86.34$, and $b = 9.5$ for the GoMa law (these were the best-fitting parameters to the unisex RP2000 mortality table analyzed in Chapter 3). Under a valuation rate of $r = 4\%$, the *annuity factor* for ages $x = 65, 75$, and 85 are $\bar{a}_{65} = 12.454$, $\bar{a}_{75} = 8.718$, and $\bar{a}_{85} = 5.234$.

Table 6.4. *IPAF $\bar{a}_x$: Price of lifetime*
$1 annual income

Starting at age x of	Interest rate r		
	4%	6%	8%
55	$15.822	$12.700	$10.480
65	$12.454	$10.474	$8.963
75	$8.718	$7.696	$6.857
85	$5.234	$4.832	$4.480

Note: GoMa mortality with $m = 86.34$ and $b = 9.5$.

The intuition should be clear. The older the annuitant at the point of "annuitization," the lower is the value of each dollar of lifetime income. These numbers can obviously be scaled up. A pension annuity that pays $650 per month—which is $7,800 per year—has a value of $(12.454)(7800) = \$97,141$ at age 65. This number is not far from the $100,000 premium of Table 6.1 that entitled a 65-year-old male annuitant to $655 for life. The reason the two premiums are not exactly equal is likely due to different interest rates, mortality estimates, and commissions embedded within the quoted annuity price. We will return to this issue later.

If we increase the GoMa parameter from $\lambda = 0$ to $\lambda = 0.01$ while maintaining the same values as before of m, b, and r, then the annuity factors are reduced to $\bar{a}_{65} = 11.394$, $\bar{a}_{75} = 8.181$, and $\bar{a}_{85} = 5.026$. The actuarial reason for this is that a positive λ parameter increases the instantaneous force of mortality and thus projects shorter life spans. This means the insurance company pays less, which reduces the annuity factor at all annuitization ages.

Table 6.4 provides a bird's-eye view. As the table shows, the same qualitative results follow when we increase the interest rate r from 4% to 6% while maintaining $\lambda = 0$, $m = 86.34$, and $b = 9.5$. In this case we have $\bar{a}_{65} = 10.474$, $\bar{a}_{75} = 7.696$, and $\bar{a}_{85} = 4.832$. This is identical to the impact of higher interest rates on the value of a (mortality-free) fixed-income bond.

Finally, if instead of using a GoMa value of $m = 86.34$ we increase the modal value to $m = 90$ while retaining the dispersion parameter $b = 9.5$, then the annuity factors increase to $\bar{a}_{65} = 13.753$, $\bar{a}_{75} = 10.094$, and $\bar{a}_{85} = 6.434$. The higher values are obviously due to the longer life span. Under these parameters, the value of a pension annuity that pays $650 per month is $(13.753)(7800) = \$107,273$ at age 65, which is higher than the $100,000 premium of Table 6.1.

With these numerical examples out of the way, let us push the algebra one step further. If we substitute $\lambda = 0$, the annuity factor in equation (6.12) can be simplified to

$$\bar{a}_x = \frac{b\Gamma(-rb, b\lambda(x))}{e^{(m-x)r - b\lambda(x)}}.$$

This is the pure Gompertz (no Makeham) case. In fact, if we let $r = 0$ as well, then the equation for the annuity factor collapses to an even simpler

$$\bar{a}_x = E[T_x] = \frac{b\Gamma(0, b\lambda(x))}{e^{b\lambda(x)}},$$

which oddly enough is the expected remaining lifetime under the Gompertz law of mortality. Why is this so? Well, examining (6.3) reveals the seeds of this identity. Indeed, go ahead and plug in a value of $r = 0$ in equation (6.3); you will obtain the definition of the ERL, which is $E[T_x]$.

For example, under the same $m = 86.34$ and $b = 9.5$, computing the annuity factor under a 0% interest rate yields $\bar{a}_{45} = 36.445$ years at age 45, $\bar{a}_{55} = 27.189$ at age 55, and $\bar{a}_{65} = 18.714$ at age 65. In sum, then, implicit in the annuity factor $\bar{a}_x$ is an interest rate r as well as the GoMa parameters λ, m, b.

6.7 How Is the Annuity's Income Taxed?

When you purchase a life annuity and then receive periodic income from the policy, there are certain tax consequences that you must be aware of. First, it is important to distinguish between annuities that are purchased as part of a pension plan—for example, within tax-sheltered savings accounts—and annuities that are purchased outside of a pension plan. The general rule is that, if the funds used to purchase the annuity have not yet been taxed, then all income from the annuity is taxed as ordinary interest (i.e., salary) income. On the other hand, if the annuity was purchased with after-tax funds, then the periodic income you receive will be a blended mix of interest and returned principal. A portion of this income will be taxable and a portion will be tax free. It is therefore common to hear the term *exclusion ratio* (or *excluded amount*) to denote the fraction of income that is not included in taxable income and the term *inclusion ratio* (or *taxable amount*) to denote the balance. Here is a numerical example.

You have $100,000 inside a personal pension plan—such as an IRA or 401(k) account in the United States—and have decided to use these funds to purchase a life annuity, which pays $100000/\bar{a}_{65} = \$8,000$ per year for life. Since you have used tax-sheltered funds to purchase the life annuity, the entire $8,000 per year is considered to be ordinary interest income and is added to your other income when determining the amount of income taxes you must pay. If you are in the (highest) 50% marginal tax bracket, then you will be left with $4,000 after tax.

If the same $100,000 were placed outside of a tax shelter (or nonqualified pension plan), then a portion of the annual $8,000 income would be excluded from income taxes and the remainder would be taxable as ordinary interest income.

The mathematics is as follows. The taxable fraction, once the life annuity is purchased at age x, is defined by

$$\rho_x = 1 - \frac{\bar{a}_x}{E[T_x^{\text{tax}}]}, \tag{6.13}$$

where $E[T_x^{\text{tax}}]$ denotes the expected remaining years of payments (i.e. lifetime) as specified by mortality tables used by the tax authorities, which are not necessarily the same tables used by the insurance company to price the pension annuity factor $\bar{a}_x$. To make this absolutely clear, $E[T_x^{\text{tax}}]$ and $E[T_x]$ can differ. In fact, under most tax jurisdictions the value of $E[T_x^{\text{tax}}]$ is less than $E[T_x]$, which means that the tax code assumes people will be living (and receiving payments) for less time than they actually do. This difference in mortality assumptions results in fewer taxes being paid than if a higher $E[T_x^{\text{tax}}]$ had been assumed.

Note that, once determined at the time of purchase, the taxable portion ρ_x will remain the same until time $E[T_x^{\text{tax}}]$. After that, some tax jurisdictions (such as the United States) will force the entire payment to be taxable. In other jurisdictions (such as Canada), the payments will still be partially tax free and ρ_x will determine the fraction that is taxable.

Here is the intuition for equation (6.13). First of all, by definition of the life annuity factor, it should be that $\bar{a}_x < E[T_x^{\text{tax}}]$. If this inequality is satisfied, then the positive ratio $\bar{a}_x/E[T_x^{\text{tax}}] < 1$ and therefore $\rho_x < 1$. In fact, the smaller is the value of $\bar{a}_x$, the greater is the taxable portion, ceteris paribus. If you are paying less for the same $1 of lifetime income, then the same dollar should be taxed more heavily. In the limit, if you paid absolutely nothing for the life annuity and so $\bar{a}_x$ was very close to 0 (because interest rates were very high), then the taxable portion ρ_x would be close to 1 and almost the entire $1 of periodic income would be taxable.

Table 6.5 provides some numerical examples of the impact of tax authorities using a different (old) mortality table for determining the taxable portion as well as the relative impact of age on the taxable portion. Observe that here the outdated mortality assumptions are reflected in a lower Gompertz parameter m^{tax}.

Table 6.5. *Taxable portion of income flow from \$1-for-life annuity purchased with non–tax-sheltered funds*

Purchase age (x)	$E[T_x]$ (years)	Cost $\bar{a}_x$	$E[T_x^{\text{tax}}]$ (years)	Taxable portion ρ_x
60	22.82	\$11.671	17.66	33.9%
65	18.71	\$10.474	13.98	25.1%
70	14.93	\$9.133	10.72	14.8%
75	11.55	\$7.696	7.93	2.95%

Notes: GoMa mortality with $m^{\text{tax}} = 80$, $m = 86.34$, $b = 9.5$, and $r = 6\%$. Taxable portion $\rho_x = 1 - \bar{a}_x/E[T_x^{\text{tax}}]$.

For example, if you purchase a life annuity (with regular, nonqualified funds) at age 60, then Table 6.5 shows that 33.9% of the income you receive would be taxable while the remaining 66.1% would be considered a return of principal and hence tax free. This 33.9% would be taxable for the next 17.66 years—that is, until you've reached (approximately) age 78. At this point, 100% of the payment would be considered taxable under the U.S. tax code, which assumes that your entire principal has been received and so what you are now getting is pure interest. However, each country has its own rules for annuity income taxation. In Canada, for instance, taxing only the 33.9% would continue until death. I will return to this topic in the next chapter, where I explain the tax arbitrage opportunity that arises as a result of annuity taxation methods.

6.8 Deferred Annuities: Variation on a Theme

Imagine a situation in which you purchase a pension annuity at age x, but the contract stipulates that it does not start providing income until age $x + u >$ x. Furthermore, if you don't actually survive to age $x + u$, you receive nothing. Clearly, the value of this deferred annuity factor should be much less than $\bar{a}_x$, since the annuity is not paying you any income during the next u years. Likewise, the value should also be less than $\bar{a}_{x+u}$, since (i) there is a chance you will not survive to age $x + u$ and (ii) the insurance company has access to your premium during this time. In fact, when you combine these two elements, you are left with a *deferred pension annuity factor* (DPAF):

$$_u\bar{a}_x := \bar{a}_{x+u}(_up_x)e^{-ru}. \tag{6.14}$$

I will omit the u subscript whenever $u = 0$ and the annuity factor is of the immediate type, so $_0\bar{a}_x := \bar{a}_x$.

Let's go over each piece of equation (6.14) separately. The first part of the right-hand side is the immediate pension annuity factor at the income-starting age of $x + u$. This, of course, must be discounted for the time value of money e^{-ru} and for mortality $(_u p_x)$, which corresponds to the probability that the x-year-old will actually survive u years to receive income. Think back to the fundamentals of insurance. If a fraction of the group will not live to age $x + u$, then the insurance "collective" can charge less than $\bar{a}_{x+u}$ by a factor of $(_u p_x)$.

Some might benefit from an alternative view in which DPAF is defined via

$$_u\bar{a}_x = \int_u^\infty \exp\left\{-\left(rt + \int_0^t \lambda(x + s)\, ds\right)\right\} dt, \qquad (6.15)$$

which differs from the IPAF definition in equation (6.3) by virtue of the u (instead of 0) in the lower bound of integration. Indeed, the payments start at time u, or age $x + u$, so the "summation" of benefits must start at u as well.

Under the GoMa law of mortality, the equation for the DPAF presented in (6.15) can again be solved in terms of the incomplete Gamma function, leading to

$$_u\bar{a}_x = \frac{b\Gamma\left(-(\lambda + r)b, \exp\left\{\frac{x - m + u}{b}\right\}\right)}{\exp\left\{(m - x)(\lambda + r) - \exp\left\{\frac{x - m}{b}\right\}\right\}}. \qquad (6.16)$$

Here is a detailed numerical example. Assume the same GoMa parameters of $\lambda = 0$, $m = 86.34$, and $b = 9.5$ as well as the valuation rate of $r = 4\%$. The expected remaining lifetime for an $x = 45$-year-old is $E[T_{45}] = 36.46$ years, which also means that the expected age at death is 81.46 years. The probability that an $x = 45$-year-old survives 20 more years to age $x = 65$ is $(_{20}p_{45}) = 0.911$ or a 91.1% chance. The TVM factor for 20 years under $r = 4\%$ is $e^{-0.04(20)} = 0.449$, which is slightly less than fifty cents on the dollar. The immediate PAF at age $x = 65$ is $\bar{a}_{65} = 12.454$ per dollar of lifetime income. Finally, multiply these three numbers together to arrive at an age-45 "value" of $_{20}\bar{a}_{45} \approx (0.911)(0.449)(12.454) \approx \$5.10$ per dollar of lifetime income, starting at age 65.

Thus, a 45-year-old who wants a pension that commences in 20 years—and is willing to forfeit all claims to the pension if they die prior to age 65—will have to pay approximately 5.1 times the desired annual income under a 4% valuation rate. Stated differently, if interest rates in the market were precisely 4% and if these deferred pension annuities were fairly priced, then a 45-year-old could purchase a retirement pension for this price. The younger the age at which the deferred pension annuity is purchased or the

Table 6.6. *DPAF* $_u\bar{a}_{45}$*: Price of lifetime*
$1 annual income for 45-year-old

Income	Interest rate r		
starting at …	4%	6%	8%
Age 55, $u = 10$	$10.354	$6.804	$4.597
Age 65, $u = 20$	$5.099	$2.875	$1.649
Age 75, $u = 30$	$1.964	$0.951	$0.465
Age 85, $u = 40$	$0.449	$0.186	$0.077

Note: GoMa mortality with $m = 86.34$ and $b = 9.5$.

older the age at which the pension annuity commences payment, the lower
is the DPAF.

Table 6.6 provides additional examples. Contrast and compare the numbers in this table to those in Table 6.4. At any given starting age, the value
of the pension annuity is much lower in the deferred case than in the immediate case.

One last point worth noting in both equations (6.16) and (6.12) is that the
terms λ and r always appear together as a sum. They are never separate in
the annuity factors. In other words, *they are interchangeable.* We can value
the DPAF or IPAF with a valuation rate of $r = 0$ and a $\lambda = 5\%$ or we can
value these factors using $r = 5\%$ and $\lambda = 0\%$, but in both cases we will
obtain the same result. In some sense this is why I have not bothered to
include $\lambda \neq 0$ examples in the numerical section, since it is always possible to increase the valuation rate r by the required amount. Of course, this
is exactly what we found in the case of an exponential model for remaining lifetime, where the IPAF was the inverse of the sum of $\lambda + r$. We shall
return to this idea later in the analysis.

6.9 Period Certain versus Term Certain

Recall from Chapter 4 on modeling fixed-income bonds that the value of
a bond paying a coupon of $c \times$ [bond face value] dollars per annum until
maturity could be valued by using the equation

$$V(c, r, T) = \frac{c}{r}(1 - e^{-rT}) + e^{-rT} \qquad (6.17)$$

per dollar of face value. Now we compare the fixed-income bond to a
period-certain annuity, which promises to provide income only for a predetermined period of time and ends thereafter. When we value these latter

Table 6.7. *Value $V(r, T)$ of term certain annuity factor vs. immediate pension annuity factor*

Length T of term	Interest rate r		
	4%	6%	8%
10 years	$8.242	$7.520	$6.883
20 years	$13.767	$11.647	$9.976
30 years	$17.470	$13.912	$11.366
IPAF $\bar{a}_{65}$	$12.454	$10.474	$8.963

products we need not adjust for mortality in any way and, in fact, can use a variation of the generic bond valuation equation (6.17). We thus define the *term certain annuity factor* (TCAF),

$$V(r, T) := V(1, r, T) - e^{-rT},$$

which in essence is the value of a coupon bond paying one dollar per year between time 0 and T but paying no face value at the end (hence the subtraction of e^{-rT} from the bond's value).

Table 6.7 provides examples of how the TCAF varies with the length of the term T and the valuation rate, regardless of the starting age. Contrast these term certain annuity factors to the immediate pension annuity factors in the bottom row. A 65-year-old who wanted to purchase a life annuity that makes annual $1 payments for the rest of his life would have to pay $10.47, assuming a valuation rate of 6%. However, if he wanted guaranteed payments of $1 made to himself or his beneficiary for a period of only 10 years then he would pay $7.52 under the same valuation rate (or $11.65 for 20 years of annual $1 payments).

Putting two concepts together, the value of an immediate pension annuity that guarantees payments for u years and makes life-contingent payments for all years beyond age $x + u$ is defined as

$$V(r, u) + (_u\bar{a}_x).$$

Another type of pension annuity is one in which the payments continue for as long as the annuitant is still alive but cease at some fixed date (after τ years). So, for example, you might purchase a pension annuity at age 50 that pays $1 per year as long as you are still alive but not past age 89. This is not exactly an annuity that pays for life. But neither is it a term certain annuity, since you must survive in order to receive payments. The notation we will use for this pension annuity factor is $\bar{a}_{x:\tau}$, which is formally defined as follows:

$$\bar{a}_{x:\tau} = \int_0^\tau \exp\left\{-\left(rt + \int_0^t \lambda(x+s)\,ds\right)\right\}dt. \qquad (6.18)$$

Note the similarity to equation (6.3), which defined the IPAF; now, however, the upper bound of integration stops at τ. Also, compare and contrast
(6.18) with the DPAF $_u\bar{a}_x$ of equation (6.15), where the upper bound went
to infinity but the lower bound was u. In that case the annuity starts at time
u, but in this case it ends at time τ. Effectively, the temporary annuity factor
$\bar{a}_{x:\tau}$ is simply the difference between the IPAF and the DPAF at age x.

6.10 Valuation of Joint and Survivor Pension Annuities

Up until now our discussion has centered on $\bar{a}_x$, the value or cost of a pension that is issued to a single life at age x. When this person dies, payments
cease. In practice, however, it is quite common for pension annuities to be
issued to couples or "joint lives" under which payments continue for as long
as at least one member of the couple survives. Thus, for example, a male
retiree who is 65—and whose female spouse is 59 years of age—might be
entitled to a pension that pays $30,000 per year to the couple for as long as
either one of them is still alive. In this section I will address how to value
and price these kinds of joint life pension annuities.

Now it would obviously be a mistake for the insurance company or pension fund to value this annuity assuming that the younger annuitant will
outlive the older annuitant, so all that matters from an actuarial standpoint
is the younger life. After all, there is a chance that a 65-year-old male will
outlive a 59-year-old female. The correct way to value the joint life annuity, which pays $1 for as long as one member of the couple is still alive, is as
follows. As before, let x denote the age of annuitant 1 and y the age of annuitant 2, and let $(_tp_x)$ and $(_tp_y)$ denote their respective survival probabilities.
Recall from Chapter 3 that if we use the basic rules of probability—and assume both deaths are independent of each other—then the probability that
the insurance company or pension fund is still making payments of $1 in t
years (i.e., that at least one of the couple is still alive) will be

$$\begin{aligned}(_tp_{x,y}) &= 1 - (1 - (_tp_x))(1 - (_tp_y))\\ &= 1 - (1 - (_tp_y) - (_tp_x) + (_tp_x)(_tp_y))\\ &= (_tp_x) + (_tp_y) - (_tp_x)(_tp_y).\end{aligned} \qquad (6.19)$$

In sum, you add the individual survival probabilities and then subtract
the product of those same numbers. For instance: if $(_{20}p_{59}) = 0.8$ and
$(_{20}p_{65}) = 0.7$, then the probability that at least one of them is still alive and

receiving payments in 20 years is $(0.8) + (0.7) - (0.8)(0.7) = 0.94$, which is obviously much higher than either's individual odds of surviving for 20 years.

What this means is that we have a shortcut for valuing and pricing joint life pension annuities—provided that the pension annuity continues paying exactly the same amount as long as at least one annuitant is still alive. This is known as a 100% joint and survivor pension annuity. Our x, y subscript notation will be used to define the generic pension annuity factor as

$$\bar{a}_{x,y} := \int_0^\infty e^{-rs}(_sp_{x,y})\, ds$$
$$= \int_0^\infty e^{-rs}(_sp_x)\, ds + \int_0^\infty e^{-rs}(_sp_y)\, ds$$
$$- \int_0^\infty e^{-rs}(_sp_x)(_sp_y)\, ds, \qquad (6.20)$$

which follows directly from the decomposition in (6.19). The joint life annuity factor issued to a couple (x, y) is equal to the sum of the two individual annuity factors at age x and age y, minus a *hypothetical* annuity factor issued to a life whose survival probability equals the product of their two independent survival curves. This last component of equation (6.20) might seem awkward and cumbersome to work with, but in some cases it boils down to an equally simple expression.

For example, assume for both lives an exponential remaining lifetime under which $(_tp_x) = e^{-t\lambda_x}$ and $(_tp_y) = e^{-t\lambda_y}$, where λ_x and λ_y denote the constant IFM for annuitant x and for annuitant y, respectively. In this case, the product $(_tp_x)(_tp_y) = e^{-t(\lambda_x + \lambda_y)}$ and hence—by the properties of the annuity factor under exponential mortality and by the derivation in (6.20)—we arrive at

$$\bar{a}_{x,y} = \frac{1}{\lambda_x + r} + \frac{1}{\lambda_y + r} - \frac{1}{\lambda_x + \lambda_y + r}. \qquad (6.21)$$

This is the sum of the two annuity factors minus a hypothetical annuity factor, where the instantaneous force of mortality is the sum of the two independent forces of mortality. For example, under an $r = 5\%$ valuation rate, if the younger (female) $\lambda_x = 1/30$ and the older (male) $\lambda_y = 1/20$, then $1/(1/30 + 0.05) = 12.0$ for the age-x factor and $1/(1/20 + 0.05) = 10.0$ for the age-y factor and $1/(1/20 + 1/30 + 0.05) = 7.5$ for the combined factor. Thus $\bar{a}_{x,y} = 12 + 10 - 7.5 = 14.5$, a value that is obviously higher than either of the individual $\bar{a}_x$ or $\bar{a}_y$ factors, so the guaranteed monthly payments are lower than they would be in the case of a single life. This is the observation we made in Table 6.3. As you can see, dealing with 100% J&S pension annuities under exponential mortality is quite simple.

Yet even under a GoMa law of mortality, where the survival probability takes on the more complicated form

$$({}_tp_x) = \exp\{-\lambda t + (e^{(x-m)/b})(1 - e^{t/b})\}, \tag{6.22}$$

we can still obtain relatively easy formulas. Recall, for example, that assuming $\lambda = 0$, $m = 80$, and $b = 10$ implies that there is a $({}_{20}p_{65}) = 24\%$ chance that a 65-year-old (male) will survive for 20 more years. In contrast, when $m = 90$ and $b = 10$, there is a $({}_{20}p_{59}) = 75\%$ chance that a 59-year-old (female) will survive for 20 more years. Obviously, the female has a much better chance than the male of being alive in 20 years to receive the pension income. In this case, the relevant "both survive" probability will be:

$$({}_tp_{x,y}) = \exp\{-(\lambda_1 + \lambda_2)t + (e^{(x-m_1)/b_1})(1 - e^{t/b_1})$$
$$+ (e^{(y-m_2)/b_1})(1 - e^{t/b_2})\}, \tag{6.23}$$

where λ_1, m_1, b_1 are the GoMa parameters for the first life and λ_2, m_2, b_2 are those for the second life. Equation (6.23) is just the product of equation (6.22) under the relevant parameters. This latter expression is then placed into equation (6.20) in the last integral. The calculus needed to integrate the expression might be messy, but it is doable.

In fact, a closely related case is the situation in which the pension annuity is issued to a couple but now the income ceases as soon as *either* of the annuitants dies. This is the opposite of the 100% J&S case and of course would result in a much lower annuity factor. In this case, the relevant probability that the insurance company will still be making payments in t years is the probability that both are still alive, which is exactly the $({}_tp_y)({}_tp_x)$ we used in equations (6.20) and (6.23). Thus, under exponential mortality, for an x-year-old and a y-year-old to purchase a 0% J&S pension annuity, which pays nothing after the first death, the cost is $7.50 per dollar of lifetime income when $\lambda_x = 1/30$, $\lambda_y = 1/20$, and $r = 5\%$.

Finally, in between these two extremes (of income termination vs. 100% continuation after the first death) is the case in which an income *reduction* occurs upon the first death. For example, a 75% J&S pension annuity would pay $1 until the first death and then $0.75 upon the death of annuitant 1 until annuitant 2 dies. This is quite common for pensions, where the income is reduced by K (which may equal 25%, 40%, or even 50%) upon the first death. In this case, the $K\%$ J&S annuity factor must be calculated explicitly as follows:

$\bar{a}_{x,y}$

$$= \int_0^\infty e^{-rs}[(_sp_x)(_sp_y) + (_sp_x)(1 - (_sp_y))K + (1 - (_sp_x))(_sp_y)K]\,ds$$

$$= \int_0^\infty e^{-rs}(_sp_x)\,ds + \int_0^\infty e^{-rs}(_sp_y)\,ds$$

$$+ (1 - 2K)\int_0^\infty e^{-rs}(_sp_x)(_sp_y)\,ds. \tag{6.24}$$

Notice the similarity between this equation and (6.20); they differ only in the third and final integral. The intuition for the bracketed expression in (6.24) is as follows. The first product term $(_sp_x)(_sp_y)$ denotes the full \$1 payment that is made to the couple as long as they are both alive. The second term $(_sp_x)(1 - (_sp_y))K$ denotes the partial \$K payment that is made if the younger (female) annuitant of age x at issue survives but the older (male) annuitant of age y at issue does not survive. Finally, the third term $(1 - (_sp_x))(_sp_y)K$ denotes the partial \$K payment that is made if the older (male) annuitant survives the younger (female) annuitant.

To further convince yourself that equation (6.24) is correct, assume that $K = 100\%$; then we are back to the original 100% J&S case presented in equation (6.20). In this case, the relevant bracketed portion of the integrand in equation (6.24) collapses to $(_sp_x)(_sp_y) + (_sp_x) + (_sp_y) - 2(_sp_x)(_sp_y)$, which is precisely $(_sp_x) + (_sp_y) - (_sp_x)(_sp_y)$ and the relevant integrand for (6.20). This should be even more obvious from the second line of the same equation.

Finally, equation (6.24) is general enough to cover the situation in which the continuation payment made to the survivor upon the first death depends on who dies first. For example, if the male dies earlier then the payment might be reduced to $K_f\%$, but if the female dies earlier then the payment might be reduced to $K_m\%$. Then, instead of K we would use K_f and K_m (as appropriate) in equation (6.24).

6.11 Duration of a Pension Annuity

Akin to the concept of duration (and convexity) in the case of generic fixed-income bonds is the same idea defined within the context of annuity factors. The duration D of the annuity factor is the (negative) derivative with respect to the valuation rate r, scaled by the annuity factor $\bar{a}_x$ itself. The formal and explicit definition of the annuity factor duration is

Table 6.8 *Duration value D (in years) of immediate pension annuity factor*

Starting at age x of	Interest rate r		
	4%	6%	8%
55	11.76	10.26	8.99
65	9.13	8.21	7.39
75	6.49	5.99	5.55
85	4.10	3.88	3.68

Note: GoMa mortality with $m = 86.34$ and $b = 9.5$.

$$D(x, u, r, \lambda, m, b) := \frac{-\dfrac{\partial}{\partial r} \bar{a}_x}{\bar{a}_x}. \tag{6.25}$$

I use the same symbol D for duration that was used also for generic fixed-income bonds but with the understanding that the additional terms (x, u, r, λ, m, b) will clarify the context in which the duration is calculated. When mortality obeys a simple exponential distribution, the duration parameter can be easily computed as

$$D(x, 0, r, \lambda, m, b) = \frac{1}{r + \lambda}. \tag{6.26}$$

Oddly enough, in the case of exponential mortality this duration parameter D is equal to the annuity factor $\bar{a}_x$ itself! Thus, a small change in rates Δr will change the annuity factor by $-\Delta r \times \bar{a}_x$. For example, if the valuation rate increased by 1% then the original annuity factor $\bar{a}_x = \$10$ would change by $\$10 \times (-1\% \times \$10) = -\$1$, resulting in a new annuity factor of \$9.

More generally, under a GoMa law of mortality, the calculus doesn't work out as nicely and the expression for $D(x, \tau, r, \lambda, m, b)$ is, well, a mess. Fortunately, we are able to obtain some (numerical) values by taking derivatives symbolically, using mathematical software, and evaluating the results; see Table 6.8.

For example: assuming GoMa mortality at age 55, the annuity factor under an interest rate of $r = 4\%$ is \$15.82 per dollar of lifetime income. The GoMa duration number of 11.76 years shown in the table is lower than the annuity factor (in contrast to the case of exponential mortality). If the valuation rate increases from $r = 4\%$ to $r = 4.5\%$, then the duration approximation states that the annuity factor will decline by $(0.005)(11.7597) = 5.879\%$

from a value of \$15.82 to a value of \$14.89 per dollar of annual lifetime income. How good is this approximation? Well, by (6.12) the correct value of the annuity factor under an $r = 4.5\%$ valuation rate is $\bar{a}_{55} = 14.93$ per dollar of annual lifetime income. It should come as no surprise that the duration approximation overestimates the extent to which the annuity factor declines when the valuation rate increases. As we saw, this is the nature of the duration (first-derivative) approximation to any valuation function.

Along the same lines, we can compute the duration of a deferred pension annuity factor and compare it with the duration of an immediate pension annuity factor purchased at the same age. For instance, under the same GoMa parameters as before, the duration of an IPAF at age $x = 55$ under an $r = 5\%$ valuation rate is $D = 10.98$ years. Interestingly enough, the duration of a DPAF at the same age $y = 55$ and valuation rate $r = 5\%$—but deferred for $\tau = 10$ years until a starting age of $x = 65$—is $D = 18.65$ years. Why? The answer lies in the payment structure. Recall that duration is a weighted average or a "center of gravity" for a series of payments. When the annuity is deferred by τ years, the income is pushed off into the future and so the duration is increased as well. Don't confuse the value of the annuity factor itself—which is much lower for a DPAF than for an IPAF—with the duration, which already includes a scaling element to adjust for price.

What about convexity? You can go through an even messier exercise to compute the second derivative of the annuity factor,

$$K(x, u, r, \lambda, m, b) := \frac{\frac{\partial^2}{\partial r^2}\bar{a}_x}{\bar{a}_x};$$

this equation can be handled symbolically in several computer languages. An example of a convexity value is $K = 195.497$ when $x = 55$, $r = 5\%$, and the GoMa parameters are $\lambda = 0$, $m = 86.34$, and $b = 9.5$. But when $x = 45$ and $\tau = 10$ under the same valuation rate of $r = 5\%$, the convexity value is $K = 515.11$. The numbers are different but the pattern is the same as before. Longer deferral periods increase both the duration and the convexity of the annuity factor. Table 6.9 provides a summary of duration and convexity values for annuities with various deferral periods.

6.12 Variable vs. Fixed Pension Annuities

Pension annuities can be paid out in "units" as opposed to dollars. In such a case, the pension annuity is often labeled an immediate *variable* annuity

Table 6.9. *Pension annuity factor at age x = 50*
when r = 5%

Deferral period	Value $_u\bar{a}_{50}$	Duration D	Convexity K
0 years	$15.229	12.058 years	237.23
10 years	$7.477	19.839 years	453.15
20 years	$3.087	27.439 years	787.19
30 years	$0.895	35.073 years	1246.84

Note: GoMa mortality with $m = 86.34$ and $b = 9.5$.

(IVA) as opposed to an immediate *fixed* annuity (IFA). Note that immediate variable annuities are distinct from and should not be confused with deferred variable annuities, which are tax-deferred accumulation policies that allow the investor to allocate funds to risky or variable investment funds. I will return to the topic of deferred variable annuities in Chapter 11.

To better understand the mechanics of an immediate variable annuity—and as a precursor to our technical discussion about risk and return characteristics—here is a helpful way to visualize the product. Imagine a payout annuity that is paid in shares instead of cash. Essentially, each month during retirement, instead of getting a check for $1,000 you get 10 shares of XYZ Corporation, regardless of what these shares are actually worth.

Of course, no one can eat shares of XYZ Corp. or buy food with those shares, so the insurance company provides you the added service (at no risk) of converting these shares to cash—based on their value at the time of payment. Thus, if the shares happened to appreciate during that month, you would receive a higher annuity payout than for the previous month; if the shares depreciated, you would get less. This is the essence of an immediate variable annuity.

Obviously, when one initially purchases the IVA, the insurance company offering the product will take the premium paid in and immediately invest the funds in shares of XYZ Corp. As a result, the insurance company is indifferent to the movement of XYZ shares—in other words, it does not care if their value goes up or down—since it de facto makes payments to you in XYZ Corp. shares. Sure, the periodic income of the IVA is in cash, but they are just converting those shares to cash on the day they send you the check. The insurance company is certainly not in the business of speculating on the stock of XYZ Corp. They completely hedge this exposure by setting up actuarial reserves that are held in XYZ shares.

Now, let us consider this transaction from the point of view of the insurance company. What happens if people start living much longer than expected? Will the insurance company run out of XYZ shares?

As with an immediate fixed annuity, the insurance company is required to make those share-based payments to all survivors as long as they are alive. So, a prudent company will make sure to continuously monitor the reserves that are being held and ensure they have enough money set aside to make good on these obligations. This is the main function of the insurance company. They evaluate mortality risk, price it, and hedge against it.

What happens if the XYZ Corp. tanks? Each month, the annuitant receives the value of XYZ shares. If the share price continues to decline each month then the annuitant will receive less and less. But, as long as the XYZ Corp. doesn't hit zero, the annuitant will get something at the end of each month. They can never technically run out of money.

Of course, linking your payout annuity to one particular company is ridiculously risky. Common sense dictates that we invest prudently by holding a diversified portfolio or collection of stocks and bonds. In practice, IVAs are actually linked to well-diversified funds or broad-based market indices.

So, instead of the XYZ Corp., imagine an equity-based fund whose net asset value (NAV) is currently $1 per unit. The unit fluctuates each day. In any given day, week, month, or year the price can increase or decrease relative to the previous period. Instead of receiving fixed annuity payments or fixed payments in shares, you get fixed payments in "fund units." Every month, the insurance company promises to send you the value of 50 fund units. The insurance company converts these fund units into cash using the NAV.

Is this annuity fixed or floating? Well, as Einstein pointed out in his theory of relativity, it all depends on your frame of reference. If you take my analogy to the extreme, all payout annuities are fixed. They are fixed in an asset of reference and converted to the cash value.

Here is the mathematics. An investment of W premium dollars into an immediate *variable* annuity will entitle the annuitants to a lifelong payment of $W/\bar{a}_x$ units per year—where the NAV is normalized to a value of $1—as opposed to dollars per year. As before,

$$\bar{a}_x := \int_0^\infty e^{-ht}(_tp_x)\, dt, \tag{6.27}$$

but in this case the valuation rate r has been replaced with the rather arbitrary h. You will see why in a moment, but for now simply note that this is often called the *assumed interest rate* (AIR) in the insurance lexicon.

Each payment unit entitles the individual to a variable (i.e. random) payment that depends on the performance of the chosen underlying asset (typically, an equity fund) with respect to the AIR h. If the return on the underlying asset in any one period is less than the AIR h, the variable payment will decrease. If, on the other hand, the return on the asset is greater than the AIR h, the variable payment will increase. Formally, if the price dynamics of the underlying asset are governed by a Brownian motion, then the immediate variable annuity's dollar income at time t will be

$$\frac{W}{\bar{a}_x} e^{(\nu - h)t + \sigma B_t}, \tag{6.28}$$

where B_t, ν, σ are as defined in Chapter 5. For example, in the case of exponential mortality, $\bar{a}_x = 1/(\lambda + h)$ and the income flow becomes

$$(\lambda + h) W e^{(\nu - h)t + \sigma B_t}. \tag{6.29}$$

The expression for this variable annuity income may seem obscure at first, but a comparison to the income from a fixed immediate annuity is quite illustrative. For example, if the AIR h is equal to the valuation rate (i.e., $h = r$), then the individual is entitled to an initial $(\lambda + r)W$ units. If the chosen underlying asset were a risk-free asset then $\nu - h = 0$ and $\sigma = 0$, and so each unit would pay off \$1 per year. Therefore, the total income would be exactly the same as in the fixed immediate annuity case: $(\lambda + r)W$ per year for life.

The higher the assumed interest rate h, the greater is the value of $(\lambda + h)W$. In other words, more units are acquired. This may be more desirable for retirees with higher needs in early retirement. However, this is not a free lunch, since the growth of the return process will be lower and hence the payment from each unit (initial NAV times $e^{(\nu - h)t + \sigma B_t}$) will be reduced with time. Alternatively, others may want their payments to increase at a greater rate over time (perhaps to keep up with inflation); in this case, a lower AIR would be selected. In practice, all values of h are actuarially equivalent.

In the event of Gompertz–Makeham mortality, the annual income flow per initial premium W becomes

$$W \frac{\exp\{(m - x)(\lambda + h) - \exp\{\frac{x-m}{b}\}\}}{b\Gamma\left(-(\lambda + h)b, \exp\{\frac{x-m}{b}\}\right)} \exp\{(\nu - h)t + \sigma B_t\}. \tag{6.30}$$

One way to view the AIR is as capturing the amount of future market returns that you are taking, or pricing, in advance. Table 6.10 illustrates this concept employing our usual GoMa parameters. If you are 65 years old and

Table 6.10. *Annuity payout at age x = 65 ($100,000 premium)*

AIR	Initial	Number of units	−20%	0%	+20%
0%	$445	45	$356	$445	$534
3%	$609	61	$469	$591	$713
6%	$796	80	$589	$748	$907

Note: $\lambda = 0$, $m = 86.34$, $b = 9.5$; NAV = $10.

choose a 0% AIR (which can be approximated with a very small rate for the purposes of (6.30)), your initial payment will be approximately $445. If we assume that the initial NAV of the chosen fund is $10 per unit, then you are entitled to $445/$10 = 44.5 fund units. If the market subsequently increases by 20% then the value of your units and your total payment will also increase by exactly 20%, to $534. This is because you have "taken" or "advanced" none (0%) of the portfolio's future return. However, if you select a 6% AIR, resulting in a larger initial payment of $796, and if the market subsequently increases by 20%, then you would get to keep only about 14% of this increase because you already took 6% in advance. Your actual payment will increase only to $907. Of course, this is still better than $445 or even $534 for that matter—which is what you would have received in the 0% AIR case—but over time the advantage will erode, since a higher h slows down the return growth process by decreasing the fund's expected growth rate v. Figure 6.2 illustrates this reversal of the relationship between payouts under different AIRs over time.

6.13 Further Reading

Like the earlier chapter on mortality models, the valuation of pension (life) annuities is fairly standard for actuaries and insurance "quants." Once again, the master reference is *Actuarial Mathematics* (Bowers et al. 1997). In addition, there are a number of interesting papers that are relevant to or extend some of the ideas raised in this chapter. Beekman and Fuelling (1990) extended the computation of a pension annuity factor—which is the expectation of the stochastic present value of a pension annuity—to a scenario in which the valuation rate r is itself random. (I will return to this in a later chapter.) Duncan (1952) and Biggs (1969) were the first to formulate the actuarial mathematics of a variable payout annuity that provides income in units of a fund as opposed to units of currency. The first company to adopt this innovation was the U.S.-based pension fund TIAA-CREF to provide

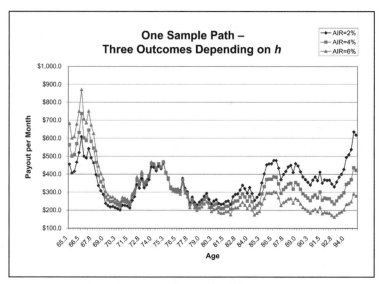

Figure 6.2

pensions for high-school teachers and university professors, and it has since been modified and used by many companies. Feldstein and Ranguelova (2001) use variable payout (income) annuities as part of a proposal to reform Social Security in the United States. Brown and colleagues (1999) examine the "fairness and efficiency" of actual annuity prices and compare their money's worth relative to bonds and other fixed-income products. They build on the methodology developed in Friedman and Warshawsky (1990) and Warshawsky (1998). The effect of adverse selection on annuity prices is examined by Finkelstein and Poterba (2002), and the impact of transaction costs is described by Sinha (1986). These papers—and many subsequent ones that have used the same ideas—are a nice example of how traditional economists use and implement some of the actuarial models I have developed in this chapter.

Along the same lines, for a brief economic history of annuities see Poterba (1997). To understand the impact of unisex pricing on the demand for annuities, see Carlson and Lord (1986). From an actuarial perspective, Frees, Carriere, and Valdez (1996) make clever use of annuity purchase data provided by a large insurance company to estimate the magnitude of the "broken heart" syndrome, based on a GoMa law of mortality. This syndrome is used to describe the higher mortality rates that are often associated with the death of a spouse. Mereu (1962) is the first paper to explicitly derive a pension annuity factor under GoMa mortality. Vanneste, Goovaerts, and Labie (1994) started a series of papers that attempt to classify and compute the entire distribution—as opposed to just the expected value alone—of the stochastic present value of a pension annuity under a variety of interest rate and mortality dynamics.

6.14 Notation

$(_u\bar{a}_{x:\tau})$—pension annuity factor at age x, where u denotes the deferral period and τ denotes the term of temporary coverage

$(\bar{a}_{x,y})$—joint and survivor annuity factor

$V(r, u)$—term certain annuity factor

6.15 Problems

PROBLEM 6.1. Using the annuity income numbers displayed in Table 6.1, locate the "best fitting" GoMa parameters λ, m, b and embedded valuation rate r that minimize the distance between the pension annuity value and the pension annuity price. Use a portion of the prices if this appears to be too complicated.

PROBLEM 6.2. Verify (via integration) the formula for the DPAF $_u\bar{a}_{x:\tau}$ under the Gompertz–Makeham law of mortality, from first principles as laid out in equation (6.2).

PROBLEM 6.3. Assuming $\lambda = 0$, $m = 86.34$, and $b = 9.5$, compute the (correct) IPAF at age 55, 65, and 75 under an $r = 4\%$ and $r = 6\%$ valuation rate. Compare this number to the incorrect value using the (biased) life expectancy method.

PROBLEM 6.4. In Problem 6.3, assume a model of exponential remaining lifetime $\Pr[T_x \geq t] = e^{-\lambda t}$ and compute the "implied IFM value" that equates the IPAF at ages 55, 65, and 75. In other words, find a number such that $\bar{a}_x = 1/(r + \lambda)$. How does the ERL compare under the two mortality assumptions?

PROBLEM 6.5. Assuming $\lambda = 0$, $m = 86.34$, and $b = 9.5$ as GoMa parameters, compute the value and (somehow) the duration of a deferred pension annuity purchased at age 62, under a valuation rate of $r = 5.5\%$, that pays $10,000 per year for life starting at age 72. Also, compute the value and duration for a C-per-year lifetime immediate pension annuity that is purchased at age 72 under the same $r = 5.5\%$ valuation rate. What value of

C allows a long position in the deferred annuity to exactly offset a short position in the immediate annuity for small changes in the valuation rate?

PROBLEM 6.6. Derive an expression for the IPAF $\bar{a}_x$ assuming that the instantaneous force of mortality satisfies the following equation:

$$\lambda(x) = \begin{cases} \frac{1}{b}e^{(x-m)/b} & \text{if } x < 95, \\ \frac{1}{b}e^{(95-m)/b} & \text{if } x \geq 95. \end{cases} \tag{6.31}$$

This is a Gompertz–Makeham law of mortality that "flattens out" and becomes constant at age 95. There is some biological evidence that this better reflects human aging toward the end of the life cycle. Using $m = 86.34$ and $b = 9.5$, compare the value of $\bar{a}_{65}$ under a standard GoMa model to the value under (6.31), using a valuation rate of $r = 5\%$. Is the annuity factor higher or lower? Please provide an intuitive explanation. By how much does the flattening affect the annuity factor? What if the pension annuity is valued at age $x = 75$?

SEVEN

Models of Life Insurance

7.1 A Free (Last) Supper?

A few years ago, a clever friend of mine borrowed $100,000 from the bank at a fixed interest rate of 5% per year. He promised to pay the loan back when he (eventually) died. The bank was willing to lend him the money under these conditions because he used part of the $100,000 to purchase a life insurance policy with a death benefit of $100,000, with the bank listed as the beneficiary. Apparently, this transaction still left him with enough money to purchase an immediate pension annuity that would cover his periodic interest payments of $5,000 each year and then some. In other words, even after buying the life insurance policy and the annuity, he still had some money left over. This sounds like a free lunch to me. In this chapter I will discuss the characteristics and valuation of various types of life insurance policies and investigate whether this transaction is possible.

7.2 Market Prices of Life Insurance

Life insurance is the mirror image of pension annuities and is the subject and focus of this chapter. The word "life" insurance is a misnomer, since this type of insurance pays off only upon death. But then "death insurance" is a much tougher sell even for marketing specialists.

Table 7.1 provides a sample of actual life insurance quotes. It displays the fixed annual premiums that males and females would have to pay at various ages in order to obtain $100,000 of life insurance coverage that would pay off at death. These numbers are averages of the best (i.e. lowest) 3–5 U.S. insurance company quotes in the early part of 2005.

The *term* of the insurance policy is the amount of time during which the coverage is in effect. For example, if you purchase a 10-year term insurance

Table 7.1. *U.S. monthly premiums for a $100,000 death benefit*

Term of insurance	Age 30		Age 50		Age 70	
	M	F	M	F	M	F
5 years	$12.71	$11.53	$19.65	$15.30	$105.65	$59.27
10 years	$8.21	$7.68	$17.95	$14.57	$102.51	$55.96
20 years	$11.01	$9.68	$27.56	$21.19	$207.54	$128.07
30 years	$15.47	$12.88	$46.23	$33.15	$307.33	$259.50
Term-to-100[a]	$33.51	$27.27	$103.60	$81.51	$373.83	$299.07

[a] Canadian data, "regular health," nonsmoker.
Source: Compulife, "preferred health" applicant, nonsmoker.

policy then you will pay premiums (each month) for 10 years, and if you die anytime during the 10 years your beneficiary will receive $100,000. If you die one instant after the ten years are over, they get nothing. In Table 7.1, the only insurance that truly covers you for life is "term-to-100," which covers you to age 100. Although this type of insurance is not available in the United States, the "no-lapse universal life" policy can serve as an alternative.

Many obvious—and some not so obvious—observations emerge from Table 7.1. For any given term, a male of any age must pay a higher monthly premium than a female for the same coverage. Of course, the differences in mortality account for this observation. Next, both males and females (of any age) pay more for 30 years of coverage than they would pay for 20- or 10-year term life insurance. However, what may appear counterintuitive is that a 5-year policy is actually more expensive than a 10-year and sometimes even a 20-year policy. This irregularity is likely due to a combination of several factors. First, the lack of insurer competition may be resulting in higher premiums for 5-year policies, since consumers tend to be more interested in longer-term insurance. Second, the insurer may be trying to amortize all of the costs associated with offering this policy over a shorter period of time. See also Section 7.15, which explores an additional factor that contributes to the price differences.

7.3 The Impact of Health Status

The insurance prices you pay actually depend on something we have not stressed before: your health status. Table 7.2 illustrates the impact of health on the premium a 50-year-old would pay. For example, a 50-year-old male who is in exceptional health would pay only $23.85 per month for a 20-year

Table 7.2. *U.S. monthly premiums for a $100,000 death benefit—*
50-year-old nonsmoker

Term	Health status							
	Average		Above average		Excellent		Exceptional	
(years)	M	F	M	F	M	F	M	F
5	$27.61	$20.68	$25.16	$17.49	$19.65	$15.30	$15.37	$12.11
10	$23.54	$18.38	$22.64	$17.94	$17.95	$14.57	$14.86	$12.48
20	$38.69	$28.65	$35.30	$26.73	$27.56	$21.19	$23.85	$17.90

Source: Compulife, ⟨www.term4sale.com⟩.

policy whose death benefit is $100,000. In contrast, a 50-year-old male in only average health would have to pay $38.69 for the same contractual terms. As you can see, the 62% markup is quite a substantial incentive to prove you are in exceptional health (if you are) when purchasing life insurance. In the lingo of our mortality laws, the IFM curve $\lambda(x)$ for a very healthy individual is "lower" than the IFM curve for a less healthy individual. Without abusing the notation too much, you can imagine a whole family of IFM curves $\lambda(x, i)$, where the index $i = 1, \ldots, n$ captures the health of the individual at age x.

With regard to health status, it is important to recognize the *adverse selection* that may occur as a result of information asymmetries between the insurance applicant and the insurance company. That is, the applicant may be affected by or predisposed to a health condition yet may withhold this information from the insurer. As a result this applicant will be undercharged for the actual level of risk undertaken by the insurer. In fact, potential evidence of adverse selection was revealed in the Tillinghast Older Age Mortality Study (Tillinghast 2004), which stated that the number of deaths resulting from cancer was higher during the early years of life insurance policy terms than during the later years.

I will return to the cost of changing health in Chapter 10, but for now it is important to note the substantial impact of health on insurance premiums, which is something we did not experience (and is quite rare) for pension annuities.

7.4 How Much Life Insurance Do You Need?

There are two approaches to determining how much life insurance a person requires. The first approach—the income approach—looks at how much money you can expect to earn over the course of your working life; this is your *human capital*, which can be viewed as an asset that you possess as a result of your natural and acquired skills and abilities. Then, you subtract taxes (since the death benefit is not taxable), subtract the expenses you would have incurred had you been alive, and set that as the amount of insurance you require.

The second approach is the expense approach. As its name suggests, this method looks at the expenses that your family will incur over the course of their lives. You then buy insurance to cover those expenses rather than to replace your income. As you can imagine, there will be a wide variation between the amounts of insurance you think you need if you use the (family) expense method as opposed to the income approach. And the larger your income, the larger this gap will be.

Thus, for example, if you make $100,000 per year and expect this number to remain fairly constant in real terms (after inflation) for the rest of your life, then the income approach might lead to about $1,000,000 in life insurance coverage, which arguably could be the present (discounted) value of your wages at some interest rate (akin to our life-cycle calculations in Chapter 2). The expense approach would compute the costs of family living expenses, such as food and education, which might only be $500,000. In this case, any number between $500,000 and $1,000,000 would be acceptable as a life insurance policy.

This brings me to another important concept of insurance. Although the pricing of insurance is a rigorous and scientific discipline, determining the amount of insurance coverage that you require is not. Many people mistakenly believe that you can never have too much insurance. I disagree. I think that there is an upper bound (the income approach) and a lower bound (the expense approach), and anything in between is fair game. Further, regardless of whether you take the income or the expense approach, your insurance needs will change over time. Obviously, families' expenses will decline substantially as their children grow up and leave the nest. Likewise, the discounted value of wages and other income will decline with time. So there is really no justification for buying more and more life insurance as you age.

I therefore find it quite puzzling that the size of one's life insurance policy has become a status symbol in the corporate world. Executives in their 60s boast of life insurance policies worth $10 million to which their spouses and/or beneficiaries would be entitled. This strikes me as a waste of insurance premiums—and I would advise sleeping with one eye open! They may be very important and knowledgeable executives with lifelong experience and wisdom, but the present value of their salaries is nowhere near $10 million and the present value of their families' expenses is even lower. In the absence of other (non–human capital) reasons, to which I shall return momentarily, there is no need to have more life insurance as you age.

Insurance is not a good *investment* on a pre-tax basis because the expected discounted value of the benefits you receive is lower than the premiums you pay; otherwise the insurance company would never make a profit. Yet it is a good *hedge* because the uncertainty in the insurance payout is negatively correlated with your human capital.

7.5 Other Kinds of Life Insurance

In general, there are two basic (and quite different) categories of life insurance: temporary and permanent.

Temporary life insurance, also known as *term life,* is a no-frills way of insuring yourself for a specific period of time—for example, one, five, or ten years. This is the type of insurance for which we listed quotes in Table 7.1. When the temporary life insurance can be automatically renewed every year at increasing rates, it is called annual renewable term (ART) insurance; when the premiums are constant for a longer term, it is referred to as level premium term insurance. In the latter case, as I explained earlier, your monthly premiums are guaranteed for the term of the insurance, and the insurance coverage ends at the end of the term.

The important characteristics of a term policy are its temporary nature and its lack of a savings component. This might seem an odd comment at first, since insurance should have nothing to do with savings. But you will see in a moment that permanent life insurance does have a savings component.

Temporary coverage, of course, is great for temporary needs. For example, it may be advisable for young couples, with considerable human capital to protect, who have just purchased a house and financed it with a large mortgage, have dependents, and so forth. They may have term life insurance of perhaps 8–10 times their annual salaries. Some financial advisors believe that, as these individuals age, this factor can be reduced to 6–8 times their annual salaries, and then perhaps even to 4–6 times—but never less. Of course, renewing the term insurance will cost more as you age because the probability of dying increases. In fact, in order to ensure they can continue to buy temporary coverage at all, some purchase term insurance with a guaranteed renewable clause. This means that, even if their health deteriorates, when the original period is over they can purchase a replacement policy (for the same or lower amount of coverage) without having to undergo a medical examination, which the insurance company usually requires in order to reduce adverse selection.

So much for temporary insurance coverage. What is permanent coverage? This type of coverage is usually referred to as *whole life,* universal life, or level life insurance. There are various types and flavors of permanent coverage, but the main idea is that your monthly or quarterly insurance premiums also contain a savings component. So, if you pay $100 per month, perhaps $60 goes toward the insurance premiums while the remaining $40 goes to a side savings fund and grows on a tax-deferred basis.

Why the savings? With (short) term insurance, the cost of buying a new policy would increase each year because the probability of dying increases as you age. Remember, as shown in Table 7.1, insurance is more expensive at older ages. In fact, by the time you are 80 the premiums are prohibitively expensive—assuming you can find a seller. Level or permanent insurance is a system whereby you overpay in the early years in order to subsidize the later years. Although the premiums are also fixed for a level life insurance policy (as its name suggests), level insurance premiums are higher than term premiums for the first part of your life whereas term premiums exceed level premiums later on. This is where the savings come in. Since you are overpaying in the early years, the excess over the pure premiums is being invested in a side fund. In fact, this tax-deferred savings component is what often gives rise to non–human capital reasons for purchasing insurance. For example, the tax shelter provides an efficient method of accumulating savings to finance the tax bill on your appreciated physical assets that your estate may face upon your death.

In some cases, you can actually control where those excess premiums are invested. For example, you may be able to choose to invest in insurance company mutual funds or bonds. As you age, some of the savings will be depleted to make up for the fact that your annual level premiums are lower than what they should be. With these so-called variable policies, you can withdraw (or cash in) the excess savings at any time, so you have access to an emergency fund in times of need.

In sum, were it not for income taxes and the possibility that your insurability might change over time, buying life insurance would be a simple decision. Everybody would be advised to "buy term and invest the difference."

7.6 Value of Life Insurance: Net Single Premium

We start by computing the net single premium (NSP), which is the amount that must be paid in one lump sum to acquire the insurance protection. In

Section 7.12 I present results for the net periodic premium (NPP), which is the name given when the insurance premiums are paid in installments.

Conceptually, here is the main idea behind the pricing of life insurance. Say the valuation rate is $r = 5\%$ and the insured person dies at time $T = 10$ years; then the discounted value of the death benefit at time 0 is $e^{-(0.05)10} = \$0.606$ per dollar of face value. Stated differently, if a \$1 death benefit were desired then an initial premium of 0.606 dollars invested at a rate of $r = 5\%$ would grow to \$1 at the time of death, which would be enough to pay the death benefit to the beneficiary. If, on the other hand, the insured person dies at time $T = 20$ years, then the discounted value of the death benefit is a much lower $e^{-(0.05)20} = \$0.368$ per dollar of face value. In this case, an initial premium of 0.368 dollars is sufficient.

One does not require a large leap of faith to generalize this statement by saying that, when the remaining lifetime random variable is T_x, the stochastic discounted value of a \$1 death benefit at a valuation rate r is

$$A_x = e^{-rT_x}. \tag{7.1}$$

Intuitively, the *realized* discounted value will be very low—and hence a small premium would have been sufficient ex post—if the realized value of T_x is large. On the other hand, if the realized value of T_x is very small, then the ex post discounted value of the death benefit would be much higher, since the money did not have enough time to compound and grow.

The stochastic discounted value A_x is the life insurance counterpart to the stochastic discounted value a_x for the pension annuity. Recall that a_x was defined by the integral relationship

$$a_x = \int_0^{T_x} e^{-rt}\, dt. \tag{7.2}$$

At first glance, the stochastic discounted value of the life insurance benefit in equation (7.1) is "simpler" than (7.2) since there is no integral or summation sign to compute for life insurance. However, any euphoria will be short-lived because the process of evaluating the expectation of A_x, which is unavoidable for an unbiased actuarial premium, involves a fair dose of calculus.

Indeed, in a manner parallel to our definition by $\bar{a}_x = E[a_x]$ of the pension annuity factor, we define the NSP as

$$\bar{A}_x = E[e^{-rT_x}] = \int_0^\infty e^{-rt} f_x(t)\, dt, \tag{7.3}$$

where $f_x(t)$ denotes the probability density function (PDF) of the remaining lifetime random variable T_x. The intuition is as follows. Starting from the perspective of the current age (x), we must add up all possible discounted values e^{-rt} as weighted by $f_x(t)$, the probability of death at that instant. The sum (integral) of these discounted values is the net single premium. Stated differently: If the insurance company receives the fair actuarial premium $\bar{A}_x$ for life insurance coverage at age x, then the discounted value of their expected profit is $E[A_x - \bar{A}_x] = 0$.

Readers with some background in mathematical analysis might recognize the expression in (7.3) as the Laplace transform or moment generating function (MGF) of the random variable T_x. The relevance of this insight is that, if one has the Laplace transform or MGF of the remaining lifetime random variable, then the net single insurance premium can be obtained simply by plugging in the valuation rate r.

7.7 Valuing Life Insurance Using Pension Annuities

As I warned previously, computing $\bar{A}_x$ requires that we perform some more calculus. The method of integration by parts, which is at the heart of calculus, leads to a helpful shortcut for valuing the NSP for life insurance. Recall the basic relationship

$$\frac{d}{dt}(u(t)v(t)) = u(t)dv(t) + v(t)du(t)$$

$$\Longleftrightarrow \int u(t)\,dv(t) = u(t)v(t) - \int v(t)\,du(t), \qquad (7.4)$$

where both $u(t)$ and $v(t)$ are general functions of t and where $du(t), dv(t)$ denote derivatives with respect to t. This is the product rule: Take derivatives with respect to one term $u(t)$ and then with respect to the other term $v(t)$; then add them together.

With this insight we can use equation (7.3) and substitute $u(t) = e^{-rt}$ and $dv(t) = f_x(t)\,dt$ in the integrand. In this case, $du(t) = -re^{-rt}$ and $v(t) = F_x(t)$ owing to the relationship between the PDF and CDF (cumulative distribution function) of the remaining lifetime random variable. This leads us to the general relationship

$$\int e^{-rt}f_x(t)\,dt = e^{-rt}F_x(t) - \int F_x(t)(-re^{-rt})\,dt. \qquad (7.5)$$

The integral we are interested in evaluating can be transformed into an integral involving the CDF $F_x(t)$ and the simple discount factor e^{-rt}. Then the right-hand side of (7.5) can be written as

$$e^{-rt}F_x(t) - r\left(\int (1 - F_x(t))e^{-rt}\, dt - \int e^{-rt}\, dt \right) \qquad (7.6)$$

by artificially adding and then subtracting the extra integral term $\int e^{-rt}\, dt$. We then recognize $(_tp_x) = (1 - F_x(t))$ in the integrand of the first integral as the conditional survival probability. In the end, this leaves us with:

$$\int e^{-rt}f_x(t)\, dt = e^{-rt}F_x(t) - r\left(\int (_tp_x)e^{-rt}\, dt - \int e^{-rt}\, dt \right). \qquad (7.7)$$

When evaluated from the lower bound of $t = 0$ to the upper bound of $t = \infty$, this leads to a very recognizable expression:

$$\bar{A}_x := \int_0^\infty e^{-rt}f_x(t)\, dt = 1 - r\bar{a}_x. \qquad (7.8)$$

Equation (7.8) is quite remarkable and extremely useful. The NSP for the life insurance policy is equal to 1 minus the immediate pension annuity factor multiplied by the valuation rate r.

Thus, for example, if you already have a formula or expression for $\bar{a}_x$ and you need a value for $\bar{A}_x$, you need only multiply by r and subtract from 1. This is true regardless of the specific law of mortality $\lambda(x)$, the age x, or the valuation rate r. As you can imagine, I will "milk" this relationship many times in the analysis. We will use this trick to obtain explicit expressions for $\bar{A}_x$ using the work done in Chapter 6 to obtain $\bar{a}_x$. In addition, this shortcut is applicable to deferred (or delayed) insurance—which I have yet to introduce—as well as to computing the duration and convexity of $\bar{A}_x$.

Note that $\bar{a}_x < 1/r$ regardless of the actual mortality law as long as there is some chance of dying prior to infinity. Equations (7.9) and (7.10) demonstrate why. The value of a bond that pays an annual coupon of $1 perpetually can be stated as

$$V(1, r, \infty) = \int_0^\infty e^{-rt}\, dt = \frac{1}{r}. \qquad (7.9)$$

Contrast this with the value of a pension annuity paying $1 per year:

$$\bar{a}_x = E\left[\int_0^{T_x} e^{-rt}\, dt \right]. \qquad (7.10)$$

The integration from 0 to ∞ in (7.9) will clearly outweigh the integration from 0 to T_x in equation (7.10); hence the former integral's value is greater, implying that $\bar{a}_x < 1/r$. It is only in the limit with zero mortality that the annuity factor converges to $1/r$. Now look back at equation (7.8). Since $\bar{a}_x < 1/r$, it follows that $r\bar{a}_x < 1$ and so $1 - r\bar{a}_x > 0$. The life insurance net single premium should (obviously) be greater than zero. In the limit, however, when the person is very young and the instantaneous force of mortality curve $\lambda(x)$ is very low, the expression $r\bar{a}_x \approx 1$ and the NSP will be close to zero. The inverse relationship between $\bar{A}_x$ and $\bar{a}_x$ should be intuitive as well. The more you have to pay for life insurance, the less you should have to pay for a pension annuity (and vice versa).

7.8 Arbitrage Relationship

There is yet another way to arrive at the expression in (7.8). Let's return to the story that opened this chapter (but reducing the amounts for clarity). My friend borrowed \$100 from a bank at an interest rate of r. This loan was structured as interest only, so that each year the borrower had to pay $100r$ in interest payments ($100r\,dt$ in continuous time). The loan principal was due and payable when the borrower dies. To cover this risk, he was forced to purchase a life insurance policy—with the bank as beneficiary—and had to pay $100\bar{A}_x$ for this coverage. He then purchased a life annuity to cover the interest payments of $100r\,dt$, which should have cost $100r\bar{a}_x$ (as you may recall from Chapter 6). The remainder after paying for life insurance and pension annuity was:

$$100 - 100\bar{A}_x - 100r\bar{a}_x. \tag{7.11}$$

You should convince yourself that, at least on a pre-tax basis, this should equal zero (or less); otherwise, there is a clear arbitrage opportunity available for riskless profit. In fact, it is possible to take this one step further and, by appealing to competitive markets, force the inequality into an equality between the two sides.

Thus, arbitrage opportunities that arise from varying assumptions of mortality and returns among the companies selling insurance and those selling annuities will not last long. And even though misalignments in pricing can exist when a poor credit rating forces an insurer to lower its premiums, any potential profit would not qualify as an arbitrage opportunity because of the implicit default risk.

Indeed, by dividing all terms by 100 and then isolating the NSP, this also implies the fundamental relationship between the NSP and the annuity factor: $\bar{A}_x = 1 - r\bar{a}_x$. Another way of expressing this relationship is

$$\frac{\bar{A}_x}{\bar{a}_x} = \frac{1}{\bar{a}_x} - r. \tag{7.12}$$

The ratio $\bar{A}_x/\bar{a}_x$ has its own special meaning and interpretation, to which we will return later.

7.9 Tax Arbitrage Relationship

While on the subject of arbitrage, I wish to discuss a situation in which an arbitrage opportunity would actually be available. As mentioned in Chapter 6, in some sense the taxation of annuity income is quite lenient (even in the United States). In fact, in Canada it is possible to purchase for W_0 dollars a life annuity that pays $W_0/\bar{a}_x$ for life and then use part of the periodic proceeds to purchase (for $W_0\bar{A}_x/\bar{a}_x$) a life insurance policy and still have enough left over on an after-tax basis to earn more than what the money would earn in the bank. This is called a "mortality swap" and is effectively a tax arbitrage opportunity.

Using the language of mathematics, we have

$$\frac{W_0}{\bar{a}_x} - \tau_{\text{tax}}(\rho_x)\frac{W_0}{\bar{a}_x} - W_0\frac{\bar{A}_x}{\bar{a}_x} > W_0 r(1 - \tau_{\text{tax}}), \tag{7.13}$$

where

$$\rho_x = 1 - \frac{\bar{a}_x}{E[T_x^{\text{tax}}]}.$$

Hence (7.13) can be simplified to

$$\frac{1}{\bar{a}_x} - \tau_{\text{tax}}\left(1 - \frac{\bar{a}_x}{E[T_x^{\text{tax}}]}\right)\left(\frac{1}{\bar{a}_x}\right) - \frac{\bar{A}_x}{\bar{a}_x} > r(1 - \tau_{\text{tax}}), \tag{7.14}$$

which means that you get more from the combination of annuity and insurance than from investing in a risk-free bond paying an after-tax interest rate of $r(1 - \tau_{\text{tax}})$, where τ_{tax} denotes the marginal tax rate of the annuitant.

One might wonder how this opportunity can persist, and the answer likely lies in the lobbying efforts by seniors and insurance companies for continuation of the more favorable tax treatment accorded to annuity income during retirement. So, although certain restrictions do apply when making the transaction, this tax quirk lives on.

7.10 Value of Life Insurance: Exponential Mortality

Under exponential mortality, where the IFM curve $\lambda(x) = \lambda$, the NSP becomes

$$\bar{A}_x = 1 - \frac{r}{r + \lambda} = \frac{\lambda}{r + \lambda}. \tag{7.15}$$

For example: when the life expectancy is $1/\lambda = 20$ and the valuation rate is $r = 5\%$, the net single premium is equal to $\bar{A}_x = 0.05/0.10 = 0.5$ per \$1 of life insurance protection. If the valuation rate doubles to $r = 10\%$, the NSP becomes $\bar{A}_x = 0.05/0.15 = 0.333$ per \$1 of life insurance protection. As you would expect, increasing the valuation rate r tends to reduce the NSP and increasing the IFM λ will increase the NSP.

7.11 Value of Life Insurance: GoMa Mortality

Under the GoMa law of mortality, the value of $\bar{A}_x$ can be expressed as

$$\bar{A}_x = 1 - \frac{rb\Gamma\left(-(\lambda + r)b, \exp\left\{\frac{x-m}{b}\right\}\right)}{\exp\left\{(m - x)(\lambda + r) - \exp\left\{\frac{x-m}{b}\right\}\right\}}, \tag{7.16}$$

where I have merely used the relationship $\bar{A}_x = 1 - r\bar{a}_x$ and then plugged in the relevant pension annuity factor from Chapter 6.

For example, using our favorite $m = 86.34$, $b = 9.5$, and $\lambda = 0$ GoMa parameters from that chapter, the NSP under an $r = 6\%$ valuation rate is $\bar{A}_{35} = \$0.0846$ at age 35, $\bar{A}_{45} = \$0.1445$ at age 45, and $\bar{A}_{65} = \$0.3715$ at age 65. Each of these premiums will buy \$1 of life insurance protection. Thus, for a death benefit of \$100,000, a 35-, 45-, and 65-year-old would pay \$8,460, \$14,449, and \$37,155, respectively. Quite obviously, at younger ages where $\lambda(x)$ is small the life insurance cost is minimal, and at advanced ages where $\lambda(x)$ is higher the cost is higher as well. As a means of comparison, the pension annuity factor at the same ages and valuation rates would be $\bar{a}_{35} = 15.257$, $\bar{a}_{45} = 14.259$, and $\bar{a}_{65} = 10.474$ per dollar of lifetime annual income. Table 7.3 summarizes the NSP values for various ages and interest rates under these same mortality parameters.

Of course, none of the numbers in Table 7.3 are comparable to the "real world" numbers in Table 7.1 or Table 7.2, where quotes were based on monthly premiums, because $\bar{A}_x$ corresponds to a net single premium paid in advance. So how does one go about pricing insurance that is paid by installments?

Table 7.3. *Net single premium^a for $100,000
of life insurance protection*

Initiated at age x	Interest rate r		
	4%	6%	8%
35	$17,892	$8,460	$4,376
45	$25,916	$14,449	$8,616
55	$36,711	$23,800	$16,161
65	$50,185	$37,155	$28,298

^{a} NSP $= $100,000 \times \bar{A}_x$.
Note: GoMa mortality with $m = 86.34$ and $b = 9.5$.

7.12 Life Insurance Paid by Installments

When determining what annuity payment an individual is entitled to, we divide the initial lump-sum payment by the appropriate annuity factor in order to spread the premium over the remaining lifetime, taking into account mortality and interest. Similarly, when the insurance is paid over time as opposed to all at once, the premium must be amortized or spread over the life of the insured. In the event of coverage that lasts a lifetime, the $\bar{A}_x$ must be converted into a *net periodic premium*,

$$\text{NPP} := \frac{\bar{A}_x}{\bar{a}_x}. \tag{7.17}$$

Remember that $\bar{A}_x/\bar{a}_x = 1/\bar{a}_x - r$, so the NPP can be computed by taking the inverse of the pension annuity factor and then subtracting the valuation rate. In the case of exponential mortality this collapses to NPP $= \lambda$, which (oddly enough) does not depend on the valuation rate; it is purely a function of the instantaneous force of mortality. In the case of GoMa mortality, the NPP expression can again be computed quite easily. Table 7.4 provides a picture of how the net periodic premiums change with initial age and valuation rate under GoMa mortality.

We are now in a better position to compare numbers with Table 7.1. However, we first digress with some further remarks about term life insurance.

7.13 NSP: Delayed and Term Insurance

Up to this point in our discussion of pricing life insurance, I have focused on the valuation of life insurance policies that provide coverage immediately upon payment of the initial lump sum. However, in some cases the

Table 7.4. *Net periodic premium^a for $100,000 of life insurance protection*

Initiated	Interest rate r		
at age x	4%	6%	8%
35	$871.63	$554.51	$366.10
45	$1,399.27	$1,013.32	$754.27
55	$2,320.21	$1,874.00	$1,542.10
65	$4,029.72	$3,547.26	$3,157.28

^{a} NPP $= \$100,000 \times (\bar{A}_x/\bar{a}_x)$.
Note: GoMa mortality with $m = 86.34$ and $b = 9.5$.

life insurance is paid for now even though coverage doesn't start for another u years. The pricing equation for this variation of life insurance is

$$(_u\bar{A}_x) := \int_u^\infty e^{-rt} f_x(t)\, dt. \tag{7.18}$$

In the case of term life insurance, coverage starts immediately but is valid for only a predetermined period of time. In this case, equation (7.19) is appropriate:

$$\bar{A}_{x:\tau} := \int_0^\tau e^{-rt} f_x(t)\, dt. \tag{7.19}$$

These two definitions parallel the expressions for the familiar annuity factors:

$$(_u\bar{a}_x) := \int_u^\infty e^{-rt}(1 - F_x(t))\, dt; \tag{7.20}$$

$$\bar{a}_{x:\tau} := \int_0^\tau e^{-rt}(1 - F_x(t))\, dt. \tag{7.21}$$

The NPP for temporary insurance can be computed by $\bar{A}_{x:\tau}/\bar{a}_{x:\tau}$ for reasons that should be intuitive.

7.14 Variations on Life Insurance

I will now present an example in which the general formula for the net single premium is

$$\int_u^\tau e^{-rt} f_x(t)\, dt = (e^{-r\tau} F_x(\tau) - e^{-ru} F_x(u))$$
$$- r\left(\int_u^\tau (_t p_x) e^{-rt}\, dt - \int_u^\tau e^{-rt}\, dt \right). \tag{7.22}$$

This is identical to equation (7.7) except it takes into account the period of u years during which no coverage takes place. The expression can also be written using formal notation as

$$(_u\bar{A}_{x:\tau}) = (e^{-r\tau}F_x(\tau) - e^{-ru}F_x(u)) - r(_u\bar{a}_{x:\tau}) - (e^{-r\tau} - e^{-ru}). \quad (7.23)$$

Equation (7.23) can be used to compute a wide variety of temporary and permanent life insurance policy values. Recall that, in the case of GoMa mortality, the CDF function $F_x(t) = 1 - \exp\{-\lambda t + e^{(x-m)/b}(1 - e^{t/b})\}$, which collapses to $F_x(0) = 0$ when $t = 0$ and where $F_x(\infty) \to 1$ as $t \to \infty$.

Thus, in order to obtain the NSP for a 10-year term life insurance policy at age $x = 45$, we must perform the following calculations. First, recall that

$$\bar{a}_{45:10} = \bar{a}_{45} - (_{10}\bar{a}_{45}), \quad (7.24)$$

which means that a 10-year temporary pension annuity is equal to an immediate pension annuity minus a 10-year deferred pension annuity. When $m = 86.34$, $b = 9.5$, $\lambda = 0$, and the valuation rate is $r = 5\%$, this works out to $\bar{a}_{45} = 16.16$ and $(_{10}\bar{a}_{45}) = 8.36$, so $\bar{a}_{45:10} = 7.80$ per dollar of yearly income. It is important to remember that $7.80 is the value of a pension annuity for an $x = 45$-year-old that pays income for 10 years (provided the insured is still alive). At the end of the 10 years, payments stop. The $7.80 value can be compared to the value of a 10-year term certain annuity with no life-contingent component under an $r = 5\%$ interest rate. The discounted value of this generic annuity would be

$$7.869 = \int_0^{10} e^{-0.05t}\, dt := V(0.05, 10),$$

which is slightly higher than $7.80 owing to the (small) probability that the 45-year-old will die prior to age 55.

Continuing on our quest to compute the value of a 10-year term life insurance policy that pays $100,000 upon death, we have

$$\bar{A}_{45:10} = (e^{-(0.05)10}F_{45}(10) - e^{-(0.05)0}F_{45}(0)) - (0.05)(7.8)$$
$$- (e^{-(0.05)(10)} - 1)$$
$$= 0.017873$$

and so the NSP for a $100,000 policy is $1,787 up front. Finally, if we amortize this over 10 years by dividing by the $\bar{a}_{45:10}$ annuity factor, the result is $1,787/7.8 = $229 per year for 10 years.

Table 7.5. *Model results: $100,000 life insurance—
Monthly premiums for 50-year-old by health status*

Term	Health status (m-values)		
(years)	$m = 86.34$	$m = 96.34$	$m = 100$
5	$24.84	$8.67	$5.90
10	$32.07	$11.22	$7.63
20	$52.14	$18.49	$12.61

Note: $b = 9.5, r = 6\%$.

Now you can finally and directly compare our model results with the numbers in Table 7.1. But first, since the table is dealing with "preferred health" applicants, it makes more sense to use a higher value of m for GoMa mortality. I will therefore choose $m = 96.34$ (instead of our usual 86.34), which is an additional ten years of (average) life, but the dispersion value of $b = 9.5$ will remain unchanged. When $x = 70$ and $r = 5\%$, the value of $(\bar{A}_{45:\overline{10}|}/\bar{a}_{45:\overline{10}|})$ times $100,000 is $1,105 per year, which is $92 per month for a 10-year term policy. When $x = 50$, the values are $136 per year and $11.30 per month. As we observed when pricing life annuities, our model results differ from the quoted numbers in Table 7.1. The numbers are slightly higher, which is most likely due to commissions and company profits. Table 7.5 provides summary values.

A number of intuitive results emerge from Table 7.5. First, it is easy to create a robust mix of monthly life insurance premiums simply by moving the GoMa value of m up or down by a few years. Adding an additional 15 years to m can reduce the life insurance premium by 70%. Healthy individuals should and do pay much less for insurance. Note that I have not distinguished between males and females in Table 7.5. Indeed, from a modeling perspective the only difference between the two genders is a value of m and perhaps a small value of b. Finally, note that a longer term for the insurance policy (denoted by τ in the equations) will also result in higher premiums.

Observe, however, that I have not managed to precisely replicate the relationship between term length and premiums for the market quotes displayed in Table 7.2. The market quotes for 5-year terms were (counterintuitively) higher than for 10- or 20-year terms. At the time I attributed this to "other" costs such as fees and commissions that must be amortized over a shorter period of time, as well as to a lack of competition. But part of the story involves lapsation and the fact that some people "abandon" their insurance prior to its term ending. If the insurance company can rely on this fact in advance, this effectively lowers the insurance cost for everyone.

7.15 What If You Stop Paying Premiums?

When paying for life insurance via the installment method of $\bar{A}_x/\bar{a}_x$ per year, the only way to make absolutely sure that your beneficiaries will receive the death benefit is by continuing to pay your insurance premiums until the last possible moment. Under a generic term insurance contract, if you stop making those payments for any reason at all and your policy *lapses,* your beneficiaries will lose all claims to the death benefit. Unfortunately, many consumers lapse their policy and give up on making payments long before the term is over. This behavioral fact is so persistent and predictable that insurance companies actually rely on it when pricing their term insurance policies. If they know that a fraction of the group will lapse their insurance coverage, the company can charge the group less overall. Implicitly, some of the people dying will not receive any benefits, since they will have discontinued their policies prior to death. This might sound odd at first, so here is a model to help understand the pricing and valuation implications.

Allow me to return to our classic expression for the net single premium $\bar{A}_x$. Imagine that some fraction of the group of policy holders "do not qualify" to receive the death benefit of $1. I will model the rate at which individuals leave the insured group by using a hazard rate denoted $\eta(t)$, with the usual proviso that $H_x(t)$ denotes the CDF and $h_x(t)$ the PDF of the remaining "unlapsed time" random variable L, so that $H_x(t) := \Pr[L \leq t]$. In this case, the lapse-adjusted NSP would be

$$(_u\bar{A}^\eta_{x:\tau}) := \int_u^\tau e^{-rt}f_x(t)(1 - H_x(t))\,dt$$

$$= (_u\bar{A}_{x:\tau}) - \int_0^\infty e^{-rt}f_x(t)H_x(t)\,dt, \qquad (7.25)$$

where (with my sincere apologies) the new superscript η on the $\bar{A}_x$ indicates that we are working with a lapse curve $\eta(t)$. The intuition for equation (7.25) is straightforward. The only way the insurance policy will pay the death benefit at time t is if the insured is unlapsed. The probability of being unlapsed is $1 - H_x(t)$, which is akin to the probability of being "undead." Therefore, the only difference between the integrand in equation (7.25) and the conventional and expected $e^{-rt}f_x(t)$ is the additional term $1 - H_x(t)$. It should come as no surprise that $({}_u\bar{A}^\eta_{x:\tau}) \le ({}_u\bar{A}_{x:\tau})$, since a fraction of the people paying the (adjusted) NSP will not be collecting their death benefit. These "deserters" effectively subsidize the premiums for everyone else. Of course, if the insurance premium were paid up front then there would be no lapse to talk about, since the entire amount has already been paid. This is also the case if the insurance policy is purchased as a part of a more complicated structure such as the mortality swap discussed in Section 7.9. This is why it might be more appropriate to think of $1 - H_x(t)$ as the probability of being "a member of the group" to qualify for the death benefit at time t. Later, once I convert the calculations to a periodic premium, we can legitimately use L as an "unlapsed time" random variable. Another point worth mentioning is that I am using the subscript x on the CDF $H_x(t)$ and the PDF $h_x(t)$ in order to remind the reader that one's propensity to leave the insured group might depend on biological age as well as the time elapsed since the original policy was acquired.

Now we must hand over the mathematics to the rules of calculus and integration by parts. The final expression for $({}_u\bar{A}^\eta_{x:\tau})$ will depend on the precise structure of the $H_x(t)$ function. The easiest possible case is when the unlapsed time random variable has a constant instantaneous hazard rate η, which leads to the CDF of $H_x(t) = 1 - e^{-\eta t}$ and a modified NSP of

$$({}_u\bar{A}^\eta_{x:\tau}) := \int_u^\tau e^{-(r+\eta)t} f_x(t)\, dt. \tag{7.26}$$

In this case the lapse rate η can be absorbed or added into the valuation rate r, and the valuation formula for (say) GoMa mortality can be used with $r + \eta$ instead of just r. The process of converting the NSP into a periodic annual premium would proceed along the same lines. I define the modified pension annuity factor as

$$({}_u\bar{a}^\eta_{x:\tau}) := \int_u^\tau e^{-rt}(1 - F_x(t))(1 - H_x(t))\, dt$$

$$= \int_u^\tau e^{-rt} \exp\left\{-\int_0^t (\lambda(x+s) + \eta(x+s))\, ds\right\} dt, \tag{7.27}$$

where I have written both $H_x(t)$ and $F_x(t)$ in terms of their primitive definitions based on instantaneous hazard rates and mortality forces. Again, when $\eta(x+t) = \eta$, the instantaneous hazard rate can also be absorbed into the valuation rate r, and the valuation equations then proceed as before. Of course, when $\eta(x+s)$ is a more complicated function of time, there is no choice but to roll up our sleeves and compute the integrals in equations (7.26) and (7.27) by brute force.

Table 7.6. *$100,000 life insurance—Monthly premiums for 50-year-old by lapse rate*

Term	Assumed lapse rate (η)		
(years)	$\eta = 3\%$	$\eta = 5\%$	$\eta = 10\%$
5	$24.68	$24.57	$24.30
10	$31.24	$30.71	$29.45
20	$47.15	$44.20	$38.13

Note: $m = 86.34, b = 9.5, r = 6\%$.

When $m = 86.34$, $b = 9.5$, and $\lambda = 0$ under a $r = 6\%$ valuation rate, the net periodic premium for an $x = 50$-year-old is $\bar{A}_{45:20}/\bar{a}_{45:20} = 0.06257$ per year for a $1 death benefit. This translates into $625.70 per $100,000 death benefit, or $625.7/12 = \$52.14$ per month, which is consistent with the numbers in Table 7.5. If I now assume that, in each instant, $0.05dt$ of the surviving group lapse and stop paying their insurance premiums, then I can replace $r = 6\%$ by $r + \eta = 11\%$ in the valuation equation for GoMa mortality. This leads to $530.38 per year, which is $530.38/12 = \$44.20$ per month—a reduction of approximately 20% in the required insurance premium.

To recap, the lapse-adjusted annual premium for a τ-year term insurance policy is

$$\frac{e^{-(r+\eta)\tau}F_x(\tau) - r\bar{a}_{x:\tau} - e^{-(r+\eta)\tau} + 1}{\bar{a}_{x:\tau}}, \qquad (7.28)$$

where the valuation rate for all pension annuity calculations must be replaced by $r + \eta$ and the temporary pension annuity factor $\bar{a}_{x:\tau}$ can be computed via $\bar{a}_x - ({}_u\bar{a}_x)$, both of which are easily available in analytic format.

Table 7.6 provides a simple example of the impact of lapsation on pricing. Observe that when the term of the policy is 5 years, the impact of assuming a lapse rate is minimal; for instance, when the lapse rate is assumed to be 5%, the difference in monthly premiums is less than 30 cents. However, as the term of the policy is increased—even though the actual premium goes up due to the increased probability of death—the impact of lapsation is more pronounced. Assuming an $\eta = 10\%$ lapse rate reduces the monthly premium by almost $9 per month. In general, the impact of lapse assumption is proportionally much greater under longer-term policies. This is fully consistent with the actual quotes displayed in Table 7.1.

Once again, it is important to stress that our mathematical life is being made much easier by assuming a constant lapse rate η so that $H_x(t) = 1 - e^{-\eta t}$. In practice, the lapse rate curve $\eta(x+t)$ is more complicated and depends on economic conditions, but the qualitative impact remains.

7.16 Duration of Life Insurance

As in the case of pension annuities, we can compute the duration of the net single premium and net periodic premium by using the following relationship and the calculus chain rule:

$$\frac{\partial}{\partial r}\bar{A}_x = \frac{\partial}{\partial r}(1 - r\bar{a}_x) = -\left(r\frac{\partial}{\partial r}\bar{a}_x + \bar{a}_x\right). \qquad (7.29)$$

Recall from Section 6.11 that the duration of a pension annuity is defined as $D_{\text{annuity}} = -(\partial \bar{a}_x/\partial r)/\bar{a}_x$, which implies that we can substitute $-D_{\text{annuity}}(\bar{a}_x) = \partial \bar{a}_x/\partial r$ in the relevant part of equation (7.29). And, since the tradition is to define duration D as the "negative" of this expression scaled by $\bar{A}_x$, we are left with

$$D_{\text{insurance}} = -\frac{\frac{\partial}{\partial r}\bar{A}_x}{\bar{A}_x} = \frac{\bar{a}_x}{\bar{A}_x}(1 - rD_{\text{annuity}}). \qquad (7.30)$$

Another way to look at this is by explicitly recognizing that

$$\frac{\partial}{\partial r}\bar{A}_x = \int_0^\infty \frac{\partial}{\partial r}e^{-rt}f_x(t)\,dt = -\int_0^\infty te^{-rt}f_x(t)\,dt, \qquad (7.31)$$

since we are allowed to interchange the integral and derivative signs. We are left with a "mess" similar to that in the previous chapter when we attempted to compute duration for the annuity. Compare the numbers in Table 7.7 with those in Table 6.8 (for pension annuities) and notice how the duration values are all lower.

Let us do a simple example of duration for life insurance under an exponential remaining lifetime. In this case, since the NSP is

$$\bar{A}_x = 1 - \frac{r}{r+\lambda} = \frac{\lambda}{r+\lambda},$$

it is easy to take the derivative of this expression with respect to r and then scale by $\bar{A}_x$. This operation leaves us with

$$D_{\text{insurance}} := -\frac{\frac{\partial}{\partial r}\left(\frac{\lambda}{\lambda+r}\right)}{\frac{\lambda}{\lambda+r}} = \frac{1}{r+\lambda}. \qquad (7.32)$$

Table 7.7. *Duration value D (in years) of NSP*
for life insurance

| Initiated | Interest rate r | | |
at age x	4%	6%	8%
55	22.825	20.512	18.209
65	15.753	14.304	12.948
75	9.912	9.159	8.446
85	5.534	5.220	4.927

Note: GoMa mortality with $m = 86.34$ and $b = 9.5$.

Oddly enough, the duration of the NSP is equal to the pension annuity factor. If interest rates change by Δr, then the NSP will change by approximately $-\Delta r \times D_{\text{insurance}}$ percent. For example, when $r = 0.05$ and $\lambda = 1/20$, the NSP is $(1/20)/(0.05 + 1/20) = 0.5$, which is $50 per $100 of death benefit. But when $r = 0.055$ under the same $\lambda = 1/20$, the NSP is $(1/20)/(0.055 + 1/20) = 0.476$, which is $47.60 per $100 of death benefit. You pay less because the interest rate is higher. Now, at a value of $r = 0.05$, by (7.32) the duration of the NSP is $1/(0.05 + 1/20) = 10$ units. Thus, under the duration approximation developed in earlier chapters, $-\Delta r \times D = -(0.005)(10) = -0.05$ and hence the new (after the change in interest rate) value of the NSP should be $50 - $50(0.05) = 47.50, which is not far from the exact value of $47.60 per $100 of death benefit.

How does lapsation affect duration? Well, if we price the same exponential life net single premium under a constant η lapse rate then we can replace the interest rate r with $r + \eta$, which leads to an NSP of $\bar{A}_x^\eta = \lambda/(r + \eta + \lambda)$ and a lapse-adjusted duration of

$$D_{\text{insurance}}^\eta := -\frac{\frac{\partial}{\partial r}\left(\frac{\lambda}{\lambda+r+\eta}\right)}{\frac{\lambda}{\lambda+r+\eta}} = \frac{1}{r+\lambda+\eta}. \qquad (7.33)$$

Notice that the numerator is the same as the non–lapse-adjusted duration in (7.32) and that the denominator is larger by η units, which serves to reduce the duration of the net single premium. Intuitively, a change in interest rates will have a smaller impact on the NSP because a fraction of the population is assumed to lapse and thus does not receive the death benefit. Of course, the concept of lapsation for a single premium doesn't make much sense—why in the world would anyone lapse after they have paid the entire premium up front? To truly make use of this concept, we must divide the lapse-adjusted NSP $\bar{A}_x^\eta$ by the lapse-adjusted annuity factor $\bar{a}_x^\eta$ to arrive

Table 7.8. *Modeling a book of insurance policies over time*

Age	Lives	Deaths	In (premium)	Out (death)	Reserve
90	10,000	1,506	$18,926,119	$15,055,701	$4,840,781
91	8,494	1,408	$16,076,659	$14,084,133	$7,905,767
92	7,086	1,293	$13,411,079	$12,926,554	$9,483,230
93	5,793	1,162	$10,964,584	$11,615,650	$9,880,546
94	4,632	1,020	$8,766,193	$10,195,205	$9,407,572
95	3,612	872	$6,836,636	$8,717,902	$8,359,164
96	2,740	724	$5,186,675	$7,241,679	$6,998,671
97	2,016	582	$3,816,107	$5,824,892	$5,544,371
98	1,434	452	$2,713,681	$4,520,802	$4,160,649
99	982	337	$1,858,068	$3,372,178	$2,955,125
100	645	241	$1,219,846	$2,406,989	$1,982,037
101	404	164	$764,296	$1,636,063	$1,251,078
102	240	105	$454,653	$1,053,299	$739,886
103	135	64	$255,304	$638,467	$407,748
104	71	36	$134,467	$361,983	$208,032
105	35	19	$65,958	$190,553	$97,485
106	16	9	$29,894	$92,383	$41,526
107	7	4	$12,409	$40,880	$15,821
108	2	2	$4,672	$16,347	$5,197
109	1	1	$1,578	$5,842	$1,281
110	0	0	$473	$1,843	$0

Note: NPP $= \$1,893$, $r = 5\%$, benefit $= \$10,000$.

at a lapse-adjusted net periodic premium; in the exponential case the result is exactly λ, which is independent of interest rates and lapse rates. This, once again, is a feature of constant hazard rates. Call it the peculiarities of lobster premiums (cf. Section 3.8).

7.17 Following a Group of Policies

In this section I will explain why $\bar{A}_x / \bar{a}_x$ is a reasonable price to charge for life insurance—when the premiums are paid on an ongoing basis—by building a "model life office" in which premiums flow in, death benefits are paid out at the end of the year, administrative costs are ignored, and an insurance reserve builds over time to pay for the death benefits. See Table 7.8.

Obviously, 90 is not a typical age at which people purchase life insurance, but the point is to illustrate how the books of the business evolve. In the table I assume that all of the premiums come in at the beginning of the year and that all death benefits are paid out at the end of the year. This is a very rough approximation. Indeed, in a continuous-time model, the premiums of $\bar{A}_x/\bar{a}_x$ would be paid into the company on an ongoing basis—hence the company would not have access to all the funds from the beginning of the year—and the outflow benefits would be payable as death claims occur, which would also restrict the company's use of funds in the interim. All in all, this would imply that the company can charge less than our formula's $1,893 to cover all the claims.

Note that, in the table, the number of deaths were generated by a pure GoMa mortality of $m = 86.34$ and $b = 9.5$ with $\lambda = 0$. The probability of an x-year-old surviving one year is $\exp\{e^{(x-m)/b}(1 - e^{1/b})\}$, and the probability of death is 1 minus this number. The reserve grows or shrinks as a result of either receiving payments—number of lives at the start of the year times the premium of $1,893—or satisfying the claims: number of deaths times $10,000.

Observe how the reserve increases to roughly $10 million and then starts to decline. The rate we have used for asset growth is precisely $r = 5\%$, the valuation rate used to derive the $1,893 premium.

7.18 The Next Generation: Universal Life Insurance

One more type of life insurance that we should discuss in more detail is universal life insurance (UL), which is increasing in popularity and has some interesting features. In some sense, universal life insurance is the most general type of life insurance policy available. It combines elements of tax-sheltered savings, investment asset allocation, and adjustable human capital protection. At the "big picture" level, policyholders deposit a flexible (ongoing) payment into the policy and the insurance company withdraws a fraction of the account value to pay for the life insurance portion. There is no direct link between the amount the policyholder deposits into the account and the amount the insurance company uses for protection or insurance coverage. This is quite different from a term life insurance policy, where by definition the amount being sent to the insurance company is precisely the amount used to cover the insurance. With UL, the two aspects are detached. The policyholder might decide to deposit $10,000 into a UL policy that pays a $100,000 death benefit. In the first year, the insurance company would withdraw or use $500 from the account to pay for the mortality costs of the death benefit, but the remaining $9,500 would remain in the account. Think of it as a basic open-ended mutual fund linked to an insurance policy. The remaining $9,500 would grow in value (tax deferred) at money market rates; and if the variable universal life (VUL) policy is purchased, the remaining funds can be allocated by the policyholder amongst the universe of available investments (e.g., stocks, bonds, cash) and the account would then grow (or shrink) over time.

The policyholder can change the face value or death benefit at any time—as long as sufficient funds remain in the policy account to pay for the ongoing death benefit. As the policyholder ages, the amount withdrawn from the account to pay for the mortality cost would increase and in some cases might drive the savings portion of the account to zero. Note that in the absence of any "no-lapse" guarantees, an account that falls to zero is lapsed and coverage ends. At any time, the UL/VUL policyholder can surrender or withdraw the investment funds from the account, although there may be "surrender" charges as well as adverse tax implications.

From a mathematical point of view, the UL/VUL policy can be fully and best described by the way in which the market value M_t of this policy *changes* over time. In the simplest case of a policy offering a choice between only two investments—a risky stock fund and a risk-free bond fund—I will denote the change by

$$dM_t = (\theta_t \mu + (1 - \theta_t)r - f)M_t\,dt + \theta_t \sigma M_t\,dB_t + I_t\,dt - D_t\bar{\lambda}_t\,dt. \quad (7.34)$$

Here the policy is defined over the time interval $[0, T]$, M_t denotes the formal account value, and $M_t(1 - \xi_t)$ denotes the *cash surrender value* after all penalties are paid. The applied deferred surrender charge ξ_t is based on a curve that starts at ξ_0 and declines toward zero over time.

I will address each part of equation (7.34) in order. First, the asset allocation "vector" θ_t denotes the portion of the account value that is invested in risky equity and is expected to earn μ per annum; $1 - \theta_t$ denotes the portion allocated to the risk-free rate r. Next, the asset-based fee is denoted by f and is paid continuously in time. For instance, each year the UL account might be charged $f = 50$ basis points for investment management fees. The term I_t denotes the insurance deposit made by the policyholder at time t. This number is not fixed or forced in advance; rather, it is up to the policyholder to decide how much should be placed in the account at any given time. The only requirement is that there be enough to pay for the insurance coverage.

The death benefit that is paid if death occurs and time t is represented by D_t, and $\bar{\lambda}_t$ is the mortality cost, which is multiplied by the death benefit D_t and is withdrawn from the account on an ongoing basis. Note that $\bar{\lambda}_t$ need not necessarily be the instantaneous force of mortality at time t, which is why a bar appears over the hazard rate to distinguish the two. For example, the policyholder might want to pay a fixed premium for the next 10 years, in which case $\bar{\lambda}_t = (\bar{A}_{x:\overline{10}})/(\bar{a}_{x:\overline{10}})$ during the time period $t = 0, \ldots, 10$. Then, at the end of the 10 years, the policyholder can decide whether to reduce the death benefit D_t or to pay for the insurance using the instantaneous cost $\bar{\lambda}_t = \lambda_t$.

7.19 Further Reading

The material presented in this chapter is fairly basic from the standpoint of actuarial mathematics. Thus, the references cited in earlier chapters on pension annuities and mortality modeling are relevant here as well.

For a practitioner's overview of the life insurance industry, I suggest reading Baldwin (2002). As for the issue of how much life insurance a person needs—as well as the interaction of this need with other "moving parts" in one's portfolio—this is a long-standing question in the field of insurance economics, starting with Yaari (1965) and Fischer (1973). Both papers are heavily cited classics in the (personal) insurance economics literature. However, I will postpone (to Chapter 9) a more in-depth discussion regarding the demand for insurance and the microeconomic foundations of human capital protection. In this chapter, I have tried to focus exclusively on the actuarial valuation of life insurance as opposed to the analysis of *why* people would buy these instruments. See Chen and colleagues (2006) for a theory that ties together the optimal asset allocation and life insurance portfolio over the human life cycle.

The tax arbitrage strategy that involves life insurance and pension annuities is described and analyzed in greater detail in Charupat and Milevsky (2001). A related paper by Philipson and Becker (1998) uses a GoMa model for mortality to price life insurance policies and then "inverts" the equation to solve for the implied hazard rates using actual market prices and insurance quotes.

7.20 Notation

$(_u\bar{A}_{x:\tau})$—net single premium for a life insurance policy sold to an individual at age x, where u denotes the deferral period and τ denotes the term of temporary coverage

7.21 Problems

PROBLEM 7.1. Confirm the duration numbers for the life annuity NSP by integrating the relevant expression.

PROBLEM 7.2. Recall that $\bar{A}_{x:\tau}$ denotes the value of life insurance (NSP) that covers you for the next τ years. Derive an expression for $\lim_{\tau \to 0} \bar{A}_{x:\tau}$, but don't get carried away with fancy math. Think about what this means.

PROBLEM 7.3. A "critical illness" insurance policy pays a fixed "illness benefit" if the insured individual is afflicted with any one of a list of insured illnesses during the term of the insurance. For example, if the insured is diagnosed with cancer, has a stroke, or suffers a heart attack within 10 years, the insurance company will pay a lump sum of $100,000 in benefits. A recent innovation in this market has been a return-of-premium clause, which stipulates that—at maturity of the insurance term or upon death—if the insured did not claim any benefits then the sum of the premiums will be returned. For example, if the annual premiums are $5,000 and if the insured individual died after 5 years of paying premiums without having claimed any benefits, then the named beneficiary will receive $25,000 back from the insurance company. Likewise, if the insured dies after 8 years of paying premiums (but without having claimed any benefits) then the beneficiary will receive $40,000 under this "return of premium" guarantee. Finally, if the insured does not file a claim for 15 years and is still alive, then the insurance company will refund the entire $75,000. Please devise a model to price this insurance policy. Assume that the instantaneous force of mortality (IFM) curve satisfies the GoMa parameters $m = 86.34$, $b = 9.5$, and $\lambda = 0$, but assume that the hazard rate for covered illnesses is constant at a rate of $\eta = 0.03$ per year. Also, given a valuation rate of $r = 5\%$, compute the "value" of this critical illness insurance policy (assuming an illness benefit of $100,000).

EIGHT

Models of DB vs. DC Pensions

8.1 A Choice of Pension Plans

Would you like to have a pension that promised to pay you 60%–70% of your final salary for the entire duration of your retirement? Or would you rather be part of a pension arrangement that places 6% of your salary each year in a savings account and then lets you do whatever you want with the accumulated funds when you retire? This is the essence of the *defined bene- fit* (DB) versus *defined contribution* (DC) dilemma facing many individuals and corporations. Figure 8.1 provides a diagram of the two basic pension extremes and the various subcategories within the DB and DC world. On the leftmost side, the DB pension agreement—where the future benefit is defined—can be structured as an unfunded pay-as-you-go (PAYGO) plan in which current workers pay the pensions (via payroll and employment taxes) of retirees. In contrast, a funded DB plan is one in which funds are con- tributed and accumulated over time to pay the benefits of retirees. Whether the plan is fully funded, overfunded, underfunded, or PAYGO, there is a well-defined formula that links the actual retirement benefits to the number of years of work. In most cases, the financial risk (investment and longevity risk) is in the hands of the plan sponsor. They must make sure that, what- ever they do with the funds, there is enough to pay pensions to retirees. And, barring any default on their obligation, they can be "on the hook" for a very long time.

A defined contribution plan does not explicitly promise a level of benefits during retirement but instead can be viewed as a regular savings account in which employers and sometimes employees contribute on a regular basis. For example, under certain plans the employer fully or partially matches employee contributions. Regardless of the plan design, only the contri- bution payments are defined, relieving the sponsor of the investment and

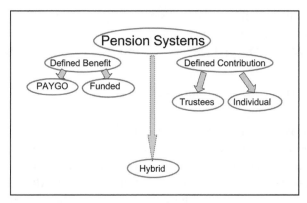

Figure 8.1

longevity risks. These accumulations grow over time at some (random) rate of return. Whatever these funds grow to at the time of retirement will determine the amount of the pension. The investments and portfolio allocations within DC plans can be managed by professional trustees, or they can be managed by the individuals themselves.

Finally, hybrid pensions combine aspects of both DB and DC plans. A hybrid plan can, for example, guarantee a floor or minimal pension in retirement using a DB-type formula and then supplement this pension using a DC-type formula that depends on realized investment performance.

Most individuals who have a formal pension plan through work or from government-provided plans are not allowed to choose their type of pension contract. Some employers offer DC plans, while others offer DB plans or some hybrid combination. However, in a growing number of recent cases either DB plans are closed to new entrants, or employees who are currently in one type of pension plan are allowed to switch to the other type under predetermined parameters for the "exchange rate" between the two plans. One of the largest such offers to switch was made to each of the 600,000 employees of the State of Florida a few years ago. This trend seems to be gaining momentum in other states and private sector companies. Either way, it is important to develop an analytic framework for comparing and contrasting the two extreme pension arrangements.

8.2 The Core of Defined Contribution Pensions

To understand the "core" of the difference between these two plans, I will start at the very end by displaying the two main equations for DC and DB pension plans.

When you retire from a DC pension—at age x or after T years of employment and participation in the plan—the annual retirement income (i.e. pension) you are entitled to is specified by the following formula:

$$[\text{DC pension income}] := \frac{\int_0^T c(s)e^{g(s)(T-s)}w(s)\,ds}{\bar{a}_x},\qquad(8.1)$$

where $c(s)$ is the contribution rate, $g(s)$ the realized investment growth rate, and $w(s)$ the wage or salary—all of which are parameterized by time s. Finally, $\bar{a}_x$ is the familiar pension annuity factor that converts a lump sum in the numerator into a periodic income flow. It is important to note that (8.1) is backward looking and meant to be used at retirement for computing a retirement income benefit under the pension plan. Heuristically, you meet with the "plan" or human resource administrator one instant prior to retirement, when you are just about to turn x years old. Their job is then to integrate the sum of the contributions $c(s)w(s)$ against the credit investment rate $g(s)$ from initial time $s = 0$ to retirement time $s = T$. The annual income is expressed in year-T dollars.

Allow me to walk through a basic example so that you can develop some intuition. Assume that you are just about to turn $x = 65$ years old, the point at which you will be retiring from the labor force and will start to draw a pension. You have been working for the same company for the last $T = 30$ years and have been earning a constant $w(s) = \$50,000$ each year. Note that if there has been any price or wage inflation during the last 30 years, which likely there was, then your salary has been falling in real (inflation-adjusted) terms. Assume that each year you and/or your employer contributed 7% of your salary to a defined contribution pension fund and that this fund earned $g(s) = 10\%$ during each of the 30 years. I know that most of this is quite unrealistic, but bear with me for a moment. In this case, the funds in your DC account will have accumulated to

$$0.07 \int_0^{30} 50000 e^{(0.10)(30-s)}\,ds = 667994 \qquad(8.2)$$

dollars at retirement. Equation (8.2) "adds up" the 7% pension contribution plus investment gains for the entire 30-year period. Finally, the $667,994 is divided by the $\bar{a}_{65} = 11.395$ pension annuity factor to yield a retirement income of $58,622 per year. The pension annuity factor was obtained by using our favorite $m = 86.34$, $b = 9.5$, and $r = 5\%$ parameters. Observe that this is a very nice pension. Your salary was $50,000 per year, which means that your pension has replaced $\$58,622/\$50,000 = 117\%$ of your pre-retirement income. Remember, though, that the $58,622 is in nominal terms, which means that inflation will erode its purchasing power as you move through your retirement years. The same type of calculation can be done with nonconstant values of $c(s)$, which (for example) can be 7% when you are relatively junior and 12% as you move up through the ranks. Or, the same calculation can be done under a time-varying investment rate $g(s)$ or with time-varying wages. In the end, it will all come down to an integral similar to that in (8.1).

A few caveats are in order. First, not all DC pension plans provide the benefit in the form of a pension annuity. Many plans offer their pension-aries only a lump sum (the numerator of equation (8.1)) and then supply the phone number of a "decent" insurance company that can actually provide the pension annuity. It is up to the individual to buy the pension annuity and convert their lump sum—for example, $667,994—into a true retirement income. As you can imagine, many retirees, when faced with a lump sum and the option to annuitize, choose not to purchase the pension annuity. Instead, they manage the money themselves and draw down their account to support their standard of living. When retirees can "take the money and run," in some jurisdictions there are regulatory guidelines on how much the retiree can spend each year—the government doesn't want them gambling their money away—and what they can invest in.

Another point worth emphasizing is inflation. There are a few DC (as well as DB) pension plans that provide a real, inflation-adjusted pension annuity instead of a nominal pension annuity. Other plans offer a nominal annuity that increases by a fixed and predetermined rate each year. Either way, the mathematics of equation (8.1) are identical except that the valuation rate is modified to account for the inflation protection. For instance, in the previous example I used an $r = 5\%$ nominal valuation rate to "value" the pension annuity. However, if the pension annuity will make payments in inflation-adjusted terms, then I would use a real valuation rate to obtain the annuity factor. Suppose the real interest rate in the economy is $r = 2.5\%$; then I would obtain a pension annuity factor of $\bar{a}_{65} = 14.362$ instead of $\bar{a}_{65} = 11.395$. This higher number would be used in the denominator of (8.1) and would result in an initial retirement income of $667,994/14.362 = $46,511$ per year. Initially this might appear much worse than the $58,622 resulting from the $r = 5\%$ valuation rate. However, on an actuarial basis they are equivalent! This is because the $46,511 is in real terms while the $58,622 is in nominal terms. Over time, the buying power of the $58,622 pension will decline as inflation erodes its purchasing value, while the buying power of the $46,511 will remain exactly the same since it will increase every year to match changes in the Consumer Price Index (CPI). Of course, this assumes that the CPI is an appropriate measure for retiree inflation (this was discussed in Chapter 6). The bottom line is that you can receive your retirement income pension in a variety of formats depending on your need and preferences.

The key insight from the DC side of the story is that there are no guarantees concerning what the income will be or what the value of the denominator in (8.1) will be come retirement time. The only guarantee within a DC plan is the contribution rate $c(s)$ of funds being poured into your retirement savings (pension) account. If after 30 years the realized value of $g(s)$ is low then you will have less retirement income; it's as simple as that. The investment risk is in your hands. Of course, the flip side is that if you are a good investor (or just plain lucky) and the realized return $g(s)$ is high, then your pension will be much larger. Stepping back to time 0—as opposed to the age and time of retirement—your pension income is a random variable that can be expressed as

$$\frac{\int_0^T c(s)\exp\{B^{(v,\sigma)}_{(T-s)}\}w(s)\,ds}{\bar{a}_x}. \tag{8.3}$$

Here $B_t^{(v,\sigma)}$ is the familiar Brownian motion term (introduced in Chapter 5) representing the total return that will have been earned on the contributions made at time s, and $w(s)$ denotes the random and unpredictable wage or salary over the T years of work. In fact, some might argue that even the denominator in equation (8.3) should be viewed as stochastic since interest rates and perhaps even GoMa parameters are unknown so far in advance of retirement. This is a legitimate point, and we will return to the "stochasticity" of annuity factors in Chapter 10.

I would urge you to think carefully about each of the terms within (8.3) and about how each contributes to the overall pension equation. At first glance, it might seem strange to integrate $B^{(v,\sigma)}_{(T-s)}$ in the exponent of the integrand. But after thinking about this for a while you should realize that, when s is very small, the savings component will be growing over an entire path of 30 years, for example. However, as s gets larger, the path over which we integrate gets smaller (since the contribution is made later), which is why only the reduced portion is used.

In sum, I have just laid down the mathematical foundation of a DC pension plan formula. The main ingredients are the contribution rate $c(s)$, the wage process $w(s)$, and the earnings path $g(s)$. At retirement, these elements are all known with certainty, but before this date—when market returns are unknown—all we have is a random variable for the pension.

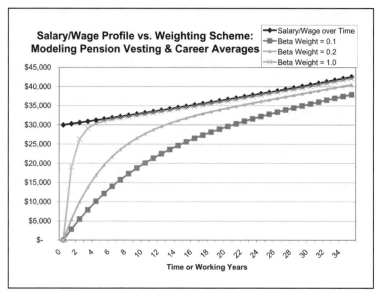

Figure 8.2

8.3 The Core of Defined Benefit Pensions

In contrast to the DC pension formula, the DB formula focuses on and provides a guarantee of actual retirement income. In the DB case, there is no numerator or denominator but rather a direct formula:

$$[\text{DB pension income}] := \alpha T \beta \int_0^T e^{-\beta(T-s)} w(s)\, ds, \qquad (8.4)$$

which I will abbreviate as

$$[\text{DB pension income}] := \alpha T \omega(T). \qquad (8.5)$$

Here α is the pension benefit accrual rate, and the new "salary weighting function" is defined by

$$\omega(T) = \beta \int_0^T e^{-\beta(T-s)} w(s)\, ds, \qquad (8.6)$$

which allows the company some flexibility in linking pensions to your average salary.

Once again we have a number of moving parts, so I will explain each term individually. Figure 8.2 provides a graphical illustration of the salary weighting function. The greater the value of β, which is determined by the company, the more weight is placed on recent or final wages versus the overall path of wages. For example, when $\beta = 0.1$, the value of the $\omega(t)$ function starts quite low and then slowly increases over time as the wage increases. However, when $\beta = 1$ (and in theory it can go as high as infinity), the $\omega(t)$ function quickly moves to a number that is close to $w(t)$. In some sense, $\omega(t)$ and $w(t)$ are the same after a while.

The point in all of this is to capture a stylized feature of most DB pension plans: namely, that retirement income benefits are computed by multiplying the number of years of credit service T by the accrual factor α and then by the "average" salary over the working period. Some companies use an actual average of the entire T-year period, while others use an average of the last few years or perhaps even the "best earning" years. The purpose of the function $\omega(T)$ was to capture the diversity of averaging methods in a parsimonious and easy-to-use manner.

In fact, when the function for salary or wages satisfies a simple exponential growth equation,

$$w(t) = we^{kt} \tag{8.7}$$

(where k is an annual growth rate), then the salary weighting function defined in equation (8.6) can be integrated explicitly to yield

$$\omega(T) = \frac{\beta w}{\beta + k}(e^{kT} - e^{-\beta T}). \tag{8.8}$$

When $k = 0$ (a flat wage profile) the function collapses to $w(1 - e^{-\beta T})$, which rapidly converges to the salary value itself as $e^{-\beta T}$ becomes very small.

So, for example, let $w = \$30,000$ and suppose it grows each year by $k = 1\%$. Then, for $\beta = 0.1$, equation (8.8) leads to a value of $\omega(30) = \$35,456$; when $\beta = 0.2$ we have $\omega(30) = \$38,497$; and if $\beta = 1$ then $\omega(30) = \$40,095$, which is extremely close to $30000e^{(0.01)(30)} = \$40,496$, the actual salary at retirement. And, if the DB pension stipulates an accrual rate of $\alpha = 1\%$ for each year of employment, then at retirement the retiree will be entitled to a nominal pension income of $(30)(0.01)(35456) = \$10,637$ under a $\beta = 0.1$ weighting, $(30)(0.01)(38497) = \$11,549$ under a $\beta = 0.2$ weighting, and $(30)(0.01)(40095) = \$12,028$ under a $\beta = 1.0$ weighting.

Thus, we have finally reached the point where meaningful comparisons can be made between DB and DC plan benefits.

Table 8.1 displays a range of retirement income values for a DC pension plan. Once again, we imagine someone right before retirement and calculate the amounts shown based on the realized investment return g and the periodic contribution rate c. All values are in nominal terms. Thus, with

Table 8.1. *DC pension retirement income*

DC rate of contribution	Assumed investment returns		
	$g = 3\%$	$g = 5\%$	$g = 7\%$
$c = 4\%$	$5,105	$7,203	$10,452
$c = 6\%$	$7,658	$10,805	$15,678
$c = 8\%$	$10,210	$14,407	$20,904
$c = 10\%$	$12,763	$18,009	$26,130
$c = 12\%$	$15,315	$21,610	$31,356

Notes: $m = 86.34$, $b = 9.5$, $\lambda = 0$, $r = 3.5\%$. Initial salary of $30,000, $T = 30$ years of work, and $k = 1\%$ salary growth yielding final salary of $40,496.

Table 8.2. *DC pension: Income replacement rate*

DC rate of contribution	Assumed investment returns		
	$g = 3\%$	$g = 5\%$	$g = 7\%$
$c = 4\%$	12.6%	17.8%	25.8%
$c = 6\%$	18.9%	26.7%	38.7%
$c = 8\%$	25.2%	35.6%	51.6%
$c = 10\%$	31.5%	44.5%	64.5%
$c = 12\%$	37.8%	53.4%	77.4%

Note: See notes to Table 8.1.

an initial salary of $w = \$30,000$ and a salary growth rate of $k = 1\%$, the final salary at the end of $T = 30$ years of work is $w(30) = \$40,496$. Under these parameters, the retirement income is obtained by dividing the retirement value of the account by the pension annuity factor, which in this case is $\bar{a}_{65} = 13.043$ under an $r = 3.5\%$ valuation rate. For example, if $c = 10\%$ of salary is contributed to the account—either by the employer or the employee—and if these contributions are invested and grow at $g = 7\%$ per annum (for 30 years), then the retirement income will be $26,130 per year. This, again, is in nominal terms. Lower contribution rates and lower investment returns result in a lower pension. As I have mentioned many times, in reality the value of g will not be known until retirement. This places the risk squarely in the hands of the pensioners.

Alternatively, the same information can be displayed by converting the numbers in Table 8.1 to replacement rates; to do this we divide the retirement income by the final wage—see Table 8.2, where each entry is divided by the $40,496. Obviously, the larger the replacement rate, the more income one has in retirement. In this example, if investment returns (set by

Table 8.3. *DB pension retirement income*

DB rate of accrual	Salary weighting scheme		
	$\beta = 0.1$, average of $35,457	$\beta = 0.2$, average of $38,497	$\beta = 1$, average of $40,095
$\alpha = 1.00\%$	$10,637	$11,549	$12,028
$\alpha = 1.25\%$	$13,296	$14,436	$15,036
$\alpha = 1.50\%$	$15,955	$17,323	$18,043
$\alpha = 1.75\%$	$18,615	$20,211	$21,050
$\alpha = 2.50\%$	$26,592	$28,872	$30,071

Notes: All numbers are in nominal terms. Initial salary of $30,000, $T = 30$ years of work, and $k = 1\%$ salary growth yielding final salary of $40,496.

the capital market) are $g = 7\%$ and if the contribution rate (set by the plan documents) is 12%, then the replacement rate will be 77.4% of the final pre-retirement income. This number is obtained by dividing $31,356 by $40,496, which was the final salary in the year prior to retirement.

Replacement rates are a good segue into the parallel analysis of DB plans, since the product of working years and accrual rates lends itself naturally to a replacement rate. For example, if $T = 30$ years and the accrual rate is $\alpha = 1.75\%$, then $(0.0175)(30) = 52.5\%$; the formula specifies a replacement rate of 52.5% of the weighted average salary, denoted by $\omega(30)$.

The case of a DB pension is illustrated in Table 8.3. For example, under a $\beta = 1$ weighting scheme and an $\alpha = 1.75\%$ accrual rate, the retirement pension income will be $21,050 per year of retirement. As intuition should dictate, the lower the value of β and the lower the value of α, the lower the retirement pension income. Table 8.4 converts these numbers to replacement ratios like those shown for DC plans in Table 8.2. Note that the replacement rate is very close to αT for high values of β, where $T = 30$ years in all cases.

In sum, Tables 8.1–8.4 provide a range of perspectives on the retirement income one may be entitled to under a DB or DC pension. Without knowledge of future investment returns and wages, it is impossible to argue that one plan is inherently better or worse than the other.

8.4 What Is the Value of a DB Pension Promise?

Most of the previous discussion centered on retirement income and what you are entitled to once retired. I would like to step back from retirement

Table 8.4. *DB pension: Income replacement rate*

DB rate of accrual	Salary weighting scheme		
	$\beta = 0.1$, average of $35,457	$\beta = 0.2$, average of $38,497	$\beta = 1$, average of $40,095
$\alpha = 1.00\%$	26.3%	28.5%	29.7%
$\alpha = 1.25\%$	32.8%	35.6%	37.1%
$\alpha = 1.50\%$	39.4%	42.7%	44.5%
$\alpha = 1.75\%$	46.0%	49.9%	52.0%
$\alpha = 2.50\%$	65.6%	71.3%	74.3%

Note: See notes to Table 8.3.

by a few years. Imagine that you are y years old and have worked for τ years at your current job that offers a defined benefit pension plan, where $0 < \tau \leq T$. The DB plan allows you to retire at age x (e.g., 65 years of age) so that $x - y = T - \tau$ by definition.

I will use Υ to denote the current value or worth of what you are entitled to at retirement age x, and there are three possible ways to measure this quantity. The first measure of the firm's pension obligation to their employees is called the retirement benefit obligation (RBO), the second is the projected benefit obligation (PBO), and the third is the accumulated benefit obligation (ABO). Here is the formal definition of all three quantities:

$$\Upsilon_y^{\text{RBO}} = e^{-r(x-y)}\alpha T\omega(T)\bar{a}_x, \tag{8.9}$$

$$\Upsilon_y^{\text{PBO}} = e^{-r(x-y)}\alpha \tau \omega(T)\bar{a}_x, \tag{8.10}$$

$$\Upsilon_y^{\text{ABO}} = e^{-r(x-y)}\alpha \tau \omega(\tau)\bar{a}_x. \tag{8.11}$$

Before I get into the similarities and differences between these three possible measures, notice that once you have worked at the company for the full T years and you are x years old, then all three expressions collapse to the simple and intuitive $\alpha T\omega(T)\bar{a}_x$. This is your annual DB retirement income entitlement—years of service multiplied by the accrual factor multiplied by the final salary weight—multiplied by the pension annuity factor. This is a lump-sum value at retirement.

Prior to retirement, however, there are three possible ways to characterize the firm's obligation or commitment to you. The RBO discounts the lump-sum value by a valuation rate of r for $x - y$ years to arrive at an age-y value (assuming you will be entitled to your full pension benefits). In contrast, the ABO takes a more pragmatic view of the relationship between you

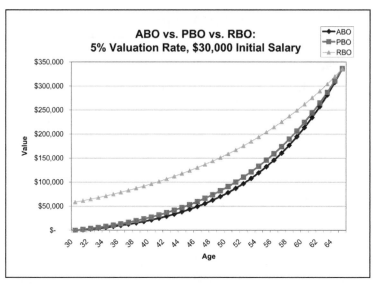

Figure 8.3

and your employer. The ABO calculation counts the number of years τ you have already worked and multiplies by the salary average $\omega(\tau)$ to that date and then assumes that you are fired or terminated immediately. In this case you will have earned only $\alpha\tau\omega(\tau)$ in retirement income, which leads to a lump-sum value at retirement of $\alpha\tau\omega(\tau)\bar{a}_x$; discounted to age y, this is precisely $\Upsilon_y^{\text{ABO}} = e^{-r(x-y)}\alpha\tau\omega(\tau)\bar{a}_x$. In contrast to a deferred annuity, the employee would not have to "survive to retirement" in order to receive the pension benefit. The computed value of the benefit would be available to your beneficiary if something happens between age y and retirement age x.

Now, some of you might rightfully argue that the ABO is a biased or inaccurate measure of what the employee's DB pension promise is worth, since they are not in fact being terminated at the time of the valuation. Indeed, they may end up working for the full T years until age x, which then entitles them to a total retirement pension of $\alpha T\omega(T)$ per year. This is why we have a third measure of pension value, the projected benefit obligation. The PBO takes a compromise view. At age y, which is time $T - \tau$, the employee has indeed worked only for τ years but is projected to have a salary weight of $\omega(T)$ at retirement. This middle view implies that as an employee you have earned $\alpha\tau$ worth of the total αT of the $\alpha T\omega(T)$ you receive in retirement.

Figure 8.3 provides a graphical illustration of the relationship between the three possible measures of the value of the pension promise at age y.

Table 8.5. *Current value of sample retirement pension by valuation rate and by type of benefit obligation*

Valuation rate	ABO	PBO	RBO	$\bar{a}_{65}$
$r = 5\%$	\$43,399	\$53,008	\$123,685	11.394
$r = 7\%$	\$24,686	\$30,152	\$70,355	9.669
$r = 9\%$	\$14,271	\$17,431	\$40,672	8.339

Notes: $m = 86.34$, $b = 9.5$, $k = 1\%$; $\alpha = 2\%$, $\beta = 1$. Assumes 45-year-old worker with 15 years of pension service, earning \$34,855 annually and planning to retire at age 65.

The underlying parameters for this particular figure are the standard $m = 86.34$ and $b = 9.5$, which lead to the pension annuity factor of $\bar{a}_{65} = 11.3949$ at retirement. The initial salary of $w = \$30,000$ grows by $k = 1\%$ each year until it reaches $w(35) = \$42,572$ at age $x = 65$. The salary weighting function under a $\beta = 1$ leads to $\omega(35) = \$42,151$. Finally, $\alpha = 2\%$ per each year of credited service in the DB plan. This leads to $(0.02)(35)(42151)(11.3949) = \$336,214$, the lump-sum value at retirement. Using our notation, $\Upsilon_{65} = \$336,214$ for the RBO, PBO, and ABO. This is the point (age) at which the three curves meet.

As the current age y declines, all three curves go down in value, which is to be expected under the "algebraic rules" for present value calculations. Notice that the PBO and ABO are relatively close to each other. The RBO curve lies well above the other two and starts off at a much higher level. On the first day of employment—for example, at age $y = 35$—the RBO value immediately assumes 35 years of work in the discounted value calculation. Clearly, this is an overly optimistic view of the employment contract. In contrast, the ABO is often called a "wind-up" measure of the pension obligation. If a DB pension plan were terminated, the ABO would be the best estimate of what it would cost to purchase pension annuities to fulfill this obligation. It captures what the employee "owns."

The distinction between the ABO, PBO, and RBO measures is critical to understanding some of the accounting issues that arise. To get a better sense of the interaction between the values, Table 8.5 lists some numerical examples. The table assumes a 45-year-old employee who has credited service for $\tau = 15$ years in a DB pension plan that provides a retirement income benefit of $\alpha = 2\%$ times the final salary weight for each year of service. The salary weighting function $\omega(T)$ uses $\beta = 1$ (which, recall, is heavily tilted toward the final salary $w(T)$). In Table 8.5, the salary is assumed to increase by $k = 1\%$ each year, which will take it from the current $w(15) =$ $34,855 to $w(35) =$ $42,572 at retirement.

Observe the impact of the valuation rate r on the ABO, PBO, and RBO as a result of the $e^{-r(x-y)}$ in equations (8.9), (8.10), and (8.11), respectively. The right-most column of the table displays the pension annuity factor under the various valuation rate assumptions of 5%, 7%, and 9%. It should come as no surprise that $\bar{a}_{65}$ also declines as the valuation rate r increases.

For example, under an $r = 9\%$ valuation rate, the accumulated benefit obligation after 15 years of work is a mere $14,271 at age 45. In contrast, if the valuation rate is reduced to $r = 5\%$ then the RBO is $123,685, which is almost ten times more.

So what is the pension promise really worth? The truth is that I don't have an answer. It is not about mathematics anymore. It comes down to accounting, economics, and even legal and ethical issues. Can the employer terminate any employee at any time and prevent them from accruing any more pension credits? In that case, the ABO might be the most appropriate measure of what a pension is worth. On the other hand, if the labor relationship is more than just a "spot market" transaction and if there are implicit contracts between the employer and the employee, then perhaps the PBO or even the RBO is a better measure of pension value.

8.5 Pension Funding and Accounting

A related and equally vexing question is how an employer should "fund" the DB pension. In a DC plan, the answer is trivially obvious. The funding is precisely the contribution or cash flow $c(s)w(s)$ that must be added to the pension fund account each year. In the case of a DB plan, there is no natural economic obligation to "invest" or "fund" a portion of the ABO, PBO, or RBO while the employee is still working. In theory the company could wait until the employee retires and then pay the retirement pension of $\alpha T\omega(T)$ from corporate revenues. This would be the ultimate unfunded DB pension plan. If you think about it, this would save the company a large sum of money today because pension contributions for active employees—as opposed to retired employees—can add up to billions of dollars per year. Why not put it off until the payment must be made?

In practice the pension industry is heavily regulated, and most private sector companies cannot "wait and worry" to pay the pension once the employee retires. In the United States, for example, there is a substantial body of law that governs exactly how pensions must be funded. The companies

Table 8.6. *Change in value (from age 45 to 46) of sample retirement pension by valuation rate and by type of benefit obligation*

Valuation rate	ΔABO	ΔPBO	ΔRBO
$r = 5\%$	$5,756	$6,433	$6,341
$r = 7\%$	$3,839	$4,342	$5,101
$r = 9\%$	$2,552	$2,913	$3,830

Note: $m = 86.34$, $b = 9.5$, $k = 1\%$; $\alpha = 2\%$, $\beta = 1$.

Table 8.7. *Change in pension value at various ages assuming $r = 5\%$ valuation rate*

Age y at retirement	ΔABO	ΔPBO	ΔRBO
35	$2,012	$2,562	$3,659
45	$5,252	$5,947	$6,032
55	$12,640	$12,646	$9,945
65	$28,626	$25,535	$16,397

Notes: $m = 86.34$, $b = 9.5$, $k = 1\%$; $\alpha = 2\%$, $\beta = 1$. Assumes 30-year-old worker with starting salary of $30,000.

have no choice and they must set aside—today—a sum of money in a pension fund even though you will not be retiring for another 10, 20, or even 30 years. These funds are contributed to a stand-alone legal entity called the pension plan, and the money actually grows tax deferred, within limits, until the funds are needed to pay pensions.

This is exactly where the ABO and PBO come into play. They are more than a theoretical curiosity; they determine how much must be contributed to these funds. Table 8.6 provides us with a first step in understanding pension funding, as it illustrates how the ABO, PBO, and RBO change over time. More specifically, it displays the change (also known as "Delta") in the ABO, PBO, and RBO after one additional year of work. For example, under an $r = 5\%$ valuation rate, the ABO will increase from $43,399 at age $y = 45$ to $49,155, which is an increase of ΔABO = $5,756. The change in the PBO would be $6,433, and the change in the RBO would be $6,341.

Table 8.7 provides a different perspective on the change. It picks one particular valuation rate, $r = 5\%$, and examines the impact of age alone on the

Table 8.8. *Change in PBO from prior year*

Age y at valuation	Salary	Costs			Service (% of salary)
		Interest	+ Service	= ΔPBO	
35	$31,538	$418	$2,143	$2,562	6.80%
45	$34,855	$2,413	$3,534	$5,947	10.14%
55	$38,521	$6,820	$5,826	$12,646	15.13%
65	$42,572	$15,929	$9,606	$25,535	22.56%

Note: $r = 5\%, k = 1\%; \alpha = 2\%, \beta = 1.$

Table 8.9. *Change in ABO from prior year*

Age y at valuation	Salary	Costs			Service (% of salary)
		Interest	+ Service	= ΔABO	
35	$31,538	$301	$1,711	$2,012	5.42%
45	$34,855	$1,956	$3,296	$5,252	9.46%
55	$38,521	$6,109	$6,531	$12,640	16.95%
65	$42,572	$15,770	$12,856	$28,626	30.20%

Note: $r = 5\%, k = 1\%; \alpha = 2\%, \beta = 1.$

change in the ABO, PBO, and RBO. For example, between the ages of $y = 34$ and $y = 35$, the ABO increases by $2,012. Between age $y = 44$ and $y = 45$ the ABO increases by $5,252, and from age $y = 64$ to age $y = 65$ the ABO increases by $28,626. The intuition for these changes comes directly from Figure 8.3. The ABO, PBO, and RBO increase with time. The rate at which the values increase is time dependent, and this rate is precisely what is being measured in Table 8.7.

Table 8.8 and Table 8.9 take a closer look at the changes in the PBO and ABO, decomposing the ΔABO and ΔPBO in two components. The first part is the *interest* component or cost, and the second part is the *service* component or cost. The interest cost is the change in ABO or PBO that is attributable to one more year of the time value of money. Mathematically, if last period's benefit obligation is denoted by Υ_t, then the interest component of next period's obligation is $\Upsilon_t r \, dt$. In contrast, the service component is the portion of the change that is due to an increase in service.

For example, from age $y = 34$ to age $y = 35$, the ABO increases by $2,012. Of this sum, $301 is attributed to the (valuation) interest of 5% on last year's $5,876 ABO, and the remaining $1,711 service component comes from the additional year in the ABO calculation; in other words, it is from using $\tau = 5$ instead of $\tau = 4$ in the ABO formula. Here is another way to think about it. If the managers of the pension fund had set aside exactly \$5,876 when the employee was $y = 34$ years old and if this sum of money had grown by the valuation rate of $r = 5\%$ during the next year, then the managers need only contribute or fund \$1,711 in the subsequent year in order to bring the assets of the fund to the new required ABO level of \$7,888. The service component or cost of \$1,711 is equal to 5.42% of the 35-year-old's salary of \$31,538. By age $y = 55$, the service component of the change in the ABO has now increased to about 17% of the salary. At age $y = 65$, the service component is 30% of the salary.

Let me say this once again to reiterate how central it is to our main story. If a DB pension fund is 100% funded to either the PBO or ABO level and if the fund's assets earn the valuation rate during the subsequent year, then the managers will only have to "add" the service cost to the fund to bring the value up to the new ABO or PBO. I remain agnostic as to whether companies "should" fund up to the ABO or PBO. Note how the service component of the PBO is a larger fraction of the salary—compared to the service component of the ABO—early on in the life cycle. But, as time goes on, the service component of the ABO becomes higher than the PBO's as a percentage of salary.

Formally speaking, a pension *funding method* describes the manner under which defined benefit pension sponsors contribute to the pension fund over time so that sufficient reserves are available upon the employees' retirement. As I mentioned, in theory there are infinitely many ways in which to fund a pension. The sponsors could wait until one instant prior to the employee's retirement and then deposit or contribute $\bar{a}_x$ times the pension income to the plan. Alternatively, they could contribute the entire RBO right away and then invest the funds at the valuation rate until it grows to the required $\bar{a}_x \times [\text{pension income}]$ at retirement. An even more extreme funding method is the PAYGO system, under which the sponsors provide benefits to retirees when they are due and payable; thus, an actual fund is never accumulated.

In practice, a funding method must balance the needs and interests of current and future shareholders against current and future employees, taking into account both regulatory and tax requirements. In fact, even the intuitively simple method of contributing the aforementioned service cost— assuming the fund earns the valuation rate from year to year—is fraught with problems because it creates an uneven pattern of expenses over time. Some companies and pension sponsors might prefer to smooth the contributions so that approximately the same percentage of salary is contributed to the pension plan over the course of an individual's employment. Also, while it is convenient to think of the assets of and contributions to the pension plan on a per-employee basis, these decisions are actually made in aggregate and thus depend on the distribution of employees and of their ages and salaries within the plan.

Indeed, pension actuaries have developed and now implement a number of "rational" funding methods, which are meant to develop sufficient assets to equal liabilities upon retirement. These methods have a variety of (nondescriptive) names: the unit credit funding method, entry age funding method, attained age funding method, and aggregate cost funding method. Regardless of the exact name, the unifying theme for all these actuarial funding methods—besides accumulating a steady base of assets to pay liabilities—is smoothing fluctuations in financial markets when the funds' investment performance does not match the assumed valuation rate and so there is an unfunded actuarial liability.

And finally, while on the subject it is important to discuss a number of additional benefits that might be part of the pension promise. For example, many plans guarantee that upon retirement the pension income will continue for as long as one member of a couple is still alive, not only while the retired employee is living. This provision is obviously meant to protect the spouse of the employee, which makes perfect sense from the perspective of financial planning and wealth management. However, this also makes the pension promise more expensive, since the annuity factor at retirement is no longer $\bar{a}_x$ but the presumably larger joint and survivor factor $\bar{a}_{x,y}$ introduced in the previous chapter, where x is the age of the employee at retirement and y is the age of the employee's spouse. In this case, the ABO, PBO, and RBO would all be higher at any moment in time prior to retirement.

Other factors that might contribute to increases in ABO, PBO, and RBO values—and hence to the value of the pension guarantee—are life (and even health) insurance benefits that the employee's beneficiary might be entitled to in the event of the employee's early death. I leave all of these complicated and important issues to other sources on the actuarial aspects of pensions.

8.6 Further Reading

In this chapter I have only scratched the surface of material that one can cover on pension funding, valuation, and accounting. Indeed, pension actuaries must study for many years to learn all the rules and regulations on the subject, and it is well beyond the scope of this book to delve into these matters in any depth. In the United States, for example, a large body of literature and analysis has centered around the Employee Retirement Income

Security Act (ERISA), which among other things dictates the funding requirements for private (i.e. corporate) pension plans. At the same time, I would be remiss if I did not mention that many of the assumptions and practices used by traditional pension actuaries have recently come under attack by financial economists because they do not properly account for risk. If you are interested in reading more about defined benefit pension valuation, accounting, and funding through the prism and history of financial economics, I recommend you start with Treynor (1977), Ezra (1980), Black and Dewhurst (1981), Bodie, Marcus, and Merton (1988), Barret (1988), and Ippolito (1989), and then conclude with Babbel, Gold, and Merrill (2002) as well as Gold (2005).

Note also that in this chapter I have adopted the notation and framework of Sundaresan and Zapatero (1997), in which the defined benefit salary weighting function is parameterized by the constant β. Indeed, the function can capture a wide spectrum of salary weighting schemes, although it obviously lacks the ability to precisely model a pension that pays out based on (say) the five best years or the last six months of salary. However, given the scope of this particular chapter, I felt it was more important to maintain analytic simplicity than practical realism. For those readers who are interested in a more detailed description of the types of salary weighting schemes and their actuarial implications—but in a relatively accessible manner—I recommend the book by Booth et al. (1999). For those interested in a more detailed description of the various pension funding methods, please see the concise monograph by Berin (1989).

The field of defined contribution pensions—by virtue of their simplicity and transparency—has not generated as much formal academic literature as there is on defined benefit pension. However, for a deeper understanding of the options available within these plans and the peculiar choices and decisions that people make within them, I suggest Stanton (2000), Benartzi and Thaler (2001), and Brown and Warshawsky (2001). For a life-cycle view of pension plan selection—in other words, whether DB or DC is better for individuals—see McCarthy (2003). For a more mathematical analysis of the options that are embedded within DB and DC plans, see Sherris (1995), Pennacchi (1999), or Friedman and Shen (2002).

8.7 Notation

α—accrual factor or portion of average salary contributed to the pension fund

β—weighting factor used in determining average salary over years worked

Υ_y—measure of the firm's pension obligation to the worker at the current age y, which can be stated as the retirement, projected, or accumulated benefit obligation

8.8 Problems

PROBLEM 8.1. *Making two plans equivalent.* Derive a formula that "solves" for the contribution rate c in a DC plan, so that a DB pension $\{\alpha, \beta\}$ provides the same retirement income benefit. Assume a time horizon T and an investment rate g.

PROBLEM 8.2. In a DC plan, assume that $c(s) = 0.09e^{-(0.1)s}$ (which means that contributions to the plan decline over time), that $w(s) = 30000e^{(0.02)s}$, and that $g(s) = 8\%$. Please derive the retirement income from this plan, assuming the individual is $y = 35$ now and plans to retire at age $x = 65$.

PROBLEM 8.3. What is the service component of the change in the RBO? Why?

PROBLEM 8.4. Derive an expression for the interest component and service component of a change in the ABO and PBO over a small amount of time dt.

PROBLEM 8.5. You are the head of risk management at a large insurance company that sells both life insurance and pension annuities. In general, you are selling pension annuities to people between the ages of 60 and 80 using GoMa mortality parameters of $m = 90$ and $b = 9.5$; you are selling life insurance to people between the ages of 30 and 50 using the GoMa mortality parameters $m = 80$ and $b = 9.5$. Your use of different "modal" values is due to the different clientele and to adverse selection issues.

As a risk manager, you are worried that your actuaries may have misestimated how long people will live. I would like you to investigate and discuss how the company can use insurance to hedge against mispricing of annuities and vice versa. More specifically, how much (notional value of) life insurance would the company have to sell a $y = 45$-year-old in order to hedge the uncertainty in the pension annuity sold to the $x = 70$-year-old? Build the hedge so that, if m increases, gains on the life insurance portfolio offset losses on the pension annuity portfolio and vice versa. Think duration!

PART TWO

WEALTH MANAGEMENT:
APPLICATIONS AND IMPLICATIONS

NINE

Sustainable Spending at Retirement

9.1 Living in Retirement

Jorge Guinle—the famous Brazilian playboy—died on Friday the fifth of March 2004 in Rio de Janeiro. Jorge was born to one of the wealthiest families in Brazil, and he spent a large part of his life dating famous Hollywood starlets such as Rita Hayworth, Lana Turner, and Marilyn Monroe. This hobby was quite expensive and apparently he squandered most of his family's fortune well before he died at the age of 88. In fact, in an interview a few years before his death, Jorge said: "The secret of living well is to die without a cent in your pocket. But I miscalculated, and the money ran out too early."

I do not know whether Mr. Guinle spent too much, invested too poorly, or lived too long. All three factors likely contributed to his unfortunate situation, and the objective of this chapter is to carefully model the chances of "dying without a cent in your pocket" using the probability tools developed in the last few chapters. More specifically, I will compute the probability that, under a given asset allocation and spending policy, you will run out of money while still alive.

To better understand the nature of risk management during retirement, the triangle in Figure 9.1 provides a graphical illustration of the relationship between (what I consider to be) the three most important factors in retirement planning: spending rates, investment asset allocation, and mortality considerations. If you spend and consume too much (or underestimate the impact of inflation on your long-term needs), or if you invest poorly (taking too much risk or too little risk), or if you underestimate your longevity and the time to be spent in retirement, then the probability of ruin in retirement increases.

The topic of sustainable withdrawal and spending rates has been the focus of academic and practitioner research over the years. But this field

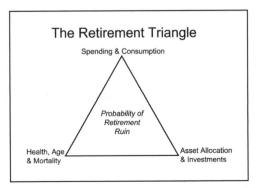

Figure 9.1. *Source:* Copyright 2005 by the CFA Institute, *Financial Analysts Journal,* Charlottesville, VA. Reprinted with permission.

has developed a renewed sense of urgency as a wave of North American Baby Boomers approaches retirement and seeks wealth management guidance on "what's next" for their savings plans.

Many financial planners and advisors have resorted to Monte Carlo simulations (similar to those described in Section 2.8) in order to illustrate financial life cycles. The problem with these and similar Monte Carlo–based studies is that they (i) can be difficult to replicate, (ii) are quite time consuming to generate if done properly using the required number of simulations, and (iii) provide very little financial or pedagogical intuition on the trade-off between risk and return during retirement,

Therefore, in this chapter I address the issue of sustainable spending rates from a different and perhaps novel perspective. I start by linking the three factors of Figure 9.1 in a parsimonious and intuitive manner by using the "probability of retirement ruin" as a risk metric that gauges the relative impact of these factors and the trade-offs between them. This is similar to the probability of shortfall—that a stock portfolio will do worse than a risk-free investment—presented in Chapter 5. Thus, for example, if a retiree increases her spending rate while maintaining the same investment allocation then the probability of retirement ruin will increase, all else being equal. However, if a retiree's health suddenly deteriorates (not the most comforting thought) then the probability of retirement ruin will obviously decline, assuming the same asset allocation and spending rate are maintained. My point is that, by using retirement ruin probabilities and the relatively simple analytic approximation developed in this chapter, retirees and their advisors can better understand the link between the factors affecting risk without resorting to complicated simulations.

In the first step toward developing the analytic approximation, I introduce the concept of a stochastic present value (SPV) and use this to provide an expression for the probability that an initial corpus (nest egg) will be depleted under a fixed consumption rule when the rate of return and the horizons are both stochastic. I stress the dual uncertainty for returns and horizons, which is something that has not received much attention in the portfolio management literature as it pertains to retirees.

The analysis is based on the aforementioned SPV and a continuous-time approximation under lognormal returns and exponential lifetimes. In the case of an investor with an infinite horizon (perpetual consumption), this formula is exact. In the case of a random future lifetime, the formula is based on moment matching approximations, which target the first and second moment of the "true" stochastic present value. The results are remarkably accurate when compared with more costly and time-consuming simulations.

I will also provide several numerical examples to demonstrate the versatility of the closed-form expression for the stochastic present value in determining sustainable withdrawal rates and their respective probabilities. This formula can easily be implemented in Excel or any other spreadsheet using a variety of portfolio risk–return parameters, ages, and withdrawal rates, and it reproduces results that are within the margins of error from extensive Monte Carlo simulations.

This chapter first casts the mathematics of the sustainable spending problem within the context of a traditional "present value of future cash flows" calculation, derives a closed-form analytic expression for the probability that a given spending rate is sustainable, and provides extensive numerical examples over a variety of ages and spending rates.

9.2 Stochastic Present Value

Recall from Chapter 2 that, if you invest your money in a portfolio earning $R\%$ per annum and plan to consume a fixed real (after-inflation) dollar each year until some horizon denoted by T, then the present value (PV) of your consumption at initial time 0 would be computed as

$$\text{PV} = \sum_{i=1}^{T} \frac{1}{(1+R)^i} = \frac{1 - (1+R)^{-T}}{R}, \tag{9.1}$$

but only if the horizon and investment rate of return are known with absolute certainty. Thus—in a deterministic world—if you start retirement with a nest egg greater than the PV in equation (9.1) times your desired consumption, then your money will last for the rest of your life. If you have less than this amount, you will be "ruined" at some age prior to death. Note that as T goes to infinity, which I call the endowment case, the PV converges to

$1/R$. At $R = 0.07$ (=7% effective annual rate), the resulting PV is 14.28 times the desired consumption. An endowment fund that wants to sustain a payout of \$1 per year forever—when investment returns are assumed to be a constant 7% forever—will require \$14.28 in initial capital. Hence, if it wants to sustain a payout of \$100 per year then the fund will need \$1,428 of initial capital.

Of course, human beings have a random (and finite) life span—which is the core model of Chapter 3—and any exercise that attempts to compute required present values at retirement must account for this uncertainty. From a retirement spending perspective, a 65-year-old might live 20 more years or 30 more years or only 10 more years. How should this uncertainty affect the withdrawal rate?

Should a 65-year-old plan for the 75th percentile, the 95th percentile, or the end of the mortality table? What T-value should be used in equation (9.1)? The same question applies to the investment return R: What is a reasonable number to use? The average real investment returns from a broadly diversified portfolio of equity during the last 75 years has been in the vicinity of 6%–9% (as discussed in Chapter 5), but the year-by-year numbers can vary widely.

So, in contrast to the trivial deterministic case—where both the horizon and the investment return are known with certainty—here these variables are stochastic, and the analogue to equation (9.1) is a stochastic present value:

$$\text{SPV} = \frac{1}{1 + \tilde{R}_1} + \frac{1}{(1 + \tilde{R}_1)(1 + \tilde{R}_2)} + \cdots + \frac{1}{\prod_{j=1}^{\tilde{T}}(1 + \tilde{R}_j)}$$

$$= \sum_{i=1}^{\tilde{T}} \prod_{j=1}^{i} (1 + \tilde{R}_j)^{-1}, \tag{9.2}$$

where the new variable $\tilde{T}$ denotes the random time of death (in years) and the new $\tilde{R}_j$ denotes the random investment return in year j. Without any loss of generality, $\tilde{T} = \infty$ is the infinitely lived endowment or foundation situation. I touched upon these ideas in Chapter 3 with regard to the present value of a life-cycle plan, and in this chapter I am focusing exclusively on retirement.

If the consumption/withdrawals take place once per month or once per week, the random variables $\tilde{R}_j$ and $\tilde{T}$ are adjusted accordingly. And if the return frequency is infinitesimal then, of course, the summation sign in equation (9.2) converges to an integral while the product sign is converted into a continuous-time diffusion process.

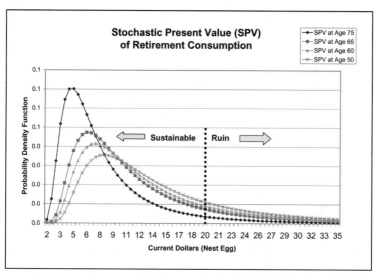

Figure 9.2. *Source:* Copyright 2005 by the CFA Institute, *Financial Analysts Journal,* Charlottesville, VA. Reprinted with permission.

The intuition behind the equation is as follows. Looking forward, we must sum up a random number of terms in which each denominator is also random. The first item discounts the first year of consumption at the first year's random investment return. The second item discounts the second year's consumption (if the individual is still alive) at the product of the first and second years' random investment return, and so on.

The SPV defined by equation (9.2) can be visualized as in Figure 9.2. One can think of the stochastic present value as a random variable with a probability density function (PDF) that depends on the risk–return parameters of the underlying investment-generating process as well as on the random future lifetime. If you start retirement with an initial endowment or nest egg of $20 and intend to consume $1 (after inflation) per annum, then the probability of sustaining this level of consumption is equal to the probability that the SPV is less than $20. In the figure, this corresponds to the area under the curve to the left of the ray emanating from $20 on the x-axis. The probability of ruin is the area under the curve to the right of this $20 ray. The precise shape and parameters governing the SPV depend on the investment and mortality dynamics, but the general picture is remarkably similar to Figure 9.2. This family of SPVs is defined over positive numbers, is right skewed, and at zero is equal to zero.

The four distinct curves in Figure 9.2 denote differing random life spans. In the first plot the (unisex) individual is 50 years old; in the second, 60; in the third, 65; and in the last, 75. As the individual ages, the SPV of future (planned) consumption shifts toward the left (relative to the same $20 mark) because chances are that $20 is enough to sustain this standard of living when starting consumption at an older age.

Now I move on to the main goal of this chapter, which is to obtain a closed-form expression for the distribution of the SPV. Remember that the model developed in Chapter 5 assumed that investment returns are generated by a lognormal distribution, also known as the geometric Brownian motion diffusion process. (In that chapter I spent some time discussing whether this is a reasonable assumption for security prices, and I will not revisit those justifications here.)

9.3 Analytic Formula: Sustainable Retirement Income

Before I come to the main part of the story, I will review quickly the three important probability distributions that play a critical role in our calculations of sustainability. The first is the ubiquitous lognormal (LN) distribution, the second is the exponential lifetime (EL) distribution, and the third is the (perhaps lesser-known) reciprocal Gamma (RG) distribution. The connection between these three will become evident in this section. For more detailed information I urge the reader to revisit Chapters 3 and 5.

First, the investment total return denoted by R_t between time 0 and time t is said to be *lognormally* distributed with parameters $\{\mu, \sigma\}$ if the expected total return is $E[R_t] = e^{\mu t}$, the logarithmic volatility is $SD[\ln R_t] = \sigma\sqrt{t}$, and the probability law can be written as $\Pr[\ln R_t < x] = N\big((\mu - \frac{1}{2}\sigma^2)t, \sigma\sqrt{t}, x\big)$, where $N(\cdot)$ denotes the cumulative normal distribution (introduced in Chapter 3). For example, a mutual fund or portfolio that is expected to earn an inflation-adjusted and continuously compounded return of $\mu = 7\%$ per annum with a logarithmic volatility of $\sigma = 20\%$ has a $N(0.05, 0.20, 0) = 40.13\%$ chance of earning a negative return in any given year. But if the expected return is a more optimistic 10% per annum, the chances of losing money are reduced to $N(0.08, 0.20, 0) = 34.46\%$. Recall from Chapter 5 that, whereas the expected value of the lognormal random variable R_t is $e^{\mu t}$, the median value (geometric mean) is a lower $e^{(\mu - \sigma^2/2)t}$. And by definition the probability that a lognormal random variable is less than its median value is precisely 50%. Again, the gap between the expected value $e^{\mu t}$ and the median value $e^{(\mu - \sigma^2/2)t}$ is always greater than zero, proportional to the volatility, and increasing in time.

In this chapter I will also use the by-now familiar *exponential lifetime* random variable. Recall that the remaining lifetime random variable T is said to be exponentially distributed with mortality rate λ if the probability law for T can be written as $\Pr[T > s] = e^{-\lambda s}$. The expected value of the remaining lifetime random variable is $E[T] = 1/\lambda$, and the median value (the 50% mark) can be computed via $\text{Med}[T] = \ln[2]/\lambda$. Again, the expected value is greater than the median value. As argued in Chapter 3, the exponential assumption is a most convenient one for future lifetime random variables. Even though human aging does not quite conform to an exponential—or constant force of mortality—assumption, I will show that, for the purposes of estimating a sustainable spending rate, it does a remarkably good job of capturing the salient features.

The reciprocal Gamma distribution will also play a key role. A random variable denoted by X is said to be *reciprocal Gamma* distributed with parameters $\{\alpha, \beta\}$ if the probability law for X can be written as

$$\Pr[X < x] := \frac{\beta^{-\alpha}}{\Gamma(\alpha)} \int_0^t y^{-(\alpha+1)} e^{(-1/y\beta)} \, dy. \tag{9.3}$$

The cumulative distribution function (CDF) displayed in equation (9.3) plays the same role as the CDF of the normal or lognormal distribution. The definition of the reciprocal Gamma random variable is such that the probability an RG random variable X is greater than or equal to x is equivalent to the probability that a Gamma random variable is less than $1/x$. The CDF of a Gamma random variable is available in all statistical packages—even in Excel—and thus should be easily accessible to most readers. The precise syntax would be as follows: for $\Pr[X \geq x]$, type GAMMADIST(1/x,alpha, beta,TRUE); and for $\Pr[X < x]$, type 1-GAMMADIST(1/x,alpha,beta, TRUE).

The reciprocal Gamma distribution is central to the analysis and the models developed in this chapter, which is why it is important to develop some intuition for how it differs from the normal distribution (reviewed in Chapter 3). First of all, the RG—like all statistical distributions—can be visualized graphically as a function that maps values into probabilities and whose area under the plotted curve integrates to a value of exactly 1. Like the normal distribution, the RG can take on very large values but with small probability. Yet in contrast to a normal random variable, which can take on negative values, the RG random variable can only take on values between zero and positive infinity. Thus, whereas the domain of the normal distribution is $(-\infty, \infty)$, the domain of the RG distribution is $(0, \infty)$. This is an important difference between the two densities, particularly when we move on to computing actual probabilities. To compute the $\Pr[X < x]$ for a normal variable, we must integrate the relevant PDF from the lower bound of $-\infty$ to the upper bound x. But in the RG case, we integrate only from a lower bound of 0 to x.

Figure 9.2 (in Section 9.2) provides a rough picture of the probability density function of the RG random variable under various parameter values. At the lower left-hand side of the picture, the value of the PDF at zero is zero. At the right-hand side of the picture, the value of the PDF at large (infinite) values is also zero. Between the two extremes, the PDF rises to a unimodal hump and then falls again toward zero.

Like the normal distribution, which is governed by two parameters (traditionally the mean and variance), the RG distribution also has two degrees of freedom. These two parameters α, β, which are both assumed positive, determine the shape and rate of decline of the PDF. These parameters do not have an immediate statistical interpretation, but the α, β values can be converted into mean and variance (i.e., first and second moments) of the RG distribution. For example, if $\beta = 1$ and $\alpha = 5$, then the probability that an RG random variable takes on a value less than $x = 0.25$ is $\Pr[X < 0.25] = 62.88\%$. However, if the governing parameter is changed from $\alpha = 5$ to $\alpha = 2$, the relevant probability is $\Pr[X < 0.25] = 9.16\%$. Notice that by reducing the value of α we are pushing more mass toward the right tail of the distribution. In the high-α case approximately 37% of the mass is to the right of $x = 0.25$, but in the low-α case a much higher 91% is to the right of $x = 0.25$. These numbers all come from Table 14.5, and I urge the reader to scan that table in order to better understand the behavior of the reciprocal Gamma distribution.

Finally, the expected (mean) value or first moment of the reciprocal Gamma distribution is $E[X] = (\beta(\alpha - 1))^{-1}$, and the second moment is $E[X^2] = (\beta^2(\alpha - 1)(\alpha - 2))^{-1}$. For example, within the context of this chapter, a typical parameter pair is $\alpha = 5$ and $\beta = 0.03$. In this case, the expected value of the RG variable is $1/((0.03)(4)) = 8.33$, and the probability that the RG random variable is greater than or equal to, say, 8 is 40.37%. In contrast, if we decrease α from a value of 5 to a value of 4, then the relevant expected value becomes $E[X] = 11.11$ and the probability then becomes $\Pr[X \geq 8] = 59.84\%$.

9.4 The Main Result: Exponential Reciprocal Gamma

With the mathematical background behind us, my primary claim is that if one is willing to assume lognormal returns in a continuous-time setting, then the stochastic present value (displayed graphically in Figure 9.2) is actually reciprocal Gamma distributed in the limit. In other words, the probability that the SPV is greater than or equal to the initial wealth w—which is equivalent to the probability of retirement ruin—is the simple-looking

$$\Pr[\text{SPV} \geq w] = \text{GammaDist}\left(\frac{2\mu + 4\lambda}{\sigma^2 + \lambda} - 1, \frac{\sigma^2 + \lambda}{2} \;\middle|\; \frac{1}{w}\right), \qquad (9.4)$$

where $\text{GammaDist}(\alpha, \beta \mid \cdot)$ denotes the CDF of the Gamma distribution evaluated at the parameter pair α, β. The precise Excel syntax is as follows: GAMMADIST([spending rate as a fraction of wealth],alpha,beta,TRUE). The familiar pair μ, σ are the expected return and volatility parameters from the investment portfolio, and λ is the mortality rate. The expected value of the SPV—based on the reciprocal Gamma representation—is $(\mu - \sigma^2 + \lambda)^{-1}$. For the precise derivation of the exponential reciprocal Gamma (ERG) equation, see Section 9.10.

Here is how to apply the formula. Start with an investment (endowment, nest egg) fund containing $20 to be invested in an equity fund that is expected to earn $\mu = 0.07$ per annum with a volatility or standard deviation of $\sigma = 0.20$ per annum. Assume that a (unisex) 50-year-old with a median remaining lifetime of 28.1 years intends to consume $1 (after inflation) per annum for the rest of his or her life. Recall from Chapter 3 that if the median life span is 28.1 years then by definition the probability of survival for 28.1 years is exactly 50%, which implies that our instantaneous force of mortality parameter is $\lambda = \ln[2]/28.1 = 0.0247$. By (9.4) our probability of retirement ruin, which is the probability that the stochastic present value of $1 consumption is greater than or equal to $20, is approximately 26.8%. In the language of Figure 9.2, if we evaluate the SPV at $w = 20$ then the area to the right has a mass of 0.268 units. The area to the left—which is the probability of sustainability—has a mass of 0.732 units. Naturally, different values of w will result in different probabilities of ruin.

9.5 Case Study and Numerical Examples

A newly retired 65-year-old has a nest egg of $1,000,000, which must provide income and must last for the remainder of this individual's natural life. In addition to expected Social Security benefits of $14,000 per annum and a defined benefit (DB) pension from an old employer providing $16,000 per annum (with both payments adjusted for inflation each year) the retiree estimates the need for an additional $60,000 from the investment portfolio. The $60,000 income will be coaxed from the million-dollar portfolio via a systematic withdrawal plan (SWiP) that sells off the required number of shares/units each month using a reverse dollar-cost average (DCA) strategy. All of these numbers are prior to any income taxes and thus do not distinguish between tax-sheltered plans and taxable plans—a significant matter not addressed here. What is important to note is that the $90,000 consumption plan will be satisfied with $30,000 from a de facto inflation-adjusted life annuity and the remaining $60,000 from a SWiP.

In our previous lingo, I am interested in whether the stochastic present value of the desired $60,000 income per annum is probabilistically less than the initial nest egg of $1 million. If so, the standard of living is sustainable. If, however, the SPV of the consumption plan is greater than $1 million, then the retirement plan is deemed unsustainable and the individual will eventually face ruin unless consumption is reduced. Once again, the basic philosophy of this chapter is that the SPV is a random variable and so the proper analysis comes down to probabilities.

Tables 9.1–9.3 list an extensive range of consumption/withdrawal rates across various ages so readers can gauge the impact of these factors on the ruin probability. The first column in each table displays the retirement age x; the second column displays the median age at death, $x + \text{Med}[T]$ (based on actuarial mortality tables); and the third column computes the implied mortality rate λ from this median value. With a λ-value in hand and given μ and σ as indicated, the table evaluates the SPV of various spending rates ranging from $2 to $10.

The first group of entries (lines 1–3) within Table 9.1 provides results in the case of a retiree who would like the spending to last forever (hence the median age at death is infinity); this applies also to an endowment or foundation with an infinite horizon. The probability of ruin ranges from a low of 15% ($2 spending) to a high of 92% ($10 spending) if investments are made in an equity-based portfolio that is expected to earn a (lognormal) return with a mean value of $\mu = 7\%$ and a volatility of $\sigma = 20\%$ per annum.

Back to our retiree: according to Table 9.1, if the 65-year-old invests the million-dollar nest egg in the same equity-based portfolio and withdraws $60,000, then the exact probability of ruin—that is, the probability that the plan is not sustainable—is 25.3%. Roughly one out of four retirees who adopt this retirement consumption plan will be forced to reduce their standard of living during retirement. By "exact probability of ruin" I mean the outcome from discounting all future cash flows using the correct (unisex) actuarial mortality table starting at age 65.

In the table, just above this exact 25.3% number I list the result using the ERG approximation formula, which is based on an exponential future lifetime implemented within equation (9.4). Observe that the approximate answer is a slightly higher 26.2% probability of ruin. Here the gap between the exact and approximate number is less than 0.9%, which inspires additional confidence in our ERG formula (9.4).

Table 9.1. *Probability of retirement ruin given (arithmetic mean)*
return μ of 7% with volatility σ of 20%

Age x at retirement	Median age at death	Mortality rate λ		Spending rate (per $100)					
				$2	$4	$5	$6	$9	$10
N.A.	∞	0.00%	A	15.1%	45.1%	58.4%	69.4%	89.1%	92.5%
			E	15.1%	45.1%	58.4%	69.4%	89.1%	92.5%
			D	0.0%	0.0%	0.0%	0.0%	0.0%	0.0%
55	83.0	2.48%	A	4.3%	18.0%	26.7%	35.7%	60.2%	66.8%
			E	2.8%	18.0%	28.7%	39.6%	66.7%	73.0%
			D	1.4%	0.0%	−2.0%	−3.9%	−6.5%	−6.3%
65	83.9	3.67%	A	2.6%	12.3%	18.9%	26.2%	48.3%	54.9%
			E	1.0%	9.4%	16.8%	25.3%	50.5%	57.4%
			D	1.6%	2.8%	2.1%	0.9%	−2.2%	−2.5%
70	84.6	4.75%	A	1.8%	9.0%	14.2%	20.1%	39.5%	45.8%
			E	0.5%	5.7%	11.0%	17.6%	39.6%	46.4%
			D	1.3%	3.2%	3.2%	2.6%	−0.1%	−0.6%
75	85.7	6.48%	A	1.1%	5.7%	9.3%	13.6%	29.0%	34.4%
			E	0.2%	2.9%	6.10%	10.5%	27.7%	33.7%
			D	0.9%	2.8%	3.2%	3.1%	1.2%	0.7%
80	87.4	9.37%	A	0.5%	3.0%	5.1%	7.7%	18.0%	21.9%
			E	0.1%	1.2%	2.8%	5.2%	16.6%	21.1%
			D	0.5%	1.8%	2.3%	2.5%	1.4%	0.8%

Note: A = approximate answer, E = exact answer, D = A − E.
Source: Copyright 2005 by the CFA Institute, *Financial Analysts Journal*, Charlottesville, VA. Reprinted with permission.

Now I would argue that, regardless of whether one uses the exact or the approximate methodology, a 25% chance of retirement ruin—which is only a 75% chance of success—should be unacceptable to most retirees. Table 9.1 indicates that lowering the desired consumption or spending plan by $10,000 to a $50,000 SWiP reduces the probability of ruin to 16.8% (using the exact method) or 18.9% (using the approximation); if the spending plan is further reduced to $40,000, the probability of ruin shrinks to 9.4% (exact) or 12.3% (approximate). Retirees (together with a financial planner or analyst) can determine whether these odds are acceptable in light of their tolerance for risk.

In the other direction, if the same individual were to withdraw (the entire) $90,000 annually from the million-dollar portfolio, then—using the 7% mean and 20% volatility portfolio parameters—the probability of ruin would be 50.5% (exact) or 48.3% (approximate).

To develop an intuition for these numbers, note that the mean or expected value of the SPV of $1 of real spending is $1/(\mu - \sigma^2 + \lambda)$, where μ and σ are the investment parameters and λ is the mortality rate parameter associated with a given median future lifetime. For a (unisex) 65-year-old, the median future lifetime is 18.9 years according to the RP2000 Society of Actuaries mortality table. To derive the 50% probability point with an exponential distribution, we must solve the equation $e^{-18.9\lambda} = 0.5$, which leads to $\lambda = \ln[2]/18.9 = 0.0367$ as the implied rate of mortality.

Returning to the mean value of the SPV, if $\mu = 7\%$ and $\sigma = 20\%$ then this works out to $1/(0.07 - 0.04 + 0.0367)$, which is an average of $15 for the SPV per dollar of desired consumption. Thus, if the retiree plans to spend $90,000 per annum, it should come as no surprise that a nest egg of only 11 times this amount is barely enough to give even odds. Note that the expected value of the SPV decreases in $\{\mu, \lambda\}$ and increases in σ. The impact of portfolio parameters should be obvious: higher mean is good, higher volatility is bad. The benefit of a higher mortality rate λ comes from reducing the anticipated life span and hence the length of time over which the withdrawals are taken.

Now, if the same individual were to delay retiring by five years—or, more precisely, to begin consuming from the nest egg at age 70—then the same $60,000 consumption plan would result in a 17.6% (exact) or 20.1% (approximate) probability of ruin according to Table 9.1. The increased sustainability of the same plan (compared with the roughly 25% probability if this individual were to retire at age 65) is due to the reduced future life span and hence the lower stochastic present value of consumption. Think back to the expected value of the consumption plan. At age 70 the median future life span is only 14.6 years, which leads to a higher λ and hence a lower value for $E[\text{SPV}]$. The retiree can start retirement with less or can consume more.

Tables 9.2 and 9.3 provide results under various portfolio investment parameters using the ERG approximation from equation (9.4). In Table 9.2 I have reduced the expected investment return from 7% to 5% but left the volatility at 20%. In this case all the corresponding probabilities are higher than in Table 9.1 because a higher volatility can only make things worse. In Table 9.3 I have reduced the volatility from 20% to 10% and kept the expected return at 5%. For example, the 65-year-old withdrawing $60,000 annually from a million-dollar portfolio has a 39.8% probability of ruin under a $\mu = 5\%$ and $\sigma = 20\%$ investment regime, compared to a 26.2% probability of ruin under a $\mu = 7\%$ and $\sigma = 20\%$ regime, where the difference is clearly due to the 200-basis-point loss in returns. But if the $\mu = 5\%$ investment return is matched with a (more reasonable) $\sigma = 10\%$

Table 9.2. *Probability of retirement ruin given μ of 5% with σ of 20%*

Age x at retire-ment	Median age at death	Mortality rate λ	Spending rate (per $100)					
			$2	$4	$5	$6	$9	$10
N.A.	∞	0.00%	42.8%	73.9%	82.8%	88.8%	97.1%	98.1%
55	83.0	2.48%	11.5%	32.8%	43.4%	53.1%	74.9%	80.0%
65	83.9	3.67%	6.7%	22.3%	31.1%	39.8%	62.2%	68.1%
70	84.6	4.75%	4.4%	16.1%	23.3%	30.8%	51.9%	58.0%
75	85.7	6.48%	2.4%	10.0%	15.1%	20.8%	38.7%	44.4%
80	87.4	9.37%	1.1%	5.0%	8.0%	11.5%	24.1%	28.6%

Table 9.3. *Probability of retirement ruin given μ of 5% with σ of 10%*

Age x at retire-ment	Median age at death	Mortality rate λ	Spending rate (per $100)					
			$2	$4	$5	$6	$9	$10
N.A.	∞	0.00%	2.1%	40.7%	66.7%	84.5%	99.3%	99.8%
55	83.0	2.48%	1.0%	10.8%	20.1%	31.2%	63.9%	72.4%
65	83.9	3.67%	0.7%	7.0%	13.2%	21.0%	47.9%	56.4%
70	84.6	4.75%	0.5%	5.0%	9.5%	15.3%	37.3%	45.0%
75	85.7	6.48%	0.3%	3.1%	6.0%	9.9%	25.8%	31.9%
80	87.4	9.37%	0.2%	1.7%	3.2%	5.4%	15.0%	19.1%

volatility, then by Table 9.3 the probability of ruin shrinks to 21%. The intuition once again comes down to the expected value of the SPV of $1 spending: $1/(\mu - \sigma^2 + \lambda)$. If $\mu = 5\%$ and $\sigma = 10\%$ then $\mu - \sigma^2$ in the denominator is 0.04, but if $\mu = 7\%$ and $\sigma = 20\%$ then the same term is only 0.03, which ceteris paribus increases the SPV and so lowers the sustainable spending rate. Note that Table 9.3 does not provide uniformly lower probabilities of ruin. For high levels of consumption, a more aggressive ($\mu = 0.07$, $\sigma = 20\%$) portfolio may lead to better odds of sustainability than the more conservative ($\mu = 0.05$, $\sigma = 10\%$) portfolio.

One can think of a number of ways in which to manipulate this formula. For example, our main equation (9.4) can be inverted to compute a "safe" rate of investment return based on a given tolerance for probability of ruin. This idea is akin to some recent applications of shortfall as a measure of risk in the context of portfolio management. Along the same lines, the impact of the expected return μ on the sustainability of a given withdrawal strategy can easily be "stress tested."

Table 9.4(a). *Maximum annual spending given tolerance for*
5% probability of ruin

Age x at retirement	Mortality rate λ	Expected investment return μ					
		3%	4%	5%	6%	7%	8%
N.A.	0.00%	$0.004	$0.103	$0.352	$0.711	$1.145	$1.635
55	2.48%	$0.526	$0.859	$1.247	$1.680	$2.148	$2.647
65	3.67%	$0.923	$1.296	$1.710	$2.157	$2.633	$3.135
70	4.75%	$1.310	$1.707	$2.135	$2.592	$3.074	$3.576
75	6.48%	$1.958	$2.380	$2.825	$3.293	$3.779	$4.284
80	9.37%	$3.080	$3.525	$3.988	$4.466	$4.959	$5.465

Note: Investment return volatility $\sigma = 20\%$.

Table 9.4(b). *Maximum annual spending given tolerance for*
10% probability of ruin

Age x at retirement	Mortality rate λ	Expected investment return μ					
		3%	4%	5%	6%	7%	8%
N.A.	0.00%	$0.016	$0.211	$0.584	$1.064	$1.610	$2.204
55	2.48%	$0.884	$1.340	$1.846	$2.391	$2.967	$3.568
65	3.67%	$1.461	$1.953	$2.482	$3.039	$3.622	$4.225
70	4.75%	$2.008	$2.521	$3.063	$3.629	$4.216	$4.820
75	6.48%	$2.911	$3.445	$4.002	$4.576	$5.168	$5.774
80	9.37%	$4.452	$5.007	$5.578	$6.162	$6.758	$7.366

Note: Investment return volatility $\sigma = 20\%$.

Likewise, Tables 9.4(a)–(c) invert or "solve for" the sustainable spending rate that results in a given probability of ruin. The mathematics of this
operation are quite straightforward. One simply uses the inverse function
for the Gamma distribution applied to the relevant probability—say 5%,
10%, or 25%—under the given alpha and beta coefficients, and the result is
the maximum spending rate.

For example, if the retiree is willing to assume or "live with" a ruin probability of only 5%, which means that a 95% chance of sustainability is
desired, then the most a 65-year-old can consume under a $\mu = 5\%$ assumed return is $1.71 per initial nest egg of $100 (assuming 20% volatility).
On the other hand, if the retiree is willing to tolerate a 10% chance of ruin,
then the maximum consumption level increases from $1.71 to about $2.48
per $100. A retiree who can tolerate a 25% chance of ruin can consume as
much as $4.30 per $100 of capital. Of course, all these numbers are in real

Table 9.4(c). *Maximum annual spending given tolerance for 25% probability of ruin*

Age x at retirement	Mortality rate λ	Expected investment return μ					
		3%	4%	5%	6%	7%	8%
N.A.	0.00%	$0.102	$0.575	$1.213	$1.923	$2.675	$3.455
55	2.48%	$1.866	$2.561	$3.288	$4.039	$4.808	$5.593
65	3.67%	$2.845	$3.563	$4.304	$5.063	$5.836	$6.622
70	4.75%	$3.748	$4.480	$5.229	$5.993	$6.769	$7.555
75	6.48%	$5.212	$5.957	$6.715	$7.484	$8.262	$9.049
80	9.37%	$7.677	$8.434	$9.201	$9.975	$10.756	$11.544

Note: Investment return volatility $\sigma = 20\%$.

terms and are based on the ERG approximation and an assumption of lognormal investment returns. But the intuition should be the same regardless of the return-generating process or the specific law of mortality. Namely, the higher the age and the higher the mortality rate (λ), the more the individual can consume. Consumption can also increase with higher expected returns and greater tolerance for increased probability of ruin.

Observe once again the strong impact of age (or health status) on the sustainable spending rate for any given expected return and level of tolerance for ruin. When the mortality rate is zero—that is, when consumption is needed perpetually—the sustainable spending rate can change (with respect to consumption from age 80 until death) by more than $5 per $100, depending on the expected return and tolerance assumptions.

Another interesting insight comes from examining the interplay between the parameters in our formula. Reducing the fixed mortality rate λ by 100 basis points—which increases the median remaining lifetime from $\ln[2]/\lambda$ to $\ln[2]/(\lambda - 0.01)$—has the "probability equivalent" effect of increasing the portfolio return by 200 basis points and increasing the portfolio variance by 100 basis points; both lead to the same statistical results. Recall that our α, β parameter arguments in equation (9.4) can be expressed as a function of $\mu + 2\lambda$ and $\sigma^2 + \lambda$. Thus, a longer life span (i.e., a lower mortality rate) is interchangeable with decreasing the portfolio return and portfolio variance relative to the baseline. In aggregate, however, a longer life span increases the probability of ruin and reduces the probability that a given level of wealth is enough to sustain retirement spending.

Figure 9.3 provides a graphical perspective for the results in Tables 9.4 but takes a slightly different approach. It fixes a probability of ruin tolerance level—for example, 1%, 5%, or 10%—and then displays the minimum initial wealth needed to support a $1-for-life consumption stream with the

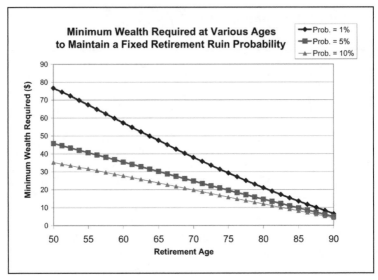

Figure 9.3

given probability. For example, if you are 70 years old and want 99% confidence that you will not run out of money during retirement, then—using precise unisex mortality rates of $m = 87.8$ and $b = 9.5$ (GoMa parameters) rather than the ERG approximation—you must start with approximately $W_0 = \$40$, which can be read from the vertical axis. On the other hand, if you are content with a 95% chance of success then approximately $W_0 = \$25$ is enough.

In the next chapter, which discusses longevity insurance and the role of pension annuities in a retirement portfolio, you will see how these numbers compare with the sum needed at retirement to purchase lifetime income from an insurance company. It should come as no surprise that you will need much less to generate the same retirement income, since you are ceding control of the assets in the event of death.

Finally, it is important to stress that in the $\lambda = 0$ (infinite horizon) case our result is not an approximation: it is a theorem that the SPV is, in fact, reciprocal Gamma distributed. If you remain unconvinced that what is effectively the "sum of lognormals" in equation (9.4) can converge to the inverse of a Gamma distribution, I urge you to simulate the SPV for a reasonably long horizon and then conduct a Kolmogorov–Smirnov (KS) goodness-of-fit test of the inverse of these numbers against the Gamma distribution, with the parameters given by $\alpha = (2\mu + 4\lambda)/(\sigma^2 + \lambda) - 1$ and $\beta = (\sigma^2 + \lambda)/2$. As long as the volatility parameter σ is not too high relative to the expected

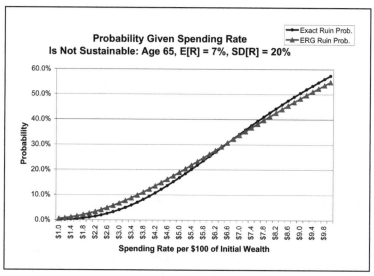

Figure 9.4. *Source:* Copyright 2005 by the CFA Institute, *Financial Analysts Journal,* Charlottesville, VA. Reprinted with permission.

return μ, we obtain convergence of the relevant integrand. Thus, it is only in the random life span that our result is approximate, though it is correct to within two moments of the true SPV density. To illustrate this graphically, Figure 9.4 provides a stylized illustration—under a 7% mean and 20% volatility—of the approximation error from using the ERG formula based on an exponential future lifetime when the true future lifetime random variable is actually more complicated. Here "true" refers to the probability of ruin obtained using numerical methods for solving the relevant partial differential equation (PDE).

Figure 9.4 displays the retirement ruin probability (i.e., the probability that the spending rate is not sustainable) starting at age 65 for a range of consumption rates from $1 to $10 per original $100 nest egg. For low consumption rates, the ERG formula slightly overestimates the probability of ruin and thus gives a more pessimistic picture of the sustainability of spending. At higher consumption rates, the exact retirement ruin probability is higher than that claimed by the approximation. Yet there is only a relatively small error gap between the two curves that at worst is no more than 3%–5%. The two curves are at their closest—which implies that the approximation is at its best—when the spending rate is between $5 and $7 per original $100, which (coincidentally) is precisely the range over which sustainable spending is currently debated.

Table 9.5. *Probability of ruin for 65-year-old male given collared portfolio under a fixed spending rate*

	$4	$5	$6
No downside protection	7.3%	13.7%	21.3%
−5% against +6.6%	1.5%	6.0%	16.8%
−10% against +12.8%	4.1%	9.7%	18.3%

9.6 Increased Sustainable Spending *without* More Risk?

Can you increase your sustainable spending rate without taking on additional risk? Believe it or not, the answer to this question is Yes. Let me explain. A retiree who invests "too much" money in risky equity funds will run the risk of retirement ruin if markets perform poorly during the first few years of retirement. On the other hand, investing "too little" in the equity fund runs the same risk of retirement ruin but this time because there is insufficient portfolio growth to sustain the spending rate. It seems that you are "damned if you do and damned if you don't."

However, there is a third alternative: use derivative securities to reduce the dispersion of portfolio returns—both positive and negative—and thus concentrate investment returns around a central value that, in most cases, will improve the sustainability of the portfolio. For those new to the concept of financial options, a derivative instrument is one whose value is based on (derived from) the value of some underlying investment such as a stock. Specifically, buying a *call option* gives an individual the right (but not the obligation) to purchase an investment at a predetermined price, whereas buying a *put option* guarantees the holder the right to sell the underlying investment at a predetermined price. Purchasing put options on a portfolio's assets thus guarantees a minimum return when the assets are finally sold. Combining puts and calls in a "retirement collar" allows one to sell a call with a strike price of K_c, for example, and then use the proceeds to purchase a put with a lower strike price K_p. Hence, if the asset's market price falls below K_p, your loss is limited because you have the right to sell it at a price of K_p. However, if the asset's value increases above K_c then you will have to sell it to the call's holder at the K_c price, thus limiting the gains you could have earned on the portfolio.

Table 9.5 provides an example of how this would work. Imagine that you decide at retirement to allocate your $100 nest egg (which can arbitrarily be scaled up or down) and to consume $4 annually from this nest egg. If all of

Table 9.6. *Probability of ruin for 65-year-old female given collared portfolio under a fixed spending rate*

	$4	$5	$6
No downside protection	8.4%	15.4%	23.5%
−5% against +6.6%	1.5%	6.0%	16.8%
−10% against +12.8%	5.9%	14.1%	25.1%

the money is invested in equity-based products, then the probability of retirement ruin (the probability that the standard of living is not sustainable) is 7.3% for a male (and 8.4% for a female; see Table 9.6) using the methodology described earlier. However, if you purchase a 3-month put option that is 5% out of the money—which means that the strike price is initially $95—and if you fund this purchase by selling a call option that is 6.6% out of the money, then the put–call combination will reduce the dispersion of your portfolio and thus will reduce the probability of ruin to 1.5% for a male and 2.4% for a female. Note that these scenarios ignore transaction costs and assume that the 3-month options are rolled over upon expiration (at the same price).

The intuition for this result is that when "very bad" investment returns are removed or purged from future scenarios, the stochastic present value is shifted to a lower value and so the same initial sum of money has a much higher probability of sustaining a given standard of living.

It is important to recognize that this collar strategy of buying puts funded by selling calls is not a free lunch. As I have demonstrated, the strategy reduces the probability of retirement ruin by limiting the magnitude and frequency of (large) negative returns, but this comes at the expense of reducing the portfolio's upside potential. Although the portfolio's income will last longer if its depletion is delayed via "collaring," the portfolio cannot increase in value as rapidly as the uncollared or unprotected portfolio.

Figure 9.5 illustrates this graphically. Starting from time $t = 0$, two lines are plotted. The first (upper) line represents the expected value of wealth $E[W_t]$, from time $t = 0$ to $t = 40$, assuming a 100% allocation to risky equity that is expected to earn $\mu = 7\%$ with a standard deviation of $\sigma = 20\%$. The second (lower) line represents the expected value of wealth assuming that the 100% equity allocation is protected by a collar whose 3-month put option is 5% out of the money. (Recall that this means the most a portfolio can lose during any given quarter is 5%.) The put is funded by selling a 3-month call option that is out of the money. You can see that,

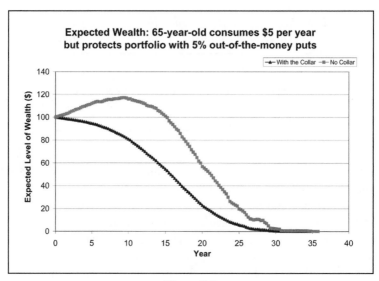

Figure 9.5

although both curves start off at a normalized value of 100, the expected level of wealth for the uncollared portfolio is uniformly higher throughout the 35–40-year horizon. Thus, the downside risk (variance or standard deviation) is reduced, but so is the upside potential.

It might seem odd that using derivative securities such as puts and calls can have such a dramatic impact on the probability of retirement ruin. After all, the assumed asset allocation and consumption patterns remain exactly the same, so why is the stochastic present value of consumption so much lower? Figure 9.6—which was created based on Monte Carlo simulations—provides an additional perspective and yet another way to understand these intriguing results. Recall that, according to the main formula (9.4), if a 65-year-old male invests his entire nest egg in (risky) equities that are expected to earn a 5% (inflation-adjusted) geometric mean return then the probability of retirement ruin—if he consumes $7 each year—is approximately 30%.

However, my simulations indicate that if this 65-year-old male gets lucky by earning a 10% compound annual return during his first decade of retirement, then the conditional probability of retirement ruin drops from about 30% to about 7%. In other words, if I artificially force the portfolio's investment return to be exactly 10% each year between ages 65 and 75 and *then* let the investment return vary randomly for the remaining part of his life, the probability of retirement ruin is reduced. This should come as no surprise. If investment returns are better than anticipated, the odds of sustainability

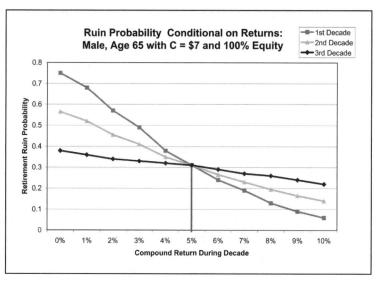

Figure 9.6

will be better as well. Likewise, if I force the investment return during the
first decade of retirement as being 0%, then the probability of retirement
ruin increases from 30% to about 75%. Once again, the qualitative aspects
of this result should be expected.

However, what is interesting is that, when I perform the exact same
"conditioning" for the second or third decade of retirement, the impact on
the probability of retirement ruin is much less than in the previous (first-
decade) case. Notice that fixing the compound annual return during the
second decade at 10% reduces the probability of ruin not to 7% but only to
15%; if instead the third decade's return is set at 10%, then the ruin probability drops only to 25%. It is much better to earn an abnormally high rate
of return in the first decade of retirement than in the second or third decade.
Of course, the opposite is true of low investment returns. If you earn a 0%
compound annual return during your second decade of retirement (from age
75 to 85) then the retirement ruin probability is high at 60% but not as high
as if that 0% were earned in the first decade of retirement, for in that case
the probability of ruin would be close to 75%.

The main insight from this picture and the underlying analysis is that the
first decade of retirement is the most crucial one in determining whether your
retirement plan will be successful. Intuitively, a poor performance from the
market when you have a lot of wealth at stake has a more detrimental impact overall. Thus, it makes sense that purchasing downside protection in

the form of put options—funded by selling call options—will reduce the probability of retirement ruin. In some sense, it is like conditioning the investment performance on a higher number, which improves the odds. The implications of this insight go far beyond arguing the benefits of using put options to protect a retirement portfolio. In fact, any financial or insurance product that can create similar downside investment protection will increase a portfolio's sustainability.

It is easy to verify these results with a simple spreadsheet. Create a column (vector) of random investment returns representing the year-by-year performance of a portfolio during 30 possible years of retirement. For each sequence of 30-year investment returns, compute the (stochastic) present value of a particular consumption stream—for example, $7 per year. Do this a few hundred times and count the number of times the present value is higher than your initial wealth of $100. This is your probability of retirement ruin, assuming you die in exactly 30 years. Now, go back to the spreadsheet and put an "IF statement" in place of the first 10 years of portfolio investment returns. Namely, if the investment return is less than a given floor (i.e., the strike price of the put option you purchased), force the investment return to be the floor for that year. Likewise, if the investment return is greater than a given ceiling (i.e., the strike price of the call you have written), force the investment return to be the ceiling for that year. Remember that the relationship between the floor (which protects your portfolio) and the ceiling (which you have given away) should be determined in a fair economic manner. As before, discount your consumption by this path of returns to obtain a stochastic present value. Do this a few hundred times and compute the number of times the present value is greater than your initial $100 retirement nest egg.

The results will show that your present values are lower and thus your retirement ruin probability is reduced. If you then try the same exercise for the second and third decade of retirement, the odds still improve—as shown in the figure—but they will not be as good as when the portfolio is protected during the first decade. In fact, in the extensive simulations I have run together with a number of my colleagues and graduate students, it seems that the first *seven* years of retirement are the most critical in affecting the probability of retirement ruin.

9.7 Conclusion

A casual search on the Web reveals close to a dozen on-line calculators—most sponsored by financial services companies—that purport to compute via Monte Carlo simulations a sustainable withdrawal rate (and asset allocation) for retirees. A number of these calculators are plagued by opacity in the details of their stochastic generating methodology, and most conduct an absurdly small number of simulations when compared with the tens of thousands needed for convergence. Moreover, the uncertainty generated by the randomness of human life is often either ignored or merely alluded to outside of the formal model. Indeed, the "black box" and time-consuming nature of obtaining results do little to enhance a pedagogical understanding of retirement income. The same issues are relevant in the endowment business, where trustees and other decision makers must trade off current spending against future growth.

The distinction between traditional Monte Carlo simulations and the analytic techniques promoted in this chapter is more than just a question of academic tastes and techniques. For example, the *Wall Street Journal*—in an article entitled "Tool Tells How Long Nest Egg Will Last" (31 August 2004)—described the benefits of analytic PDE-based solutions over Monte Carlo simulations. Clearly, retirement income mathematics has gone mainstream. And though Monte Carlo simulations will continue to have a legitimate and important role within the field of wealth management and retirement planning, I believe that a simple, easy-to-use, and baseline formula can serve as a sanity check or a calibration point for more complicated simulations. At the risk of overselling, this is akin to having a Black–Scholes formula for the price of a call or put option: although many of the underlying assumptions are questionable, it still enables a deep understanding of the embedded risk and return trade-offs and can live side-by-side with more sophisticated option pricing models based on simulations.

For example, we can use formula (9.4) to find that a (unisex) 65-year-old retiree who invests a portfolio in the market and expects to earn a real (after-inflation) 7% with a volatility of 20% and who consumes $4 annually per $100 of initial portfolio value will be "ruined" 10 times out of 100. However, if the same retiree withdraws a more aggressive $6 per $100 then the probability of ruin increases to about 25 times out of 100. This level of consumption is clearly not sustainable. As an upper bound, a retiree should be spending no more than $(\mu - \sigma^2 + \lambda)$ percent of the initial nest egg, where μ is the expected return, σ is the volatility, and $\lambda = \ln[2]/m$ for m a median future lifetime. This spending rate would be sustainable "on average" but not much better.

Note that most of these numbers are in line with results from a variety of simulation studies—for example, the widely used Ibbotson Associates retirement wealth simulator—even though they were produced by a single formula in a fraction of the time.

Our hero, of course, is the (reciprocal) Gamma distribution, which should take its rightful place beside the lognormal density in the pantheon of probability distributions that are of immediate relevance to financial practitioners and portfolio managers. The same formula can also be used to show how annuities reduce ruin and increase sustainability.

9.8 Further Reading

This chapter draws heavily from—and is an extended and more technical version of—Milevsky and Robinson (2005). Indeed, the question of sustainable spending rates as they pertain to retirement pensions has been explored by a number of authors and from various perspectives. An article by Arnott (2004) lamented the lack of academic research on sustainable spending. The "simulation or bootstrap" approach was used in Ho, Milevsky, and Robinson (1994), Bengen (1994, 1997), Khorasanee (1996), Cooley, Hubbard, and Walz (1998), Milevsky (1998), Jarrett and Stringfellow (2000), Pye (2000, 2001), Ameriks, Veres, and Warshawsky (2001), Albrecht and Maurer (2002), Blake, Cairns, and Dowd (2003), and Smith and Gould (2005), among others. An alternative analytic approach (based on the lognormal distribution) is proposed in McCabe (1999); Milevsky and Robinson (2000) provide a more complicated moment matching technique; and Huang, Milevsky, and Wang (2004) discuss the PDE approach to the problem. For an extension of retirement ruin probabilities to a dynamic model, see Browne (1999) or Young (2004) for a deterministic horizon. For yet another perspective on dynamic asset allocation to maximize spending rates within the context of endowments, see Dybvig (1999). For an earlier proof of (9.4) for zero λ, see Dufresne (1990). Finally, for a comprehensive treatment of ruin probabilities, see Asmussen (2000).

9.9 Problems

PROBLEM 9.1. Create a simulation spreadsheet in Excel that computes the probability of lifetime ruin. Start the simulation at age 65. Generate 40 random (lognormal) investment returns for the next 40 years of retirement. Generate a random future lifetime—for example, 22 years—and then compute the present value of a given consumption plan under a particular realization of the investment sequence. Compare the analytic approximation to the empirical probabilities. How good (or bad) is the formula?

PROBLEM 9.2. Assume you have just retired and are planning to spend 5% (adjusted for inflation) of your nest egg each year. You are investing in a portfolio with a real expected return of $\mu = 7.5\%$ and a volatility of $\sigma = 18\%$. Compute the probability of retirement ruin under a median remaining lifetime of $m = 20$ years and of $m = 30$ years.

9.10 Appendix: Derivation of the Formula

The main formula presented in this chapter connected the instantaneous mortality rate λ, the investable asset's expected return μ, the investable asset's volatility σ, and the initial spending rate $1/w$ to the probability of ruin $\Pr[SPV \geq w]$. The formula was presented in equation (9.4) and formed the basis of many numerical examples and case studies throughout the chapter. I have argued that the formula yields a good approximation of the true probability of ruin and that it can be used to calibrate or benchmark more complicated simulations. In this appendix I will sketch the precise steps that lead to this formula.

I start by assuming that the investable asset (mutual fund, index fund, etc.) obeys the basic geometric Brownian motion model, denoted by

$$dS_t = \mu S_t dt + \sigma S_t dB_t, \qquad S_0 = 1. \tag{9.5}$$

Recall from Chapter 5 that the solution to this stochastic differential equation (SDE) can be written formally as

$$S_t := e^{(\mu - \sigma^2/2)t + \sigma B_t} = e^{\nu t + \sigma B_t}, \tag{9.6}$$

where μ is the arithmetic mean and ν is the geometric mean (a.k.a. the growth rate).

This underlying asset forms the basis of the retirement income portfolio from which the quantity $1dt$ dollars is being withdrawn, continuously in time, from an initial wealth of w. Therefore, the dynamics of the investment portfolio satisfy a related SDE:

$$dW_t := dS_t - 1dt = (\mu W_t - 1)dt + \sigma W_t dB_t, \qquad W_0 = w. \tag{9.7}$$

The investment portfolio W_t starts off at a value of $W_0 = w$ at time $t = 0$ and then fluctuates over time as per the dynamics given by (9.7). The drift of the retirement portfolio process is $\mu W_t - 1$, which differs from the drift μS_t of the investable asset itself. The investable asset S_t is expected to grow over time because the expected return $\mu > 0$, but it is quite likely that the retirement portfolio will shrink over time—especially if $\mu W_t < 1$.

The solution to the SDE for W_t can be written explicitly as

$$W_t = e^{\nu t + \sigma B_t}\left[w - \int_0^t e^{-\nu t - \sigma B_t}\, dt \right], \qquad W_0 = w; \tag{9.8}$$

by (9.6), this can be rewritten as

$$W_t = S_t\left[w - \int_0^t S_t^{-1}\,dt\right], \qquad W_0 = w. \tag{9.9}$$

To confirm that equations (9.8) and (9.9) actually do satisfy the SDE in (9.7), you can take derivatives of either equation using the stochastic calculus (Ito) version of a derivative.

My main objective is to compute the probability of retirement ruin, which can be expressed mathematically as

$$\phi(w) := \Pr\left[\inf_{0 \le s < T} W_s \le 0 \mid W_0 = w\right]. \tag{9.10}$$

It is the probability that the lowest value of the stochastic process W_t hits or breaches a value of zero at some point prior to the random time of death T. The function $\phi(w)$ is an explicit function of the initial level of retirement wealth w, or the initial spending rate $1/w$, and an implicit function of the mortality dynamics governing T as well as the portfolio parameters μ, ν, σ. Naturally, the greater the value of w, the lower the probability of retirement ruin. I will prove that the probability of retirement ruin in equation (9.10) can be expressed as the probability that a suitably defined stochastic present value function is greater than w.

Now let us look carefully at equation (9.9) and the probability that it will reach a value of zero. The process W_t consists of two parts multiplied by each other. The first portion S_t can never be negative, since it is an exponential function of Brownian motion, and so the process W_t will hit zero if and only if the second portion equals zero. The quantity in brackets starts off at time 0 at a value of w, since the integral $\int_0^t (S_t^{-1})\,dt$ is equal to zero at time 0. The only way the quantity in brackets can equal zero is if the integral portion $\int_0^t (S_t^{-1})\,dt$ grows from zero to a value of w. Note that this integral is monotonically increasing in the upper bound of integration t; therefore, once $\int_0^t (S_t^{-1})\,dt$ exceeds w, it will never go back under w. This means that we can rewrite the retirement ruin probability strictly in terms of S_t alone:

$$\phi(w) := \Pr\left[\int_0^T e^{-\nu t - \sigma B_t}\,dt \ge w\right]. \tag{9.11}$$

The integral in equation (9.11) is precisely the stochastic present value introduced in the body of this chapter. The probability of retirement ruin is equivalent to the probability that the SPV is greater than or equal to the initial retirement wealth. This problem is now reduced to finding an appropriate probability distribution for the integral, defined by

$$X_T := \int_0^T e^{-vt - \sigma B_t} \, dt, \tag{9.12}$$

where the probability of retirement ruin is:

$$\phi(w) = 1 - \Pr[X_T < w]. \tag{9.13}$$

Note that an explicit distribution function is not available for X_T when $T < \infty$, but we can use moment matching techniques to locate an approximating distribution that shares the first two moments of the true distribution.

To obtain these moments, I start by defining the following intermediate variables: $v = v_0 = \mu - \sigma^2/2$, $v_1 = \mu - \sigma^2$, $v_2 = \mu - 3\sigma^2/2$, and $v_3 = \mu - 2\sigma^2$; this implies that $v_0 \geq v_1 \geq v_2 \geq v_3$. I will assume the most restrictive case that $v_3 > 0$, which in turn implies that the expected return μ is sufficiently larger than the volatility σ; this is required for convergence of the SPV integral defined by (9.12). To compute moments, I switch the integral and expectations signs, which yields

$$M_t^{(1)} := E[X_t] = \int_0^t e^{-v_1 s} \, ds = \frac{1 - e^{-v_1 t}}{v_1} \tag{9.14}$$

as the first moment of the stochastic present value (to a fixed time) and

$$
\begin{aligned}
M_t^{(2)} &:= E[X_t^2] \\
&= \frac{2}{v_3} \int_0^t (e^{-v_1 s} - e^{-2v_2 s}) \, ds \\
&= \frac{2}{v_3} \left(\frac{1 - e^{-v_1 t}}{v_1} - \frac{1 - e^{-2v_2 t}}{2v_2} \right)
\end{aligned} \tag{9.15}
$$

as the second moment of the SPV (to a fixed time). The time index on both $M_t^{(1)}$ and $M_t^{(2)}$ indicates that we are integrating up to time t, which is fixed; I will return to the random horizon (where $t = T$) in a moment. Note also that, when $t \to \infty$ and the SPV is over an infinite horizon, the first and second moments converge to $M_\infty^{(1)} = (v_1)^{-1}$ and $M_\infty^{(2)} = (v_1 v_2)^{-1}$ or, using the original parameters μ, σ, to $M_\infty^{(1)} = (\mu - \sigma^2)^{-1}$ and $M_\infty^{(2)} = ((\mu - \sigma^2)(\mu - 3\sigma^2/2))^{-1}$.

When $\Pr[T > t] = e^{-\lambda t}$, which is the exponential mortality case, the relevant moments are

$$M_\lambda^{(1)} := E[X_\lambda] = \int_0^\infty e^{-(v_1 + \lambda)s} \, ds = \frac{1}{v_1 + \lambda} \tag{9.16}$$

and

$$M_\lambda^{(2)} := E[X_\lambda^2] = \frac{2}{v_3} \int_0^\infty (e^{-(v_1+\lambda)s} - e^{-(2v_2+\lambda)s})\, ds$$

$$= \frac{2}{v_3}\left(\frac{1}{v_1+\lambda} - \frac{1}{2v_2+\lambda}\right)$$

$$= \frac{2}{(v_1+\lambda)(2v_2+\lambda)}, \tag{9.17}$$

since $2v_2 - v_1 = v_3$. Using the original parameters μ and σ in place of the values v_1 and v_2, we are left with

$$M_\lambda^{(1)} = \frac{1}{\mu + \lambda - \sigma^2} = \frac{1}{\tilde{\mu} - \tilde{\sigma}^2}, \tag{9.18}$$

$$M_\lambda^{(2)} = \frac{2}{(\mu + \lambda - \sigma^2)(2\mu - 3\sigma^2 + \lambda)} = \frac{2}{(\tilde{\mu} - \tilde{\sigma}^2)(2\tilde{\mu} - 3\tilde{\sigma}^2)}, \tag{9.19}$$

where the modified expected return and volatility variables are $\tilde{\mu} := \mu + 2\lambda$ and $\tilde{\sigma}^2 := \sigma^2 + \lambda$, respectively. In sum, I have just derived the first and second moments of the SPV under exponential mortality.

I will now choose the reciprocal Gamma distribution as our candidate for approximating the SPV and will locate parameters α, β that match these moments. The reason I have selected the RG distribution as the approximator is that, in the limit, the distribution of X_∞ actually does converge to the reciprocal Gamma density. See Dufresne (1990) and Milevsky (1997) for a proof and for the references therein.

Recall that a random variable is RG distributed with parameters α, β if the probability law for X can be written as

$$\Pr[X < x] := \frac{\beta^{-\alpha}}{\Gamma(a)} \int_0^x y^{-(\alpha+1)} e^{(-1/y\beta)}\, dy, \tag{9.20}$$

where α and β are the free parameters. The expected (mean) value or first moment of the reciprocal Gamma distribution is $E[X] = (\beta(\alpha-1))^{-1}$, and the second moment is $E[X^2] = (\beta^2(\alpha-1)(\alpha-2))^{-1}$. The first two moments of the RG distribution, which are denoted generically by $M^{(1)}$ and $M^{(2)}$, are

$$M^{(1)} = \frac{1}{\beta(\alpha-1)}, \qquad M^{(2)} = \frac{1}{\beta^2(\alpha-1)(\alpha-2)}. \tag{9.21}$$

This imposes a natural condition for the existence of the second moment—namely, that $\alpha > 2$. Equation (9.21) induces a one-to-one relationship between the parameters α, β and the moments $M^{(1)}, M^{(2)}$. Indeed, one can invert the moment equations and solve for the implied α, β parameters, which leads to

$$\alpha = \frac{2M^{(2)} - M^{(1)}M^{(1)}}{M^{(2)} - M^{(1)}M^{(1)}}, \qquad \beta = \frac{M^{(2)} - M^{(1)}M^{(1)}}{M^{(2)}M^{(1)}}. \tag{9.22}$$

So, because we know the first two moments of the SPV, we can invert them and then solve for the α, β values just displayed. The result of this moment matching approximation is

$$\Pr[X_\lambda \leq w] = \mathrm{RG}(\tilde{\alpha}, \tilde{\beta} \mid w)$$

$$:= 1 - \frac{\tilde{\beta}^{-\tilde{\alpha}}}{\Gamma(\tilde{\alpha})} \int_0^w x^{-(\tilde{\alpha}+1)} e^{-(1/x\tilde{\beta})} \, dx, \tag{9.23}$$

where now $\tilde{\alpha} = 2\tilde{\mu}/\tilde{\sigma}^2 - 1$ and $\tilde{\beta} = \tilde{\sigma}^2/2$. I will pause for a moment to let this statement sink in, since it is the basis of the approximation that I used within the actual chapter.

For those readers who are struggling to understand the intuition behind the lifetime ruin probability, start by thinking about what happens when $\sigma \to 0$ in the SPV defined by equation (9.4). In this case, the two RG parameters collapse to values of $\tilde{\alpha} = 2\mu/\lambda + 3$ and $\tilde{\beta} = \lambda/2$. The expected value of the SPV is $(\mu + \lambda)^{-1}$. Now, let us use W_t to denote the wealth of a retiree who invests and consumes \$1 per year. This W_t process will obey the ordinary differential equation (ODE)

$$dW_t = (\mu W_t - 1)dt, \quad W_0 = w, \ W_t \geq 0, \tag{9.24}$$

where μ is the arithmetic (continuously compounded) return. Without any loss of generality, we can define this equation up to the point of ruin $W_{t^*} = 0$. The solution to the ODE is

$$W_t = \begin{cases} (w - 1/\mu)e^{\mu t} + 1/\mu & \text{if } t < t^*, \\ 0 & \text{if } t \geq t^*, \end{cases} \tag{9.25}$$

where t^* is the time of ruin. This value can be obtained exactly by solving

$$\left(w - \frac{1}{\mu}\right)e^{\mu t} + \frac{1}{\mu} = 0 \iff t^* = \frac{1}{\mu}\ln\left[\frac{1}{w\mu - 1}\right]. \tag{9.26}$$

Now, if the initial value of the function/process W_0 is arbitrarily set equal to $w = (\lambda + \mu)^{-1}$, then the ruin time t^* can be simplified to

$$t^* = \frac{1}{\mu}\ln\left[1 + \frac{\mu}{\lambda}\right]. \tag{9.27}$$

Moreover, if $\mu = \lambda$ then the value of $t^* = \ln[2]/\lambda$, which is exactly the *median* life span. In the limit as $\mu \to 0$, the ruin time is precisely the life expectancy $1/\lambda$ because

$$\lim_{\mu \to 0} \frac{1}{\mu} \ln\left[1 + \frac{\mu}{\lambda}\right] = \frac{1}{\lambda}. \tag{9.28}$$

Finally, the probability of not surviving to the point at which W_t hits zero is

$$1 - \exp\{-\lambda t^*\} = 1 - \exp\left\{-\frac{\lambda}{\mu} \ln\left[1 + \frac{\mu}{\lambda}\right]\right\}. \tag{9.29}$$

I refer the interested reader to Huang et al. (2004) for further analysis and discussion of the robustness and accuracy of this approximation as compared to one derived using a PDE-based technique.

TEN

Longevity Insurance Revisited

10.1 To Annuitize or Not To Annuitize?

The pension plan at my university will present me with a very difficult choice when I reach retirement. At that time I must decide whether I want to receive my benefits in the form of an immediate pension annuity (which the university will provide for the rest of my life) or to take the money out in one lump sum and assume the responsibility for retirement income myself. This is an all-or-nothing decision. I can't leave part of the money in, nor can I reverse my decision after I retire. If I take the pension annuity, I will never be able to access the funds, and if I withdraw the money, I can never rejoin the university pension plan and convert the balance into a pension annuity. So if I take the lump-sum payout but then later want an annuity, my only option will be to go to an established insurance company and purchase a (retail) pension annuity directly. In this case, the price I must pay for the lifetime income will depend on the insurance company and their pricing assumptions, but it will certainly provide me with less income than what I could have received from my university pension plan because of the difference between group pricing and individual pricing. Thus, if I truly want to receive my benefits in the form of a pension annuity, I'm much better off doing this via my university pension plan. Hence the gut-wrenching dilemma!

This situation is obviously quite extreme and scary compared to the decision that most retirees face, but it is at the heart of prudent financial planning toward the end of the human life cycle. *Should you annuitize?* This question and its various answers are the topic of this chapter. I might be tempted to avoid the pension annuity altogether because it is clearly irreversible, illiquid, and nonmarketable. The funds cannot be accessed under any circumstances, regardless of whether it is needed for emergencies, a bequest, or any other reason—unless I pay extra for a guaranteed period certain.

Fixed-payout annuities also face inflation risk and the risk of locking in a low fixed income during periods of low interest rates. This can be partially alleviated through inflation or cost-of-living adjustments or through the purchase of immediate variable payout annuities (IVA). However, some individuals are not comfortable with the fluctuating income of IVAs. And though the income from a life annuity would last for the rest of my life (and possibly longer, if I purchase one with survivorship benefits), I could instead manage and invest the money myself and create my own income stream—that is, self-annuitize.

In earlier chapters I talked about the valuation of pension annuities and the mathematics behind the mortality and interest rate components. In this chapter I take a deeper look at the topic of longevity insurance and discuss why anyone would choose to lock in an irreversible pension annuity.

10.2 Five 95-Year-Olds Playing Bridge

Let us begin our discussion of longevity insurance with a simple story that illustrates the benefits of this concept. A 95-year-old grandmother loves playing bridge with her four best friends on Sunday every few months. Coincidentally, all five of them are aged exactly 95 years, are quite healthy, and have been retired—and playing bridge—for 30 years. Recently, the cards have become rather tiresome, and the grandmother has decided to juice up their activities. Last time they met, she proposed that they each place $100 on the kitchen table. "Whoever survives 'til the end of the year gets to split the $500," she said. "And, if you don't make it, you forfeit the money.... Oh yeah, don't tell the kids." Yes, this is an odd gamble, but you will see my point in a moment.

In fact, they all thought it was an interesting idea and agreed to participate, but they felt it was risky to leave $500 on the kitchen table for a whole year. Hence they decided to put the money in a local bank's one-year term deposit, paying 5% interest for the year.

So what will happen next year? Roughly speaking, there is a 20% chance that any given member of the bridge club will die during the next year. This, in turn, implies an 80% chance of survival. Virtually anything can happen during the next 12 months of waiting (in fact, there are six possible scenarios), but the odds are that, on average, four 96-year-olds will survive to split the $525 pot at year's end.

Note that each survivor will receive $131.25 as their total return on the original investment of $100. The 31.25% investment return contains 5% of the bank's money and a whopping 26.25% of what I call *mortality credits*. These credits represent the capital and interest "lost" by the deceased and "gained" by the survivors.

The catch, of course, is that the nonsurvivor forfeits any claim to the funds. The beneficiaries of the deceased might be frustrated with this outcome, but the survivors get a superior investment return. From the perspective of retirement planning, all five bridge players get to manage their lifetime income risk in advance and without having to worry about what the future will bring.

I think this story does a nice job of translating the benefits of longevity insurance (a.k.a. pension annuities) into investment rates of return. There is no other financial product that guarantees such high rates of return, conditional on survival.

We can take this scenario one step further. What if the grandmother and her club decided to invest the $500 in the stock market—or in some risky NASDAQ high-tech fund—for the next year? Moreover, what happens if this fund or subaccount collapses in value during the year and falls 20% in value? How much will the surviving bridge players lose? Well, if you are thinking "nothing" that is absolutely the correct answer. They divide the remaining $400 amongst the surviving four and so receive their original $100 back.

Such is the power of mortality credits. They subsidize losses on the downside and enhance gains on the upside. In fact, I would go so far as to say that once you wrap true longevity insurance around a diversified portfolio, the annuitant can actually afford to tolerate more financial risk.

Of course, real-world annuity contracts do not work in the way described here. The grandmother's policy is actually a *tontine* contract, which she would have to renew each year if she wanted to continue. In fact, the surviving 96-year-olds have the option to take their mortality credits and go home. In practice, annuity contracts are for life and these credits are spread and amortized over many years of retirement. But the basic insurance economics underlying the contract are exactly as I have described.

In sum, pension/life annuities provide a unique and peculiar kind of insurance. It is virtually the only insurance policy that people acquire and actually hope to use! Although we are willing to pay for home insurance, disability insurance, and car insurance, we never want to exercise or use the policy: after all, who wants their house to burn down (or to break a leg or crash a car)? Yet the "insurable event" underlying pension annuities is living a long and prosperous life. Perhaps this is why the industry marketers

Table 10.1. *Algebra of fixed tontine vs.*
nontontine investment

	End-of-year payoff	
Invesment now	Alive	Dead
$100 (nontontine)	$100(1 + R)$	$100(1 + R)$
$100 (tontine)	$\frac{100}{(_1p_x)}(1 + R)$	0

have yet to achieve much success in selling these products—they are still accustomed to scaring us. I hope simple tales like this can help retirees and their financial advisors understand the benefits, risks, and returns from buying longevity insurance.

10.3 The Algebra of Fixed and Variable Tontines

I will now present the mathematics behind the example of Section 10.2. My specific objective is to measure the impact of age on the so-called mortality credits. What if a group of 50-year-olds entered into such an arrangement? Would the financial gains or benefits for the survivors be as high? Table 10.1 provides a general answer.

As usual, I will let $(_1p_x)$ denote the one-year probability of survival for someone currently aged x. In our story, $(_1p_{95}) = 80\%$ for each of the 95-year-old females, and this is pretty close to the Gompertz–Makeham (GoMa) values under the parameters we have been using throughout the book. From the individual's perspective, a $100 investment will grow to $100(1 + 0.05) = 105$ at the end of one year. This will be split amongst the surviving 80%, which leads to a gain of $105/(0.8) = 131.25$ per survivor, or a one-year investment return of 31.25%. Of course, in the event of death, the end-of-period payoff will be zero and the investment return will be -100%. If we average the four ladies (survivors) who are getting 31.25% and the one lady (deceased) who gets -100%, we are left with exactly $(4(31.25) - 100)/5 = 5\%$, which is the 5% return from the bank. There is no magic or sleight of hand in the algebra. The "dead" subsidize the investment returns of the "living"; the survivors are "eating" other people's money.

At this point, you will notice that the same analysis can be done at any age using the same $R = 5\%$ (effective annual) interest rate. Thus, Table 10.2 shows the mortality credits at age $x = 30, 50, 60, 65, 70, 75, 80, 85,$ and 90. To be precise, I will use our favorite GoMa parameters of $m = 86.34$ and

Table 10.2. *Investment returns from fixed tontines given survival to year's end*

Age	Survival $(_1p_x)\%$	Payoff $\frac{\$100}{(_1p_x)}(1+R)$	Mortality credits $10000\left(\frac{1}{(_1p_x)}-1\right)(1+R)$
30	99.97%	$105.03	3.1 b.p.
50	99.76%	$105.25	25.4 b.p.
60	99.31%	$105.73	73.1 b.p.
65	98.83%	$106.24	124.0 b.p.
70	98.03%	$107.11	210.8 b.p.
75	96.69%	$108.59	359.3 b.p.
80	94.46%	$111.15	615.3 b.p.
85	90.81%	$115.63	1,062.6 b.p.
90	84.94%	$123.61	1,861.0 b.p.

Notes: b.p. = basis points. GoMa mortality with $m = 86.34$ and $b = 9.5$; $R = 5\%$.

$b = 9.5$ with $\lambda = 0$. Recall that, under GoMa mortality with $\lambda = 0$, the survival probability is given by the functional form

$$(_tp_x) = \exp\{e^{(x-m)/b}(1 - e^{t/b})\}. \tag{10.1}$$

In this case, Table 10.1 can be extended to the following numbers. A 50-year-old who invests $100 in a one-year tontine will lose the entire $100 by dying during that year. But if the 50-year-old survives to age 51 then the $100 will grow to $105 plus an additional $0.25, which is the principal plus interest of the $(1 - 0.9976) = 0.24\%$ who die during the year. Stated differently, if 10,000 50-year-old investors each place $100 in a tontine fund that earns 5% during the year, then the $1,050,000 "pot of money" will be split amongst the 9,976 survivors and leave each with a total cash flow of $1050000/9976 = \$105.25$, which is 0.25% more than the 5% return. This is a mortality credit of (approximately) 25 basis points. At age 70, the mortality credit is close to 211 basis points and at age 90 it is 1,861 basis points (see Table 10.2).

Another way to think about the results in Table 10.2 is by focusing on those individuals who do not enter into a tontine agreement—instead allocating their money to traditional investments—and still survive to the end of the year. A 50-year-old would have to earn 25 basis points above the "valuation rate" of 5% to be as well off as someone who purchased the tontine. At age 75, the same (reluctant) investor who did not purchase the tontine would have to earn 359 basis points above the valuation rate just to

Table 10.3. *Algebra of variable tontine vs.*
nontontine investment

	End-of-year payoff	
Investment now	Alive	Dead
$100 (nontontine)	$100(1 + X)$	$100(1 + X)$
$100 (tontine)	$\frac{100}{(_1 p_x)}(1 + X)$	0

keep up. At age 85 it becomes an (insurmountable) 10% above the valuation rate: the individual would have to earn a rate higher than 15% just to keep up.

The same idea can be applied to variable returns. Instead of investing $100 in a riskless deposit that earns R, the investor (i.e., the tontine group) can place the money in a "risky fund" earning X, which is random. Assuming that the fraction $(_1 p_x)$ of the group survived, the total return to the survivors at year's end would be $100(1 + X)/(_1 p_x)$, rather than the quantity of $100(1 + R)/(_1 p_x)$ that would be applicable in the fixed case.

Table 10.3 shows the payoff matrix under the alive and dead states as a function of whether the individual purchased a risky asset or rather a tontine "wrapped around" a risky asset. If the market does well—for example, if $X = 20\%$—the survivors get $120/(_1 p_x)$. On the other hand, if the market fares poorly (say, $X = -20\%$) then the survivors get $80/(_1 p_x)$.

On a more formal level, assuming $(_1 p_x)$ people survive to the end of the year, the expected return from the "risky tontine" would be $(1 + E[X])/(_1 p_x) - 1$, which by definition is higher than $E[X]$ because $(_1 p_x) < 1$. Likewise, the standard deviation of the return from the risky tontine conditional on $(_1 p_x)$ individuals surviving is $SD[X]/(_1 p_x)$, which is also larger than $SD[X]$ itself. Note that both the mean and the standard deviation (volatility) are larger. The natural question is: "Is the extra risk worth it?" In other words, if all I care about is making sure I have enough money to last for the rest of my natural life and if I don't care about giving up the option of leaving a bequest, do these extra mortality credits influence my asset allocation? The next section will answer this question.

10.4 Asset Allocation with Tontines

To understand this concept in a more rigorous manner, imagine a situation in which you have $W_0 = \$100$ that you would like to allocate between a "safe bonds" fund yielding an interest rate of R during the next year and a "risky stocks" fund yielding (a random) X during the next year. Assume that your allocation proportion is denoted by the symbol θ, which can range from $\theta = 0\%$ to $\theta = 100\%$, allocated to the risky investment fund. In general, if W_0 denotes your initial investment or wealth, then at year's end you will have a total of

$$W_1 = W_0(\theta(1 + X) + (1 - \theta)(1 + R)). \tag{10.2}$$

For example, if you allocate $\theta = 60\%$ to stocks and $1 - \theta = 40\%$ to bonds and if the safe bonds fund is paying $R = 5\%$ per year, then an initial investment of $W_0 = 100$ will become $W_1 = 100((0.6)(1 + 0.2) + (0.4)(1.05)) = 114.0$ if the *realized* return from risky stocks were $X = 20\%$. But if the realized return from risky stocks were negative at $X = -20\%$ then the portfolio would be worth $W_1 = 100((0.6)(1 - 0.2) + (0.4)(1.05)) = 90.0$, which is a loss of 10% in portfolio value.

Let the expected investment return from the risky stock be denoted by $E[X] = v$, the volatility or standard deviation of this return be $SD[X] = \sigma$, and the investment return X itself be normally distributed. Then the end-of-year portfolio value will also be normally distributed with

$$E[W_1] = W_0(\theta(1 + v) + (1 - \theta)(1 + R)) \tag{10.3}$$

and

$$SD[W_1] = W_0 \theta \sigma. \tag{10.4}$$

For instance, in the aforementioned case where $R = 5\%$ and $\theta = 60\%$, if the risky stock satisfies $v = 11\%$ and $\sigma = 20\%$ then $E[W_1]/W_0 - 1 = 8.6\%$ and $SD[W_1]/W_0 = (0.6)(0.2) = 12\%$. Observe that I subtracted 1 from the ratio $E[W_1]/W_0$ in order to convert the total return into a rate of return.

Now, let me examine the probability of earning a certain threshold return, similar to the concept or shortfall risk discussed in Chapter 5. We seek

$$\max_{\theta} E[W_1] \tag{10.5}$$

subject to the constraint that

$$\Pr[W_1 \leq W_0] \leq \varepsilon. \tag{10.6}$$

In other words, we are looking for the "best" value of θ such that the expected value of the portfolio at the end of the year is at its highest level— subject to the condition that the probability of losing money is less than ε. Note that our "objective function" $E[W_1]$ is linear in the choice variable θ

as long as $v > R$, which makes perfect sense. Intuitively, since $E[X] = v > R$ by definition, our natural inclination—and the formal solution to this problem—is to increase θ as much as possible until $\Pr[W_1 < W_0] = \varepsilon$ exactly, which is the point at which the constraint has become binding. We are therefore reduced to locating the largest value of θ under which $\Pr[W_1 < W_0] = \varepsilon$.

So let us focus on the probability of shortfall in question. Recall from Chapter 5 that the probability of a standard normal random variable "taking on" a value less than or equal to c is

$$\Phi(c) = \int_{-\infty}^{c} \frac{1}{\sqrt{2\pi}} e^{-z^2/2} \, dz. \tag{10.7}$$

The probability that a nonstandard normal random variable will take on a value less than or equal to c is $\Phi((c - v)/\sigma)$, where v is the mean and σ is the standard deviation. In our case, the probability that the portfolio W_1 is worth less than its initial value W_0 is

$$\Phi\left(\frac{W_0 - W_0(\theta(1 + v) + (1 - \theta)(1 + R))}{W_0 \theta \sigma} \right), \tag{10.8}$$

where the numerator is the difference between the initial value W_0 and the portfolio's expected value $E[W_1]$ from equation (10.3) and where the denominator is the portfolio value's standard deviation $SD[W_1]$ from equation (10.4). Again, we are looking for the largest value of θ—which will become our optimum θ^*—such that the probability of shortfall is exactly equal to ε. After some basic cancellations and simple algebra, we can invert the function $\Phi(\cdot)$ and search for the largest value of θ such that

$$\frac{1}{\theta \sigma} - \left(\frac{1 + v}{\sigma} + \frac{1 + R}{\theta \sigma} - \frac{1 + R}{\sigma} \right) = \Phi^{-1}(\varepsilon), \tag{10.9}$$

where $\Phi^{-1}(\varepsilon)$ denotes the inverse of the normal cumulative distribution function evaluated at ε. For example, a tolerance value of $\varepsilon = 0.01$ leads to $\Phi^{-1}(0.01) = -2.326$, while $\Phi^{-1}(0.10) = -1.281$ and obviously $\Phi^{-1}(0.5) = 0$. All these numbers correspond to the z-value for which the "area to the left of z" is equal to ε.

Collecting terms and simplifying further lead us to

$$-\left(\frac{v - R}{\sigma} \right) - \frac{R}{\theta \sigma} = \Phi^{-1}(\varepsilon), \tag{10.10}$$

which—by isolating the choice variable θ—finally yields

$$\theta^* = \frac{R}{-\sigma\Phi^{-1}(\varepsilon) - (v - R)}. \qquad (10.11)$$

There are a number of technical conditions for this to work. First and foremost: $-\sigma\Phi^{-1}(\varepsilon) - (v - R) > 0$, which means that $(v - R)/\sigma < -\Phi^{-1}(\varepsilon)$.

In conclusion, if I want to allocate my portfolio between a risk-free asset and a risky asset so that my expected portfolio return is at its highest yet the risk of losing money is bounded by $\varepsilon\%$, then the optimal allocation will be θ^* as presented in equation (10.11).

Now let me investigate the same problem when the asset allocation decision takes place within the tontines described in previous sections. In this case the R variable is replaced by $(1 + R)/(_1p_x) - 1$, the v variable is replaced by $(1+v)/(_1p_x)-1$, and the standard deviation σ of the risky asset is replaced by $\sigma/(_1p_x)$. The mathematics of the problem proceeds exactly as before, but this time I replace the v- and σ-values with their tontine-adjusted numbers.

Another way to think about this is by examining the tontine-adjusted portfolio mean and standard deviation via:

$$E[W_1^{\text{tontine}}] = W_0(\theta(1 + v) + (1 - \theta)(1 + R))/(_1p_x), \qquad (10.12)$$

$$\text{SD}[W_1^{\text{tontine}}] = W_0\theta\sigma/(_1p_x). \qquad (10.13)$$

The optimization problem remains the same, except that the probability constraint must now be written as:

$$\Phi\left(\frac{W_0 - W_0(\theta(1 + v) + (1 - \theta)(1 + R))/(_1p_x)}{W_0\theta\sigma/(_1p_x)}\right) \le \varepsilon. \qquad (10.14)$$

Going through similar algebra as before—and canceling the $(_1p_x)$ wherever possible—we are left with the problem of locating the largest value of θ such that

$$\frac{(_1p_x)}{\theta\sigma} - \left(\frac{1+v}{\sigma} + \frac{1+R}{\theta\sigma} - \frac{1+R}{\sigma}\right) = \Phi^{-1}(\varepsilon), \qquad (10.15)$$

which can be simplified to

$$\frac{(_1p_x) - (1+R)}{\theta} - (v - R) = \sigma\Phi^{-1}(\varepsilon). \qquad (10.16)$$

This then leads to

$$\theta^{**} = \frac{R + (1 - (_1p_x))}{-\sigma\Phi^{-1}(\varepsilon) - (v - R)}. \qquad (10.17)$$

Table 10.4. *Optimal portfolio mix of stocks and safe cash*

Loss tolerance	θ^*	Allocation to stocks θ^{**} (age-75 tontine)	θ^{**} (age-60 tontine)
$\varepsilon = 1\%$	12.34%	20.51%	14.04%
$\varepsilon = 5\%$	18.59%	30.90%	21.15%
$\varepsilon = 10\%$	25.47%	42.33%	28.98%
$\varepsilon = 20\%$	46.16%	76.71%	52.53%
$\varepsilon = 25\%$	66.76%	110.95%	75.97%

Note: $E[X] = 11\%$, $\text{SD}[X] = 20\%$, $R = 5\%$; $(_1p_{60}) = 99.31\%$, $(_1p_{75}) = 96.69\%$; $m = 86.34$, $b = 9.5$.

The structure of equation (10.17) matches that of (10.11) except for the numerator, where (10.17) contains an additional $(1 - (_1p_x))$ term. This additional term will become larger—and hence increase the optimal value of θ^{**}—as the survival probability declines.

Table 10.4 provides numerical estimates of θ^{**} and θ^* (with and without tontines, respectively) under a variety of loss tolerance levels ε. The main result is the rapid increase in risk taking once the investment options are offered within a tontine structure. For example, if all you are willing to tolerate is a 10% chance of losing any money by the end of the year, then without a tontine you should allocate only 25.47% of your wealth to the risky asset X; the remaining 74.53% should be placed in the risk-free R asset. On the other hand, if you are making the exact same asset allocation decision within a tontine, the optimal allocation to the risky asset increases to 28.98% if you are 60 years old and to 42.33% if you are 75 years old. Remember that the older age implies a lower probability of survival $(_1p_x)$ and hence a higher investment return value of $(1 + v)/(_1p_x) - 1$, even if this is at the expense of a higher standard deviation $\sigma/(_1p_x)$.

Of course, the discussion so far—in terms of asset allocation and mortality credits—has taken place within the context of a simple (and currently unavailable) tontine insurance in which contracts are terminated and then possibly renegotiated each year. (One has to wonder why insurers have not yet developed the equivalent short-term annuities.) As you recall, in exchange for one lump sum $\bar{a}_x$, the annuitant receives a dollar of income for the rest of his life. This stream of income consists of three parts: the return of principal, the interest, and other people's money (the mortality credits). It is therefore much harder to isolate the precise value of these mortality credits as in Table 10.2, given the multiperiod nature of the contract. In the next section, however, I will introduce an equivalent idea that should help generalize the concept of mortality credits from tontines to annuities.

10.5 A First Look at Self-Annuitization

Although most of the mathematics in this book has been in the language of continuous time, I will now deviate for a bit and perform some of the calculations in discrete time. More specifically, I will examine pension annuities that pay out \$1 at the end of the year as opposed to paying $1dt$ continuously. The reason for working (just briefly) in discrete time is to capture the essence of our mortality credits in a fresh and perhaps more accessible way.

The basic market pricing definition of a \$1-per-year pension annuity in discrete time is

$$a_x = \sum_{t=1}^{\infty} \frac{(_tp_x)}{(1+R)^t}, \tag{10.18}$$

where R denotes the effective annual valuation rate used by the insurance company to discount cash flows and $(_tp_x)$ denotes the conditional probability that an individual aged x will attain age $x + t$. I am (again) ignoring all proportional insurance loads, premium taxes, sales commissions, and distribution fees that would be added to (or multiplied by) the pure actuarial premium when arriving at a market price for the pension annuity. Notice that there is no bar over the a_x since this is not a continuous annuity but rather a discrete (annual) one.

Now, imagine that—instead of purchasing a pension annuity and paying a_x for the promise of \$1 per year for life—the retiree decides to *delay* purchasing the life annuity for one year (until age $x + 1$). Now, in order to afford the exact same life annuity stream in one year, the annual investment return G earned by the retiree must satisfy the following inequality:

$$a_x(1+G) - 1 \geq a_{x+1}. \tag{10.19}$$

In other words, the life annuity premium at age x invested at a rate G, minus the \$1 consumption at the end of the year, must be greater than or equal to the market price of the annuity at age $x + 1$. Re-arranging equation (10.19) in terms of the portfolio investment return G, we obtain the condition for beating the rate of return from the annuity over one year:

$$G \geq \frac{a_{x+1}}{a_x} + \frac{1}{a_x} - 1. \tag{10.20}$$

The right-hand side of equation (10.20) is the threshold annual investment return necessary for what I would consider a successful deferral decision. Now using the actuarial identity

$$(_tp_{x+n}) = \frac{(_{n+t}p_x)}{(_np_x)} \qquad (10.21)$$

(which is true regardless of whether I am working in discrete or continuous time—think of the definition in terms of the instantaneous force of mortality curve), we can rewrite a_{x+1} in terms of a_x and then, using (10.20), rewrite the condition for beating the annuity's rate of return as

$$G \geq \frac{1+R}{(_1p_x)} - 1. \qquad (10.22)$$

Thus, if you can earn at least G percent, you should have enough money to consume $1 at the end of the year and then purchase an identical annuity with the remaining funds. Equation (10.22) should be recognized as the investment return plus the "mortality credit" from the tontine, and this formulation is crucial to my main thesis. The intuitive condition for beating the multiperiod annuity is that $G \geq (1 + R)/(_1p_x) - 1$. Hence, I hope to have succeeded in illustrating how the concept of mortality credits applies to more than just a simple one-period tontine. In fact, the concept can be generalized far beyond a single year. Let us now return to continuous time by way of an intuitive example.

10.6 The Implied Longevity Yield

A 65-year-old male can convert a $100,000 lump-sum premium into a pension annuity by going to any one of the many insurance companies that offer competitive quotes. At the time of writing, companies were quoting a payout ranging from a high of $690 per month to a low of $633 per month. The average was about $678.22 per month, and I will use this figure hereafter. These quotes assumed he was interested in acquiring 10 years of guaranteed payments and that the remaining payments would continue as long as he lived. If he wanted a longer guarantee period—or, say, payments that continued (to his spouse) after his death—then the monthly payout would be lower. In contrast, by settling for a shorter guarantee period he would receive more income per month.

Recall from Section 6.9 that an annuity with a 10-year (payment certain) guarantee has two components. The guaranteed portion is similar to a portfolio of zero-coupon bonds. The other portion continues to make payments to the annuitant after the end of the payment certain period—but only if the annuitant survives the guaranteed period.

All else being equal, a 75-year-old male could convert a $100,000 premium into a much higher monthly payment ranging from $1,002 per month to $948 per month depending on the insurance company. In this case, the average of the five best quotes was $975.90 per month.

Now here is my main argument. If a 75-year-old male wanted to purchase a life annuity with a *zero*-year guarantee paying the original $678.22 per month, he would have to pay only $(678/976) \times 100000 = \$69{,}396$ or roughly 70% of the original cost. The same annuity would be cheaper if purchased later. A 65-year-old needs a $100,000 premium to generate $678 for life (with 10 years of certain payments) whereas a 75-year-old requires only $69,396.

In the language of continuous-time mathematics, the quantity $100000/\bar{a}_{65}$ (that is, the annual income generated by a $100,000 premium annuitized at age 65) will cost $(100000/\bar{a}_{65})\bar{a}_{75}$ at age 75, and this cost must be less than $100,000 because $\bar{a}_{75} < \bar{a}_{65}$.

What would happen if the 65-year-old male decided to forgo the purchase of a life annuity and instead invested the $100,000, withdrawing the same $678.22 per month for the next 10 years? This strategy is called self-annuitization. What would be the portfolio investment return needed to withdraw $678.22 per month *and* still have $69,396 at the end of 10 years to purchase an identical annuity?

This value is known as the *Implied Longevity Yield* (ILY).† In our example (for age 65), the ILY works out to 5.90% (I will demonstrate shortly how to compute this number). So, if the 65-year-old can earn an annual return of 5.90%, he will be able to purchase the exact same life annuity at age 75 as he could have at age 65. The equivalent calculations for a female yield an ILY of 5.46%. In comparison, 4.73% was the applicable risk-free rate at the time. The ILY value for males (resp. females) was approximately 117 (resp. 73) basis points above the bond yield.

How can this number be used? There are several important applications for such a metric and thus good reasons for it to be computed and reported on an ongoing basis. The ILY should help consumers understand (and decompose) exactly what they are getting when they purchase a life annuity. In fact, one can obtain ILY values (using the same algorithm) to compare any two ages. One might compute the ILY for someone aged 70 or 75 who

---

† The "Implied Longevity Yield"—and its acronym, "ILY"—are registered trademarks and the property of CANNEX Financial Exchanges.

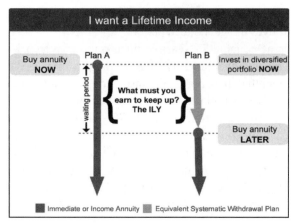

Figure 10.1. *Source:* Copyright 2005 by CANNEX Financial Exchanges. Reprinted with permission.

is contemplating purchasing a life annuity versus waiting to age 80 or 85. In the same manner, consumers can compute the ILY from taking a defined benefit pension at any age.

Resuming our standard notation, let $(_u\bar{a}_x)$ denote the price of a deferred life annuity that is sold to an individual aged x and that pays \$1 per annum for life (in continuous time) starting at time u. If the annuitant does not survive to age $x + u$ then the estate or beneficiaries receive nothing. Along the same lines, recall from Chapter 6 that $V(r, u)$ denotes the price of a term-certain (with no mortality component) annuity paying \$1 per annum (in continuous time) for u years. For example: the cost of a life annuity paying \$5,000 per annum (10 years payment certain) and purchased by a 65-year-old is denoted by $5000(V(r, 10) + (_{10}\bar{a}_{65}))$.

The theoretical basis of the Implied Longevity Yield metric is as follows. We compute the internal rate of return that an x-year-old would have to earn on the nonannuitized portfolio over the next u years in order to replicate the income payout from the annuity *and* still be able to acquire the same income pattern at age $x + u$ (assuming that current pricing remains unchanged). Figure 10.1 provides a graphical illustration of what we are trying to compute.

To understand the analytic dynamics of self-annuitization, I begin once again with a hypothetical retiree who has W_0 dollars in marketable wealth. If this individual were to annuitize—that is, to convert a stock of wealth W into a lifetime flow—then she would be entitled to W/a_1 per annum for life, where a_1 is shorthand for the relevant pension annuity factor at the relevant age. If, in contrast, the retiree decided not to purchase the life annuity and instead self-annuitized—by investing the funds at a "fixed" rate of interest denoted by g and consuming in continuous time at the annuity rate W/a_1—then the wealth dynamics would satisfy the ordinary differential equation

$$dW_t = \left(gW_t - \frac{W_0}{a_1}\right)dt, \quad W_t \geq 0. \tag{10.23}$$

In words, the instantaneous change in the value of the portfolio would be the sum of the interest gain (gW_t) minus the withdrawal for consumption purposes (W_0/a_1). Remember that the investment return g is assumed to be constant (nonstochastic) over time. The solution to (10.23) is

$$W_t = \left(W_0 - \frac{W_0}{ga_1}\right)e^{gt} + \frac{W_0}{ga_1}, \quad W_t \geq 0, \tag{10.24}$$

where g can always be selected so that $W_t > 0$ for all values of t. However, if this investment portfolio must contain enough funds to purchase the same exact annuity flow at age $x + u$, then the following relationship must hold:

$$\frac{W_0}{a_1}a_2 = \left(W_0 - \frac{W_0}{ga_1}\right)e^{gu} + \frac{W_0}{ga_1}, \tag{10.25}$$

where a_2 is shorthand for the relevant pension annuity factor at age $x + u$. The intuition behind equation (10.25) is as follows. The right-hand side describes the evolution of wealth under a consumption rate of W_0/a_1 and an interest rate of g. The annuity factor a_2 represents the cost of acquiring "a dollar for life" at some future age $x + u$. The cost of acquiring the original life annuity flow W_0/a_1 at age $x + u$ is exactly the value of the left-hand side, $(W_0/a_1)a_2$.

We are therefore searching for a value of g that equates both sides: if g is too small then the left-hand side will be "too expensive," but if g is too large then the individual can afford a better annuity. Finally, dividing by W_0 and multiplying by a_1, we arrive at

$$a_2 - \left(a_1 - \frac{1}{g}\right)e^{gu} - \frac{1}{g} = 0. \tag{10.26}$$

The value of g^* that solves (10.26) will be the Implied Longevity Yield. It is the rate that must be earned on nonannuitized wealth in order to be as well-off after u years, *assuming a_2 is known with certainty*. Just to make sure this point is clear: we are implicitly assuming that the current pension annuity factor $\bar{a}_{x+u}$ (see Section 6.8) can be used as a proxy for the (random) future annuity factor when this person reaches age $x + u$. In other words, we are assuming the pension annuity factor does not change over time.

I will now demonstrate equation (10.26) using the numerical example presented in the previous section. A 65-year-old male is quoted an average monthly payout of $678.22 per initial premium of $100,000 with a 10-year payment certain period. The continuous-time annuity factor is approximated as $100000/(12 \times 678.216) = 12.2871$, which in our notation is $a_1 = 12.2871$ per dollar-for-life. On the same exact date, a 75-year-old is quoted an average monthly payout of $976 per premium of $100,000 with a zero-year payment certain period. This means that it would cost the 75-year-old approximately $69,497 to purchase the same annuity that the 65-year-old would be entitled to; in this case the annuity factor is $100000/(12 \times 975.904) = 8.5391$, which is $a_2 = 8.5391$ per dollar-for-life.

We are searching for the g that the 65-year-old would have to earn on his discretionary investment portfolio in order to beat the annuity's return yet still consume the exact same income on an ongoing basis. The situation we are faced with is equation (10.26) with $u = 10$ years, $x = 65$, and g the unknown return variable:

$$8.5391 - \left(12.2871 - \frac{1}{g}\right)e^{10g} - \frac{1}{g} = 0. \tag{10.27}$$

The solution (which must be computed numerically or approximated using (10.34)) is $g^* = 0.0590$, which is an ILY value of 5.90%. As stated previously, the 65-year-old male would have to earn 5.90% per annum each year for the next 10 years in order to beat the return from the annuity. Thus, the value of the ILY on the date in question is 5.90% for males. The same calculation can be done for females using the average payouts listed earlier. In this case, $a_1 = 13.3706$ and $a_2 = 9.7875$ for a value of $g^* = 5.465\%$. Naturally, the g^*-value is lower since mortality rates are lower and since the (expected) horizon over which the payments are being returned is longer.

Table 10.5 provides the average monthly payout for males and females of various ages under different guarantee periods. These figures can, in turn, be used to calculate ILY values for a number of combinations of age and "period certain." Tables 10.6–10.8 illustrate once again that an annuity paying out a specified monthly income will fall in price with increasing age and that the comparable ILY value is always higher for males than for females. Keep in mind, however, that getting a "better deal" on both annuity factors does not guarantee that the ILY will increase.

Table 10.5. *Monthly income from immediate annuity*
($100,000 premium)

Age	Gender	Period certain		
		0-year	10-year	20-year
60	M	$582	$569	$536
60	F	$546	$539	$519
70	M	$741	$689	
70	F	$674	$644	
80	M	$1,075		
80	F	$967		

Note: Amounts listed are averages of best U.S. companies as of March 2005.
Source: CANNEX financial exchanges.

Table 10.6. *Cost for male of $569 monthly*
from immediate annuity

Age	Period certain		
	0-year	10-year	20-year
60	$97,816	$100,000	$106,204
70	$76,892	$82,675	
80	$52,984		

Implied Longevity Yield (age x to age y)
Age 60 to age 70	5.06%
Age 70 to age 80	5.58%
Age 60 to age 80	4.97%

Notes: Amounts listed are averages of best U.S. companies as of March 2005. For comparison, U.S. Treasury yield curve rates are 4.38% for 10 years and 4.80% for 20 years.
Source: CANNEX financial exchanges.

There is a close relationship between these ILY values and the actuarial mortality credits described earlier. To see this connection explicitly, I analyze the simplest possible case of annuity pricing—namely, when the valuation rate is constant at r, the force of mortality is constant at $\lambda(x) = \lambda$ for all ages, and all annuities are life-only with no guarantee period. In this case, the annuity pricing equation collapses to

$$\bar{a}_x = \int_0^\infty e^{-(r+\lambda)s} \, ds = \frac{1}{\lambda + r} \tag{10.28}$$

Table 10.7. *Cost for female of $539 monthly from immediate annuity*

	Period certain		
Age	0-year	10-year	20-year
60	$98,712	$100,000	$103,874
70	$80,054	$83,756	
80	$55,779		

Implied Longevity Yield (age x to age y)
Age 60 to age 70   4.93%
Age 70 to age 80   5.18%
Age 60 to age 80   4.86%

Note: See Table 10.6 notes.
Source: CANNEX financial exchanges.

Table 10.8. *Should an 80-year-old annuitize?*

Age	Gender	Period certain	Monthly income	ILY
80	M	5-year	$995	7.58%
85	M	0-year	$1,352	
80	F	5-year	$917	6.71%
85	F	0-year	$1,231	

Note: For comparison, U.S. Treasury yield curve rate is 4.02% for 5 years.
Source: CANNEX financial exchanges, March 2005.

regardless of the age x. Using our shorthand notation, both a_1 and a_2 are therefore equal to $(r + \lambda)^{-1}$ because exponential mortality (and a constant mortality rate) is synonymous with no aging.

The fundamental equation for the ILY is then

$$\frac{1}{\lambda + r} - \left(\frac{1}{\lambda + r} - \frac{1}{g} \right) e^{gu} - \frac{1}{g} = 0, \qquad (10.29)$$

whose solution is precisely $g = r + \lambda$ regardless of the value of u. In other words, the self-annuitization strategy must earn (and the ILY value must be) at least λ above the pricing rate r in order to purchase the same annuity income flow in the future.

In sum, under the special exponential mortality case, the ILY spread above the pricing rate $g - r$ is exactly the instantaneous mortality rate λ.

Under a more general law of mortality, the relationship would not be as direct and would obviously depend on the deferral period u, which is why we consider the ILY an extension of the traditional concept of mortality credits.

Technically, we can use numerical techniques to solve for the unknown g-value by treating the left-hand side of (10.26) as a function $f(g)$ and then searching for the root of $f(g) = 0$. We use the often-called Newton–Raphson (NeRa) algorithm to find the appropriate g. The NeRa algorithm is based on Taylor expansion of the function $f(x)$ in the neighborhood of a point x:

$$f(x + \varepsilon) \approx f(x) + f'(x)\varepsilon + \frac{f''(x)}{2}\varepsilon^2 + \cdots . \tag{10.30}$$

For small enough values of ε, the terms beyond $f'(x)\varepsilon$ are of second-order importance and so $f(x + \varepsilon) = 0$ implies

$$\varepsilon = \frac{-f(x)}{f'(x)}. \tag{10.31}$$

Thus, when we are trying to locate a value of g such that $f(g) = 0$, we start with an initial $g = g_0$ and then use the NeRa algorithm to pick the next value of g, so that

$$g_{i+1} = g_i - \frac{f(g_i)}{f'(g_i)}. \tag{10.32}$$

We continue this process until $|g_{i+1} - g_i| < \varepsilon$ for ε sufficiently small (which in our case is three significant digits after the decimal point).

In fact, looking back at equation (10.26), we can approximate the exponential term e^{gu} over small values of g with the quadratic form $1 + gt + \frac{1}{2}(gt)^2$. Using this approximation and then collecting terms, the implied longevity yield is the value of g that solves

$$-\left(\tfrac{1}{2}a_1 u^2\right)g^2 + \left(\tfrac{1}{2}u^2 - a_1 u\right)g + (a_2 + u - a_1) = 0. \tag{10.33}$$

The solution to this quadratic equation in g is

$$g^* = \frac{(u - 2a_1) + \sqrt{u^2 + 4a_1(u + 2a_2 - a_1)}}{2ua_1}. \tag{10.34}$$

In our earlier case (male 65), for which $a_1 = 12.2871$ and $a_2 = 8.5391$, the exact value of the ILY is $g^* = 5.900\%$ using the NeRa method. Using (10.34), we obtain

$$g^* = \frac{(10 - 24.5742) + \sqrt{100 + 49.1484(10 + 17.0782 - 12.2871)}}{2(10)(12.2871)}$$
$$= 0.05771,$$

which is an ILY value of 5.771%, a mere 13 basis points lower than the true value. Our quadratic approximation consistently underestimates the true value of g^* by 10–20 basis points.

10.7 Advanced-Life Delayed Annuities

Consistent with the main theme of this chapter, this section explores the financial risk–return properties of a "concept" product known as an advanced-life delayed annuity (ALDA). This is a variant of a pure deferred annuity contract that is paid by installments, is linked to consumer price inflation, and locks in longevity insurance. Reduced to its essence, the product would be acquired at a young age—and small premiums would be paid over a long period of time—but the ALDA would not begin paying its inflation-adjusted and life-contingent income until the annuitant reached the advanced age of 80, 85, or even 90. Figure 10.2 illustrates the timing of these cash flows.

The product would have no cash value and no survival or estate benefits, and it could not be commuted for cash at any age. Of course, these stringent design requirements might be impossible to attain in the current regulatory environment. But in theory these features—combined with standard actuarial, interest, and (possibly) lapsation discounting—would reduce the ongoing premium for this insurance to mere cents on the dollar. The ALDA and its derivatives are closely related to a DB pension and would be intended for those who don't have a pension (or perhaps as an option within a DC-style pension).

From a slightly different perspective, this type of product is akin to buying car, home, or health insurance with a large deductible, which is also the optimal strategy (and common practice) when dealing with catastrophic risk. By analogy, the ALDA's longevity insurance would kick in only if the longevity risk became substantial and financially unsupportable. Indeed, the raison d'être of life-contingent annuities is the acquisition of mortality credits, which at advanced ages are substantial and unavailable from any competing asset class. During the early years of retirement—when most pension decisions are made—the magnitude of these credits is quite small once survivor benefits, insurance fees, and antiselection (i.e., annuitant vs. population) costs are included. In contrast, the ALDA would entitle the holder to insurance against the risk of outliving assets, but only when the assets actually run the risk of being depleted later in life.

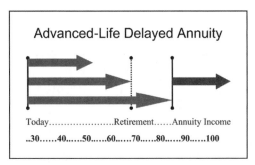

Figure 10.2

I start the discussion by letting $_u\bar{a}_{x:\tau}$ denote the deferred, "temporary" pension annuity factor, which is the cost of a financial contract that pays an inflation-adjusted, life-contingent \$1 per annum from time 0 (i.e., age $x + u$) to time τ (i.e., age $x + u + \tau$); this was first introduced in Chapter 6. I will suppress the symbol $\tau = \infty$ and use $\bar{a}_x$ when dealing with a complete life annuity that pays until death. Implicit in the expression is a real interest rate (or curve) denoted by r, and the retirement or pension income flow is adjusted for realized inflation each year. Thus, in nominal terms, the life annuity initially pays \$1 per annum and then increases by the realized rate of the Consumer Price Index (CPI). For most of this section, the ALDA purchase age will range from $x = 35$ to $x = 45$ and the ALDA commencement age will range from $x + u = 65$ to $x + u = 85$.

Specifically, the deferred pension annuity factor that we are interested in is $(_u\bar{a}_x)$, which represents the net single premium at age x for a \$1-per-annum ALDA benefit:

$$\text{NSP} := (_u\bar{a}_x) = \int_u^\infty e^{-rt}(_tp_{x+u})\, dt. \tag{10.35}$$

By construction, the NSP at age $x < x + u$ for an ALDA benefit of \$1 per annum is the annuity factor $\bar{a}_{x+u}$, discounted for the probability of survival and the time value of money (TVM). Mathematically, we have

$$\text{NSP} = e^{-r(u)}(\bar{a}_{x+u})(_up_x), \tag{10.36}$$

where the first term captures the u years of interest, the second term represents the annuity factor commencing at age $x + u$, and the third term is the conditional probability that someone currently aged x will survive for u more years. Note that equation (10.36) is consistent with the idea that there are no payments made to beneficiaries should the primary annuitant die between the initial acquisition age x and the benefit commencement age $x + u$.

Table 10.9. *ALDA: Net single premium ($_u a_x$) required at age x to produce $1 of income starting at age x + u*

Age x	x + u (years)			
	70	75	80	85
$r = 3.25\%$ *(real)*				
35	$3.642	$2.376	$1.412	$0.731
40	$4.294	$2.802	$1.665	$0.861
45	$5.070	$3.308	$1.965	$1.017
$r = 2\%$ *(real)*				
35	$6.346	$4.325	$2.687	$1.456
40	$7.029	$4.790	$2.976	$1.612
45	$7.796	$5.313	$3.301	$1.788
$r = 1\%$ *(real)*				
35	$9.951	$7.013	$4.509	$2.532
40	$10.484	$7.388	$4.750	$2.667
45	$11.061	$7.795	$5.012	$2.814

Note: GoMa mortality with $m = 90$ and $b = 9.5$.
Source: Copyright 2005 by the Society of Actuaries, Schaumburg, IL. Reprinted with permission.

Adding a survivorship benefit would increase the NSP and reduce the appeal of the product from a personal risk management perspective. Note that some of the ALDA-like products that have recently been created by U.S. insurance companies for the 401k (DC pension) market contain survivorship benefits and cashable options—for example, the ability to sell the units at some commuted value—which completely eliminates the mortality credits during the accumulation phase.

Note the focus on real (after-inflation) versus nominal returns in the pricing and valuation of the annuity factor. The real interest rate r is implicitly used in two places in the valuation equation. The first is to discount a single cash flow prior to the annuity commencement date—which covers the next u years—and the second is to price the annuity and discount the repeated cash flows that occur after age $x + u$. Thus, in practice one could envision using slightly different interest rates during the deferral versus payout periods. Indeed, one could go a step further and use a real yield curve r_t as opposed to a single interest rate, which would conform to capital market pricing techniques.

To provide some numerical intuition for the simple valuation of the ALDA, I offer the following example under GoMa mortality with $m = 90$, $b = 9.5$, and three different (real) valuation rates r; see Table 10.9. I use a slightly higher $m = 90$ value (compared to $m = 86.34$ used elsewhere) to reflect the healthy nature of anyone likely to purchase the ALDA. Thus, for example, if we start (i.e., purchase the ALDA in one lump sum) at age $x = 35$ and if benefits commence at age $x + u = 85$, then the NSP from (10.36) is $0.73 in current dollars. This pure deferred lifetime annuity will pay $1 in inflation-adjusted terms each year, commencing at age 85, in exchange for a premium payment of less than $1 today. The $0.73 resulted from multiplying the age-85 annuity factor of $\bar{a}_{85} = 6.679$ by the 0.556 probability of survival to age 85 and then by the 0.1969 TVM factor. Of course, the annuity factors would look quite different under different assumed real interest rates. For instance, Table 10.9 displays the NSP of a *unisex* annuity purchased at age x and given a variety of annuity commencement ages $x + u$ under a variety of different real interest rates. As one would expect, for any given combination of x and u, the annuity factor increases as the real rate r decreases, meaning that each dollar-per-year received after u years is more expensive to acquire initially.

For reference purposes, the assumed life expectancy at the initial purchase age was $E[T_{35}] + 35 = 84.7$, $E[T_{40}] + 40 = 84.8$, and $E[T_{45}] + 45 = 84.9$, respectively. Likewise, the implied life expectancy at the annuity commencement age was 87.6, 88.9, 90.7, and 92.9 at ages 70, 75, 80, and 85, respectively.

Payment for ALDA would not be made in one lump sum. Rather, the annuitant would make a series of inflation-adjusted, nonrefundable, and noncashable payments between the ages of x and $x + u$ that would entitle the recipient to a real $1 per annum for life commencing at age $x + u$. In practice, this would be implemented by linking both the periodic premiums and the benefits to the same consumer price index so that all cash flows could be discounted using the same unit of account. I emphasize that the pure actuarial pricing of this product would *not* require any assumptions about future inflation or nominal rates. Both premiums and benefits would be variable in nominal terms but fixed in real terms.

The NSP or $(_u\bar{a}_x)$ must be actuarially amortized over the u years, contingent on survival. Using our previous notation and assuming no lapsation, the net periodic premium for ALDA is

$$\text{NPP} = \frac{(_u\bar{a}_x)}{(\bar{a}_{x:\tau})}, \tag{10.37}$$

where the numerator is the NSP and the denominator effectively spreads these payments over the $\tau = u$ years between the initial purchase age x and the ALDA commencement age $x + u$. Intuitively, for any given purchase age x, the longer the deferral period u, the greater the annuity factor $\bar{a}_{x:\tau}$ and the lower the ongoing periodic premium. Similarly, as emphasized in the earlier discussion, it is quite conceivable that the pricing interest rate r in the denominator's factor will differ from (be greater than) the pricing rate in the numerator's factor. This is because in practice a nonflat yield curve will result in different (constant) interest rate approximations, depending on the period that is being discounted. Regardless, each r is a real (after-inflation) rate.

Here are some examples under the same pricing conditions considered previously. If the initial purchase age is $x = 35$ and the annuity commencement age is $x + u = 85$, then (under an $r = 3.25\%$ real interest rate) the NPP needed to create a \$1-per-annum real lifetime annuity is precisely \$0.0312 per annum. In other words, a mere three cents each year—paid over a period of 50 years—will generate an annual income flow of \$1 for life (after age 84), a factor of 32 times the ongoing premium. I can scale this quantity up or down and declare that, for each \$100 of premium per week, month, or year, the ALDA will pay a pension of \$3,200 per week, month, or year. If instead of using ages 35 and 85 I use ages 40 and 80—while retaining the same interest rate of $r = 3.25\%$ percent—then the NPP becomes \$0.0779, which is a factor of 12.8 times the ongoing premium. Finally, if I increase the interest rate to $r = 4\%$ then the premium that must be paid by the 40-year-old becomes \$0.061, a factor of 16.2. Table 10.10 converts the NSP values of Table 10.9 into payout factors that are the reciprocal of the NPP. Once again, a decreasing interest rate results in a lower income multiple, as shown in Table 10.10 under real valuation rates of 2% and 1%.

Table 10.10 includes the extreme case in which the commencement age is $x = 90$. For example, in this case a 35-year-old would receive 77.70 real dollars starting at age 90 for each real dollar paid from age 35 (when the interest rate is 3.25%). The number would drop by more than half to 32.50 real dollars per year for life under a lower $r = 1\%$ pricing rate. Thus, with yields on inflation-protected zero-coupon bonds (a.k.a. TIPS) in the 2%–2.5% vicinity at the time of this writing, one would expect to see market prices for ALDAs somewhere between the lower and upper extremes of 1% and 3.25% seen in the table.

Whether or not a 35-year-old would actually persevere and pay premiums for 55 years is debatable, which brings us to the topic of lapsation. Although everyone who purchases (or starts) an ALDA likely has the full intention of holding the product to maturity, it is unreasonable to assume that *all* survivors will continue to pay premiums until the commencement date. In fact, if the product is structured with absolutely no cash value and/or no ability to scale down the income benefit by reducing premiums, there is a high probability that people will (irrationally) lapse the product

Table 10.10. *ALDA income multiple: Dollars received during retirement per dollar paid today*

Age	$x = 70$	$x = 75$	$x = 80$	$x = 85$	$x = 90$
$r = 3.25\%$ (real)					
$y = 35$	5.6	9.2	16.1	32.0	77.7
$y = 40$	4.4	7.2	12.8	25.7	62.6
$y = 45$	3.3	5.6	10.1	20.4	49.9
$r = 2\%$ (real)					
$y = 35$	3.9	6.2	10.5	20.2	47.3
$y = 40$	3.1	5.1	8.7	17.0	39.9
$y = 45$	2.4	4.1	7.1	14.0	33.2
$r = 1\%$ (real)					
$y = 35$	2.9	4.5	7.6	14.3	32.5
$y = 40$	2.4	3.8	6.5	12.4	28.3
$y = 45$	1.9	3.2	5.5	10.5	24.3

Note: GoMa mortality with $m = 90$ and $b = 9.5$.
Source: Copyright 2005 by the Society of Actuaries, Schaumburg, IL. Reprinted with permission.

prior to the benefit commencement age. As a result, this lapsation phenomena must be taken into account in the original pricing.

From a pricing perspective, one can assume the existence of an instantaneous lapse-rate curve—which is akin to a force of mortality—that determines the probability the contract will be lapsed as a function of the number of years since initiation. This curve will most likely start at a level close to zero, increase as time evolves, then start to decline again as the ALDA nears the commencement date. The psychological justification would be that, on an aggregate level, as individuals see the payoff horizon approaching they are less likely to become disillusioned with the product. Denoting the lapse rate curve by η, we can define the cumulative probability of lapsing prior to time t as

$$H_x(t) := \Pr[L_x < t] = 1 - e^{-\eta t}. \qquad (10.38)$$

This is akin to the cumulative probability of death function. It is critical to stress that, if the premium is paid in one lump sum (up front), then the lapsation factor is irrelevant because the premium has become a sunk cost. Finally, the lapse-adjusted net periodic premium can be defined as

$$[\text{lapse-adjusted NPP}] = \frac{e^{-\eta u} \int_u^\infty e^{-rt}(_t p_x)\, dt}{\int_0^\tau e^{-rt}(_t p_x)(e^{-\eta t})\, dt}. \qquad (10.39)$$

Table 10.11. *Lapse-adjusted ALDA income multiple*

Age	$x = 70$	$x = 75$	$x = 80$	$x = 85$	$x = 90$
$r = 3.25\%$ *(real)*					
$y = 35$	8.7	15.3	29.2	63.4	168.4
$y = 40$	6.3	11.2	21.6	47.0	125.3
$y = 45$	4.4	8.1	15.7	34.5	92.3
$r = 2\%$ *(real)*					
$y = 35$	5.9	10.0	18.4	38.5	98.0
$y = 40$	4.4	7.7	14.3	30.1	76.8
$y = 45$	3.3	5.8	10.9	23.2	59.5
$r = 1\%$ *(real)*					
$y = 35$	4.3	7.2	12.9	26.2	64.8
$y = 40$	3.4	5.7	10.4	21.3	52.7
$y = 45$	2.6	4.4	8.2	17.0	42.4

Note: GoMa mortality with $m = 90$ and $b = 9.5$; lapse rate $\eta = 2\%$.
Source: Copyright 2005 by the Society of Actuaries, Schaumburg, IL.
Reprinted with permission.

The lapsation curve will affect the periodic premium in two partially off-setting ways: it will reduce the numerator by virtue of the smaller number of people who will end up using the product, but it will also reduce the denominator by virtue of the reduced size of the group that actually covers (funds) the actuarial present value of the ALDA benefit. The net effect will be a total reduction in the NPP regardless of the precise shape of the lapsation curve. Indeed, for most reasonable specifications, the premiums will decline quite substantially. One could envision a wide range of lapsation specifications, each leading to its own premiums. For illustrative purposes, in the following examples I take a simpler approach—in order to demonstrate the impact of even a small lapse rate—and display the relevant income payout factors assuming a constant 2% lapse rate each year.

The only difference, then, between Table 10.10 and Table 10.11 is the latter's assumption that, each year, 2% of the ALDA population ceases to make payments (for reasons other than mortality). I emphasize again that this is a crude approximation; actual lapsation behavior in the case of such a product would depend on the number of years remaining until commencement date as well as on other, health-related factors. Despite the simplicity, a number of interesting facts emerge from Table 10.11. Income multiples increase by a factor of 2–3, and this effect becomes even more pronounced at more distant commencement dates.

10.8 Who Incurs Mortality Risk and Investment Rate Risk?

The foregoing description and pricing mechanics are predicated on the ability of the insurance company to guarantee the pricing rate and the mortality table. In practice, if the insurance company offering the ALDA were to earn less than the pricing rate and/or experience mortality that was worse than assumed, the company would obviously face the potential of severe losses. This raises the question of whether the ALDA should have a participating structure in which a minimal income payout factor would be guaranteed and then, depending on investment performance and mortality experience, the income would be increased. Indeed, this kind of arrangement—which involves an additional level of risk sharing—is at the heart of some products that have recently been introduced in the North American marketplace. Thus, for example, a commercially viable version of the ALDA would guarantee an implicit real rate of at least 2% applied to the Annuity 2000 mortality table and then, depending on future financial and economic conditions, would increase benefits on a periodic basis. The extent to which this minimum guarantee is calibrated would depend on a number of factors, including the insurance company's ability to hedge part of its mortality risk (i.e., the risk of underestimating longevity) by using life and health insurance products in their portfolio with the opposite exposure.

Expanding on the topic of mortality risk considerations, the insurance company selling an ALDA would be taking a long position in mortality rates by fixing the life-contingent payments for up to half a century in advance. Indeed, if experienced mortality (hazard) rates were to decline to a level that is lower than what was priced in advance—that is, if people live longer than expected—then the insurance company could be in for substantial losses. Thus, even if the pricing assumed a very conservative (real) interest rate and even if the reinvestment risk were mitigated by hedging in the capital markets, it would be difficult if not impossible to avoid the uncertainty of mortality rates.

In fact, this is not a concern just for ALDAs. Insurance companies and reinsurers alike are concerned about guaranteeing mortality on the sale of immediate (let alone delayed) annuities. This is due to the perceived risk that unknown (and nonquantifiable) medical discoveries might increase human life spans beyond currently projected mortality tables, perhaps even leaving the insurance company paying annuities to infinitely lived Methuselahs. To cover this contingency, insurance companies selling variable payout annuities commonly impose an explicit mortality risk charge on a perpetual asset basis.

Some actuaries and financial economists argue that in-force life insurance might serve as a hedge against this (diversifiable) risk, but others are quick to dismiss the so-called basis risk implicit in this strategy because the target group for each class of policy is distinct. Immediate annuities are sold to the old, whereas life insurance is purchased by the young (for the most part). Thus, it is plausible that an increase in population longevity will adversely affect the liabilities of the annuity book of business but only marginally affect the profitability of the insurance book. Furthermore, another concern is that the duration and especially the lapsation characteristics of the two liabilities are mismatched and hence cannot properly hedge each other. Thus, it is unclear to what extent one side of the business could offset the other, so I leave this particular issue for further research.

Yet oddly enough—and here is the main point of this section—ALDAs might not be terribly sensitive to changes (or misestimates) in mortality assumptions and hence might not pose as much longevity risk to the insurance company as one would expect a priori. Most actuaries are familiar with the counterintuitive argument that a book of payout annuities sold to a 35-year-old is less exposed to mortality risk than one sold to a 75-year-old. The former's price or value is similar to that of a fixed-income perpetuity, where the annuity factor is $\bar{a}_x \approx 1/r$, while the latter is closer to a medium-term bond. At early issue ages and for long deferral periods, the dominant concern is reinvestment and interest rate risk. The same is true for ALDAs, and I offer the following numerical example to illustrate this concept.

Assume that an insurance company has just sold an ALDA to a (unisex) 45-year-old and that the benefit pays an inflation-adjusted \$10,000 per year starting at age 90. Long-term interest rates in the market are 3% (real) and the insurance company prices the ALDA by subtracting a profit margin of one percentage point from the 3% to arrive at an annual premium of \$301.47 per year for the next 45 years (using our Gompertz parameters without lapsation and an adjusted $r = 2\%$ pricing rate).

Now let us further assume that the insurance company misestimated mortality and that mortality rates decline by 20% more than anticipated (or, stated differently, that mortality improves by 20% more than what was projected at the time of sale). The 20% can be modeled as a shock to the instantaneous force of mortality (IFM) curve, one that immediately shifts the IFM from λ_x to a modified $0.8\lambda_x$ at all ages. This might appear simplistic, but it has the desired effect. To put this in perspective, the shifting of the mortality rate curve translates the conditional probability of survival to age 90 from the assumed $_{45}p_{45} = 37.11\%$ to a realized $_{45}p_{45} = 45.25\%$ for an individual who is currently 45 years old. These numbers are obtained under the usual methods: integrating only 80% of the Gompertz IFM curve, evaluating the integral between zero and the survival time, and then raising to the exponent.

If we translate this into prices under the same $r = 2\%$ (which is 3% minus the 100-basis-point spread), then the insurance company should have charged a \$412.15 premium for the ALDA as opposed to the \$301.47 per year it is committed to. Stated differently, if we solve for the implied interest rate that equates the \$301.47 premium to the model price under the modified mortality curve $0.8\lambda_x$, then the insurance company's 100-basis-point profit spread is reduced to a mere 4.2 basis points. This should not be surprising since a 20% improvement in experienced mortality (i.e., reduction in mortality rates) will obviously reduce profits. Our model simply quantifies this intuition by converting the 20% figure into basis points.

However, the interesting fact is what happens when I do the exact same exercise—pricing the ALDA under one mortality assumption and then immediately shocking the IFM curve to a lower level—at younger issue ages. One would think that the longer the deferral period the greater the so-called risk to the insurance company in misestimating the true curve. It turns out that ceteris paribus the situation is reversed, which is my main point. An ALDA that commences paying \$10,000 at age 90 requires an annual premium of \$301.47 if purchased at age 45 but of only \$211.50 if at age 35 (under the full curve used previously). If the company misestimates mortality by the same 20% factor, with hindsight the ALDA premiums should have been \$291.13 at age 35. In other words, under the true (new) mortality curve, the insurance company undercharged the 35-year-old by the difference between \$291.13 and \$211.50 per year. Hence the company is losing \$79.63 per year, relative to what they should have charged. Finally, if we invert and solve for the implied interest rate under the shifted IFM curve, the equivalent profit spread drops from 100 basis points to 19 basis points. Obviously, the product is less profitable ex post, but the interesting and relevant fact is that the spread has dropped by less than when the ALDA was sold to the 45-year-old. Recall that, for the 45-year-old, the same mortality misestimate led to a 4-basis-point profit spread. There are many ways to quantify the profitability (or lack thereof) of an ALDA, but I interpret this evidence to imply that a longer deferral period does not necessarily lead to greater longevity risk for the insurance company.

Table 10.12 provides a summary of this analysis by comparing the revised profit spread under a variety of ALDA purchase and commencement ages. Thus, although misestimating mortality can obviously be very costly—and should be a concern in the pricing of any life-contingent instrument—my

Table 10.12. *Profit spread (in basis points) from sale of ALDA given mortality misestimate of 20%*

Purchase age	Starting age	
	85	90
35	38.4	19.0
40	32.9	12.2
45	26.6	4.1

Notes: GoMa mortality with $m = 90$, $b = 9.5$, and IFM $= 0.8\lambda_x$. For comparison, the intended profit spread was 100 basis points.
Source: Copyright 2005 by the Society of Actuaries, Schaumburg, IL. Reprinted with permission.

main argument is as follows. All else being equal, an earlier ALDA purchase age reduces the sensitivity to misestimating experienced mortality; hence longer deferral periods need not translate into greater mortality risk for the insurance company.

10.9 Further Reading

For an entertaining and in-depth history of the tontine concept, which was invented and promoted by Lorenzo Tonti around 1650, see the monograph by Jennings and Trout (1982). Indeed, the early tontines were similar to that of the five grandmothers of Section 10.2. A number of countries (including France, Holland, and England) issued tontines as a substitute for government debt to pay for wars, revolutions, and the like. The tontines paid a reasonably competitive interest (coupon) rate of 5%–7%; in addition, the survivors would receive the coupon payments of the deceased. In some cases the tontine payments were contingent on lives other than those of the investors themselves. Clever investors such as the Genevan bankers association selected a group of young and healthy "names" and were able to earn abnormal rates of return—while providing these names with the best medical care—until the French livre collapsed from inflationary pressures. Apparently Queen Marie Antoinette and her husband King Louis XVI were popular names used by annuitants, and their deaths cost investors over six million livres. Indeed, Lorenzo Tonti himself was for seven years jailed in the infamous Bastille, but I digress.

For those who are interested in a more recent analysis of the pros and cons of government-issued tontines—which now live under the respectable name of "survivor bonds"—please see Blake and Burrows (2001) and the references therein. The concept of the implied longevity yield (ILY) can be traced to Milevsky (1998) and is calibrated to a database of Canadian annuity quotes in Milevsky (2005a). The ILY can also be seen as an extension of actuarial mortality credits; see Broverman (1986) for more details. The paper by Chen and Milevsky (2003) provides additional examples of asset and product allocation models involving conventional assets and annuities; see Reichenstein (2003) for applications of this concept. The ALDA is explored in Milevsky (2005b), on which much of the material is based. Finally, Warner and Pleeter (2001) describe an experiment that involves the choice between lump-sum and annuity-based pensions. They estimate the subjective discount rate (mentioned in a number of places throughout this book) and find that it ranges from 15% to 20% and possibly higher depending on wealth, education, and age.

10.10 Notation

θ—the fraction of assets that are allocated to a variable tontine

$\Phi^{-1}(\varepsilon)$—inverse of the normal CDF evaluated at ε

10.11 Problems

PROBLEM 10.1. You are $y = 35$ years old and are contemplating the purchase of a deferred pension annuity (DPA) that will start providing income at age $x = 70$, assuming you survive. If you do not survive then you get nothing. Use a standard GoMa law of mortality with $m = 86.34$ and $b = 9.5$ to compute $({}_{35}\bar{a}_{35})$ under an $r = 5\%$ valuation rate. Now assume that—instead of buying the DPA 35 years before your expected retirement date—you invest the sum $({}_{35}\bar{a}_{35})$ in a savings account earning a fixed deterministic return of g in continuous time. What value of g ensures that you have enough money in 35 years to purchase the same exact retirement income at age 70? In other words, what rate must your investment earn to have exactly $(\bar{a}_{70})$ in 35 years? Is this larger than the valuation rate r? Why (or why not)?

PROBLEM 10.2. Continuing with the previous problem, assume you invest the funds $({}_{35}\bar{a}_{35})$ in the stock market, which earns a random (annualized)

nominal return of $E[\tilde{g}] = 9\%$ with a standard deviation of $SD[\tilde{g}] = 20\%$ per year. What is the probability you will have enough to purchase the $(\bar{a}_{70})$ annuity at age 70? What happens if mortality improves to $m = 90$ by the time you purchase the annuity in 35 years? What is the probability you will have enough to purchase the pension annuity in this case?

PROBLEM 10.3. You are 65 years old and are considering the purchase of a pension annuity that would provide annual income of $c = 100000/\bar{a}_{65}$ starting immediately. Your alternative is to invest the $100,000 in a mutual fund earning a random return $\tilde{g}$ (where $E[\tilde{g}] = 9\%$ annually and $SD[\tilde{g}] = 20\%$) and to withdraw c each year; this is called self-annuitization. Assume that the force of mortality is constant at $\lambda = 3.67\%$. What is the probability you will run out of money while you are still alive?

PART THREE

ADVANCED TOPICS

ELEVEN

Options within Variable Annuities

11.1 To Live and Die in VA

In this chapter I will focus on exotic options and derivative securities that are embedded within tax-sheltered saving policies called *deferred* variable annuities, which are distinct from the immediate variable annuities discussed in previous chapters. In the United States, a variable annuity (VA) contract is similar to an open-ended mutual fund ("unit trust" in the United Kingdom) except that all investment gains are tax-sheltered until the money is withdrawn or annuitized. Moreover, a variable annuity has a unique form of investment protection: in the event of death, the variable annuity will pay out the greater of the account market value and the original investment grown at a fixed rate. More recent versions of variable annuities have additional guarantees—such as living benefits—that I will discuss a bit later.

Call and put options are the building blocks of most derivative securities and thus are at the heart of most structured products in finance. As described in Chapter 9, a call option provides the holder with the right but not the obligation to purchase (or call) an underlying security at some fixed price (the strike price). If we let S_t denote the price of the underlying security at time t, then a call option pays off

$$\max[S_t - X, 0],$$

where X is the strike price. A put option gives the holder the right but not the obligation to sell (or put) the underlying security at some fixed price. The put option pays off

$$\max[X - S_t, 0],$$

where again X is the strike (or sale) price and S_t is the *spot price* of the underlying security at time t. An American option can be exercised at any

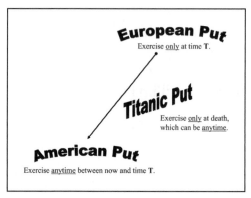

Figure 11.1. Three types of puts

time $t \leq T$, where T is the maturity, whereas a European option can be exercised only at maturity $t = T$. Obviously, the value of an American option should be at least as much as the value of a European option since the rights of the latter are contained within the former. See Figure 11.1.

I label the options that mature at a random time of death "Titanic" options because they are somewhere between American- and European-style options. A famous result in financial economics is the Black–Scholes/Merton (BSM) valuation formula for the price of a European put and call option, which can be written as

$$\text{BSP}(T) = Xe^{-rT}\Phi(-d_2) - S_0 e^{-kT}\Phi(-d_1) \tag{11.1}$$

and

$$\text{BSC}(T) = S_0 e^{-kT}\Phi(d_1) - Xe^{-rT}\Phi(d_2), \tag{11.2}$$

respectively. Here $\Phi(z)$ denotes the standard normal cumulative distribution function (or the "area under the curve" from negative infinity to z), k denotes any dividends (expressed as a yield) that are paid on the underlying security, and d_1 and d_2 are defined by

$$d_1 = \frac{\ln[S_0/X] + \left(r - k + \frac{1}{2}\sigma^2\right)T}{\sigma\sqrt{T}}, \qquad d_2 = d_1 - \sigma\sqrt{T}. \tag{11.3}$$

Often the strike price X is set equal to the original security spot price S_0, which is then arbitrarily set to $S_0 = 1$, so the $\ln[S_0/X]$ term become zero. In other cases the strike price increases over time at a (guaranteed) rate $g \geq 0$. If $X = e^{gT}$ then the put formula can be simplified to

$$\text{BSP}(T) = e^{(g-r)T}\Phi(-d_2) - e^{-kT}\Phi(-d_1) \tag{11.4}$$

with

$$d_1 = \frac{\left(r - k - g + \frac{1}{2}\sigma^2\right)T}{\sigma\sqrt{T}}, \qquad d_2 = d_1 - \sigma\sqrt{T}, \tag{11.5}$$

in which case the put option value will be expressed as a percentage of the underlying security.

Either way, the formula is based on the assumption that the underlying security price "obeys" or satisfies the equations of (Brownian) motion specified in Chapter 5, namely, that

$$\frac{\Delta S_{i+1}}{S_i} = \left(v + \frac{1}{2}\sigma^2 - k\right)\Delta t + \sigma\Delta N\left(0, \sqrt{\Delta t}\right). \tag{11.6}$$

This implies that the proportional change in the value of the state variable is equal to the sum of two terms. The first term is a deterministic increase of $\mu := v + \frac{1}{2}\sigma^2$ minus a dividend yield of k, multiplied by the incremental change in time Δt. The second term is the random component. In the continuous-time limit, (11.6) converges to the following stochastic differential equation (SDE):

$$\frac{dS_t}{S_t} = \left(v + \frac{1}{2}\sigma^2 - k\right)dt + \sigma dB_t$$
$$= (\mu - k)dt + \sigma dB_t. \tag{11.7}$$

I have elaborated on the intuition behind this equation in Chapter 4. Table 11.1 provides some numerical examples for the BSM (put) formula under a variety of maturity values t.

A quick-and-dirty explanation for "where" the valuation formula comes from can be obtained by going through the calculus:

$$\text{BSM}(t) = \int_{-\infty}^{\infty} \max[X - S_0 e^{\tilde{g}T}, 0]\, d\tilde{g}, \tag{11.8}$$

where $\tilde{g}$ is the normally distributed "annualized growth rate" (but assuming that $E[\tilde{g}] = r + \frac{1}{2}\sigma^2$ instead of the usual $E[\tilde{g}] = \mu + \frac{1}{2}\sigma^2$) and $\text{SD}[\tilde{g}] = \sigma/\sqrt{T}$. In terms of notation, I will write $E^*[\tilde{g}] = r + \frac{1}{2}\sigma^2$ when the expectation uses $\mu = r$ and $E[\tilde{g}] = \mu + \frac{1}{2}\sigma^2$ when the expectation uses the standard μ. Remember, yet again, that we replace the arithmetic mean μ with r.

Table 11.1. *BSM put option value as a function of spot price and maturity—*
Strike price = $100

Spot price	Maturity t (years)						
	1	2	3	4	5	6	7
$10	$84.28	$78.89	$73.82	$69.05	$64.57	$60.35	$56.39
$20	$74.38	$69.09	$64.12	$59.46	$55.11	$51.06	$47.30
$30	$64.47	$59.29	$54.47	$50.03	$45.99	$42.33	$39.00
$40	$54.58	$49.56	$45.08	$41.15	$37.68	$34.61	$31.85
$50	$44.70	$40.13	$36.36	$33.20	$30.47	$28.07	$25.92
$60	$35.01	$31.41	$28.67	$26.41	$24.43	$22.68	$21.09
$70	$25.94	$23.81	$22.20	$20.79	$19.51	$18.31	$17.19
$80	$18.08	$17.56	$16.95	$16.27	$15.54	$14.80	$14.06
$90	$11.87	$12.65	$12.81	$12.68	$12.38	$11.99	$11.54
$100	$7.38	$8.95	$9.62	$9.87	$9.88	$9.74	$9.51
$110	$4.38	$6.24	$7.19	$7.68	$7.90	$7.94	$7.87
$120	$2.50	$4.31	$5.36	$5.98	$6.33	$6.50	$6.55
$130	$1.39	$2.96	$3.99	$4.66	$5.09	$5.34	$5.47
$140	$0.75	$2.02	$2.97	$3.65	$4.10	$4.40	$4.58
$150	$0.40	$1.37	$2.22	$2.86	$3.32	$3.64	$3.86
$160	$0.21	$0.93	$1.66	$2.25	$2.70	$3.03	$3.26
$170	$0.11	$0.63	$1.24	$1.77	$2.20	$2.53	$2.77
$180	$0.05	$0.43	$0.93	$1.40	$1.80	$2.11	$2.36
$190	$0.03	$0.29	$0.70	$1.11	$1.48	$1.78	$2.01
$200	$0.01	$0.20	$0.53	$0.89	$1.22	$1.50	$1.73

Note: Risk-free rate = 6%, dividend yield = 1%, volatility = 25%.

11.2 The Value of Paying by Installments

One of the many unique aspects of derivative securities that are embedded within life and pension annuity products is that—in contrast to over-the-counter and exchange-traded financial derivatives, where the option premium is paid up front—the payment for these derivatives is made in installments. These installments are often structured as an asset-based fee that is proportional to the account value itself. In other words, you don't really know what you will end up paying (and the company takes the risk of not knowing what fees they will be receiving). Thus, for example, you might pay 1% of the market value of the asset, charged and withdrawn monthly by multiplying the account value by $0.01/12$. I stress that this is quite different from what happens when buying a generic call or put option, where the premium (of, say, 5% or 10% of the notional value) is paid as soon as the contract is initiated.

My objective in this section is to value the ongoing stream of proportional insurance/derivative fees and then discount this cash flow to time 0 so I can eventually compare the present value of the benefits you receive from these various guarantees to the present value of the costs that you pay for them. As in the rest of the book, I will discount these fees assuming they are paid and deducted from the account in continuous time until some deterministic or stochastic maturity horizon. At a crude level I am trying to address the following question: What is the discounted value of the 1% or 2% insurance fee you will be paying on your investment account—which is currently worth \$10,000, for example—during the next 5, 10, or 20 years? On the one hand, given that we do not know exactly how this investment account will perform over time, it should be difficult to value 1% or 2% of a random stream. However—and here is the counterintuitive aspect of this exercise—we can actually obtain a present value by "self-replication" arguments. Moreover, the risk-neutral present value does not depend on interest rates.

I compute the discounted value of the insurance/derivative risk charge by treating the stochastic cash flows as a contingent claim on the underlying account value. The insurance company can be viewed as having a long position in the continuous-flow fee derivative. The derivative remains alive as long as the policyholder has not died or lapsed the policy. Therefore, we can model the general risk-neutral evolution of the underlying account or asset price via the usual

$$dS_t = (r_t - k_t)S_t\,dt + \sigma(S_t, t)S_t\,dB_t, \qquad S_0 = 1, \qquad (11.9)$$

where B_t is the by-now familiar Brownian motion, r_t is a (possibly stochastic) interest rate (but assumed independent of S_t), k_t is the insurance/derivative fee, and $\sigma(S_t, t)$ represents the (possibly stochastic) volatility of the underlying security. The integral representation of equation (11.9) is:

$$S_t = S_0 + \int_0^t (r_u - k_u)S_u\,du + \int_0^t \sigma(S_u, u)S_u\,dB_u. \qquad (11.10)$$

In the special case of geometric Brownian motion—which was the core of the presentation in Chapter 5—the volatility parameter $\sigma = \sigma(S, t)$ is constant.

I now need to define a new "money market" investment account, which is denoted by

$$R_t = \exp\left\{\int_0^t r_s\,ds\right\} \qquad (11.11)$$

and can be viewed as the future value of one dollar that is invested at a rate of r_t. When this rate is constant the future value factor will be $R_t = e^{rt}$, but when the rate is stochastic the future value will be random. The interesting result—which I will soon prove—is that, regardless of how complicated one makes the interest rate dynamics for r_t, the expected (risk-neutral) discounted value of the proportional fees k_t will be identical!

To show this, let K_t denote the stochastic value (discounted to time 0) of insurance/derivative fees collected until time t. By construction, we have

$$dK_t = R_t^{-1} k_t S_t dt. \qquad (11.12)$$

The quantity $k_t S_t dt$ can be viewed as the instantaneous earnings of the insurance company that is charging the proportional fee of k_t, while the R_t^{-1} factor discounts the quantity to time 0. Our main objective now is to obtain values both for K_τ and its expectation $E[K_\tau]$, where τ is a *general* stopping time for the process S_t. In English: What is the present value of paying 2% of the account value from now (time 0) until some later time τ?

By a simple chain rule, we have

$$
\begin{aligned}
d(R_t^{-1} S_t) &= -r_t R_t^{-1} S_t dt + R_t^{-1} dS_t \\
&= -r_t R_t^{-1} S_t dt + R_t^{-1} (r_t - k_t) S_t dt + R_t^{-1} \sigma(S_t, t) S_t dB_t \\
&= -R_t^{-1} k_t S_t dt + R_t^{-1} \sigma(S_t, t) S_t dB_t \\
&= -dK_t + R_t^{-1} \sigma(S_t, t) S_t dB_t. \qquad (11.13)
\end{aligned}
$$

Therefore, by re-arranging equation (11.13) and noting that (by definition) $R_0^{-1} S_0 = 1$, we obtain

$$
\begin{aligned}
K_\tau &= \int_0^\tau dK_t = -\int_0^\tau d(R_t^{-1} S_t) + \int_0^\tau R_t^{-1} \sigma(S_t, t) S_t \, dB_t \\
&= 1 - R_\tau^{-1} S_\tau + \int_0^\tau R_t^{-1} \sigma(S_t, t) S_t \, dB_t. \qquad (11.14)
\end{aligned}
$$

So the discounted value of the insurance/derivative fee up to a stopping time τ is $1 - R_\tau^{-1} S_\tau$ plus an integral term whose expectation is zero. This implies that

$$E[K_\tau] = 1 - E[R_\tau^{-1} S_\tau]. \qquad (11.15)$$

In specific cases, equation (11.14) can be solved to provide the entire distribution of the discounted value of fees. More importantly, equation (11.15) can be easily applied to a variety of stochastic maturities. Here are some examples of different maturities.

If τ is *deterministic*, $r_t = r$, $\sigma(S_t, t) = \sigma$, and $k_t = k$, then the stochastic differential equation in (11.9) can be solved to yield

$$S_t = \exp\{(r - k - \tfrac{1}{2}\sigma^2)\tau + \sigma B_\tau\}; \tag{11.16}$$

hence (11.15) can be simplified to

$$E[K_\tau] = 1 - E\big[\exp\{(-k - \tfrac{1}{2}\sigma^2)\tau + \sigma B_\tau\}\big] = 1 - e^{-k\tau}. \tag{11.17}$$

Notice that the interest rate r and the volatility σ drop out of equation (11.17), so that the risk-neutral expected discounted value of fees is invariant with respect to both parameters. For example, an insurance risk charge of $k = 0.02$ (2%) with $\tau = 20$ yields $E[K_{20}] = 0.329$, which implies that an investor with a 20-year horizon is implicitly paying 33% of the initial account value. In contrast, if $k = 0.002$ (20 basis points) then $E[K_{20}] = 0.039$, which is less than 4% of the initial account value.

If τ is *stochastic* but independent of S_t, equation (11.15) leads to expectations with respect to both random variables. In many cases $\tau = T_x$, where T_x is the remaining lifetime random variable with probability density function $f_x(t)$. Once again, with $r_t = r$, $\sigma(S_t, t) = \sigma$, and $k_t = k$, we condition on age x to obtain

$$E_x[K_{T_x}] = 1 - E_x\big[\exp\{(-k - \tfrac{1}{2}\sigma^2)T_x + \sigma B_{T_x}\}\big]$$
$$= 1 - E_x\big[E\big[\exp\{(-k - \tfrac{1}{2}\sigma^2)T_x + \sigma B_{T_x}\} \mid T = t\big]\big]$$
$$= 1 - E_x[e^{-kT}] = 1 - \int_0^\infty e^{-kt} f_x(t)\, dt, \tag{11.18}$$

which some readers might identify as (1 minus) the Laplace transform of the remaining lifetime random variable evaluated at k. In fact, when $f_x(t) = \lambda e^{-\lambda t}$, which is the exponential remaining lifetime, (11.18) leads to

$$E_\lambda[K_T] = 1 - \lambda \int_0^\infty e^{-(k+\lambda)t}\, dt = \frac{k}{\lambda + k}. \tag{11.19}$$

The λ subscript replaces the current age (x) as the "conditioning" variable. For a 65-year-old with an expected future lifetime of $E_\lambda[T] = \lambda^{-1} = 20$ years, using $k = 0.02$ as a proportional asset-based insurance/derivative fee leads to a present value of $E_\lambda[K_T] = 0.2857$, or about 28% of the initial account value. But if $k = 0.002$ then $E_\lambda[K_T] = 0.038$, which is less than 4% of the account value. Notice that both values are strictly lower than (a naïve application of) $1 - e^{k/\lambda}$. This is a consequence of Jensen's inequality, according to which $1 - E_\lambda[e^{-kT}] < 1 - e^{kE_\lambda[T]}$.

Table 11.2. *Discounted value of fees*

Charge k	Time (years)		
	10	20	30
25 b.p.	2.47%	4.87%	7.22%
50 b.p.	4.87%	9.51%	13.92%
150 b.p.	13.92%	25.92%	36.23%

Notes: b.p. = basis points. Interest rates, expected returns, and volatility are irrelevant.

Finally, under the more realistic GoMa specification of the function $f_x(t)$, by (11.18) we have

$$E_x[K_T] = 1 - \int_0^\infty e^{-kt} f_x(t)\, dt$$
$$= kb\Gamma(-bk, b\lambda(x)e^{-(m-x)k+b\lambda(x)}), \qquad (11.20)$$

where $\lambda(x) =$ GoMa force of mortality at age x and $\Gamma(a, b)$ is the incomplete Gamma function (see Chapter 3). The quantity $1 - E_x[K_T]$ can also be identified as the net single premium for a life insurance policy under a force of interest k and future lifetime density $f_x(t)$.

The reader should now have a collection of formulas that can be used to compute the (risk-neutral) present value of a random series of cash flows that result from charging $k\%$ of the account value in continuous time. This is what you pay for living and death benefits.

The key insight, once again, is that equation (11.17) does not contain any mention of the interest rate in the market. This is most counterintuitive. Normally one expects that some sort of interest rate or term structure is needed to arrive at the present discounted value of cash flows. However, when these cash flows are stated in proportional terms of an account value, the discounted value is no longer a function of the interest rate.

Table 11.2 should make this point clearly; it displays the result of paying proportional fees of 25, 50, and 150 basis points on an investment account for the next 10, 20, and 30 years. According to the table, if you plan to invest $100 in a variable annuity (or in any investment account, for that matter) for the next 20 years and if the company holding the funds charges 50 basis points per year, then the discounted value of this fee at time 0 is 9.51% of the current value of the account, or $9.51. If the fee charged is 150 basis points, then the discounted value of this fee during the next 20 years is 25.92% of the account.

Some readers might wonder how I can make this assertion without any consideration of interest rates or projected growth rates for the account. This is a legitimate concern, and let me offer the following numerical example to explain. Imagine that Mr. Pay invests $100 for the next 20 years in a portfolio that is charging 150 basis points per year while Mrs. Free invests $74.08 in an identical investment portfolio that does not charge any management fee. Mrs. Fee starts off with much less than Mr. Pay, yet both are invested in the same underlying financial instruments. After 20 years, Mrs. Free's portfolio grows to a random $74.08e^{g20}$, while Mr. Pay's portfolio grows to a random $100e^{g20-(0.015)20}$, where the extra $(0.015)20$ in the exponent denotes the 150 basis points subtracted in management fees. Observe that $100e^{-(0.015)20} = 74.08182$, whence you can confirm that Mr. Pay and Mrs. Free have the exact same amount of money after 20 years even though Mr. Pay started off with much more. This is precisely why it is justifiable to say that the present value of 150 basis points for the next 20 years is $(100 - 74.08) = 25.92\%$, regardless of interest rates or growth rates.

11.3 A Simple Guaranteed Minimum Accumulation Benefit

Returning now to the topic of guarantees inside variable annuities: one type of guarantee that is commonly selected when purchasing a VA is the guaranteed minimum accumulation benefit (GMAB). In a simple scenario, assume that today $(t = 0)$ you invest $1 in a variable annuity. The random market value of the VA at maturity is

$$S_T = S_0 e^{\tilde{g}T}, \tag{11.21}$$

where $\tilde{g}$ is the random annualized return during time $[0, T]$. The guaranteed minimum accumulation benefit is then

$$S_T^* = \max[S_T, S_0 e^{gT}] \tag{11.22}$$

$$= S_T + \max[0, S_0 e^{gT} - S_T], \tag{11.23}$$

where g is a guaranteed growth rate. The GMAB is equivalent to a long position in the asset supporting the VA plus a put option struck at the initial investment level plus the minimal interest guarantee. This put can be valued using the BSM formula from Section 11.1.

Table 11.3. *Annual fee (in basis points) needed to hedge the death benefit—Female*

Age	Type of death benefit[a]		
	Money-back	5% roll-up	Look-back
30	0.30	1.77	15.10
40	0.80	4.45	18.90
50	2.00	10.84	24.60
60	5.00	21.60	32.80
65	7.60	22.50	36.10

[a] Based on maturity at $x = 75$ years.
Note: GoMa mortality based on Tables 3.6 and 3.7; $r = 6\%$, $\sigma = 20\%$.

11.4 The Guaranteed Minimum Death Benefit

Next we examine the principal protection offered to beneficiaries upon the policyholder's death—namely, the guaranteed minimum death benefit (GMDB). In order to determine the value of this embedded option, I must first state that the no-arbitrage value of a put option that matures at a random time T_x is

$$E[E[\max[S_0 e^{gT} - S_0 e^{\tilde{g}T}, 0] \mid T]]. \tag{11.24}$$

This is equivalent to

$$\Omega_x = \int_0^\tau f_x(t)\,\mathrm{BSP}(t)\,dt, \tag{11.25}$$

where τ is the termination date of the VA death benefit guarantee. Note that $f_x(t)$ is the probability density function of the time of death and $\mathrm{BSP}(t)$ is the Black–Scholes/Merton put formula. Finally, we locate a value of k in equation (11.18) such that $E[K_{T_x}] = \Omega_x$.

When purchasing an annuity contract, one would typically be faced with a choice of different death benefit types; Table 11.3 displays several numerical examples. A 60-year-old female who purchases an annuity contract is entitled to a basic "money-back" guaranteed death benefit, where all invested funds would be returned to her beneficiaries in the event of her death. Under the usual GoMa parameters from Chapter 3, the annual fee that should be paid to the company for offering this option is 5 basis points. Alternatively, she may choose an enhanced death benefit with a 5% "roll-up," where the death benefit is guaranteed to consist of at least the original premium paid,

Table 11.4. *Annual fee (in basis points) needed to hedge the death benefit—Male*

Age	Type of death benefit[a]		
	Money-back	5% roll-up	Look-back
30	0.40	3.24	25.00
40	1.30	7.96	31.60
50	3.50	19.20	41.80
60	8.70	37.50	56.40
65	13.00	39.30	62.50

[a] Based on maturity at $x = 75$ years.
Note: GoMa mortality based on Tables 3.6 and 3.7; $r = 6\%$, $\sigma = 20\%$.

grown by an annual rate of 5%. In this case, her fee would rise to 21.6 basis points. Finally, in this example she may actually prefer a "look-back" option, where the payout to her beneficiaries would depend on the highest account value of past contract "anniversaries." This is the most valuable option, for which she must pay 32.8 basis points per year. Of course, the older the individual purchasing the annuity the more she must pay for the guarantee, since she has fewer remaining lifetime years to compensate the company for the option.

Table 11.4 displays comparable values for a male annuitant. Although our observations concerning the previous table still apply, mortality differences result in the male paying more than the female for the same guarantee.

11.5 Special Case: Exponential Mortality

For general mortality it is very difficult to obtain a closed-form solution for the GMDB option expressed in equation (11.25). However, when T_x is exponentially distributed (so that $f_x(t) = \lambda e^{-\lambda t}$), we have

$$
\Omega_x = \frac{\lambda}{2(r - g + \lambda)} \left(1 - \frac{b_2}{\sqrt{b_2^2 + 2(r - g + \lambda)}} \right)
$$
$$
- \frac{\lambda}{2(k + \lambda)} \left(1 - \frac{b_1}{\sqrt{b_1^2 + 2(k + \lambda)}} \right), \tag{11.26}
$$

where

$$
b_1 = \frac{r - g - k + \frac{1}{2}\sigma^2}{\sigma}, \qquad b_2 = \frac{r - g - k - \frac{1}{2}\sigma^2}{\sigma}. \tag{11.27}
$$

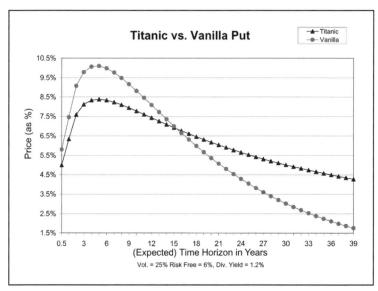

Figure 11.2

Equation (11.26) is the analogue of the BSM equation for the value of a put option, with the option's maturity now at a random (exponentially distributed) time T instead of at a fixed (deterministic) time T. The equation itself involves all the usual suspects from option pricing: the risk-free (valuation) rate r, the underlying security's investment volatility σ, the growth rate of the strike price g, the continuous insurance fees k, and the instantaneous mortality rate λ. The constants b_1 and b_2 are used as shorthand notation to simplify the main formula. Note that the subscript x in Ω_x indicates that the Titanic put option value is dependent on the purchaser's age—though only to the extent that the instantaneous force of mortality λ is higher or lower.

To better understand the intuition and properties of the Titanic option value Ω_x under exponential mortality—as defined by equation (11.26)—I offer Figure 11.2. It displays the price of a Titanic option that expires or matures at a random time T_x as compared to a generic European-style put option that matures at a deterministic time T.

Both options give the holder the right (but not the obligation) to sell an underlying security—that is currently trading for $100—at a fixed price of $100. This is an at-the-money put option in a 25% volatility environment, with a dividend yield (insurance fee) of 1.2% and a valuation rate of 6%. Using the symbols in equation (11.16), we have $\sigma = 0.25$, $r = 0.06$, $k = 0.012$, and $g = 0$, since the strike price does not change over time.

The law of mortality governing the Titanic put option gives us $\Pr[T_x > t] = e^{-\lambda t}$, which implies that $E[T_x] = 1/\lambda$. In the same figure, the European-style put option is constructed so that $T = 1/\lambda$ as well. In other words, the Titanic option *is expected to* mature at $1/\lambda$ whereas the European-style (vanilla) put option *will* mature at time $T = 1/\lambda$. For example: a European-style put option that matures in 3 years is worth approximately 9.7% of the underlying security value, whereas a Titanic put option—which is expected to mature in $E[T_x] = 3$ years under a $\lambda = 1/3$ mortality rate—is worth only 8.11% on the underlying security. As the graph illustrates, the European-style option is worth more. In fact, when $T = 5$ years, the European-style put is worth approximately 10% of the underlying account value whereas the Titanic option (with mortality rate $\lambda = 1/5$) is worth only 8.3%. Note the hump-shaped structure of the option value as a function of T (and of $E[T_x]$). As the (expected) maturity horizon increases from zero to approximately four years, the option value increases. Then, as the horizon increases, both option values decline toward zero. The European put's value declines more rapidly than the Titanic put's.

The intuition for this result is as follows. First, a European-style put option that promises only to return your \$100 at maturity should not be worth much if that maturity is 30 or 40 years from now. In contrast, the Titanic option can be viewed as a weighted average—see equation (11.15)—of the generic option value. The weighting is exponential, so some (small) weight is attached to the long horizon and some (larger) weight is attached to the short horizon. Add all these weights up and you should get the total picture. At a crude approximation, a Titanic option that matures in 5 years on average is the weighted average of a European option that matures in $1, 2, 3, \ldots$ years.

If $r = g$ and $k = 0$, then the basic formula in (11.26) further collapses to

$$\Omega_x = \frac{1}{\sqrt{1 + 8\lambda/\sigma^2}}. \tag{11.28}$$

This represents the case where the risk-free valuation rate is precisely equal to the rate at which the strike price is increasing over time. Thus, if $r = 5\%$ then the Titanic put option is assumed to have a strike price of \$1 at time zero, of \$1$e^{0.05}$ at time $t = 1$, of \$1$e^{(0.05)2}$ at time $t = 2$, and so on. The owner of a Titanic put option can sell (put) the investments back to the insurance company at progressively higher values, which are determined by the valuation rate r. Guaranteeing a risk-free return might sound too good to be true, but you must wait until death to "cash in." And, if $\lambda = 0$ and the holder never dies, $\Omega_x = 1$.

Table 11.5. *Value of exponential Titanic option*

Mortality	Volatility σ					
	5%	10%	15%	20%	25%	30%
$\lambda = 2\%$	12.40%	24.25%	35.11%	44.72%	53.00%	60.00%
$\lambda = 4\%$	8.80%	17.41%	25.63%	33.33%	40.42%	46.85%
$\lambda = 6\%$	7.20%	14.29%	21.16%	27.74%	33.94%	39.74%
$\lambda = 8\%$	6.24%	12.40%	18.43%	24.25%	29.83%	35.11%
$\lambda = 10\%$	5.58%	11.11%	16.54%	21.82%	26.92%	31.80%
$\lambda = 12\%$	5.10%	10.15%	15.13%	20.00%	24.72%	29.28%
$\lambda = 14\%$	4.72%	9.41%	14.03%	18.57%	22.99%	27.27%
$\lambda = 16\%$	4.42%	8.80%	13.14%	17.41%	21.58%	25.63%

Notes: $r = g$, $k = 0$. Value given as percentage of initial account value.

Using equation (11.28), Table 11.5 illustrates how the value of the exponential Titanic option is affected by varying values of λ and σ. As you can see, when λ is held constant, the value of the option increases with a growing volatility. Conversely, for any constant σ, the option decreases in value as λ increases. Thus, for instance, an x-year-old individual with an expected remaining lifetime of $E[T] = 10$ (which implies a $\lambda = 10\%$ mortality rate) who invests in a collection of mutual funds with a risk-free rate-of-return guarantee at death has an option that is "worth" $21.82 for each $100 investment. This assumes a portfolio volatility of $\sigma = 20\%$, which is reasonable for equity-based portfolios.

11.6 The Guaranteed Minimum Withdrawal Benefit

Another type of guarantee that has become very popular lately is the guaranteed minimum withdrawal benefit (GMWB), which is available as a "rider" to a VA policy. The GMWB rider promises to pay an annual dividend of G dollars per $100 of original investment, regardless of how the actual account performs. (Recall that the investments within the variable annuity account can move up and down depending on actual market performance.) Furthermore, this dividend or payment of G per year will continue until the entire $100 has been returned to the policyholder. So even if the VA account value collapses from $100 to nothing (say) one day after the policy is acquired, the insurance company guarantees to continue making payments of G per year until the $100 has been "paid back." Of course, as with any other VA policy, the contract holder can surrender or lapse the policy and receive the market value (minus any surrender charges).

Here is the mathematics of how to understand this unique guarantee. Let W_t denote the market value of the underlying variable annuity at any future time $t \geq 0$, with an arbitrary (but innocuous) assumption that $W_0 = 100$ dollars. Under a typical GMWB structure, the policyholder is guaranteed to be able to withdraw at most $G = 7$ dollars per annum. The guarantee remains in effect until the entire \$100 has been disbursed, which is a period of at least $100/7 = 14.28$ years. Even in the extreme scenario where the initial $W_0 = 100$ collapses to a zero value one day after the policy is purchased, the investor will be made whole—albeit over an extended period of 14.28 years. Of course, in any year the policyholder may withdraw an amount of less than $G = 7$ dollars, which would extend the life of the guarantee; conversely, withdrawing an amount greater than $G = 7$ dollars would reduce the value *and* life of the guarantee. I shall proceed by assuming the policyholder withdraws no more and no less than the $G = 7$ dollars per annum; this is called the *passive* or *static* approach. Most (if not all) insurance companies assume this type of behavior on the part of policyholders.

Following the same setup as before, I assume that the actual dynamics of the assets underlying the VA policy (i.e., prior to deduction of any insurance fees) obeys the basic stochastic differential equation

$$dS_t = \mu S_t dt + \sigma S_t dB_t. \tag{11.29}$$

The value W_t of the VA subaccount incorporates two additional effects: proportional insurance fees and withdrawals. The account value satisfies

$$dW_t = (\mu - k)W_t dt - G dt + \sigma W_t dB_t, \tag{11.30}$$

at least while $W_t > 0$. If the account value W_t ever reaches zero, it remains there. That is: equation (11.30) holds for $t < \tau_0$, and $W_t = 0$ for $t \geq \tau_0$.

The solution to the SDE (11.30) can be written as

$$W_T = \exp\left\{\left(\mu - k - \tfrac{1}{2}\sigma^2\right)T + \sigma B_T\right\}$$
$$\times \max\left[0, \left(W_0 - G \int_0^T \exp\left\{-\left(\mu - k - \tfrac{1}{2}\sigma^2\right)t - \sigma B_t\right\} dt\right)\right]. \tag{11.31}$$

The first thing to note about the dynamics in equations (11.30) and (11.31) is that—since $G > 0$, which means that the process includes forced consumption of some dollar(s)—the value of W_t can in fact hit zero at some point $t > 0$. As soon as the integral term in (11.31) exceeds W_0/G, the quantity within brackets will become negative. This is in contrast to a standard geometric Brownian motion, which is the term multiplying the bracketed portion of (11.31) that can never hit zero in finite time. The guaranteed ability to withdraw G per annum until time $T = W_0/G$ is of value *if and only if* the process W_t hits zero prior to T. Indeed, for those sample paths for which the ruin time occurs after T, the insurance option has a zero payout because the minimum withdrawal would have been satisfied endogenously, even without an explicit guarantee provided by the insurance company.

Given the importance of the ruin time in the classification and understanding of this financial guarantee, here I introduce an expression for the probability of ruin of the process W_t within the time period $[0, t]$:

$$\Pr\left[\inf_{0 \leq s \leq t} W_s = 0\right] = \Pr\left[\int_0^t \exp\{-(\mu - \alpha - \tfrac{1}{2}\sigma^2)s - \sigma B_s\}\, ds \geq \frac{W_0}{G}\right]$$

$$= \Pr\left[X_t \geq \frac{W_0}{G}\right], \tag{11.32}$$

where the new term X_t is defined as equal to the integral in the middle of (11.32). Note the analogy between the probability of ruin and the integral of the (inverse) of the geometric Brownian motion. This is yet another manifestation of the stochastic present value, which was at the core of our approximations in Chapter 9. As mentioned in the appendix of that chapter, the seemingly counterintuitive relationship between the infimum of a process and the integral of an exponential Brownian motion follows because equation (11.31) cannot reach zero until the integral X_t exceeds W_0/G. Note also that X_t is monotonically increasing in t. Thus, once X_t exceeds W_0/G we have $W_t = 0$, and it can never recover and go back above zero. It is quite easy to demonstrate that the probability of ruin is increasing in the withdrawal rate G and likewise that, the greater the time t, the higher the probability of ruin.

Assume the arithmetic average return (after money management fees but before insurance guarantee fees) is expected to be $\mu = 9\%$ per annum with a historical market volatility of $\sigma = 18\%$. Also, we let the insurance fee for this particular GMWB rider be set to $k = 0.40\%$ per annum, which is consistent with current market pricing for these products. In this case, while $W_t > 0$ the parameterized dynamics of the investment is

$$dW_t = ((0.086)W_t - 7)dt + 0.18 W_t dB_t, \qquad W_0 = 100. \tag{11.33}$$

Using numerical methods to obtain the ruin probability during the first $T = 14.28$ years yields a ruin probability of 11.7% (see Section 11.7 for references). In other words, there is approximately an 88.3% chance that the

Table 11.6. *GMWB payoff and the probability of ruin within 14.28 years*

Volatility σ	Expected return μ of subaccounts				
	4%	6%	8%	10%	12%
10%	19.0%	7.0%	1.7%	0.3%	0.04%
15%	31.4%	18.5%	9.3%	4.1%	1.60%
18%	37.8%	25.5%	15.5%	8.6%	4.40%
25%	49.9%	39.6%	30.5%	22.2%	15.50%

Note: $k = 40$-basis-point fee.

policy will survive to the end of the guaranteed horizon even if the policy-holder withdraws the maximum allowable amount each year. But if we increase the investment return volatility to $\sigma = 25\%$ per annum, the ruin probability increases to 26.2%. If we reduce the expected (arithmetic average) return to $\mu = 6\%$ and maintain a high $\sigma = 25\%$ volatility then the probability of ruin increases to 39.9%; these are clearly nontrivial amounts. Table 11.6 displays the probabilities under various risk–return combinations.

Observe that, if the expected investment return is increased to $\mu = 12\%$ with a volatility of $\sigma = 10\%$, then the probability that the withdrawals of $G = 7$ dollars per annum will actually exhaust (ruin) the policy prior to time $T = 14.28$ is less than half of a percent. Thus, an overly optimistic insurance actuary focused on real-world payout probabilities risks ignoring this event altogether.

In any case, the probability of ex ante guarantee usage ranges from 0.5% to 50%, depending on our assumptions about asset characteristics and returns, and these usage probabilities will affect the setting of traditional insurance reserves. The relevant question to a financial economist interested in the fair value of liabilities is: How much does it cost the insurance company to hedge this guarantee in the capital market?

I now illustrate how to bifurcate the product into a collection of strip bonds (or a term-certain annuity) and a complex option in the form of a so-called Quanto Asian put (QAP). Note that by definition $T = W_0/G$ (since the product terminates or matures when all the funds have been returned), so (11.31) can be written as

$$W_T = W_0 \exp\{(\mu - k - \tfrac{1}{2}\sigma^2)T + \sigma B_T\}$$
$$\times \max\left[0, \left(1 - \frac{1}{T}\int_0^T \exp\{-(\mu - k - \tfrac{1}{2}\sigma^2)s - \sigma B_s\}\,ds\right)\right];$$

here the

$$[\text{QAP option payoff}] := W_T, \qquad (11.34)$$

since the holder of the variable annuity policy is guaranteed to receive any remaining funds in the account at time $T = W_0/G$. Remember that the policyholder is also entitled to the periodic income flow in addition to the (possibly zero) maturity value of the account. The maturity value of the *periodic income* is

$$G \int_0^T e^{rt}\, dt = \frac{G}{r}(e^{rT} - 1). \qquad (11.35)$$

The no-arbitrage, time-0 present value of the GMWB cash-flow package is therefore

$$e^{-rT} E^*[W_T] + \frac{G}{r}(1 - e^{-rT}), \qquad (11.36)$$

where $E^*[\cdot]$ denotes the expectation under the option pricing measure, for which the real-world drift μ is replaced by the risk-free rate r.

Finally, for the GMWB to be fairly priced, at inception we must have that the amount invested in the product W_0 is equal to the value of the cash-flow package, where $T = W_0/G$:

$$W_0 = e^{-rT} E^*[W_T] + \frac{G}{r}(1 - e^{-rT}). \qquad (11.37)$$

Equation (11.37) is one of our main results. It states that, for the product to be fairly structured, the initial purchase price must equal the cost of the term-certain annuity plus the exotic option. For any given (r, σ) pair we can locate the (k, G) curve across which the product is fairly priced, and this implies the equality of (11.37).

I further claim that the option component is effectively a Quanto Asian put defined on the inverse of the account price process. To see this, define a new (reciprocal) process as follows:

$$Y_t = S_t^{-1} = \exp\{-(r - k - \tfrac{1}{2}\sigma^2)t - \sigma B_t\}, \qquad Y_0 = 1. \qquad (11.38)$$

One can think of Y_t as the number of VA subaccount units that one dollar can buy, similar to the number of euros or yen that one dollar can purchase in the currency market. The inverse, $S_t = Y_t^{-1}$, is the value of one VA subaccount unit in dollars, analogous to the price of one euro or one yen in U.S. dollars. Now let

$$A_T := \frac{1}{T} \int_0^T Y_t\, dt, \qquad (11.39)$$

which is an average of the reciprocal account value. The payoff from this option at maturity can now be written as

$$[\text{QAP option payoff}] := W_0 \frac{\max[1 - A_T, 0]}{Y_T}. \tag{11.40}$$

This represents W_0 units of a Quanto (fixed-strike) Asian put option. In sum, scaling everything by the initial premium, a fairly priced product *at inception* implies the relationship

$$e^{-rT} E^* \left[\frac{\max[1 - A_T, 0]}{Y_T} \right] + \frac{G}{r}(1 - e^{-rT}) = 1. \tag{11.41}$$

Given values of the other parameters, the fair insurance fee k can be obtained by solving this equation.

Thus, our main qualitative insight is that, under a static perspective, this product can be decomposed into the following items:

1. a term-certain annuity paying G per annum for a period of $T = W_0/G$ years; plus
2. a Quanto Asian put on the aforementioned reciprocal variable annuity account.

For example: with an initial deposit of $W_0 = \$100$, a guaranteed withdrawal amount of $G = 7$ dollars per annum, and an interest rate of $r = 0.06$, the time-0 cost of the term-certain annuity component is $67.15. The remaining $32.85 would be used to purchase the option, and k is determined so that this represents the fair option value. One can think of a VA with a GMWB as consisting of 67% term-certain annuity and 32% QAP option. In contrast, at a (lower) interest rate of $r = 0.05$, the cost of the term-certain annuity would be (a higher) $71.46 and only $28.54 would be used to purchase the required option.

Table 11.7 displays the required insurance fee that would lead to equality in equation (11.36) or (11.41) under a number of different volatility values. Note the fixed-point nature of the problem. Once the volatility σ, interest rate r, and guarantee rate G have been selected, we must numerically search for a fee value k that yields equality in (11.41). We price the QAP option using techniques referenced in Section 11.7. For example, if the VA guarantees a 7% withdrawal and if the pricing volatility is $\sigma = 20\%$, then the fair insurance fee would be approximately $k = 73$ basis points of assets per annum. Stated differently, a financial package that includes a stream of $7-per-annum income (in continuous time) plus a Quanto Asian put that

Table 11.7. *Impact of GMWB rate and subaccount volatility on required fee k*

Guarantee rate W_0/G	Maturity (years) $T = 1/g$	Investment volatility	
		$\sigma = 20\%$	$\sigma = 30\%$
4%	25.00	23 b.p.	60 b.p.
5%	20.00	37 b.p.	90 b.p.
6%	16.67	54 b.p.	123 b.p.
7%	14.29	73 b.p.	158 b.p.
8%	12.50	94 b.p.	194 b.p.
9%	11.11	117 b.p.	232 b.p.
10%	10.00	140 b.p.	271 b.p.
15%	6.67	272 b.p.	475 b.p.

Notes: b.p. = basis points. Assumes valuation rate of $r = 5\%$.

matures in exactly $T = 14.29$ years is a package worth precisely $W_0 = 100$ when the investment on which the option is struck is "leaking" a dividend yield of 73 basis points per annum. If the guarantee is reduced to $G = 4\%$—which implies that the product matures in $T = 25$ years—then the fair insurance fee is only 23 basis points. Likewise, if the guarantee is increased to $W_0/G = 9\%$—which implies that the product matures in $T = 11.11$ years—then the fair insurance fee is 117 basis points. The most common GMWB guarantee being offered on variable annuities is $W_0/G = 7\%$, which even under a conservative $\sigma = 15\%$ volatility implies an insurance fee of 40 basis points.

Our equating of the GMWB with a term-certain annuity plus a QAP is useful from several points of view. First of all, though I used numerical techniques to value the embedded option, this is not essential because there are a variety of other well-studied approaches to the valuation of Asian options. Second, there is an established over-the-counter market for Asian options, which raises the possibility of hedging via these products (instead of dynamic hedging). Finally, there is a body of practical experience with the hedging of Asian options, which means that the QAP and hence the GMWB are both more familiar products than they may first appear.

11.7 Further Reading

I have examined some of the derivative securities within deferred variable annuities that are associated with pension annuity policies in the United

States. The objective of this chapter was to give the reader a flavor of the types of models and issues being explored by researchers in the field, not to provide a definitive guide or reference on the embedded options. The material in this chapter draws heavily from Milevsky and Posner (2001) and from Milevsky and Salisbury (2006). Additional recommended sources on the topic of guaranteed annuity options include Ballotta and Haberman (2003) and Boyle and Hardy (2003) as well as Milevsky and Promislow (2001). The numerical solution to the ruin probability of the GMWB and the pricing of the QAP are described in Huang et al. (2004). Of course, the "bible" on derivative pricing remains the classic book by John Hull (2002); for those readers who want to "learn" option pricing, there is no better place (at least in my opinion). In their 1976 paper, Brennan and Schwartz were the first to conduct a rigorous treatment of options inside insurance contracts, which is the basis for (11.24).

In the last ten years there has been an explosion of scholarly research and academic papers that have focused on the financial options embedded within pension plans and insurance policies. It is, of course, impossible to do justice to each citable author in the field, and clearly this chapter has been biased by my own interests and research work. However, if you are interested in learning much more about pricing these types of options, I recommend *Investment Guarantees* (Hardy 2003); that book contains a much more detailed examination of alternative models to the simple Brownian motion framework used in this chapter. The merging of mortality and investment derivatives is just getting started.

11.8 Notation

Ω_x—value of a Titanic put option that promises a money-back guarantee at death, where the guarantee level (strike price) increases each year by $g\%$

$\text{BSM}(t)$—value of a generic put option that promises a money-back guarantee at time t

k—instantaneous fee that is paid for the insurance guarantee

K—discounted value of the fee that is paid for the insurance

TWELVE

The Utility of Annuitization

12.1 What Is the Protection Worth?

A few months ago I was annoyed by a phone call at home during my family dinner. The person on the other end of the line wanted to sell me an insurance policy to cover a medium-sized sailboat. For less than $200 per month, I would be protected for up to $1,000,000 in damages over the next five years. According to this salesperson, the quote was a "bargain" because insurance premiums were normally twice this amount. The reason his rates were so cheap was that the company was trying to clear out unused insurance "inventory" by the end of the year. I told him that I did not own a boat and thus had no reason to buy the insurance. But the salesperson did not give up. He went on to tell me that insurance prices were going up within a few months and that I'd better hurry before it was too late .... What did this fellow expect me to do? Buy a boat just so I could get cheap insurance?

This might sound like an odd story to tell, but my point here is that protection—whether pension annuity or life insurance policy—is worth nothing to me, regardless of the discounted or present value of the probability-adjusted cash flows, if I have no need for the protection. In this chapter I will pursue and apply this line of thinking to pension annuities and annuitization.

Allow me to make a similar point in another direction. As this is written I carry more than $1,000,000 of (term) life insurance, for which I pay premiums of a bit more than $100 per month. If anything fatal happens to me, my family will receive a lump-sum payment of $1,000,000 from a well-known and reputable life insurance company. Obviously, a million dollars could never remedy the loss of a spouse or a parent, but at least my family will not face financial ruin. I have estimated that the face value of this policy should be enough to provide them with a reasonable standard of living. Owning this insurance policy gives me a great level of comfort—or,

270

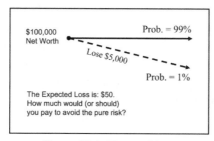

Figure 12.1. Expected loss

as the economists call it, *utility*. To be quite honest, I would be willing to pay much more than $100 per month (which is probably less than what I spend on coffee) to gain this level of utility. My personal utility of life insurance and human capital protection is very high, especially since I have four young children to support and maintain. Luckily, my insurance premiums are determined in a (relatively) free market where the various manufacturers are competing against each other to sell me their products. This drives down the premiums to very near their cost of production, as reflected in the premium factors used in previous chapters. To sum up, my utility of life insurance is much larger than my disutility of paying $100 per month.

12.2 Models of Utility, Value, and Price

I believe there are three ways to determine what a guarantee (i.e. insurance) is worth. There is the *value* or utility of the guarantee (How much comfort does it give me?), the *cost* of the guarantee (How much does it cost to manufacture?), and the *price* of the guarantee (What did you pay?).

Allow me to focus more carefully on the difference between these metrics by way of a numerical example. Assume that your net worth is $100,000 and you're worried about the possibility that the antique vase in your living room—which you bought a few years ago for $5,000—will break. Suppose the probability that this vase will break in any given year is exactly 1%. As you can see from Figure 12.1, on average your expected loss in any given year is $50. An insurance company that sells a large number of these policies to a large group of people, charging each one of them $50, can manufacture just enough reserves to cover their exposure. If it sells a hundred such policies and collects a total of $5,000 in premiums, then the one out of a hundred who breaks a vase will get the $5,000 in compensation. Think of $50 as the cost of manufacturing the protection or the guarantee to replace the vase.

However, the market price might differ from this $50 owing to a variety of competitive factors. For example, the insurance company might decide to sell these policies at a loss (for less than $50) in order (it hopes) to also sell you another, more profitable policy. Or the company might simply be trying to increase policy sales in order to offset other risks. The market price that you observe could be very different from the manufacturing cost. In most cases you pay more than the manufacturing cost, but in some cases you pay less.

Finally, from a utility perspective, protecting the vase's value could be worth (much) more to you than $50. You might be willing to pay considerably more for the peace of mind that comes from knowing it is insured. Of course, those who do not own such a vase will see absolutely no utility value in having vase insurance: to them, a $50 insurance premium is $50 too much. Returning to my initial anecdote, I can again say with certainty that a sailboat insurance policy is not worth a cent *to me*.

12.3 The Utility Function and Insurance

Is there a way of actually *quantifying* the utility, satisfaction, or comfort that an insurance policy (guarantee) provides? The answer is Yes, and this has actually been done by economists in a formal way for many years. They start by modeling the potential magnitude of loss as well as the probability of loss and then combine them using a mathematical representation called a utility function. And though the topic of utility functions properly deserves a book of its own, here are the highlights.

One of the better-known utility functions is called the *constant relative risk aversion* functional form, which can be written as

$$U(w) = \frac{1}{1-\gamma} w^{(1-\gamma)}, \quad w > 0, \tag{12.1}$$

when $\gamma \neq 1$ or defined as the logarithmic utility function $\ln[w]$ when $\gamma = 1$.

The function $U(\cdot)$ maps or transforms monetary values w into utility values $U(w)$. For example, if the coefficient of relative risk aversion is $\gamma = 0.5$ then $w = 100$ dollars provides you with 20 units of utility or satisfaction, whereas $w = 10000$ dollars leads to 200 units, which is only ten times more utility even though your wealth was multiplied by a hundred. Thus, although the utility function is increasing in the wealth argument w, the rate of increase "slows down" with wealth.

Plugging in different values of $\gamma = 3, 4, 5$ into the utility function leads to the following functional forms:

$$U(w) = \frac{1}{-2w^2}, \quad U(w) = \frac{1}{-3w^3}, \quad U(w) = \frac{1}{-4w^4}.$$

Utility functions can have negative values. The γ coefficient reflects the individual's personal level of economic risk aversion. When $\gamma = 0$ we have risk-neutral behavior; when $\gamma > 0$, risk-averse. Finally, $\gamma < 0$ characterizes risk-loving behavior. You will soon see a real-world connection between γ and risk aversion. For now, think of it as a free parameter in the utility function.

So that we may better understand the rate at which the utility value changes for increasing levels of wealth, take the following derivatives:

$$U'(w) = w^{-\gamma}, \qquad U''(w) = -\gamma w^{-(\gamma+1)}.$$

Because $w > 0$, it follows that $U'(w) > 0$ and $U''(w) < 0$. The Arrow–Pratt measure of relative risk aversion (RRA) is defined using the first and second derivatives of the utility function in the following way:

$$-w\frac{U''(w)}{U'(w)} = -w\frac{-\gamma w^{-(\gamma+1)}}{w^{-\gamma}} = \gamma. \tag{12.2}$$

The RRA measures the curvature or concavity of the utility function $U(w)$. The larger is the value of γ, the more curved is the utility function. Let us now return to the broken vase example (recall Figure 12.1) and demonstrate how utility functions can help us understand the consumer's desire to insure.

Remember, the pure (manufacturing) premium you would pay to insure against this risk is $50. But how much more of your wealth (assumed to total $100,000) would you willingly part with in order to avoid an $L = $5,000$ loss with probability $p = 0.01$? To answer this question we must compute and compare utilities. More precisely, I will solve for the the *subjective* insurance premium (or the "willingness to pay," as this is referred to by economists) I_γ under a coefficient of relative risk aversion γ that satisfies

$$U(w - I_\gamma) = E[U(\tilde{w})] = pU(w - L) + (1 - p)U(w). \tag{12.3}$$

The intuition for this equation is as follows. The left-hand side (LHS) of the equation represents the utility of wealth after purchasing the insurance to protect the vase, assuming you pay I_γ in premiums. The right-hand side (RHS) captures the utility of wealth if you do not purchase the insurance. There is a p chance that your vase will break and you will be left with only $w - L$ dollars of net worth. The utility of this outcome is $U(w - L)$. On the other hand, there is a $1 - p$ chance that you will not experience a loss and so will end the year with the same w in wealth; the utility of this outcome is simply $U(w)$. Average the two utilities together to obtain the expected utility. The subjective insurance premium I_γ is the insurance premium that would make you indifferent between having or not having insurance. If the company charges you less than I_γ then you are willing to acquire the insurance because it provides you with more utility than taking a chance and not insuring. On the other hand, if the insurance company charges you more than I_γ then you are willing to take a chance and not purchase coverage.

Let me perform a specific calculation. If $w = 100000$ of initial wealth, $L = 5000$ is the potential loss (cost of the replacing the vase), and $p = 0.01$ is the chance of breaking the vase, then we can use (12.1) and obtain the subjective insurance premium by solving

$$\frac{1}{1-\gamma}(100000 - I_\gamma)^{1-\gamma}$$
$$= (0.01)\frac{(100000 - 5000)^{1-\gamma}}{1-\gamma} + (0.99)\frac{(100000)^{1-\gamma}}{1-\gamma}. \quad (12.4)$$

The first term on the RHS is the utility of wealth after loss (of the vase) and the second term on the RHS is the utility of wealth when there is no loss; the utility of your after-loss wealth is a probability-weighted average— adjusted for risk aversion—of the two conditions. Substituting in values of $\gamma = 1, 2, 3$ leads to the following solutions: $I_3 = \$53.97$ for $\gamma = 3$, $I_2 = \$52.60$ for $\gamma = 2$, and $I_1 = \$51.28$ for $\gamma = 1$ (using the $\ln[w]$ function). Notice the markup above the fair actuarial premium of $pL = 50$ as the risk aversion increases. Table 12.1 displays a spectrum of γ-values and the corresponding subjective premiums; the positive relationship between the two variables should be obvious.

The main point is this. Depending on how risk-averse you are—as measured by the coefficient γ—you are willing to pay more or less for the insurance protection. As long as $\gamma > 0$ you are willing to pay more than the actuarial fair value (or expected loss) of the insurance policy. This is the difference between the subjective utility of insurance and the manufacturing cost or market price of that insurance. In the next section I will illustrate how this kind of utility modeling can be applied to retirement income (spending) planning and annuitization during retirement.

12.4 Utility of Consumption and Lifetime Uncertainty

I will now provide a simple two-period example that illustrates the gains in utility from having access to a life annuity market. Assume you have \$1

Table 12.1. *Relationship between risk aversion γ and subjective insurance premium I_γ*

γ	I_γ
11.0	66.772
5.0	56.853
4.5	56.114
4.0	55.388
3.5	54.674
3.0	53.972
2.5	53.282
2.0	52.603
1.0[a]	51.280
0.5	50.634
0.0	50.000
−1.0	48.761

[a] Function defined as log utility.

in net worth that you can consume (or spend) during the next two periods. The consumption amounts, denoted by C_1 and C_2, will be assumed to take place at the end of the period. Assume there is a p_1 (resp. p_2) probability that you will survive to, and consume at, the end of the first (resp. second) period. Obviously $p_2 \leq p_1$, since I do not allow for resurrections in my simple model.

The one-period interest rate is denoted by R. My objective is to maximize my discounted utility of consumption over these two possible periods. The question is: How much of my \$1 should I consume at the end of the first period versus the end of the second period? If I consume too much at the end of the first period and I end up living (with probability p_2) to the end of the second period, then I might regret not having enough to consume because I overspent in the first period. On the other hand, if I spend too conservatively in the first period, then there might be money left over (wasted) if I don't survive to the end of the second period. Does this question sound familiar?—it was at the heart of the sustainable spending rate discussion from Chapter 9. In this chapter I will focus on how utility functions and annuities interact with each other in this context.

Toward that end, I postulate logarithmic preferences, which means that individuals evaluate the interaction between risk and return by maximizing a utility function of the form $U(w) = \ln[w]$. In the absence of annuities, the objective function and budget constraints are given by:

$$\max_{\{C_1,C_2\}} E[U] = \frac{p_1}{1+\rho} \ln[C_1] + \frac{p_2}{(1+\rho)^2} \ln[C_2] \qquad (12.5)$$

$$\text{s.t.} \quad 1 = \frac{C_1}{1+R} + \frac{C_2}{(1+R)^2}, \qquad (12.6)$$

where "s.t." abbreviates "subject to" and where ρ is a new symbol that in this chapter denotes a subjective discount rate. Think of this number as a biological interest rate that determines how much (more) you value consumption today versus consumption tomorrow. The higher the value of ρ, the more you would like to "front end" your retirement benefits.

In other words, in this system I am trying to maximize expected utility but am constrained by a particular time line and limited funds. Clearly, this model does not incorporate any utility or desire for bequest, since only the "live" states are given weight in the objective function. The solution to this consumption–investment problem is obtained by creating the Lagrangian, which is an artificial "tool" that is used in order to optimize the objective function:

$$\max_{\{C_1,C_2,\lambda\}} L = \frac{p_1}{1+\rho} \ln[C_1] + \frac{p_2}{(1+\rho)^2} \ln[C_2]$$
$$+ \lambda \left(1 - \frac{C_1}{1+R} - \frac{C_2}{(1+R)^2} \right). \qquad (12.7)$$

Technically, I do not need the Lagrangian since I can always write $C_2 = (1+R)^2 - C_1(1+R)$ and convert the problem to one free variable with no constraints. Yet in the general N-period problem, this is how one would proceed, which is why I adopt the generality. The first-order condition is:

$$\frac{\partial L}{\partial C_1} = \frac{p_1}{(1+\rho)C_1} - \frac{\lambda}{1+R} = 0,$$

$$\frac{\partial L}{\partial C_2} = \frac{p_2}{C_2(1+\rho)^2} - \frac{\lambda}{(1+R)^2} = 0, \qquad (12.8)$$

$$\frac{\partial L}{\partial \lambda} = -\frac{C_1}{1+R} - \frac{C_2}{(1+R)^2} + 1 = 0.$$

Solving this system of three equations and three unknowns, I obtain the optimal values for the choice variables as

$$C_1^* = \frac{p_1(\rho R + R + \rho + 1)}{p_2 + p_1\rho + p_1}, \qquad C_2^* = \frac{p_2(1 + 2R + R^2)}{p_2 + p_1\rho + p_1}. \qquad (12.9)$$

The optimal consumption is given by equation (12.9). The ratio of consumption between period 1 and period 2 is $C_1^*/C_2^* = p_1(1+\rho)/p_2(1+R)$.

If the subjective discount rate is equal to the interest rate ($\rho = R$) then $C_1^*/C_2^* = p_1/p_2$, which is the ratio of the survival probabilities; this ratio exceeds 1. Stated differently, the individual consumes less at higher ages. This result can be generalized to a multiperiod setting. When life annuities are not available, rational utility maximizers are forced to consume less as they age, even though their time preference is equal to the market rate.

However, in the presence of an actuarially fair life annuity market (or more precisely, in this case, two one-year tontines), the budget constraint in equation (12.6) must change to reflect the probability-adjusted discount factor. This greatly expands the opportunity set for the consumer and so will increase utility. In this case the optimization model becomes

$$\max_{\{C_1, C_2\}} E[U] = \frac{p_1}{1+\rho} \ln[C_1] + \frac{p_2}{(1+\rho)^2} \ln[C_2] \qquad (12.10)$$

$$\text{s.t.} \quad 1 = \frac{p_1 C_1}{1+R} + \frac{p_2 C_2}{(1+R)^2}. \qquad (12.11)$$

Notice the difference between equation (12.11) and equation (12.6). In the first model the budget constraint has no probabilities in the numerator. In the second model—which includes the availability of annuities—the budget constraint is relaxed by having probabilities in the numerator. The intuition is that you can consume more, conditional on survival, if you are willing to give up the assets in the event of death.

In this case the Lagrangian becomes

$$\max_{\{C_1, C_2, \lambda\}} L = \frac{p_1}{1+\rho} \ln[C_1] + \frac{p_2}{(1+\rho)^2} \ln[C_2] \qquad (12.12)$$

$$+ \lambda \left(1 - \frac{p_1 C_1}{1+R} - \frac{p_2 C_2}{(1+R)^2} \right), \qquad (12.13)$$

and the first-order condition is

$$\frac{\partial L}{\partial C_1} = \frac{p_1}{C_1(1+\rho)} - \frac{\lambda p_1}{1+R} = 0,$$

$$\frac{\partial L}{\partial C_2} = \frac{p_2}{C_2(1+\rho)^2} - \frac{\lambda p_2}{(1+R)^2} = 0, \qquad (12.14)$$

$$\frac{\partial L}{\partial \lambda} = -\frac{p_1 C_1}{1+R} - \frac{p_2 C_2}{(1+R)^2} + 1 = 0.$$

The optimal consumption is denoted by C_1^{**}, C_2^{**} and is equal to

$$C_1^{**} = \frac{\rho R + R + \rho + 1}{p_2 + p_1 \rho + p_1}, \qquad C_2^{**} = \frac{1 + 2R + R^2}{p_2 + p_1 \rho + p_1}. \qquad (12.15)$$

The important point to notice is that $C_1^{**} = C_1^*/p_1$ and $C_2^{**} = C_2^*/p_2$, which implies that—in the presence of life annuities—the optimal consumption is greater in both periods. Specifically, at time 0, the individual would purchase a life annuity that pays C_1^{**} at time 1 and C_2^{**} at time 2. The present value of the two life annuities (as per the budget constraint) is \$1. In this case, the ratio of consumption between period 1 and period 2 is $C_1^{**}/C_2^{**} = (1 + \rho)/(1 + R)$. If the subjective discount rate is equal to the interest rate ($\rho = R$) then $C_1^{**}/C_2^{**} = 1$, which is the "smoothing" effect of annuities discussed earlier.

Here is a numerical example that should help illustrate the simple model. Let $R = \rho = 10\%$, and let $p_1 = 0.75$ and $p_2 = 0.40$. The individual has a 75% chance of surviving to the end of the first period and a 40% chance of surviving to the end of the second period. Hence, according to equation (12.9), the optimal consumption is $C_1^* = 0.741$ and $C_2^* = 0.395$ in the absence of annuities. The maximum utility is $E[U^*] = -0.5115$. However, in the presence of life annuities, the optimal consumption becomes $C_1^{**} = 0.987$ and $C_2^* = 0.987$ with a maximal utility of $E[U^*] = -0.01247$, which is clearly greater than the no-annuity case. To develop a sense of the benefit from annuitizing, solving equation (12.12) with a budget constraint of 0.61 instead of 1 would yield an optimal annuitized consumption of $C_1^{**} = 0.603$ and $C_2^{**} = 0.603$. In this case, the maximal utility would be the same as in the no-annuity case. Stated differently, if one were to take away 0.39 from the individual but give him access to a fairly priced life annuity, then his utility would be the same.

The model presented here obviously abstracts from many of the real-world issues that affect the decision to annuitize. For instance, the individual would be willing to give up less income (in the presence of annuities) if lower probabilities of survival were assumed. Nevertheless, I believe that the intuitive implications are worth the price in assumptions. Annuities allow individuals to consume more than they otherwise could during their retirement years. In our model, *a person would be willing to forgo up to 39% of his initial wealth in order to gain access to a fair life annuity.*

12.5 Utility and Annuity Asset Allocation

The same utility-based ideas can be applied to asset allocation between fixed and variable tontines (which, recall, pay a random sum upon survival depending on investment returns), as I now demonstrate. Assume the following utility function of wealth:

$$U(W) = Au(W_A) + Du(W_D), \tag{12.16}$$

where W_A is the end-of-period wealth of the individual, conditional on being alive, and W_D is the end-of-period wealth of the individual, conditional on being deceased. The function $u(\cdot)$ is a strictly increasing and concave utility function in wealth—with no specific functional form—while D is the weight assigned by the individual to bequest motives. By assumption, $A + D = 1$. This particular utility function allows for a difference in bequest motives across individuals.

At the beginning of the period, the retiree will allocate her initial wealth, denoted by w, among four different instruments in order to maximize expected end-of-period utility. The expectations are taken with respect to (i) the retiree's subjective probability of survival, $\bar{p}$, and (ii) the agreed-upon payoff distribution of the risky asset. The end-of-period wealth in the alive and dead states can thus be represented as

$$W_A = \alpha_1 wR + \alpha_2 wX + \alpha_3 wR/p + \alpha_4 wX/p;$$
$$W_D = \alpha_1 wR + \alpha_2 wX. \tag{12.17}$$

Combining equations (12.16) and (12.17), we find that the expected utility is of the form

$$E[U(W)] = \bar{p}AE[u(W_A)] + (1 - \bar{p})DE[u(W_D)], \tag{12.18}$$

where $E(\cdot)$ denotes consensus expectation with respect to the distribution of the risky payoff. This leads to

$$E[U(W)] = \bar{p}AE[u(\alpha_1 wR + \alpha_2 wX + \alpha_3 wR/p + \alpha_4 wX/p)]$$
$$+ (1 - \bar{p})DE[u(\alpha_1 wR + \alpha_2 wX)]. \tag{12.19}$$

Although I have not yet specified the functional form of $u(\cdot)$, I can still make some statements regarding the general decision to purchase life annuities. Specifically, I answer this question: How strong must the bequest motive be in order to avoid life annuities? Under the setup described so far, no individual will hold either a fixed or a variable tontine if the following condition is satisfied:

$$D > \left(\frac{\bar{p}/p - \bar{p}}{1 - \bar{p}} \right) A. \tag{12.20}$$

In other words, *tontines are completely avoided for a strong enough bequest motive*.

A trivial and intuitive illustration of this claim is when the individual's subjective probability of survival $\bar{p}$ is equal to the objective probability of survival p. In this case, the no-tontine condition becomes $D > A$, implying that the tontines are avoided by individuals who weigh the dead state more heavily than the alive state (i.e., who have a strong utility of bequest). Alternatively, if (say) the objective probability of survival is 75% and the individual believes that he is 10% less healthy than average, then $\bar{p} = (0.9)(0.75) = 0.675$. Then, per (12.20), if the preference for income after death is greater than 0.692 times the preference for income while alive, tontines are avoided. The less healthy an individual feels relative to the population, the lower the weight on the utility of bequest needed to shun the tontines.

The proof can be achieved by means of simple algebra. The no-tontine condition in (12.20) can be restated as

$$p > \frac{\bar{p}A}{\bar{p}A + (1 - \bar{p})D} = p^*, \qquad (12.21)$$

where the variable p^* is now denoted as a normalized weight for the states. The utility functions $u(\cdot)$ are concave, which implies that $U(\cdot)$ is concave as well. By definition, if f is a concave function then $p^*f(x)+(1-p^*)f(y) \leq f(p^*x+(1-p^*)y)$ for any $p^* \geq 0$. This constrains $E[U(W)]$ by an upper bound as follows:

$$E[U(W)] \leq E[U(\alpha_1 wR + \alpha_2 wX + p^*\alpha_3 wR/p + p^*\alpha_4 wX/p)]$$
$$\leq U(E[\alpha_1 wR + \alpha_2 wX + p^*\alpha_3 wR/p + p^*\alpha_4 wX/p])$$
$$= U(\alpha_1 wR + \alpha_2 w\mu + p^*\alpha_3 wR/p + p^*\alpha_4 w\mu/p). \qquad (12.22)$$

If $p^* < p$ then the RHS of the equality (last line) in (12.22) is maximized for $\alpha_3 = \alpha_4 = 0$. Since this value is attainable for $E[U(W)]$, we have our result that if $p^* < p$ then there is no demand for tontines, proving my claim. For completeness, in the trivial case that $\mu < R$, we have $E[U(x)] \leq U(E[x])$ and obtain that $E[U(W)]$ is less than or equal to $U(\alpha_1 wR + \alpha_2 w\mu + p^*\alpha_3 wR/p + p^*\alpha_4 w\mu/p)$. This is maximized for $\alpha_2 = \alpha_4 = 0$ and, since this value is attainable for $E[U(W)]$, our result follows.

Inequality (12.20) is a sufficient condition for there to be no demand for tontines. There are two other cases of interest. The first is when (a) the retiree's subjective probability of survival is the same as the objective probability *and* (b) the weights on the utility function are the same (i.e. $A = D$). In this case, there is no difference in utility between the states of "alive" and "dead"; the expected payoff of the fixed tontine is equal to that of the risk-free asset, while the expected payoff of the variable tontine is equal to that of the risky asset. Because the utility function used here is concave, the agent will always prefer the risk-free and risky assets (nontontines) to the fixed and variable tontines, respectively.

A second case of interest is when the individual has no utility of bequest—in other words, $D = 0$. In this case, an examination of (12.19) shows that, since $wR/p > wR$ and $wX/p > wX$ for all $p < 1$, it follows that tontines "stochastically dominate" regular assets. Therefore, individuals with no utility of bequest will always hold the annuities. This result—in the context of fixed annuities—is a well-known result in the insurance literature.

12.6 The Optimal Timing of Annuitization

In the remaining portion of this chapter, I will pursue a slightly different approach to the issue of when people should annuitize. Specifically—and as motivated by the financial option pricing paradigm—the focus of attention now is on what I shall call the "real option" embedded in the decision to annuitize. Heuristically, owing to the irreversibility of annuitization, the decision to purchase a life annuity is akin to exercising an American-style, mortality-contingent claim. It is optimal to do so only when the remaining time value of the option becomes worthless. Options derive their value from the volatility of the underlying state variables. Therefore, if one accounts for future mortality and investment uncertainty, the embedded option provides an incentive to delay annuitization until the option value has been eliminated. The option is *real* in the sense that it is not directly separable or tradeable.

Indeed, as illustrated in our discussion of utility theory, the availability of a (fair) life annuity relaxes the budget constraint, which then induces greater consumption and utility. Therefore, all else being equal, consumers annuitize wealth as soon as they are given the (fair) opportunity to do so. However, these classical arguments are predicated on the existence of a single financial asset, whose value is the basis for annuity pricing. This framework assumes de facto that the budget constraint will not improve over time. In practice, however, a risky asset is an alternative to the risk-free investment; by taking a chance in the risky asset, the future budget constraint may improve. In other words, it might be worth waiting, since tomorrow's budget constraint may allow for a larger annuity flow and greater utility. In the meantime, of course, the individual is assumed to withdraw consumption from liquid wealth, so as to mimic the life annuity. Clearly, if the volatility in the model is set equal to zero, then the option to delay has no value. Likewise, uncertainty about future interest rates, mortality, insurance loads, and product design all increase the value of the option to delay.

Stated differently, my main argument is that *retirees should refrain from annuitizing today, because they may get an even better deal tomorrow.*

So that we may price this option to wait, I propose a methodology that defines the value of the real option to defer annuitization (RODA) as the percentage increase in wealth that would *substitute* for the ability to defer. I answer the question: How much would the consumer require in compensation for losing the opportunity to wait? This number is clearly dependent on individual preferences, especially since there is no secondary market for this real option. Furthermore, the RODA option value may actually be negative, in which case I argue that the consumer is better off annuitizing right now because waiting can only destroy wealth. Of course, the availability of (low-cost) variable immediate annuities reduces the option value of waiting and should increase annuitization arrangements in the future.

12.7 The Real Option to Defer Annuitization

I illustrate the option value of deferring annuitization with a simple three-period example. Our problem starts at time 0 with a consumer who has an initial endowment or wealth of w. All consumption takes place at the end of the period, and the probabilities of dying during these periods are $q_0 < q_1 < q_2$. If the individual is fortunate to survive to the end of the third period, she consumes and immediately dies. For simplicity, I assume that both the consumer and the insurance company are aware of (and agree upon) these probabilities of death. Also for simplicity, assume that the consumer's subjective rate of time preference is set equal to the risk-free rate (we ignore income taxes).

Let c_1, c_2, c_3 denote the consumption that takes place at the end of each respective period. The variable R denotes the (risk-free) interest rate "off" which the annuities are priced. Now the optimization problem is

$$\max_{\{c_1,c_2,c_3\}} E[U_3 \mid w] = \frac{(1-q_0)u(c_1)}{1+R} + \frac{(1-q_0)(1-q_1)u(c_2)}{(1+R)^2}$$
$$+ \frac{(1-q_0)(1-q_1)(1-q_2)u(c_3)}{(1+R)^3} \qquad (12.23)$$

$$\text{s.t.} \quad w = \frac{(1-q_0)c_1}{1+R} + \frac{(1-q_0)(1-q_1)c_2}{(1+R)^2}$$
$$+ \frac{(1-q_0)(1-q_1)(1-q_2)c_3}{(1+R)^3}, \qquad (12.24)$$

where $u(c)$ is a twice differentiable utility function that is positive, increasing, and strictly concave. Specifically, I will assume the same functional form that exhibits constant relative risk aversions with $u(c) = c^{(1-\gamma)}/(1-\gamma)$ and $-cu''(c)/u''(c) = \gamma$; remember that this is the coefficient of RRA. In the event that $\gamma = 1$, the function is defined as $u(c) = \ln[c]$. Also, a utility of bequest is ignored in this material, since it could only increase the value of not annuitizing. The annuity contract is part of (12.24) by virtue of the (expected) mortality-adjusted discounting of consumption. All else being equal, higher values of q_i increase the consumption attainable in the annuity market. The same initial w can be used to finance a higher consumption stream. Likewise, setting all $q_i = 0$ in (12.24) will tighten the budget constraint and reduce the feasible consumption set. This is akin to solving the problem without annuity markets.

The Lagrangian of problem (12.23)–(12.24) is

$$\max_{\{c_1,c_2,c_3,\lambda\}} L_3 = \frac{(1-q_0)u(c_1)}{1+R} + \frac{(1-q_0)(1-q_1)u(c_2)}{(1+R)^2}$$
$$+ \frac{(1-q_0)(1-q_1)(1-q_2)u(c_3)}{(1+R)^3}$$
$$+ \lambda \left(w - \frac{(1-q_0)c_1}{1+R} - \frac{(1-q_0)(1-q_1)c_2}{(1+R)^2} \right.$$
$$\left. - \frac{(1-q_0)(1-q_1)(1-q_2)c_3}{(1+R)^3} \right), \qquad (12.25)$$

and the first-order condition is

$$\frac{\partial L_3}{\partial c_i} = 0, \quad i = 1, 2, 3, \qquad \frac{\partial L_3}{\partial \lambda} = 0. \qquad (12.26)$$

This leads to an optimal (constant) consumption of

$$c_i^* = c^* = \frac{w}{a_3}, \quad i = 1, 2, 3, \qquad E[U_3^* \mid w] = u\left(\frac{w}{a_3}\right)a_3. \qquad (12.27)$$

Here a_3 is the initial price of a \$1 life annuity that is paid over three periods and is contingent on survival:

$$a_3 = \frac{1-q_0}{1+R} + \frac{(1-q_0)(1-q_1)}{(1+R)^2} + \frac{(1-q_0)(1-q_1)(1-q_2)}{(1+R)^3}. \qquad (12.28)$$

This is a classical annuity result, stating that all retirement wealth is annuitized (i.e., held in the form of actuarial notes) and that consumption is constant across all (living) periods. As mentioned earlier, in the absence of annuity markets the budget constraint in (12.24) is tightened to equate present value of consumption and initial wealth; hence optimal consumption decreases in proportion to the probability of survival.

The constant consumption result is predicated on (a) symmetric mortality beliefs and (b) the time preference being set to the risk-free rate. If these numbers are different then the optimal consumption stream might not be constant; in some cases, it might even induce holdings of nonannuitized assets.

As an example, assume $w = 1$, $q_0 = 0.10$, $q_1 = 0.25$, $q_2 = 0.60$, $R = 0.10$, and $\gamma = 1.5$. Then $u(c) = -2/\sqrt{c}$, and

$$a_3 = 1.5789, \quad c^* = \frac{1}{a_3} = 0.63336, \quad E[U_3^* \mid 1] = u\left(\frac{1}{a_3}\right)a_3 = -3.9679.$$

If $\gamma = 1$ (log utility) then consumption remains the same because all assets are annuitized, but $\ln[1/a_3]a_3 = -0.7211$ "utiles."

My main idea is to allow the individual to consume c^* at the end of the period and then reconsider annuitization at that time. This is called self-annuitization. Meanwhile, the assets are invested and subjected to the risky return. The risky return can fall in one of two states: up (denoted with the subscript u) or down (subscript d). There is a probability p of a good return X_u and a probability $1 - p$ of a bad return X_d. So, if we wait to annuitize, then the next period's optimization problem will be one of two types.

Should the liquid assets earn a "good" return, the optimization problem will be

$$\max_{\{c_{u2}, c_{u3}\}} E[U_{u2} \mid wX_u - c^*]$$
$$= \frac{(1 - q_1)u(c_{u2})}{1 + R} + \frac{(1 - q_1)(1 - q_2)u(c_{u3})}{(1 + R)^2} \quad (12.29)$$

$$\text{s.t.} \quad wX_u - c^* = \frac{(1 - q_1)c_{u2}}{1 + R} + \frac{(1 - q_1)(1 - q_2)c_{u3}}{(1 + R)^2}. \quad (12.30)$$

In the event of a "bad" return, the second-period optimization problem becomes

$$\max_{\{c_{d2}, c_{d3}\}} E[U_{d2} \mid wX_d - c^*]$$
$$= \frac{(1 - q_1)u(c_{d2})}{1 + R} + \frac{(1 - q_1)(1 - q_2)u(c_{d3})}{(1 + R)^2} \quad (12.31)$$

$$\text{s.t.} \quad wX_d - c^* = \frac{(1 - q_1)c_{d2}}{1 + R} + \frac{(1 - q_1)(1 - q_2)c_{d3}}{(1 + R)^2}. \quad (12.32)$$

As before, the optimal consumption is constant:

$$c_d^* = \frac{wX_d - c^*}{a_2}, \qquad E^*[U_{d2} \mid wX_d - c^*] = u\left(\frac{wX_d - c^*}{a_2}\right)a_2, \qquad (12.33)$$

$$c_u^* = \frac{wX_u - c^*}{a_2}, \qquad E^*[U_{u2} \mid wX_u - c^*] = u\left(\frac{wX_u - c^*}{a_2}\right)a_2, \qquad (12.34)$$

where the two-period annuity factor is

$$a_2 = \frac{1 - q_1}{1 + R} + \frac{(1 - q_1)(1 - q_2)}{(1 + R)^2} = a_3\left(\frac{1 + R}{1 - q_0}\right) - 1. \qquad (12.35)$$

We have now arrived at the main expression:

$$E^*[U_{\text{wait}} \mid w] = \frac{1 - q_0}{1 + R}\left(pu\left(\frac{wX_u - c^*}{a_2}\right)a_2 \right.$$
$$\left. + (1 - p)u\left(\frac{wX_d - c^*}{a_2}\right)a_2 + u(c^*)\right). \qquad (12.36)$$

The utility of deferral captures the gains from taking a chance on the next period's budget constraint. Specifically, the utility of deferral weighs the next period's utility of consumption by the probability of either return state $\{u, d\}$ occurring and the probability of survival, and it then discounts for time. Hence, as long as

$$E^*[U_{\text{wait}} \mid w] > E^*[U_3 \mid w], \qquad (12.37)$$

one is better-off waiting. Finally, the value of the option to delay for one period is defined as equal to the quantity I that equates both utilities:

$$E^*[U_{\text{wait}} \mid w] = E^*[U_3 \mid w + I]. \qquad (12.38)$$

Our intuition for this result will be aided by a numerical example. I use the same parameters as in the previous example, namely: $w = 1$, $q_0 = 0.10$, $q_1 = 0.25$, $q_2 = 0.60$, $R = 0.10$, and $u(c) = -2/\sqrt{c}$. In this case, $c^* = 0.6333$ and $E[U_3^* \mid 1] = -3.9679$. If the individual is faced with a one-time decision, then the optimal consumption is 0.6333 units per period and the maximum utility is -3.9679. Now assume that the individual can defer this decision by investing w in an asset earning a stochastic return with two possible outcomes, X_u and X_d. Specifically, let $p = 0.70$ denote the probability that the nonannuitized investment factor will be $X_u = 1.45$

(which is a 45% return), so $1 - p = 0.30$ is the probability that the non-annuitized investment factor will be $X_d = 1.00$ (a 0% return). The expected investment return is therefore 31.50%.

If X_u occurs then the investor has 1.45 units at the end of the first period, from which she consumes $c^* = 0.6333$ in order to mimic the annuity. This leaves her with 0.8166 for the second-period budget constraint. However, if X_d occurs then the investor has 1.00 units at the end of the first period, from which she consumes $c^* = 0.6333$ and leaves only 0.3666 for the second-period budget constraint. Assuming she will annuitize at the end of the first period, her discounted expected utility from the decision to defer is

$$E^*[U_{\text{wait}} \mid w] = -3.9193 > -3.9679 = E^*[U_3 \mid w].$$

Furthermore, giving this individual $I = 0.02491$ at time 0 would make her indifferent between annuitizing immediately and deferring for one period. I conclude that the value of the option to delay one period is worth 2.49% of initial wealth.

A few technical comments are in order. For the deferral to make financial sense, the stochastic return from the investable asset must exceed the mortality-adjusted risk-free rate in at least one state of nature. In our context of three periods and two states of nature, X_u must be greater than $(1 + R)/(1 - q_0)$, since otherwise $E^*[U_{\text{wait}} \mid w]$ will never exceed $E^*[U_3 \mid w]$ regardless of how high p is or how low q_0 is.

One does not require abnormally high investment returns in order to justify deferral. In fact, the entire analysis could have been conducted with a stochastic interest rate R instead of a stochastic investment return (or both, for that matter). The key insight is that waiting might change the budget constraint in the consumer's favor. The budget constraint might change on the left-hand side, representing an increase (or decrease) in initial wealth, or on the right-hand side, with an increase (or decrease) in the interest rate off which the annuity is priced. As long as the risk-adjusted odds of a favorable change in the budget constraint are high enough, the option to wait has value. This insight is important because any possible change in the future price of the annuity provides an option value. This would include any changes in design, liquidity, or pricing that might improve tomorrow's budget constraint.

If $\gamma = 1$ (log utility) then the value of the one-period option is 4.26%, which is higher than if $\gamma = 1.5$. As one would expect, the lower is the level of risk aversion γ, the higher is the (utility-adjusted) incentive to take some financial risk and defer the decision to annuitize. This increases the value of the option. The same is true in the other direction. A higher aversion to risk decreases the value of the option. For a high enough value—which in our case is $\gamma = 2.1732$—the individual should not defer annuitization because the risk is too high.

Although we have not addressed this issue in our formal analysis, if the consumer has a less favorable view of her own mortality then the option to defer is even more valuable. Specifically: if q_0^O, which is used in the budget constraint to price the annuity, is lower than the subjective q_0^S used in the objective function, then the maximum utility will be reduced at time 0, which increases the value of I that yields equality in (12.38). This might go a long way toward explaining why individuals who believe themselves to be less healthy than average are more likely to avoid annuities, despite having no declared bequest motive. In our context, the individual might be speculating on next period's budget constraint in the (risk-adjusted) hope that it will improve.

Our annuities $\{a_3, a_2\}$ are priced in a profitless environment where loads and commissions are set to zero. Indeed, some studies find values per premium dollar in the 0.75–0.93 region depending on the relevant mortality table, yield curve, gender, and age. In our context, the absence of such fees would imply another incentive to defer, since X_u is then more likely to exceed the mortality-adjusted risk-free rate. This would hold true as long as the proportional insurance loads do not increase as a function of age.

Finally, although I have christened I the "option value," one must be careful to note that it is the value of the option to defer (and consume) for one period. In theory, the individual might also defer for two periods and then annuitize. To be absolutely precise, one should think of I as a lower bound on the option value, since one might consider deferring for many periods. Having considered the basic intuition in a simple three-period example, I now move on to report the results of a similar analysis in a continuous-time (multiperiod) model in which estimates are developed for the option value.

12.8 Advanced RODA Model

Without delving into much technical detail (but see Section 12.11 for references), Table 12.2 provides the results of a full-blown analysis that generalizes the results of equation (12.38) to a multiperiod framework. It displays the optimal age of annuitization and the value of the option to delay as a percentage of initial wealth, as well as the probability of consuming less at the optimal time of annuitization than if one had annuitized one's wealth immediately. I refer to this latter measure as the probability of deferral failure.

Table 12.2. *When should you annuitize in order to maximize your utility of wealth?*

Age	Optimal age	Value of delay (%)	Probability of deferral failure
$\gamma = 1$, *female* [*male*]			
60	84.5 [80.3]	44.0 [32.0]	0.311 [0.353]
65	84.5 [80.3]	33.4 [21.9]	0.346 [0.391]
70	84.5 [80.3]	22.7 [12.3]	0.385 [0.431]
75	84.5 [80.3]	12.3 [4.2]	0.429 [0.470]
80	84.5 [80.3]	3.7 [0.02]	0.473 [0.500]
85	Now [Now]	Neg. [Neg.]	N/A [N/A]
$\gamma = 2$, *female* [*male*]			
60	78.4 [73.0]	15.3 [8.9]	0.268 [0.321]
65	78.4 [73.0]	10.3 [4.3]	0.310 [0.372]
70	78.4 [73.0]	5.2 [0.8]	0.362 [0.435]
75	78.4 [Now]	1.2 [0.0]	0.428 [N/A]
80	Now [Now]	Neg. [Neg.]	N/A [N/A]
85	Now [Now]	Neg. [Neg.]	N/A [N/A]

Here is how to read and interpret the results. If you are a 75-year-old female whose coefficient of relative risk aversion is $\gamma = 1$, then the optimal age at which to annuitize is 84.5. The value of the option to delay annuitization—which, you recall, is equivalent to the payment you would demand in exchange for being forced to annuitize at age 75—is 12.3% of your wealth. For a male with the same level of risk aversion, the optimal age at which to annuitize is 80.3, and the value of the option to annuitize is worth only 4.2% of his wealth. Quite intuitively, since the male has a higher probability of death (or higher mortality credits) at age 75, it follows that the value of waiting is not as high. In general, females annuitize at older ages than males because the mortality rate of females is lower at any given age. Also, observe that individuls who are more risk averse wish to annuitize sooner, an intuitively pleasing result. Finally, our pedagogically appealing value of the option to delay annuitization—which is, in effect, equivalent to the welfare loss from annuitizing immediately—decreases as one approaches the optimal age of annuitization, as we would expect.

The probability of deferral failure, although seemingly high, is balanced by the probability of consuming more than the original annuity amount. On a utility-adjusted basis this is obviously a worthwhile trade-off, as evidenced by the behavior of the value function.

Table 12.3. *Real option to delay annuitization for a 60-year-old male who disagrees with insurance company's estimate of his mortality*

			Consumption rate (%)	
f	Optimal age of annuitization	Value of delay (%)	Before annuitization	After annuitization
−1.0	78.28	13.79	7.55	13.38
−0.8	74.58	10.54	7.95	11.79
−0.6	73.71	9.68	8.18	11.47
−0.4	73.29	9.23	8.37	11.33
−0.2	73.09	8.99	8.54	11.26
0.0	73.03	8.87	8.70	11.24
0.2	73.08	8.84	8.85	11.26
0.5	73.31	8.93	9.06	11.33
1.0	74.04	9.34	9.38	11.59
1.5	75.21	10.00	9.68	12.03
2.0	76.96	10.89	9.98	12.76
2.5	79.71	12.01	10.26	14.12
3.0	85.38	13.38	10.55	18.01

Note: Assumes that $\lambda_x^S = (1 + f)\lambda_x^O$.

12.9 Subjective vs. Objective Mortality

The setup in the previous section—as well as the simple three-period numerical example of Section 12.7—assumed that both the insurance company and the individual agreed on mortality probabilities. In other words, the insurance company used the exact same probability of survival when pricing the annuity as the individual did when discounting personal utility. In this section I will display the results from modifying the symmetric mortality assumption while maintaining the financial market assumptions from the previous example.

To create such a model, imagine that the individual's subjective force of mortality is a multiple of the company's objective force of mortality; specifically, $\lambda_x^S = (1 + f)\lambda_x^O$, in which f ranges from −1 (immortal) to ∞ (at death's door). In actuarial science this is known as the *proportional hazard* transformation. I then run through the exact same calculations as before, but with different mortality curves and rates depending on whether we are pricing annuities (λ_x^O) or computing utility (λ_x^S). Table 12.3 presents, for a 60-year-old male, the imputed value of the option to delay annuitization, the optimal age of annuitization, the optimal rate of consumption before annuitization (as a percentage of current wealth), and the rate of consumption after annuitization (also as a percentage of current wealth). For comparison, if he were to annuitize his wealth at age 60, the rate of subsequent consumption would be 8.34%.

Thus, for example, if you think you are 20% healthier than the group to whom the insurance company is selling annuities, then for you $\lambda_x^S = 0.8\lambda_x^O$ at all ages and you should annuitize at age 73.09 (as opposed to 73.03). This difference in age might seem tiny and irrelevant, but as your health assessment deteriorates further the optimal age does increase. Notice that, if you disagree with objective mortality, you delay annuitization whether you are healthier or less healthy. It seems that the optimal age of annuitization will be a minimum when the subjective and objective forces of mortality are equal. Also, the consumption rate before annuitization increases as the individual becomes less healthy, as we would expect.

12.10 Variable vs. Fixed Payout Annuities

Finally, in this section I report on the results from modeling the optimal age at which to annuitize when there are variable as well as fixed payout annuities available to retirees. Remember that the earlier sections all (implicitly) assumed that one of the reasons it was worthwhile to delay annuitization was the possibility of earning better investment returns in the open market. However, when variable payout annuities are readily available at a low cost, the so-called option value to delay is not so great. Table 12.4 illustrates this fact. More specifically, it compares the optimal ages of annuitization (and the imputed value of delaying when the individual can only buy a fixed annuity) to when the individual can buy a money mix of variable and fixed annuities.

I assume that the financial market and mortality are as previously described except as follows. For the variable annuity, the insurer has a 100-basis-point "mortality and expense risk charge" load on the return, so that the modified arithmetic return from risky assets is $\mu' = 0.11$ compared to an original μ of 0.12; and for the fixed annuity, the insurer has a 50-basis-point spread on the return, so that the modified rate of return is $r' = 0.055$ when $r = 0.06$. Assume that the individual's coefficient of RRA is $\gamma = 2$, from which it follows that 75.0% will be invested in the risky stock before annuitization and 68.7% in the variable annuity after annuitization.

Now, if you are a 65-year-old female with liquid wealth currently invested in a diversified portfolio of (68.7%) stocks and (31.3%) bonds, then the optimal age at which to annuitize is age 80.2—assuming the pension annuity does not offer a variable payout linked to the same portfolio of stocks and

Table 12.4. *When should you annuitize?—Given the choice of fixed and variable annuities*

| Age | Fixed annuity only, female [male] | | Mixture[a] of annuities, female [male] | |
	Optimal age of annuitization	Value of delay (%)	Optimal age of annuitization	Value of delay (%)
60	80.2 [75.2]	21.0 [13.4]	70.8 [64.1]	3.40 [0.6]
65	80.2 [75.2]	14.8 [7.5]	70.8 [Now]	1.30 [Neg.]
70	80.2 [75.2]	8.5 [2.5]	70.8 [Now]	0.04 [Neg.]
75	80.2 [75.2]	2.9 [0.003]	Now [Now]	Neg. [Neg.]

[a] 68.7% variable annuities and 31.3% fixed annuities.

bonds. However, if the pension annuity can be linked to the performance of those stocks and bonds (as described in Chapter 6), then the optimal age at which to annuitize is reduced to age 70.8. Note that gaining access to a variable payout annuity makes the irreversible decision relatively more appealing, since you retain more flexibility than if you are locked in to a fixed-payout product. For males this effect is even more pronounced, as the optimal age is reduced from approximately age 75 to age 65. Of course, these numbers are based on a risk-aversion level of $\gamma = 2$. If the risk aversion is only $\gamma = 1$ then the optimal age will be delayed, but if the risk aversion is increased then the RODA value (and the corresponding "best age") will be reduced.

12.11 Further Reading

The classical references on utility, life-cycle consumption, and asset allocation with lifetime uncertainty are Pratt (1964), Arrow (1965), Yaari (1965), Samuelson (1969), Merton (1971), Fischer (1973), and Richard (1975). The application of utility theory to the demand for life insurance and protection of human capital can be traced to Campbell (1980) and has recently been applied within the context of asset allocation by Chen and colleagues (2006). See Gerber and Pafumi (1999) for a comprehensive review of utility theory within the context of insurance pricing.

The application of utility theory to the demand for life annuities started with Yaari (1965). Additional references are Kotlikoff and Spivak (1981), Williams (1986), Lewis (1989), Bodie (1990), Bernheim (1991), Hayashi, Altonji, and Kotlikoff (1996), Mitchell et al. (1999), Brown and Poterba (2000), Ehrlich (2000), Brown (2001), Jousten (2001), and Davidoff, Brown, and

Diamond (2003). Also note that a review of the Lagrangian technique can be found in Salas, Hille, and Etgen (1998).

The basic utility-based consumption approach to annuitization in a simple two-period model was presented in Milevsky (2001). The application of utility theory to optimal allocation within variable and fixed payout annuities is explored from a theoretical perspective in Charupat, Milevsky, and Tuenter (2001) and is applied within the context of asset allocation in Chen and Milevsky (2003).

The advanced material in this chapter draws heavily from my joint work with Jenny Young, which is formally referenced as Milevsky and Young (2004). This chapter takes a discrete-time approach to the issue, whereas that reference extended the analysis to continuous time. The concept of an option to annuitize—which is irreversible and possibly regrettable, and hence worth delaying—can be traced to the paper by Stock and Wise (1990), who coined the phrase "option to retire." Of course, their implementation is quite different given that this chapter discusses neither labor income nor the utility of leisure, but the analogy is appropriate. The "real option" literature started with Ingersoll and Ross (1992) but likely can also be traced to the ideas of Merton (1971). The concept of an optimal time (age) at which to annuitize—and the optimality of delaying annuitization—has also been investigated by Brugiavini (1993), Yagi and Nishigaki (1993), Kapur and Orszag (1999), Dushi and Webb (2004), and Kingston and Thorp (2005). For a detailed derivation of the optimal asset allocation within the variable payout annuity, see Charupat and Milevsky (2002).

12.12 Notation

γ—coefficient of relative risk aversion

$U(W)$—utility function of wealth or consumption

λ_x^O—objective mortality rate used by the insurance company to price pension annuities

λ_x^S—subjective mortality rate used by the individual to determine personal utility from pension annuities

THIRTEEN

Final Words

During the year 2002, I was a firsthand witness to a historically unprecedented pension experiment that took place in the state of Florida. Every one of that state's more than 500,000 public employees—in addition to every new employee joining the state's payroll—was given the option of converting their traditional defined benefit (DB) pension plan into an individually managed defined contribution (DC) account. The DC investment plan was similar to a corporate-style 401(k) plan, under which the employee has full control over asset allocation and investment decisions. Florida's new Public Employee Optional Retirement Program (PEORP) was the focus of intense scrutiny by local and national media. This is because it was the largest such pension conversion in the history of the United States and was viewed by many observers as a potential laboratory for Social Security reform. Although at first the take-up rate for the DC plan was low, it is now estimated that over half of the state's new employees have decided to forgo the traditional DB pension and instead enroll in the DC investment plan.

This large-scale transition from DB pension to DC accounts is not limited to the state of Florida or the United States alone. A number of other states—including a failed attempt by California Governor Schwarzenegger—have proposed converting their public employee DB plan into either a mandatory or optional DC plan. Several countries around the world—starting most prominently with Chile in the mid-1980s—have introduced DC-style pension savings accounts as an alternative to traditional DB pensions. The impetus for this massive global shift can be attributed to a wide variety of factors, but it is primarily due to an actuarial funding crisis and demographic forces, both of which have been brewing for many years. Indeed, the economic cost of funding and maintaining DB pensions has reached unprecedented levels, driven by low interest rates, poor performance of the equity markets, and the uncertainty of increasing life spans.

Private-sector corporate pension plans have not been immune to this trend, either. As I write this in late 2005, DB pension plans in the United States have a collective funding deficit in the hundreds of billions of dollars, depending on which assumptions are used to discount these liabilities. They, too, have suffered from the same increasing longevity patterns, declining interest rates, and poor equity returns, as well as a cumbersome regulatory environment. So it is no surprise that, according to the U.S. Department of Labor, the number of private-sector DB plans in the United States has fallen from 112,208 in 1980 to 29,512 in 2003. Likewise, the number of private-sector employees covered by a DB plan fell from 30.1 million in 1980 to 22.6 million in early 2000. More telling is that the percentage of private-sector employees covered by a DB plan fell from 28% in 1980 to 7% in early 2000. In sum, defined benefit pension plans are dying. For the most part, the vacuum created by the demise of DB pension coverage has been taken up by DC-style accounts, where individuals must create their own retirement income.

Against this institutional backdrop is the fact that, beginning in 2006, the first of roughly 78 million American Baby Boomers will reach the age of 60; in fact, a Baby Boomer will be turning 60 every ten seconds. This will likely be the largest group ever to move from accumulating wealth during their working years to spending it in their retirement years.

Thus, as responsibility for generating a sustainable retirement income shifts away from governments and corporations toward individuals and their financial advisors, there is a pressing need for an underlying set of quantitative tools to assist in making informed decisions. These tools must explicitly account for the uncertainty surrounding investment returns, lifetime horizons, and the real cost of retirement income.

I hope that this book will help quantitatively inclined financial advisors— as well as the college and university instructors who train them—to develop the necessary techniques for explaining the rewards and risks of retirement income planning. Although the underlying mathematical tools may appear to be as daunting as they are beautiful, I believe that the benefits of this journey far outweigh the cost.

FOURTEEN

Appendix

This chapter contains some extended mortality and statistics tables that were referred to throughout the book.

Tables 14.1 and 14.3 are mortality tables listing q_x values, male and female, for ages 50–120; Table 14.2 offers an international comparison of q_x values at age 65.

Note the difference between the "annuitant" mortality Table 14.1 and the "insurance" mortality Table 14.3. For the most part, the q_x rates at any fixed age are lower in a mortality table that is used for pricing and valuing pension annuities than in the table used for life insurance. This difference is due to adverse selection—healthier individuals tend to purchase pension annuities rather than life insurance. Of course, individuals who have actually *qualified* for life insurance might be relatively healthier than those who simply *wanted* to purchase life insurance but did not qualify. For more information about what actuaries call "ultimate" and "select" mortality tables, see Bowers et al. (1997).

Table 14.4 provides values for the CDF of the normal distribution under a *zero* mean (μ) and standard deviation of sigma (σ). If you want to compute the probability $\Pr[X \leq x]$ under a nonzero μ, then use the numbers given $x - \mu$. For example, with $\mu = 0$ and $\sigma = 20\%$ we have $\Pr[X \leq 10\%] = 69.15\%$, but when $\mu = 5\%$ we have $\Pr[X \leq 10\%] = 59.87\%$. Intuitively, increasing the mean should reduce the probability of earning less than any given threshold. For a refresher on the CDF of the normal random variable, see Section 3.18.

Table 14.5 displays CDF values for the reciprocal Gamma distribution, assuming that $\beta = 1$. If $\beta \neq 1$ then multiply the x-value by β and use the table with β times x. For example: if you want to compute $\Pr[X \leq 10]$ when $\beta = 0.25$, then use Table 14.5 with $x = 2.5$. Thus, if $\alpha = 1.5$ and $\beta = 1$ then $\Pr[X \leq 10] = 97.76\%$, but if $\beta = 0.25$ then $\Pr[X \leq 10] = 84.95\%$.

Table 14.1(a). *RP2000 healthy (static) annuitant mortality table— Ages 50–89*

Age	Female q_x	Male q_x	Age	Female q_x	Male q_x
50	0.002344	0.005347	70	0.016742	0.022206
51	0.002459	0.005528	71	0.018579	0.024570
52	0.002647	0.005644	72	0.020665	0.027281
53	0.002895	0.005722	73	0.022970	0.030387
54	0.003190	0.005797	74	0.025458	0.033900
55	0.003531	0.005905	75	0.028106	0.037834
56	0.003925	0.006124	76	0.030966	0.042169
57	0.004385	0.006444	77	0.034105	0.046906
58	0.004921	0.006895	78	0.037595	0.052123
59	0.005531	0.007485	79	0.041506	0.057927
60	0.006200	0.008196	80	0.045879	0.064368
61	0.006919	0.009001	81	0.050780	0.072041
62	0.007689	0.009915	82	0.056294	0.080486
63	0.008509	0.010951	83	0.062506	0.089718
64	0.009395	0.012117	84	0.069517	0.099779
65	0.010364	0.013419	85	0.077446	0.110757
66	0.011413	0.014868	86	0.086376	0.122797
67	0.012540	0.016460	87	0.096337	0.136043
68	0.013771	0.018200	88	0.107303	0.150590
69	0.015153	0.020105	89	0.119154	0.166420

Table 14.1(b). *RP2000 healthy (static) annuitant mortality table— Ages 90–120*

Age	Female q_x	Male q_x	Age	Female q_x	Male q_x
90	0.131682	0.183408	106	0.307811	0.400000
91	0.144604	0.199769	107	0.322725	0.400000
92	0.157618	0.216605	108	0.337441	0.400000
93	0.170433	0.233662	109	0.351544	0.400000
94	0.182799	0.250693	110	0.364617	0.400000
95	0.194509	0.267491	111	0.376246	0.400000
96	0.205379	0.283905	112	0.386015	0.400000
97	0.215240	0.299852	113	0.393507	0.400000
98	0.223947	0.315296	114	0.398308	0.400000
99	0.231387	0.330207	115	0.400000	0.400000
100	0.237467	0.344556	116	0.400000	0.400000
101	0.244834	0.358628	117	0.400000	0.400000
102	0.254498	0.371685	118	0.400000	0.400000
103	0.266044	0.383040	119	0.400000	0.400000
104	0.279055	0.392003	120	1.000000	1.000000
105	0.293116	0.397886			

Table 14.2. *International comparison (year 2000)*
of mortality rates q_x at age 65

Country	Male	Female	Total
Austria	0.020751	0.008131	0.014009
Belgium	0.019045	0.008699	0.013608
Bulgaria	0.033951	0.016861	0.024662
Czech Republic	0.028256	0.014499	0.020679
Denmark	0.022158	0.013749	0.017788
East Germany	0.021510	0.010463	0.015632
Finland	0.019603	0.008126	0.013487
France	0.018649	0.006992	0.012446
Hungary	0.039530	0.017426	0.026788
Italy	0.017419	0.008051	0.012439
Japan	0.015900	0.006356	0.010906
Latvia	0.040380	0.015573	0.025326
Lithuania	0.037630	0.012893	0.022918
Netherlands	0.019589	0.009383	0.014308
New Zealand	0.016402	0.012824	0.014586
Norway	0.017685	0.009270	0.013337
Russia	0.050080	0.019815	0.031868
Spain	0.017548	0.006824	0.011887
Sweden	0.015217	0.008734	0.011852
Switzerland	0.014703	0.007070	0.010653
United States	0.020470	0.012929	0.016446
West Germany	0.019653	0.009085	0.014181

Source: Watson Wyatt and World Bank.

Table 14.3(a). *2001 CSO (ultimate) insurance mortality table—*
Ages 50–89

Age	Female q_x	Male q_x	Age	Female q_x	Male q_x
50	0.003080	0.003760	70	0.017810	0.025770
51	0.003410	0.004060	71	0.019470	0.028150
52	0.003790	0.00447	72	0.021300	0.031320
53	0.004200	0.004930	73	0.023300	0.034620
54	0.004630	0.005500	74	0.025500	0.038080
55	0.005100	0.006170	75	0.027900	0.041910
56	0.005630	0.006880	76	0.030530	0.046080
57	0.006190	0.007640	77	0.033410	0.050920
58	0.006800	0.008270	78	0.036580	0.056560
59	0.007390	0.008990	79	0.040050	0.063060
60	0.008010	0.009860	80	0.043860	0.070140
61	0.008680	0.010940	81	0.049110	0.078190
62	0.009390	0.012250	82	0.054950	0.086540
63	0.010140	0.013710	83	0.060810	0.095510
64	0.010960	0.015240	84	0.067270	0.105430
65	0.011850	0.016850	85	0.074450	0.116570
66	0.012820	0.018470	86	0.080990	0.128910
67	0.013890	0.020090	87	0.090790	0.142350
68	0.015070	0.021850	88	0.101070	0.156730
69	0.016360	0.023640	89	0.112020	0.171880

Table 14.3(b). *2001 CSO (ultimate) insurance mortality table—*
Ages 90–120

Age	Female q_x	Male q_x	Age	Female q_x	Male q_x
90	0.121920	0.187660	106	0.443330	0.482220
91	0.126850	0.202440	107	0.476890	0.506690
92	0.136880	0.217830	108	0.510650	0.532690
93	0.151640	0.234040	109	0.545810	0.560310
94	0.170310	0.251140	110	0.581770	0.589640
95	0.193660	0.269170	111	0.616330	0.620790
96	0.215660	0.285640	112	0.649850	0.653840
97	0.238480	0.303180	113	0.680370	0.688940
98	0.242160	0.321880	114	0.723390	0.726180
99	0.255230	0.341850	115	0.763410	0.765700
100	0.275730	0.363190	116	0.804930	0.807610
101	0.297840	0.380080	117	0.850440	0.852070
102	0.322210	0.398060	118	0.892440	0.899230
103	0.349060	0.417200	119	0.935110	0.949220
104	0.378610	0.437560	120	1.000000	1.000000
105	0.410570	0.459210			

Table 14.4. *Cumulative distribution function[a] for a normal random variable*

			Value of x				
σ	-30%	-20%	-10%	5%	10%	20%	35%
1%	0.00%	0.00%	0.00%	100.00%	100.00%	100.00%	100.00%
5%	0.00%	0.00%	2.28%	84.13%	97.72%	100.00%	100.00%
8%	0.01%	0.62%	10.56%	73.40%	89.44%	99.38%	100.00%
10%	0.13%	2.28%	15.87%	69.15%	84.13%	97.72%	99.98%
12%	0.62%	4.78%	20.23%	66.15%	79.77%	95.22%	99.82%
15%	2.28%	9.12%	25.25%	63.06%	74.75%	90.88%	99.02%
18%	4.78%	13.33%	28.93%	60.94%	71.07%	86.67%	97.41%
20%	6.68%	15.87%	30.85%	59.87%	69.15%	84.13%	95.99%
23%	9.61%	19.23%	33.19%	58.60%	66.81%	80.77%	93.60%
25%	11.51%	21.19%	34.46%	57.93%	65.54%	78.81%	91.92%
30%	15.87%	25.25%	36.94%	56.62%	63.06%	74.75%	87.83%
40%	22.66%	30.85%	40.13%	54.97%	59.87%	69.15%	80.92%
50%	27.43%	34.46%	42.07%	53.98%	57.93%	65.54%	75.80%

[a] $\Pr[X \le x] = \int_{-\infty}^{x} \left(1/\sigma\sqrt{2\pi}\right) \exp\left\{-\frac{1}{2}(y/\sigma)^2\right\} dy.$

Table 14.5. *Cumulative distribution function[a] for a reciprocal Gamma random variable*

			Value of x					
α	0.25	0.50	1.50	2.00	2.50	5.00	10.00	$E[X]$
5.00	62.88%	94.73%	99.94%	99.98%	99.99%	100.00%	100.00%	0.25
4.50	53.41%	91.14%	99.82%	99.94%	99.98%	100.00%	100.00%	0.29
4.00	43.35%	85.71%	99.51%	99.82%	99.92%	99.99%	100.00%	0.33
3.50	33.26%	77.98%	98.75%	99.48%	99.74%	99.97%	100.00%	0.40
3.00	23.81%	67.67%	96.98%	98.56%	99.21%	99.89%	99.00%	0.50
2.50	15.62%	54.94%	93.15%	96.26%	97.70%	99.53%	99.00%	0.67
2.00	9.16%	40.60%	85.57%	90.98%	93.84%	98.25%	99.00%	1.00
1.95	8.62%	39.13%	84.52%	90.20%	93.24%	98.01%	99.00%	1.05
1.90	8.09%	37.66%	83.42%	89.35%	92.58%	97.74%	99.00%	1.11
1.85	7.59%	36.19%	82.25%	88.45%	91.87%	97.44%	99.00%	1.18
1.80	7.11%	34.73%	81.01%	87.48%	91.09%	97.10%	99.11%	1.25
1.75	6.64%	33.27%	79.71%	86.45%	90.25%	96.72%	98.96%	1.33
1.70	6.20%	31.82%	78.34%	85.34%	89.35%	96.30%	98.79%	1.43
1.65	5.77%	30.38%	76.89%	84.16%	88.37%	95.82%	98.58%	1.54
1.60	5.36%	28.96%	75.38%	82.89%	87.31%	95.28%	98.35%	1.67
1.55	4.97%	27.54%	73.79%	81.55%	86.17%	94.69%	98.07%	1.82
1.50	4.60%	26.15%	72.12%	80.13%	84.95%	94.02%	97.76%	2.00
1.25	3.01%	19.48%	62.66%	71.62%	77.38%	89.42%	95.30%	4.00
1.05	2.04%	14.66%	53.74%	63.05%	69.34%	83.68%	91.71%	20.00

[a] $\Pr[X \le x] = \int_{0}^{x} (y^{-(\alpha+1)}e^{-(1/y)}/\Gamma(\alpha)) \, dy.$

Bibliography

What follows is a list of references to articles and books that were cited within the various chapters. This list is obviously not exhaustive or comprehensive and reflects more the composition of my own bookshelf and desk than the "state of the art" in the field. Nevertheless, these references were quite helpful and certainly informed my thinking as well as the particulars of this book. In some sense this list is as much an extended "thank-you" as a bibliography.

Albrecht, P. and Maurer, R. (2002), Self-annuitization, consumption shortfall in retirement and asset allocation: The annuity benchmark, *Journal of Pension Economics and Finance,* 1(3): 269–88.

Ameriks, J., Veres R., and Warshawsky, M. J. (2001), Making retirement income last a lifetime, *Journal of Financial Planning,* 14(2): 60–76.

Arnott, R. D. (2004), Editor's corner: Sustainable spending in a lower return world, *Financial Analysts Journal,* 60(5): 6–9.

Arrow, K. J. (1965), *Aspects of a Theory of Risk Bearing,* Yrjo Jahnsson Lectures, Helsinki.

Asmussen, S. (2000), *Ruin Probabilities* (Advanced Series on Statistical Science & Applied Probability), World Scientific, Singapore.

Babbel, D. F., Gold, J., and Merrill, C. B. (2002), Fair value of liabilities: The financial economic perspective, *North American Actuarial Journal,* 6(1): 12–27.

Baldwin, B. G. (2002), *The New Life Insurance Investment Advisor* (2nd ed.), McGraw-Hill, New York.

Ballotta, L. and Haberman, S. (2003), Valuation of guaranteed annuity conversion options, *Insurance: Mathematics and Economics,* 33(1): 87–108.

Barret, B. W. (1988), Term structure modeling for pension liability discounting, *Financial Analysts Journal,* 44(6), 63–7.

Baxter, M. and Rennie, A. (1998), *Financial Calculus: An Introduction to Derivative Pricing,* Cambridge University Press.

Beekman, J. A. and Fuelling, C. P. (1990), Interest and mortality randomness in some annuities, *Insurance: Mathematics and Economics,* 9(2/3): 185–96.

Benartzi, S. and Thaler, R. H. (2001), Naïve diversification strategies in defined contribution saving plans, *American Economic Review,* 91(1): 79–98.

Bengen, W. P. (1994), Determining withdrawal rates using historical data, *Journal of Financial Planning,* 7(4): 171–81.

Bengen, W. P. (1997), Conserving client portfolios during retirement, Part III, *Journal of Financial Planning,* 10(6): 84–97.

Berin, B. N. (1989), *The Fundamentals of Pension Mathematics* (rev. ed.), Society of Actuaries, Schaumburg, IL.

Bernheim, B. D. (1991), How strong are bequest motives? Evidence based on estimates of the demand for life insurance and annuities, *Journal of Political Economy,* 99(5): 899–927.

Biggs, J. H. (1969), Alternatives in variable annuity benefit designs, *Transactions of the Society of Actuaries, Part 1,* 21(61): 495–517.

Black, F. and Dewhurst, M. P. (1981), A new investment strategy for pension funds, *Journal of Portfolio Management,* 7(4), 26–34.

Blake, D. and Burrows, W. (2001), Survivor bonds: Helping to hedge mortality risk, *Journal of Risk and Insurance,* 68(2): 339–48.

Blake, D., Cairns, A. J. G., and Dowd, K. (2003), Pensionsmetrics 2: Stochastic pension plan design during the distribution phase, *Insurance: Mathematics and Economics,* 33(1): 29–47.

Bodie, Z. (1990), Pensions as retirement income insurance, *Journal of Economic Literature,* 28(1): 28–49.

Bodie, Z. (1995), On the risk of stocks in the long run, *Financial Analysts Journal,* 51(3): 18–22.

Bodie, Z., Marcus, A., and Merton, R. (1988), Defined benefit versus defined contribution plans, in Z. Bodie, J. Shoven, and D. Wise (eds.), *Pensions in the U.S. Economy* (NBER Project Report), University of Chicago Press.

Bodie, Z., Merton, R. C., and Samuelson, W. (1992), Labor supply flexibility and portfolio choice in a life cycle model, *Journal of Economic Dynamics and Control,* 16(3–4): 427–49.

Booth, P., Chadburn, R., Cooper, D., Haberman, S., and James, D. (1999), *Modern Actuarial Theory and Practice,* Chapman & Hall, New York.

Bowers, N. L., Gerber, H. U., Hickman, J. C., Jones, D. A., and Nesbitt, C. J. (1997), *Actuarial Mathematics* (2nd ed.), Society of Actuaries, Schaumburg, IL.

Boyle, P. P. (1976), Rates of return as random variables, *Journal of Risk and Insurance,* 43(4): 693–713.

Boyle, P. P. and Hardy, M. (2003), Guaranteed annuity options, *ASTIN Bulletin,* 33(2): 125–52.

Brennan, M. J. and Schwartz, E. S. (1976), The pricing of equity-linked life insurance policies with an asset value guarantee, *Journal of Financial Economics,* 3(3): 195–213.

Broverman, S. (1986), The rate of return on life insurance and annuities, *Journal of Risk and Insurance,* 53(3): 419–34.

Brown, J. R. (2001), Private pensions, mortality risk and the decision to annuitize, *Journal of Public Economics,* 82(1): 29–62.

Brown, J. R., Mitchell, O. S., Poterba, J. M., and Warshawsky, M. J. (1999), Taxing retirement income: Non-qualified annuities and distributions from qualified accounts, *National Tax Journal,* 52(3): 563–91.

Brown, J. R. and Poterba, J. M. (2000), Joint life annuities and annuity demand by married couples, *Journal of Risk and Insurance,* 67(4): 527–53.

Brown, J. R. and Warshawsky, M. J. (2001), Longevity-insured retirement distributions from pension plans: Market and regulatory issues, Working Paper no. 8064, National Bureau of Economic Research, Cambridge, MA.

Browne, S. (1999), The risk and rewards of minimizing shortfall probability, *Journal of Portfolio Management,* 25(4): 76–85.

Brugiavini, A. (1993), Uncertainty resolution and the timing of annuity purchases, *Journal of Public Economics,* 50(1): 31–62.

Buhlmann, H. (1992), Stochastic discounting, *Insurance: Economics and Mathematics,* 11: 113–27.

Campbell, J. Y., Cocco, J. F., Gomes, F. J., and Maenhout, P. J. (2001), Investing retirement wealth: A life-cycle model, in J. Y. Campbell and M. Feldstein (eds.), *Risk Aspects of Investment-Based Social Security Reform* (NBER), University of Chicago Press.

Campbell, J. Y., Lo, A. W., and MacKinlay, A. C. (1997), *The Econometrics of Financial Markets,* Princeton University Press, Princeton, NJ.

Campbell, J. Y. and Viciera, L. (2002), *Strategic Asset Allocation: Portfolio Choice for Long Term Investors,* Oxford University Press.

Campbell, R. A. (1980), The demand for life insurance: An application of the economics of uncertainty, *Journal of Finance,* 35(5): 1155–72.

Carlson, S. and Lord, B. (1986), Unisex retirement benefits and the market for annuity "lemons", *Journal of Risk and Insurance,* 53(3): 409–18.

Carriere, J. F. (1992), Parametric models for life tables, *Transactions of the Society of Actuaries,* 44: 77–99.

Carriere, J. F. (1994), An investigation of the Gompertz law of mortality, *Actuarial Research Clearing House,* 2: 1–34.

Charupat, N. and Milevsky, M. A. (2001), Mortality swaps and tax arbitrage in the Canadian annuity and insurance market, *Journal of Risk and Insurance,* 68(2): 277–302.

Charupat, N. and Milevsky, M. A. (2002), Optimal asset allocation in life annuities: A note, *Insurance: Mathematics and Economics,* 30(2): 199–210.

Charupat, N., Milevsky, M. A., and Tuenter, H. (2001), Asset allocation with mortality-contingent claims: The one period case, Working paper, Schulich School of Business, York University, Toronto.

Chen, P., Ibbotson, R., Milevsky, M. A., and Zhu, K. (2006), Human capital, asset allocation and life insurance, *Financial Analysts Journal,* forthcoming.

Chen, P. and Milevsky, M. A. (2003), Merging asset allocation and longevity insurance: An optimal perspective on payout annuities, *Journal of Financial Planning,* 16(6): 52–62.

Cooley, P. L., Hubbard, C. M., and Walz, D. T. (1998), Retirement spending: Choosing a withdrawal rate that is sustainable, *Journal of the American Association of Individual Investors,* 20(1): 39–47.

Davidoff, T., Brown, J. R., and Diamond, P. (2003), Annuities and individual welfare, Working Paper no. 03-15, Department of Economics, Massachusetts Institute of Technology, Cambridge.

de La Grandville, O. (2001), *Bond Pricing and Portfolio Analysis: Protecting Investors in the Long Run,* MIT Press, Cambridge.

Dufresne, D. (1990), The distribution of a perpetuity with applications to risk theory and pension funding, *Scandinavian Actuarial Journal,* 9: 39–79.

Duncan, R. M. (1952), A retirement system granting unit annuities and investing in equities, *Transactions of the Society of Actuaries,* 4(9): 317–44.

Dushi, I. and Webb, A. (2004), Household annuitization decisions: Simulations and empirical evidence, *Journal of Pension Economics and Finance,* 3(2): 109–43.

Dybvig, P. H. (1999), Using asset allocation to protect spending, *Financial Analysts Journal,* 55(1): 49–62.

Ehrlich, I. (2000), Uncertain lifetime, life protection, and the value of life saving, *Journal of Health Economics,* 19: 341–67.

Ezra, D. (1980), How actuaries determine the unfunded pension liability, *Financial Analysts Journal,* 36(4), 43–50.

Fabozzi, F. (1996), *Fixed Income Mathematics: Analytical and Statistical Techniques,* McGraw-Hill, New York.

Feldstein, M. and Ranguelova, E. (2001), Individual risk in an investment-based social security system, *American Economic Review,* 91(4): 1116–25.

Finkelstein, A. and Poterba, J. (2002), Selection effects in the United Kingdom individual annuities market, *Economic Journal,* 112(476): 28–50.

Fischer, S. (1973), A life cycle model of life insurance purchases, *International Economic Review,* 14(1): 132–52.

Frees, E. W., Carriere, J., and Valdez, E. (1996), Annuity valuation with dependent mortality, *Journal of Risk and Insurance,* 63(2): 229–61.

Friedman, A. and Shen, W. (2002), A variational inequality approach to financial valuation of retirement benefits based on salary, *Finance and Stochastics,* 6(3): 273–302.

Friedman, B. M. and Warshawsky, M. J. (1990), The cost of annuities: Implications for saving behavior and bequests, *Quarterly Journal of Economics,* 105(1): 135–54.

Gerber, H. U. and Pafumi, G. (1999), Utility functions: From risk theory to finance (with discussions), *North American Actuarial Journal,* 2(3): 74–100.

Gold, J. (2005), Retirement benefits, economics and accounting: Moral hazard and frail benefit design, *North American Actuarial Journal,* 9(1): 88–111.

Hardy, M. (2003), *Investment Guarantees: Modeling and Risk Management for Equity-Linked Life Insurance,* Wiley, Hoboken, NJ.

Hayashi, F., Altonji, J., and Kotlikoff, L. (1996), Risk-sharing between and within families, *Econometrica,* 64(2): 261–94.

Ho, K., Milevsky, M. A., and Robinson, C. (1994), How to avoid outliving your money, *Canadian Investment Review,* 7(3): 35–8.

Ho, K. and Robinson, C. (2005), *Personal Financial Planning* (4th ed.), Captus Press, Toronto.

Huang, H., Milevsky, M. A., and Wang, J. (2004), Ruined moments in your life: How good are the approximations? *Insurance: Mathematics and Economics,* 34(3): 421–47.

Hull, J. C. (2002), *Options, Futures and Other Derivatives* (5th ed.), Prentice-Hall, Englewood Cliffs, NJ.

Hurd, M. D. and McGarry, K. (1995), Evaluation of the subjective probabilities of survival in the health and retirement study, *Journal of Human Resources,* 30 (special issue on the health and retirement study: Data quality and early results): 268–92.

Ibbotson Associates (2005), *Stocks, Bonds, Bills and Inflation: 1926–2004,* Chicago.

Ingersoll, J. E. and Ross, S. A. (1992), Waiting to invest: Investment and uncertainty, *Journal of Business,* 65(1): 1–29.

Ippolito, R. (1989), *The Economics of Pension Insurance,* Irwin, Homewood, IL.

Jacquier, E., Kane, A., and Marcus, A. J. (2003), Geometric or arithmetic mean: A reconsideration, *Financial Analysts Journal,* 59(6): 46–53.

Jarrett, J. C. and Stringfellow, T. (2000), Optimum withdrawals from an asset pool, *Journal of Financial Planning,* 13(1): 80–92.

Jennings, R. M. and Trout, A. P. (1982), *The Tontine: From the Reign of Louis XIV to the French Revolutionary Era* (Huebner Foundation Monograph, no. 12), The Wharton School, University of Pennsylvania, Philadelphia.

Johansen, R. J. (1995), Review of adequacy of 1983 individual annuity mortality table, *Transactions of the Society of Actuaries,* 47: 211–33.

Johansson, P. O. (1996), On the value of changes in life expectancy, *Journal of Health Economics,* 15(1): 105–13.

Jousten, A. (2001), Life-cycle modeling of bequests and their impact on annuity valuation, *Journal of Public Economics,* 79(1): 149–77.

Kapur, S. and Orszag, M., (1999), A portfolio approach to investment and annuitization during retirement, Working paper, Birkbeck College, London.

Khorasanee, M. Z. (1996), Annuity choices for pensioners, *Journal of Actuarial Practice,* 4(2): 229–55.

Kingston, G. and Thorp, S. (2005), Annuitization and asset allocation with HARA utility, *Journal of Pension Economics and Finance,* 4(3): 225–48.

Kotlikoff, L. J. and Spivak, A. (1981), The family as an incomplete annuities market, *Journal of Political Economy,* 89(2): 372–91.

Lee, R. D. and Carter, L. R. (1992), Modeling and forecasting U.S. mortality, *Journal of the American Statistical Association,* 87: 659–71.

Leibowitz, M. L. and Kogelman, S. (1991), Asset allocation under shortfall constraints, *Journal of Portfolio Management,* 17(2): 18–23.

Levy, H. and Duchin, R. (2004), Asset return distributions and the investment horizon, *Journal of Portfolio Management,* 30(3): 47–62.

Lewis, F. D. (1989), Dependents and the demand for life insurance, *American Economic Review,* 79(3): 452–67.

Markowitz, H. M. (1959), *Portfolio Selection: Efficient Diversification of Investments,* Wiley, New York.

Markowitz, H. M. (1991), Individual versus institutional investing, *Financial Services Review,* 1(1): 1–8.

McCabe, B. J. (1999), Analytic approximation for the probability that a portfolio survives forever, *Journal of Private Portfolio Management,* 1(4): 14.

McCarthy, D. (2003), A life-cycle analysis of defined benefit pension plans, *Journal of Pension Economics and Finance,* 2(2): 99–126.

Mereu, J. A. (1962), Annuity values directly from the Makeham constants, *Transactions of the Society of Actuaries,* 14: 269–308.

Merton, R. C. (1971), Optimum consumption and portfolio rules in a continuous time model, *Journal of Economic Theory,* 3 (December): 373–413.

Merton, R. C. (2003), Thoughts on the future: Theory and practice in investment management, *Financial Analysts Journal,* 59(1): 17–23.

Milevsky, M. A. (1997), The present value of a stochastic perpetuity and the Gamma distribution, *Insurance: Mathematics and Economics,* 20(3): 243–50.

Milevsky, M. A. (1998), Optimal asset allocation towards the end of the life cycle: To annuitize or not to annuitize? *Journal of Risk and Insurance,* 65(3): 401–26.

Milevsky, M. A. (2001), Optimal annuitization policies: Analysis of the options, *North American Actuarial Journal,* 5(1): 57–69.

Milevsky, M. A. (2002), Space–time diversification: Which dimension is better? *Journal of Risk,* 5(2): 45–71.

Milevsky, M. A. (2005a), The Implied Longevity Yield: A note on developing an index for life annuities, *Journal of Risk and Insurance,* 72(2): 301–20.

Milevsky, M. A. (2005b), Real longevity insurance with a deductible: Introduction to advanced-life delayed annuities, *North American Actuarial Journal,* 9(4): 109–22.

Milevsky, M. A. and Posner, S. (2001), The Titanic option: Valuation of the guaranteed minimum death benefits in variable annuities and mutual funds, *Journal of Risk and Insurance,* 68(1): 93–128.

Milevsky, M. A. and Promislow, D. (2001), Mortality derivatives and the option to annuitize, *Insurance: Mathematics and Economics,* 29(3): 299–318.

Milevsky, M. A. and Robinson, C. (2000), Self-annuitization and ruin in retirement, *North American Actuarial Journal,* 4: 113–29.

Milevsky, M. A. and Robinson, C. (2005), A sustainable spending rate without simulation, *Financial Analysts Journal,* 61(6): 89–100.

Milevsky, M. A. and Salisbury, T. S. (2006), Financial valuation of guaranteed minimal withdrawal benefits, *Insurance: Mathematics and Economics,* forthcoming.

Milevsky, M. A. and Young, V. R. (2004), Annuitization and asset allocation, Working paper, IFID Centre, Toronto, ⟨www.ifid.ca⟩.

Mitchell, O. S., Poterba, J. M., Warshawsky, M. J., and Brown, J. R. (1999), New evidence on the money's worth of individual annuities, *American Economic Review,* 89(5): 1299–1318.

Modigliani, F. (1986), Life cycle, individual thrift and the wealth of nations, *American Economic Review,* 76(3): 297–313.

Olivieri, A. (2001), Uncertainty in mortality projections: An actuarial perspective, *Insurance: Mathematics and Economics,* 29(2): 239–45.

Olshansky, S. J. and Carnes, B. A. (1997), Ever since Gompertz, *Demography,* 34(1): 1–15.

Olshansky, S. J., Carnes, B. A., and Cassel, C. (1990), In search of Methuselah: Estimating the upper limits to human longevity, *Science,* 250(4981): 634–40.

Pennacchi, G. G. (1999), The value of guarantees on pension fund returns, *Journal of Risk and Insurance,* 66(2): 219–37.

Philipson, T. J. and Becker, G. S. (1998), Old-age longevity and mortality-contingent claims, *Journal of Political Economy,* 106(3): 551–73.

Poterba, J. M. (1997), The history of annuities in the United States, Working Paper no. 6001, National Bureau of Economic Research, Cambridge, MA.

Pratt, J. W. (1964), Risk aversion in the small and in the large, *Econometrica,* 32(1/2): 122–36.

Pye, G. B. (2000), Sustainable investment withdrawals, *Journal of Portfolio Management,* 26(4): 73–83.

Pye, G. B. (2001), Adjusting withdrawal rates for taxes and expenses, *Journal of Financial Planning,* 14(4): 126–36.

Reichenstein, W. (2003), Allocation during retirement: Adding annuities to the mix, *Journal of the American Association of Individual Investors,* November: 3–9.

Richard, S. F. (1975), Optimal consumption, portfolio and life insurance rules for an uncertain lived individual in a continuous time model, *Journal of Financial Economics,* 2(2): 187–203.

Rubinstein, M. (1991), Continuously rebalanced investment strategies, *Journal of Portfolio Management,* 18(1): 78–81.

Salas, S. L., Hille, E., and Etgen, G. J. (1998), *Calculus: One and Several Variables* (8th ed.), Wiley, Chichester, U.K.

Samuelson, P. A. (1969), Lifetime portfolio selection by dynamic stochastic programming, *Review of Economics and Statistics,* 51(3): 239–46.

Sherris, M. (1995), The valuation of option features in retirement benefits, *Journal of Risk and Insurance,* 62(3): 509–34.

Sinha, T. (1986), The effects of survival probabilities, transactions costs and the attitude towards risk on the demand for annuities, *Journal of Risk and Insurance,* 53(2): 301–7.

Smith, G. and Gould, D. P. (2005), Measuring and controlling shortfall risk in retirement, Working paper, Pomona College, Claremont, CA.

Stanton, R. (2000), From cradle to grave: How to loot a 401(k) plan, *Journal of Financial Economics,* 56(3): 485–516.

Stock, J. H. and Wise, D. A. (1990), Pensions, the option value of work, and retirement, *Econometrica,* 58(5): 1151–80.

Sundaresan, S. and Zapatero, F. (1997), Valuation, optimal asset allocation and retirement incentives of pension plans, *Review of Financial Studies,* 10(3): 631–60.

Tillinghast [Towers Perrin] (2004), *Tillinghast Older Age Mortality Study: Summary of Key Findings,* Stamford, CT.

Treynor, J. L. (1977), The principles of corporate pension finance, *Journal of Finance,* 32(2): 627–38.

Vanneste, M., Goovaerts, M. J., and Labie, E. (1994), The distributions of annuities, *Insurance: Mathematics and Economics,* 15(1): 37–48.

Viceira, L. M. (2001), Optimal portfolio choice for long horizon investors with non-tradable labor income, *Journal of Finance,* 56(2), 433–70.

Warner, J. T. and Pleeter, S. (2001), The personal discount rate: Evidence from military downsizing programs, *American Economic Review,* 91(1): 33–53.

Warshawsky, M. (1998), Private annuity markets in the United States: 1919–1984, *Journal of Risk and Insurance,* 55(3): 518–28.

Williams, C. A., Jr. (1986), Higher interest rates, longer lifetimes and the demand for life annuities, *Journal of Risk and Insurance,* 53(1): 164–71.

Yaari, M. E. (1965), Uncertain lifetime, life insurance, and the theory of the consumer, *Review of Economic Studies,* 32(2): 137–50.

Yagi, T. and Nishigaki, Y. (1993), The inefficiency of private constant annuities, *Journal of Risk and Insurance,* 60(3): 385–412.

Young, V. R. (2004), Optimal investment strategy to minimize the probability of lifetime ruin, *North American Actuarial Journal,* 8(4): 106–26.

Index

401(k) plans, 293

accumulated benefit obligation (ABO), 12,
173–80
accumulation phase, 8
Actuarial Mathematics (Bowers), 59, 134
advanced-life delayed annuities (ALDAs), 245
  Consumer Price Index (CPI) and, 235
  description of, 234–40
  Gompertz–Makeham (GoMa) model and,
  236–7
  hazard rates and, 241–4
  inflation and, 237–8
  instantaneous force of mortality (IFM) and,
  234–40
  lapse rate and, 238–40
  risk and, 241–4
Albrecht, P., 208
alcohol, 37
algebra, 10
Altonji, J., 291
Ameriks, J., 208
annual renewable term (ART) life insurance,
142
annuities
  advanced-life delayed annuities (ALDAs)
  and, 234–44
  bequests and, 279–80
  deferment and, 282–7
  difficult choices of, 215–16
  discrete time and, 225–6
  fixed-payout, 215–16, 290–1
  immediate fixed annuities (IFAs), 131
  immediate pension annuity factor (IPAF),
  114–15, 123, 125, 130
  immediate variable payout annuities (IVAs),
  130–2, 216

Implied Longevity Yield (ILY) and, 226–34
life insurance and, 143–60. *See also* life
  insurance
liquidity and, 215–16
mortality tables and, 295–9
optimal timing and, 281–2
options and, 249–69, 282–7
proportional hazard transformation and,
  289–90
real option to defer annuitization (RODA)
  model and, 282–9, 291
self-annuitization and, 225–34
survivor benefits and, 216–18
sustainable spending and, 193–4. *See also*
  sustainable spending
tontine contracts and, 217–25, 244–5
utility and, 270–92
variable, 130–2, 216, 249–69, 290–1
See also pension annuities
approximation bias, 67–8
arbitrage, 70–2, 147–8, 162
arithmetic average return, 86–8
Arrow, K. J., 291
Arrow–Pratt measure, 273
Asmussen, S., 208
asset allocation, 8, 12
  call option and, 202–6
  portfolio construction and, 102–4
  put option and, 202–6
  tontine contracts and, 220–5
  utility and, 278–81
assumed interest rate (AIR), 132–4

Babbel, D. F., 181
Baby Boomers, 186, 294
Baldwin, B. G., 162
Balotta, L., 269

Barret, B. W., 181
basis points, 196–7
    continuously compounded interest and, 64–6
    options and, 256–7
    tontine contracts and, 219–20
Baxter, M., 108
Becker, G. S., 162
Beekman, J. A., 134
Benartzi, S., 181
Bengen, W. P., 208
bequests, 279–80
Bernheim, B. D., 291
Biggs, J. H., 134
Black, F., 181
Black–Scholes equations, 207
Black–Scholes/Merton (BSM) valuation,
    250–1, 257–8, 260
Blake, D., 208, 245
Bodie, Z., 33, 108, 181, 291
Bond Pricing and Portfolio Analysis (de La
    Grandville), 82
bonds
    arbitrage and, 70–2
    continuous time and, 68–70
    convexity and, 76–81
    coupon, 68–70, 74, 226–7
    duration value and, 76–81
    internal yield and, 76
    market price and, 70–2
    nonflat term structure, 73–4
    Taylor's approximation and, 75–6, 79–81
    tontine contracts and, 220–5
    valuation of, 68–70
    zero, 68–70, 77, 226–7
    See also stock market
bootstrap approach, 208
Bowers, N. L., 59, 134, 295
Boyle, P. P., 108, 269
Brennan, M. J., 269
"broken heart" syndrome, 135
Brown, J. R., 181, 291
Browne, S., 108, 135, 208
Brownian motion model, 94, 96
    continuous-time stochastic processes and,
        91
    Gaussian distribution and, 91, 95, 97
    geometric (GBM), 93
    index averages/medians and, 97–9
    nondifferentiability of, 95
    nonstandard, 92–3
    options and, 251, 253, 264, 269

pensions and, 168
    portfolio construction and, 102–4
    regret probability and, 98–100
    standard deviation and, 97–9
    standard (SBM), 91
    time variance and, 92–6
Brugiavini, A., 292
Buhlmann, H., 32
Burrows, W., 245

Cairns, A. J. G., 208
calculus, 9–10, 34
    Brownian motion model and, 91–9, 102–4
    convergence and, 96
    Langrangian approach, 283, 292
    L'Hôpital's rule, 65–6
    Newton–Raphson (NeRa) algorithm, 233
    normal distribution, 62–3
    ordinary differential equations (ODEs),
        39–41, 100–1, 213
    partial differential equations (PDEs), 201,
        207–8, 214
    rate of change and, 100–1
    refresher for, 62–3
    standardizing the random variable and, 63
    stochastic differential equations (SDEs),
        100–1, 104, 209–10, 251–5, 263
    Taylor's approximation, 75–6, 79–81
    See also equations
California, 293
call option, 202–6, 249
Campbell, J. Y., 108
Campbell, R. A., 291
Canada
    Baby Boomers and, 186
    old-age dependency ratio and, 6–7
    pension annuities and, 113
    savings and, 25
CANNEX Financial Exchanges, 227n
Carlson, S., 135
Carnes, B. A., 60
Carriere, J., 135
Carter, L. R., 60
Cassel, C., 60
Charupat, N., 162, 292
Chen, P., 162, 245, 291–2
Chile, 293
cohort tables, 55–9
compound annual growth rate (CAGR), 84
compound interest. *See* interest rates
conditional probability of survival, 35–7, 48

Consumer Price Index (CPI), 85–6, 113, 168, 235
consumption
  bonds and, 69–70
  "die broke" strategy and, 18
  living standards and, 17–18, 26
  present value of, 20–2
  proportional hazard transformation and, 289–90
  real option to defer annuitization (RODA) model, 282–9
  savings exchange rate and, 22–6
  utility and, 274–8, 282–90
convexity, 76–81
Cooley, P. L., 208
cost-of-living adjustment (COLA), 113
coupon bonds, 68–70, 74, 226–7
cumulative distribution function (CDF), 40
  Black–Scholes/Merton (BSM) valuation and, 250
  hazard rates and, 52
  life insurance and, 145–7, 154–7
  mortality tables and, 295–9
  regret probability and, 98–100
  remaining lifetime and, 37–8
  sustainable spending and, 193

Davidoff, T., 291
deferred pension annuity factor (DPAF), 121–3, 125, 130
defined benefit (DB) pensions, 5, 11–12, 164, 182, 293
  accounting and, 176–80
  advanced-life delayed annuities (ALDAs) and, 234–40
  core of, 169–72
  ERISA and, 180–1
  funding and, 176–80
  interest cost and, 178
  PEORP and, 293
  service cost and, 178
  sustainable spending and, 193–4
  U.S. deficit and, 294
  valuation of, 172–6
defined contribution (DC) pensions, 5, 11–12, 164, 182, 294
  accounting and, 176–80
  advanced-life delayed annuities (ALDAs) and, 234–40
  core of, 165–9
  ERISA and, 180–1

funding and, 176–80
interest cost and, 178
PEORP and, 293
service cost and, 178
de La Grandville, O., 82
delayed insurance, 150–1
derivative securities. *See* options
Dewhurst, M. P., 181
Diamond, P., 292
"die broke" strategy, 18, 185
diffusion, 101–2
discounted value of life-cycle plan, 27–31
discount rate, 66–7
  life insurance and, 144–5
  options and, 252–7
dollar-cost average (DCA) strategy, 193–4
Dowd, K., 208
drunk gambler problem, 3–5, 14–16
Duchin, R., 108
Dufresne, D., 208, 212
Duncan, R. M., 134
duration value
  equations for, 76–81
  insurance and, 157–9
  pension annuities and, 128–30
Dushi, I., 292
Dybvig, P. H., 208

Ehrlich, I., 291
Employee Retirement Income Security Act (ERISA), 180–1
employment
  accumulation phase and, 8
  hazardous jobs and, 37
  pensions and, 164–82. *See also* pensions
equations
  advanced-life delayed annuities (ALDAs), 235, 237, 239
  arithmetic average return, 87
  Black–Scholes/Merton (BSM) valuation, 250–1
  bonds, 68–9, 73–4, 76–81
  Brownian motion model, 91–7, 102–4
  constant relative risk aversion, 272
  convexity, 76–81
  defined benefit (DB) pension, 169–70, 173
  defined contribution (DC) pension, 166, 168
  discounted value, 27–8, 30, 66–7
  drunk gambler problem, 15
  duration value, 76–81
  expected remaining lifetime (ERL), 44

equations *(cont.)*
  exponential growth, 170
  exponential reciprocal Gamma (ERG)
    distribution, 193
  future value of savings, 18–19
  Gamma function, 48, 61–2, 193
  geometric average return, 87
  Gompertz–Makeham, 47–8, 61–2, 116–17
  guaranteed minimum accumulation benefit
    (GMAB), 257
  guaranteed minimum death benefit
    (GMDB), 258–9, 261
  guaranteed minimum withdrawal benefit
    (GMWB), 263–7
  hazard rates, 51–2
  human life-cycle model, 18–22, 26–30
  Implied Longevity Yield (ILY), 229–33
  index values, 97–8
  inflation effects, 29–30
  instantaneous force of mortality (IFM),
    38–40, 116–17
  integration procedure and, 62–3
  interest rates, 64–9, 72–81
  investment regret probability, 99
  joint lifetimes, 54–5
  life insurance, 144–58
  long-term risk model, 88–9
  median remaining lifetime (MRL), 44
  moments, 42–4
  mortality rates, 37–40, 42–8, 51–7, 61–3,
    116–17, 193, 209–14
  neutral replacement rate, 26
  nominal wage, 29
  options, 250–1, 253–9, 261, 263–7
  pension annuities, 114–33, 137
  present value (PV), 20–2, 187
  probability of survival, 36
  rate of change, 100–1
  real option to defer annuitization (RODA)
    model, 282–5
  remaining lifetime, 37–8
  rule of 72, 68
  savings/consumption exchange rate, 22
  self-annuitization, 225–6
  space–time diversification, 104–6
  stochastic present value (SPV), 187–8
  sustainable spending, 187–8, 191, 193,
    209–14
  taxes, 120
  Taylor's approximation, 75–6
  tontine contracts, 219, 221–3
  utility, 272–4, 276–80, 282–5

Etgen, G. J., 292
ethnicity, 37
Euler approximation, 101–2
European options, 250, 261
Excel, 61–2
exchange rate
  neutral replacement rate and, 26–7
  pensions and, 165
  savings/consumption, 22–6
expected remaining lifetime, 44–5, 49
exponential law of mortality, 45–6
  discrete table fitting and, 49–51
  options and, 259–62
exponential lifetime (EL) distribution, 190–1
exponential reciprocal Gamma (ERG)
    distribution, 192
  equation of, 193
  formula derivation for, 209–14
  Kolmogorov–Smirnov (KS) goodness-of-fit
    test and, 200–1
  numerical examples of, 193–202
Ezra, D., 181

Fabozzi, F., 82
Factors Affecting Retirement Mortality
    (FARM) project, 60
Feldstein, M., 135
financial services industry, 9
  accumulation phase and, 8
  basis points and, 64–6, 196–7, 219–20,
    256–7
  insurable events and, 217–18. *See also* life
    insurance
  Monte Carlo simulations and, 186
  pension annuities and, 110–37. *See also*
    pension annuities
  self-annuitization and, 225–6
Finkelstein, A., 135
Fischer, S., 162, 291
Fixed Income Mathematics (Fabozzi), 82
Florida, 165, 293
France, 244
Frees, E. W., 135
Friedman, A., 181
Friedman, B. M., 135
Fuelling, C. P., 134
funding methods, 176–80
future value of savings, 18–20

gambling strategies, 3–5, 14–16
Gamma distribution, 190–1, 208
  exponential reciprocal, 192–202, 209–14

formula derivation for, 209–14
Kolmogorov–Smirnov (KS) goodness-of-fit
    test and, 200–1
mortality tables and, 295–9
Gamma function, 48–9, 61–2, 117
Gaussian distribution, 62–3, 91, 95, 97
gender
    human longevity and, 8
    joint lifetimes and, 53–5
    life insurance and, 139
    mortality and, 35, 37, 50, 295–9
    options and, 259
    pension annuities and, 111–12, 118, 127
    sustainable spending and, 189–90
geometric average return, 86–8
Gerber, H. U., 291
Gold, J., 181
Gompertz–Makeham (GoMa) model, 11
    advanced-life delayed annuities (ALDAs)
        and, 236–7
    "broken heart" syndrome and, 135
    conditional probability of survival and, 48
    discrete table fitting and, 49–51
    Gamma function and, 48–9, 61–2
    hazard rates and, 46–9, 59–62
    instantaneous force of mortality and, 46–9
    life insurance and, 149–50, 153, 162
    options and, 256, 258–9
    pension annuities and, 116–20, 129–30,
        133–7
    sustainable spending and, 200
    tontine contracts and, 218–19
Goovaerts, M. J., 135–6
Gould, D. P., 208
growth rates, 88–90
    Brownian motion model and, 91–9, 102–4
    convergence and, 96
    exponential, 170
guarantee
    cost of, 271–2
    utility and, 270–92
    value of, 271–2
guaranteed minimum accumulation benefit
    (GMAB), 257–8
guaranteed minimum death benefit (GMDB),
    258–62
guaranteed minimum withdrawal benefit
    (GMWB), 262–8
Guinle, Jorge, 185

Haberman, S., 269
Hardy, M., 269

Hayashi, F., 291
hazard rates
    advanced-life delayed annuities (ALDAs)
        and, 241–4
    exponential law of mortality and, 45–6
    general, 51–3
    Gompertz–Makeham model and, 46–9,
        59–62
    instantaneous, 51–3
    life insurance and, 162
    moments and, 41–4
    proportional hazard transformation and,
        289–90
    utility and, 289–90
health issues, 9–10
    alcohol, 37
    life insurance, 138–63. *See also* life
        insurance
    obesity, 37
    smoking, 37
    See also mortality
Hille, E., 292
Ho, K., 33, 208
Holland, 244
Huang, H., 208, 269
Hubbard, C. M., 208
Hull, John, 269
human life-cycle model, 33
    changing investment rates and, 30–2
    consumption rate and, 20–6
    discounted value and, 27–8, 30–1
    future value of savings and, 18–20
    inflation and, 28–30
    neutral replacement rate and, 26–7
    present value of consumption and, 20–2
    real vs. nominal planning and, 28–30
    savings rate and, 17–18
human longevity, 7–8, 12. *See also* longevity
    insurance; mortality
Hurd, M. D., 59

Ibbotson Associates, 108, 207–8
immediate fixed annuity (IFA), 131
immediate pension annuity factor (IPAF),
    114–15, 123, 125, 130
immediate variable annuity (IVA), 130–2, 216
Implied Longevity Yield (ILY), 12, 226–34
income
    consumption and, 20–6
    future value of savings and, 18–20. *See also*
        pensions
    human life-cycle model and, 17–33

Individual Retirement Accounts (IRAs), 119–20

inflation
  advanced-life delayed annuities (ALDAs) and, 234–40, 237–8
  life insurance and, 141
  pension annuities and, 113
  real vs. nominal planning and, 28–30
  savings and, 28–30
  stock market and, 85–6
  sustainable spending and, 185, 189
  United States and, 85–6

Ingersoll, J. E., 292

instantaneous force of mortality (IFM), 38–41
  advanced-life delayed annuities (ALDAs) and, 242–3
  Gompertz–Makeham model and, 46–9, 59–62, 116–19
  hazard rates and, 51
  life insurance and, 140, 149
  pension annuities and, 116–19, 126

interest cost, 178

interest rates, 11
  advanced-life delayed annuities (ALDAs) and, 236–7
  assumed (AIR), 132–4
  basis points and, 64–6
  continuously compounded, 64–6, 73–4
  convexity and, 76–81
  coupon bonds and, 68–70, 74
  discount factors and, 66–7
  duration value and, 76–81
  growth rate and, 88–90
  market price and, 70–2
  model value and, 70–2
  no-lapse, 139
  pension annuities and, 121–3, 132–4. *See also* pension annuities
  regret probability and, 98–100
  rule of 72 and, 67–8
  Taylor's approximation and, 75–6, 79–81
  term, 72–4, 138–9
  universal, 139
  valuation models of, 64–82
  zero bonds and, 68–70

internal yield, 76

investment, 9, 108–9
  accumulation phase and, 8
  arithmetic average return and, 86–8
  asset allocation and, 102–4
  Black–Scholes model and, 207

Brownian motion model and, 91–9, 102–4
  changing rates and, 30–2
  "die broke" strategy and, 18
  diffusion simulation and, 101–2
  drunk gambler problem and, 5
  geometric average return and, 86–8
  growth rate and, 88–99, 102–4
  human life-cycle model and, 17–33
  human longevity and, 7–8
  Implied Longevity Yield (ILY) and, 226–34
  index averages/medians and, 97–8
  mortality credits and, 216–18
  optimal timing and, 281–2
  options and, 202–6, 249–69
  pension annuities and, 110–37. *See also* pension annuities
  portfolio volatility and, 102–7
  rate of change and, 100–1
  real option to defer annuitization (RODA) model and, 282–9
  real vs. nominal planning and, 28–30
  recent stock market history and, 83–6
  regret probability and, 98–100, 104–7
  risk and, 86–8, 241–4. *See also* risk
  space–time diversification and, 104–7
  stochastic present value (SPV) and, 186–90
  sustainable spending and, 185–214. *See also* sustainable spending
  tontine contracts and, 217–25, 244–5

Investment Guarantees (Hardy), 269

Ippolito, R., 181

Jacquier, E., 108
Japan, 8
Jarrett, J. C., 208
Jennings, R. M., 244
Johansen, R. J., 59
Johansson, P. O., 59
joint and survivor (J&S) pension annuities, 112–13, 125–8
joint lifetime models, 53–5
Jousten, A., 291

Kane, A., 108
Kapur, S., 292
Khorasanee, M. Z., 208
Kingston, G., 292
Kogelman, S., 108
Kolmogorov–Smirnov (KS) goodness-of-fit test, 200–1
Kotlikoff, L. J., 291

Labie, E., 135–6
Lagrangian approach, 283, 292
Lee, R. D., 60
Leibowitz, L., 108
Levy, H., 108
Lewis, F. S., 291
L'Hôpital's rule, 65–6
life insurance, 11, 163
  advanced-life delayed annuities (ALDAs)
    and, 234–40
  amount needed, 140–2
  annual renewable term (ART), 142
  arbitrage and, 147–8, 162
  assumed interest rate (AIR) and, 132–4
  banks and, 138, 147–8
  bequests and, 279–80
  "broken heart" syndrome and, 135
  categories of, 142–3
  cumulative distribution function (CDF) and,
    145–7, 154–7
  delayed, 150–1
  discount value and, 144–5
  duration of, 157–9
  expense approach to, 141
  gender and, 139
  Gompertz–Makeham (GoMa) model and,
    149–50, 153, 162
  group policies and, 159–60
  hazard rates and, 162
  health status and, 139–40
  human longevity and, 8, 12
  income approach to, 140–1
  inflation and, 141
  installment payments and, 150
  instantaneous force of mortality (IFM) and,
    140, 149
  joint, 53–5
  market prices and, 138–9
  moment generating function (MGF) and, 145
  mortality swap and, 148
  mortality tables and, 295–9
  net periodic premium (NPP), 144, 150,
    238–40
  net single premium (NSP), 143–60, 235–8
  pension annuities and, 114–28, 130–4, 145–7
  policy lapse and, 154–7
  probability density function (PDF) and,
    145–7, 154–7
  real option to defer annuitization (RODA)
    model, 282–9
  renewing, 142–3
  subjective premiums and, 273–4
  taxes and, 143, 148, 162
  term, 142–3, 150–1
  Tillinghast Older Age Mortality Study and,
    140
  universal, 160–2
  utility and, 270–92
  valuation of, 143–7
  variations on, 151–4
living standards, 17–18, 26
Lo, A. W., 108
lognormal (LN) distribution, 190
longevity insurance
  advanced-life delayed annuities (ALDAs)
    and, 234–44
  Implied Longevity Yield (ILY) and, 226–34
  liquidity issues and, 215–16
  mortality credits and, 216–18
  risk and, 218, 241–4
  self-annuitization and, 225–6
  survivor benefits and, 216–18
  tontine contracts and, 217–25, 244–5
  See also pension annuities
Lord, B., 135
Louis XVI, King of France, 244

McCabe, B. J., 208
McCarthy, D., 181
McGarry, K., 59
MacKinlay, A. C., 108
Marcus, A., 108, 181
Marie Antoinette, Queen of France, 244
market prices
  call option and, 202–6
  interest rates and, 70–2
  life insurance and, 138–9
  pension annuities and, 110–14
  put option and, 202–6
markets. *See* stock market
Markowitz, Harry, 10, 108
matrices, 105
Maurer, R., 208
Max Planck Institute for Demographic
  Research, 7–8
median remaining lifetime, 44–5, 49
Mereu, J. A., 135
Merrill, C. B., 181
Merton, R. C., 10, 33, 181, 291–2
Mexico, 7, 25
Milevsky, M. A., 108, 162, 208, 245, 269, 292
Mitchell, O. S., 291

Modigliani, F., 33
moments, 41–4, 145
Monte Carlo simulations, 186, 204, 207
mortality, 11
    alcohol and, 37
    "broken heart" syndrome and, 135
    cumulative distribution function (CDF) and,
        37–8, 40, 52–3, 62–3
    ethnicity and, 37
    exponential, 45–6, 49–51, 149
    gender and, 35, 37, 50, 295–9
    Gompertz–Makeham (GoMa) model and,
        46–51, 59–62, 149
    hazard rates and, 41, 51–3
    IFM, 38–41, 46–9. *See also* instantaneous
        force of mortality
    Implied Longevity Yield (ILY) and, 226–34
    incomplete Gamma function and, 61–2
    instantaneous mortality rate and, 190–3,
        209–14, 232–3
    joint lifetimes and, 53–5
    labor and, 37
    life insurance and, 138–63. *See also* life
        insurance
    moments concept and, 41–4
    obesity and, 37
    ordinary differential equation (ODE)
        relationship and, 39–41
    pension annuities and, 110–37. *See also*
        pension annuities
    probability density function (PDF) and, 37,
        40–1, 52, 62–3
    probability of survival and, 35–7
    religion and, 37
    remaining lifetime and, 37–8, 44–5
    smoking and, 37
    subjective vs. objective, 289–90
    Tillinghast Older Age Mortality Study and,
        140
    tontine contracts and, 217–25, 244–5
mortality credits, 216–18
    Implied Mortality Yield (ILY) and, 226–34
mortality swap, 148
mortality tables, 60, 295–9
    cohort, 55–9
    continuous laws and, 49–51
    described, 34–5
    gender and, 35
    period, 55–9
    RP2000, 34–5, 49–50
mutual funds, 8, 249

nest eggs. *See* investment
Newton–Raphson (NeRa) algorithm, 233
Nishigaki, Y., 292
normal distribution
    Brownian motion model and, 91–9, 102–4
    cumulative distribution function (CDF) and,
        37–8, 40, 52–3, 98–100, 145–7, 154–7,
        193, 250, 295–9
    Gaussian, 62–3, 91
    growth rate and, 88–90
    Kolmogorov–Smirnov (KS) goodness-of-fit
        test and, 200–1
    mortality tables and, 34–5, 49–51, 55–9,
        295–9
    probability density function (PDF) and, 37,
        40–1, 46, 52, 62–3. *See also* probability
    sustainable spending and, 190–3

obesity, 37
old-age dependency ratio, 6–7
Olivieri, A., 60
Olshansky, S. J., 60
options, 12
    American, 249–50
    basis points and, 256–7
    Black–Scholes/Merton (BSM) valuation
        and, 250–1, 257–8, 260
    Brownian motion model and, 251, 253, 269
    call, 202–6, 249
    deferring annuitization and, 282–7
    discount rate and, 252–7
    European, 250, 261
    exponential mortality and, 259–62
    gender and, 259
    Gompertz–Makeham (GoMa) model and,
        256, 258–9
    guaranteed minimum accumulation benefit
        (GMAB) and, 257–8
    guaranteed minimum death benefit (GMDB)
        and, 258–62
    guaranteed minimum withdrawal benefit
        (GMWB) and, 262–8
    installments and, 252–7
    passive approach and, 263
    periodic income and, 266
    put, 202–6, 249–50
    Quanto Asian put (QAP), 265–8
    real option to defer annuitization (RODA)
        model and, 282–9, 291
    shortfalls and, 261
    spot price and, 249–52

stochastic differential equation (SDE) and,
251–5, 263
Titanic, 250, 261–2, 269
valuation of, 252–7
ordinary differential equations (ODEs), 39–41,
100–1, 213
Orszag, M., 292

Pafumi, G., 291
partial differential equations (PDEs), 201,
207–8, 214
passive approach, 263
PAYGO (pay-as-you-go) plans, 164, 179
payroll taxes, 25
Pennacchi, G., 181
Penrose, Roger, 9
pension annuities
advanced-life delayed annuities (ALDAs)
and, 234–44
assumed interest rate (AIR) and, 132–4
COLA and, 113
deferred pension annuity factor (DPAF)
and, 121–3, 125, 130
difficult options of, 215–16
duration of, 128–30
exclusion ratio and, 119
Gamma function and, 117
gender and, 111–12, 118, 127
generic pension annuity factor and, 126
Gompertz–Makeham (GoMa) model and,
116–20, 129–30, 133–7
immediate pension annuity factor (IPAF)
and, 114–15, 123, 125, 130
Implied Longevity Yield (ILY) and, 226–34
inclusion ratio and, 119
inflation and, 113
insurance and, 130–4, 145–7
interest rates and, 121–3
joint and survivor (J&S), 112–13, 125–8
life insurance and, 145–7. *See also* life
insurance
market prices and, 110–14
options and, 249–69
period certain vs. term certain, 123–5
self-annuitization and, 225–6
stochastic present value of a pension annuity
(SPV-PA) and, 114
survivorship and, 112–13, 125–8, 216–18
taxes and, 119–21
term certain annuity factor (TCAF) and, 124
tontine contracts and, 217–25, 244–5

valuation of, 114–19, 125–8
variable vs. fixed, 130–4
pensions
Brownian motion model and, 168
Consumer Price Index (CPI) and, 168
defined benefit (DB), 5, 11–12, 164–82,
293–4
defined contribution (DC), 5, 11–12, 164–82,
293–4
demographics and, 5–9
ERISA and, 180–1
exchange rate and, 165
Florida and, 293
human longevity and, 7–8
interest cost and, 178
market prices and, 110–14
pay-as-you-go (PAYGO), 164, 179
PEORP and, 293
plan choice and, 164–5
service cost and, 178
Social Security and, 135
TIAA-CREF and, 134–5
period tables, 55–9
Philipson, T. J., 162
Pleeter, S., 245
Posner, S., 269
Poterba, J. M., 135, 291
Pratt, J. W., 291
present value of consumption, 20–2
probability
accumulated benefit obligation (ABO) and,
173–80
arithmetic average return, 86–8
Brownian motion model, 91–9, 102–4
conditional probability of survival and,
35–7, 48
cumulative distribution function (CDF) and,
37–8, 40, 52–3, 98–100, 145–7, 154–7,
193, 250, 295–9
"die broke" strategy and, 18, 185
diffusion simulation and, 101–2
Euler approximation and, 101–2
exponential lifetime (EL) distribution and,
190–1
exponential reciprocal Gamma (ERG)
distribution and, 192–202, 209–14
Gaussian distribution, 62–3, 91, 95, 97
geometric average return, 86–8
Gompertz–Makeham model and, 46–51,
59–62
growth rate and, 91–9, 102–4

probability *(cont.)*
  investment regret and, 98–100
  Kolmogorov–Smirnov (KS) goodness-of-fit
    test and, 200–1
  lognormal (LN) distribution and, 190
  Monte Carlo simulations and, 186–7, 204,
    207
  normal distribution and, 190–3
  period/cohort tables and, 55–9
  projected benefit obligation (PBO) and,
    173–80
  real option to defer annuitization (RODA)
    model and, 282–9, 291
  reciprocal Gamma (RG) distribution and,
    190–202, 208–14
  retirement benefit obligation (RBO) and,
    173–80
  space–time diversification and, 104–7
  square mean, 44
  standard deviation, 89–90, 97–9, 103,
    217–25
  tontine contracts and, 217–25
  utility and, 271–2
  See also mortality tables
probability density function (PDF), 52, 62–3
  growth rate and, 89–90
  life insurance and, 145–7, 154–7
  ODE relationship and, 40–1
  remaining lifetime and, 37, 46
  sustainable spending and, 191–2
product innovation, 8
projected benefit obligation (PBO), 12, 173–80
Promislow, D., 269
Public Employee Optional Retirement
    Program (PEORP), 293
put option, 202–6, 249–50
Pye, G. B., 208

Quanto Asian put (QAP) options, 265–8

randomness. *See* probability
Ranguelova, E., 135
rate of change, 100–1
real option to defer annuitization (RODA)
    model, 282–9, 291
reciprocal Gamma (RG) distribution, 190–1,
    208
  exponential, 192–202
  formula derivation for, 209–14
Reichenstein, W., 245
relative risk aversion (RRA), 273, 283, 290

religion, 37
remaining lifetime, 37–8
  expected, 44–5
  exponential law of mortality and, 45–6
  Gompertz–Makeham model and, 46–51,
    59–62
  median, 44–5
  pension annuity valuation and, 114–19, 125–8
Rennie, A., 108
retirement benefit obligation (RBO), 173–80
retirement income
  demographics and, 5–9
  drunk gambler problem and, 3–5, 14–16
  pensions and, 164–82. *See also* pensions
  population demographics and, 5–9
retirement planning
  call option and, 202–6
  "die broke" strategy and, 18, 185
  discounted value and, 27–31
  human life-cycle model and, 17–33
  Implied Longevity Yield (ILY) and, 226–34
  inflation and, 28–30
  living standards and, 17–18, 26
  put option and, 202–6
  real option to defer annuitization (RODA)
    model and, 282–9, 291
  real vs. nominal, 28–30
  sustainable spending and, 185–214. *See also*
    sustainable spending
Richard, S., 291
risk, 11
  accumulation phase and, 8
  advanced-life delayed annuities (ALDAs)
    and, 234–40
  arbitrage and, 71
  arithmetic average return and, 86–8
  Brownian motion model and, 91–9, 102–4
  "die broke" strategy and, 18, 185
  diffusion simulation and, 101–2
  drunk gambler problem and, 5
  geometric average return and, 86–8
  growth rate and, 88–90
  index averages/medians and, 97–8
  investment rate, 241–4
  life insurance and, 143–54
  longevity insurance and, 218, 241–4
  long-term model for, 88–90
  market price and, 70–2
  mortality and, 36–7, 241–4. *See also*
    mortality
  optimal timing and, 281–2

options and, 249–69
pension annuities and, 130–4
portfolio construction and, 102–7
rate of change and, 100–1
real option to defer annuitization (RODA)
  model and, 282–9
recent stock market history and, 83–6
regret probability and, 98–100, 104–7
relative risk aversion (RRA) and, 273, 283,
  290
sustainable spending and, 185–214. *See also*
  sustainable spending
tontine contracts and, 217–25, 244–5
utility and, 270–92
Road to Reality, The: A Complete Guide to the
  Laws of the Universe (Penrose), 9
Robinson, C., 33, 208
Ross, S. A., 292
RP2000 table, 34–5, 49–50
Rubinstein, M., 108
rule of 72, 67–8

Salas, S. L., 292
Salisbury, T. S., 269
Samuelson, P. A., 291
Samuelson, W., 33
savings, 8, 10
  Canada and, 25
  consumption rate and, 22–6
  "die broke" strategy and, 18, 185
  future value of, 18–20
  human life-cycle model and, 17–33
  inflation and, 28–30
  life insurance and, 143
  living standards and, 17–18, 26
  options and, 249–69
  sustainable spending and, 185–214. *See also*
    sustainable spending
  United States and, 25
Schulich School of Business, 9
Schwartz, E., 269
service cost, 178
Shen, W., 181
Sherris, M., 181
Sinha, T., 135
Smith, G., 208
smoking, 37
Social Security, 135, 193
Society of Actuaries, 34, 36–7, 59–60
space–time diversification, 104–7
Spivak, A., 291

spot price, 249–52
square mean, 44
Standard & Poor's index, 83–5
standard Brownian motion. *See* Brownian
  motion model
standard deviation, 89–90, 103
  Brownian motion model and, 97–9
  tontine contracts and, 217–25
Stanton, R., 181
static approach, 263
stochastic differential equation (SDE), 100–1,
  104, 209–10, 251–5, 263
stochastic present value (SPV), 12, 186–93,
  197, 200–1, 211
stochastic present value of a pension annuity
  (SPV-PA), 114
Stock, J. H., 292
stock market, 11, 46
  arithmetic average return and, 86–8
  Brownian motion model and, 91–104
  call option and, 202–6
  cash performance and, 84–5
  geometric average return and, 86–8
  inflation and, 85–6
  mortality credits and, 217
  portfolio construction and, 102–7
  put option and, 202–6
  recent history of, 83–6
  Standard & Poor's index and, 83–5
  U.S. Treasury bills and, 84
Stringfellow, T., 208
survival. *See* mortality
sustainable spending, 12
  Baby Boomers and, 186
  Black–Scholes model and, 207
  bootstrap approach and, 208
  call option and, 202–6
  cumulative distribution function (CDF) and,
    191, 193
  defined benefit (DB) pensions and, 193–4
  dollar-cost average (DCA) strategy and,
    193–4
  examples of, 193–202
  exponential lifetime (EL) distribution and,
    190–1
  exponential reciprocal Gamma (ERG)
    distribution and, 192–202
  formula derivation for, 209–14
  gender and, 189–90
  Gompertz–Makeham (GoMa) model and,
    200

sustainable spending *(cont.)*
  Ibbotson Associates simulator and, 207–8
  inflation and, 185, 189
  instantaneous mortality rate and, 190–3, 209–14
  Kolmogorov–Smirnov (KS) goodness-of-fit test and, 200–1
  lognormal (LN) distribution and, 190
  Monte Carlo simulations and, 186–7, 204, 207
  partial differential equations (PDEs) and, 201, 207–8, 214
  probability density function (PDF) and, 191–2
  put option and, 202–6
  reciprocal Gamma (RG) distribution and, 190–3
  research focus on, 185–6
  Social Security and, 193
  stochastic present value (SPV) and, 12, 186–93, 197, 200–1, 211
  systematic withdrawal plan (SWiP) and, 193–4
  taxes and, 193–4
  without additional risk, 202–6
systematic withdrawal plan (SWiP), 193–4

taxes
  arbitrage and, 162
  exclusion ratio and, 119
  inclusion ratio and, 119
  life insurance and, 143, 148, 162
  mortality swap and, 148
  options and, 249–69
  payroll, 25
  pension annuities and, 119–21
  sustainable spending and, 193–4
Taylor's approximation, 75–6, 79–81
T-bills, 84
term certain annuity factor (TCAF), 124
term insurance, 142–3, 150–1
Thaler, R. H., 181
Thorp, S., 292
TIAA-CREF, 134–5
Tillinghast [Towers Perrin], 55
Tillinghast Older Age Mortality Study, 140
time value of money (TVM), 10
Titanic options, 250, 261–2, 269
Tonti, Lorenzo, 244
tontine contracts
  asset allocation with, 220–5

fixed, 218–20
Gompertz–Makeham (GoMa) model and, 218–19
risk and, 217–25, 244–5
standard deviation and, 221–5
utility and, 279–81
variable, 218–20
"Tool Tells How Long Nest Egg Will Last" (*Wall Street Journal*), 207
Treynor, J. L., 181
Trout, A. P., 244
Tuenter, H., 292
Turkey, 7

United Kingdom, 244, 249
United Nations, 6–7
United States, 25, 165
  Baby Boomers and, 186, 294
  defined benefit (DB) pensions and, 293–4
  defined contribution (DC) pensions and, 293–4
  ERISA and, 180–1
  inflation and, 85–6
  IRAs and, 119–20
  no-lapse universal life insurance and, 139
  old-age dependency ratio and, 6–7
  options and, 249–50, 268–9
  pension annuities and, 114, 119–20, 176–7
  PEORP and, 293
  savings and, 25
  Social Security and, 135
  Standard & Poor's index and, 83–5
unit trust, 249
universal life insurance, 160–2
U.S. Department of Labor, 294
U.S. Treasury bills, 84
utility
  Arrow–Pratt measure and, 273
  asset allocation and, 278–81
  bequests and, 279–80
  as comfort, 270–1
  constant relative risk aversion and, 272
  consumption and, 274–8, 282–90
  deferring option and, 282–7
  hazard rates and, 289–90
  lifetime uncertainty and, 274–8
  models of, 271–2
  mortality and, 289–90
  negative function values and, 273
  optimal timing and, 281–2
  price and, 271–2

probability and, 271–2
proportional hazard transformation and, 289–90
quantifying of, 272–4
real option to defer annuitization (RODA) model and, 282–9, 291
relative risk aversion (RRA) and, 273, 283, 290
tontine contracts and, 279–81
value and, 271–2
variable annuities and, 290–1
wealth levels and, 273–4

Valdez, E., 135
valuation
    advanced-life delayed annuities (ALDAs) and, 236–44
    arbitrage and, 70–2
    Black–Scholes/Merton (BSM), 250–1, 257–8, 260
    bonds and, 68–70, 75–6
    defined benefit (DB) pensions and, 172–6
    Implied Longevity Yield (ILY) and, 226–34
    interest rates and, 64–82
    market price and, 70–2
    options and, 249–57
    pension annuities and, 114–19, 125–8
    Taylor's approximation and, 75–6, 79–81
    tontine contracts and, 217–25, 244–5
Vanneste, M., 135–6
variable annuities, 269
    description of, 249–52

exponential mortality and, 259–62
guaranteed minimum accumulation benefit (GMAB) and, 257–8
guaranteed minimum death benefit (GMDB) and, 258–62
guaranteed minimum withdrawal benefit (GMWB) and, 262–8
installments and, 252–7
utility and, 290–1
Vaupel, James, 7–8
Veres, R., 208
Viceira, L., 33, 108
volatility. *See* risk

Wall Street Journal, 207
Walz, D. T., 208
Wang, J., 208
Warner, J. T., 245
Warshawsky, M. J., 135, 181, 208
Watson Wyatt, 7
Webb, A., 292
Web sites, 34, 60, 206–7
Williams, C. A., Jr., 291
Wise, D. A., 292
World Economic Forum, 7

Yaari, M. E., 33, 162, 291
Yagi, T., 292
York University, 9
Young, V. R., 208, 292

zero bonds, 68–70, 77, 226–7